Webster's AMERICAN SIGN LANGUAGE Dictionary

ELAINE COSTELLO, PH.D.

ILLUSTRATED BY
LOIS LENDERMAN
PAUL M. SETZER
LINDA C. TOM

RANDOM HOUSE REFERENCE
NEW YORK TORONTO LONDON SYDNEY AUCKLAND

Originally published as *Random House Webster's Pocket American Sign Language Dictionary*, which was a revised and updated work based on the *Random House American Sign Language Dictionary* originally published in hardcover in 1994.

Published in the United States by Random House Reference, an imprint of The Random House Information Group, a division of Random House, Inc., New York, and simultaneously in Canada by Random House of Canada Limited, Toronto.

Illustration: Lois Lenderman, Paul M. Setzer, Linda C. Tom

Trademarks

A number of entered words which we have reason to believe constitute trademarks have been designated as such. However, no attempt has been made to designate as trademarks or service marks all terms or words in which proprietary rights might exist. The inclusion, exclusion, or definition of a word or term is not intended to affect, or to express a judgment on, the validity or legal status of the word or term as a trademark, service mark, or other proprietary term.

Printed in the United States of America

ISBN-13: 978-0-307-29069-4
ISBN-10: 0-307-29069-7

10 9 8 7 6 5 4 3 2 1

New York • Toronto • London • Sydney • Auckland

Contents

How to Use This Dictionary

How to Find a Sign

Complete Entries

All entries are presented in large boldface type in a single alphabetical listing, following a strict letter-by-letter order.

Cross References

A cross-reference entry, at its own alphabetical listing, sends the reader to one or more complete entries, where signs will be found.

How to Make a Sign

Illustrations

Formation of the sign is illustrated at every complete entry.

In a sequence of pictures, the illustrations in a circle focus on some significant portion of the movement, often the final position of the hands. The reader should execute the signs in the order shown, from left to right.

Descriptions

Each illustration is supplemented by a description in terms of the four component parts of a sign: (1) handshape, (2) location in relation to the body, (3) movement of the hands, and (4) orientation of the palms.

Within the description, italicized terms such as *A hand* and *C hand* refer to handshapes shown in the chart of the Manual Alphabet (p. 388). Terms such as *1 hand* or *10 hand* refer to handshapes for numbers. Other special handshapes, such as *bent hand*, *open hand*, and *flattened C hand*, are shown on page vii.

Hints

Beginning most descriptions is a bracketed memory aid, or *hint*. These hints help the reader understand the nature of the sign and better remember how it is made.

An *initialized sign* is formed with the handshape for the relevant letter in the English term, taken from the American Manual Alphabet (see chart on p. viii).

Fingerspelled signs use the Manual Alphabet to spell out a short word or abbreviation.

An occasional reference is made to "the finger used for feelings." Signs made with the bent middle finger often refer to concepts of sensitivity, feelings, or personal contact. Allusions to the "male" and "female" areas of the head indicate that signs referring to men, such as **father** and **uncle**, begin at or are made near the forehead, whereas signs referring to women, such as **mother** and **aunt**, begin at or are made near the chin.

Abbreviations Used in This Dictionary

adj.	adjective
adv.	adverb
conj.	conjunction
interj.	interjection
n.	noun
pl. n.	plural noun
prep.	preposition
pron.	pronoun
v.	verb
v. phrase	verb phrase

Handshapes Used in This Dictionary

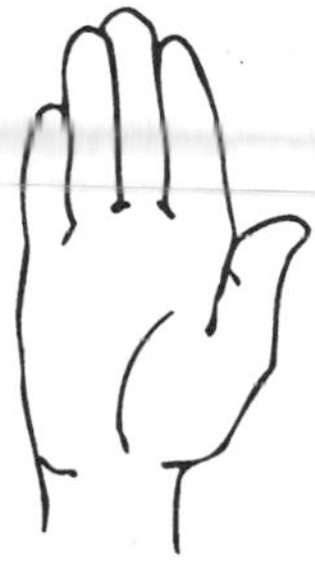

Open

Bent

Curved 5

Flattened C

Bent V

Modified X

Flattened O

Modified C

Curved 3

Numbers: Cardinals and Ordinals

Cardinal Numbers

Numbers are formed by holding the dominant hand comfortably in front of the shoulder with the palm either forward or in, depending on the context for using the number. When counting objects up to five, the palm should face in toward the signer. However, when expressing age or time, the palm should face forward.

The following are the signs for numbers from zero to 30. From the numbers from 31 to 99, the signs follow a regular pattern. For those numbers, sign each digit of the numeral moving the hand slightly to the right, such as for 34, sign *3* followed by *4*. For 60, sign *6* followed by *zero*. For numbers where both digits are the same (e.g., 44), bounce the hand slightly in place while holding the four handshape.

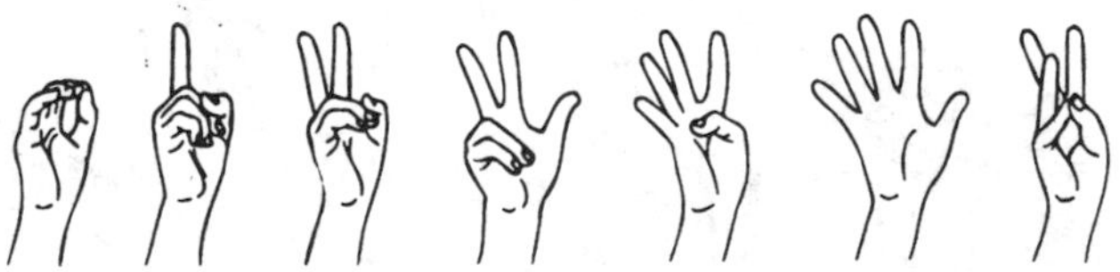

0 1 2 3 4 5 6

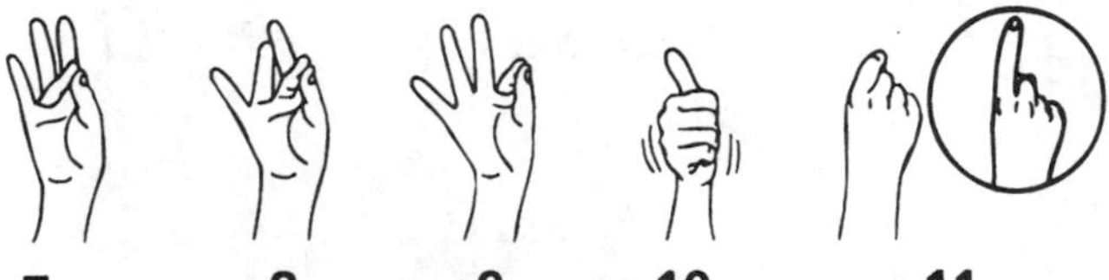

7 8 9 10 11

12

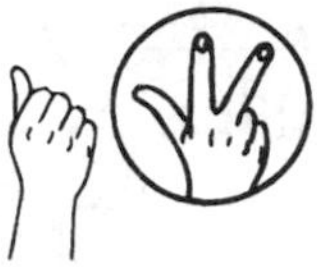

13

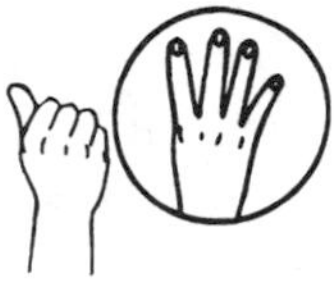

14

15

16

17

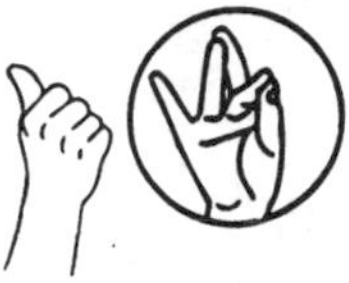

18

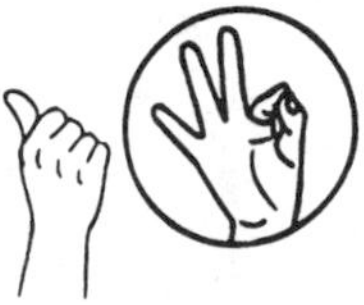

19

20

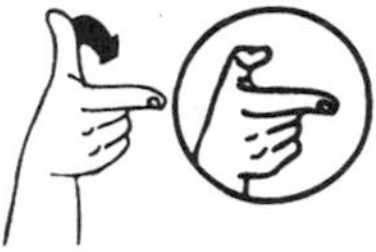

21

22

23

24

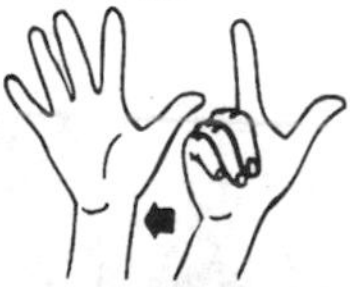

25

26

27

28

29

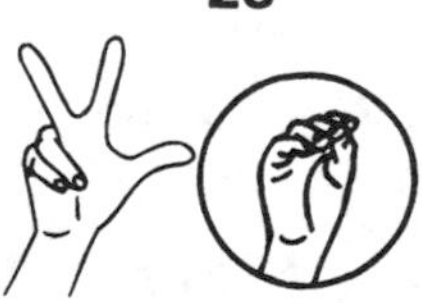

30

Numbers

The following are signs for hundred, thousand, and million. When signing numbers over one hundred, the numbers are signed just as they are spoken. For example, 283 is signed *two-hundred + eighty + three.* Similarly, 5,690 is signed *five-thousand + six-hundred + ninety.*

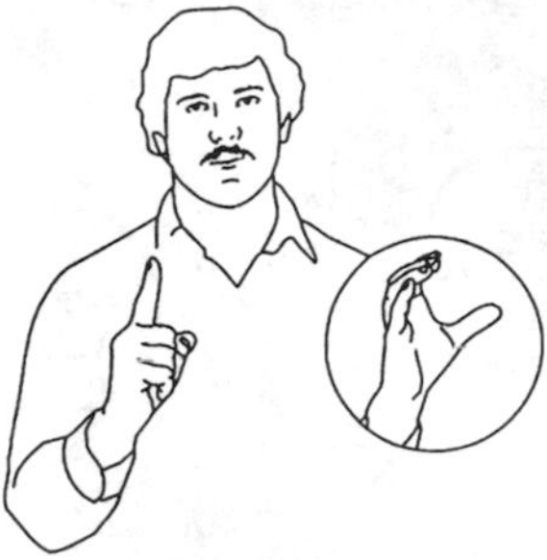

one-hundred

thousand

million

When giving an address, sign the numbers in the manner in which an address is usually spoken. For example, 3812 Charles Avenue is signed *thirty-eight + twelve.*

Money is also signed in the same order that it is spoken, except for dollar amounts under ten dollars, which are signed by using the corresponding ordinal (see p. 516). For example, "eight dollars" is signed with the sign used for *eighth*. For larger amounts, the sign *dollar* is used after the dollar amount, just as it is spoken. For example, $86.17 is signed *eighty-six* + *dollar* + *seventeen*. For cents under a dollar, sign the cents sign followed by the amount. For example, 45¢ is signed *cents* + *forty-five*.

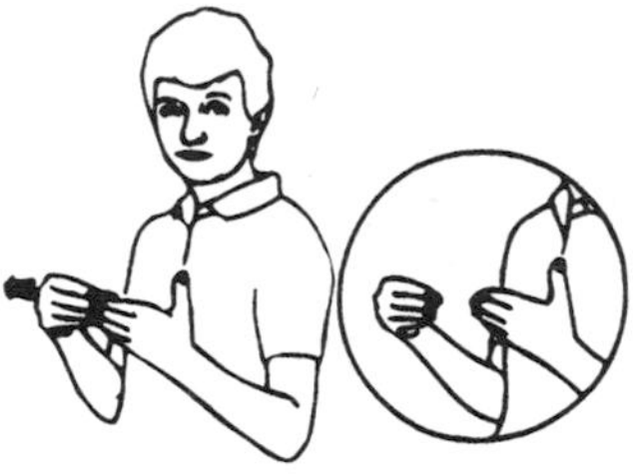

dollar

Fractions are formed by signing the top number of the fraction and then dropping the hand slightly to form the bottom number of the fraction. The following are two examples of fractions.

one-half

one-third

Numbers

Ordinal Numbers

The following signs are used when expressing order or rank in a series. Hold the hand comfortably in front of the right shoulder, twisting the wrist when forming each sign. The same signs are used for dollar amounts under ten dollars.

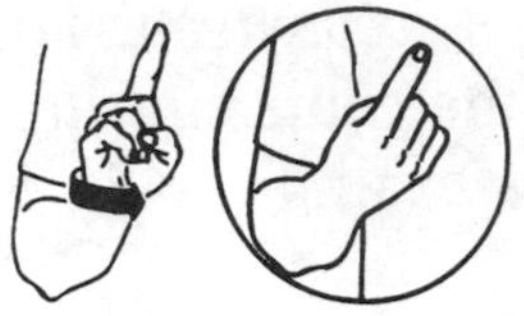

first

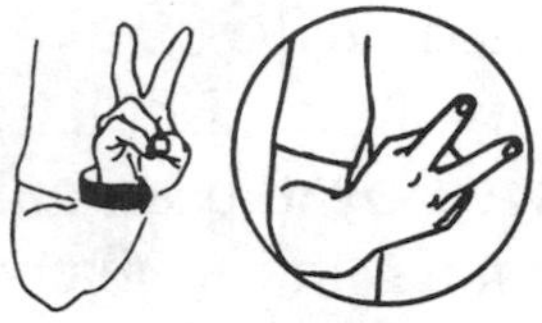

second

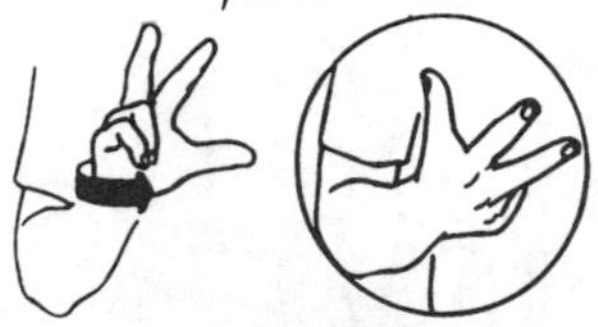

third

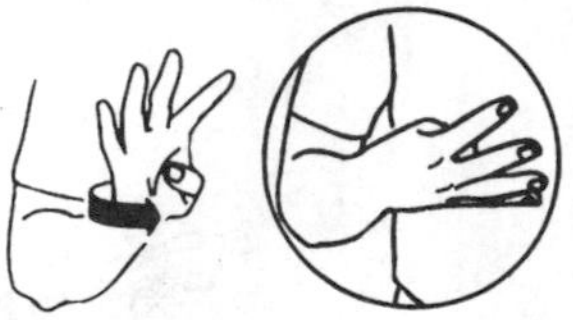

fourth

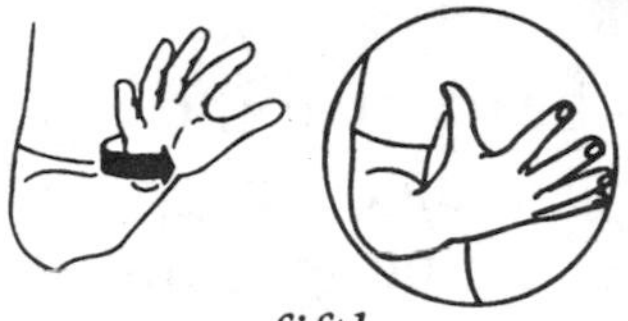

fifth

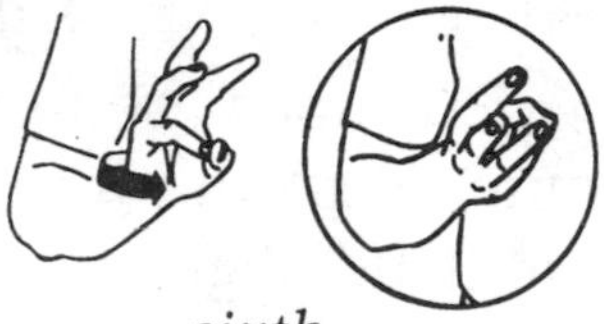

sixth

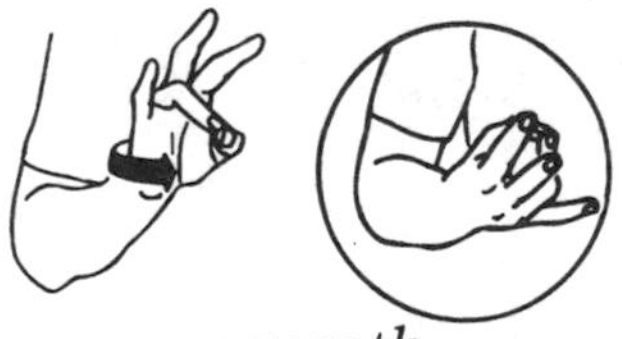

seventh

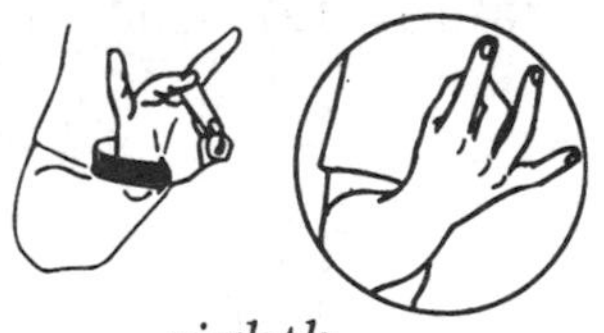

eighth

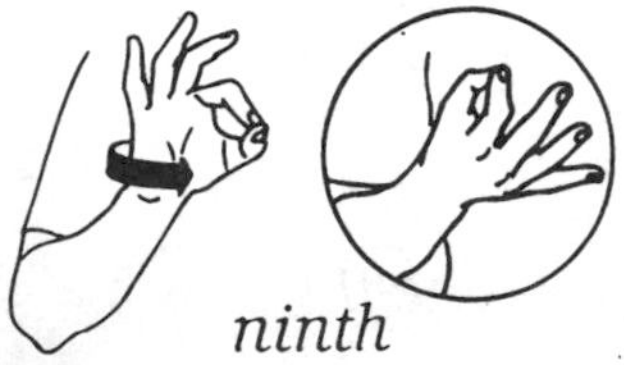

ninth

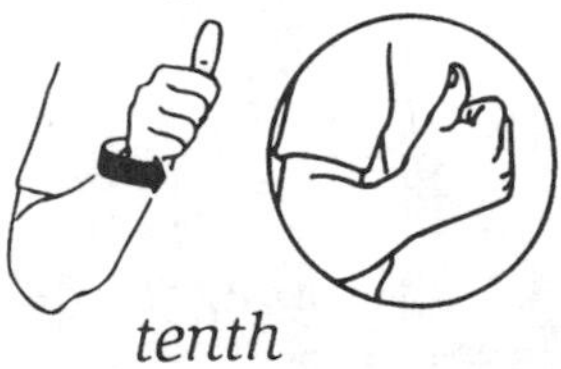

tenth

abandon *v.* Related form: **abandonment** *n.* Same sign used for: **discard, evict, expel, forsake, throw out.**

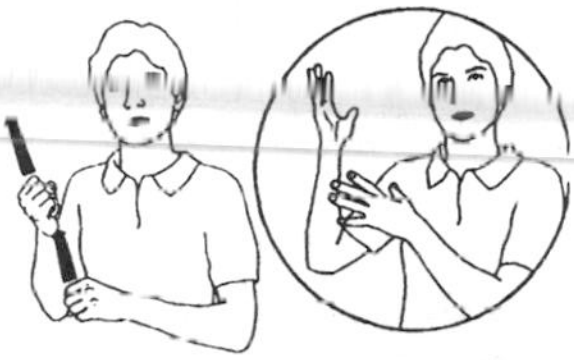

[Natural gesture of giving up hope] Beginning with both *S hands* in front of the chest, both palms facing in and the right hand above the left hand, quickly throw the hands upward to the right while opening into *5 hands* in front of the right shoulder, ending with the palms facing back and the fingers pointing up.

---

abbreviate *v.* See sign for BRIEF.

---

ability *n.* See sign for SKILL.

---

able *adj.* See sign for SKILL.

---

abolish[1] *v.* See sign for DAMAGE. Shared idea of destruction.

---

abolish[2] *v.* See signs for ELIMINATE[1], REMOVE[1].

---

abort *v.* See signs for ELIMINATE[1], REMOVE[1]. Related form: **abortion** *n.*

---

about *adv.* See signs for ALMOST, APPROXIMATELY.

---

above *prep., adv.* Same sign used for: **over.**

[Indicates area above] Beginning with the right *open hand* on the back of the left *open hand,* both palms facing down, bring the right hand upward in an arc, ending several inches above the left hand.

absent *adj., v.* Related form: **absence** *n.* See also signs for DISAPPEAR[1], SKIP. Same sign used for: **drain, extinct, gone, miss, missing.**

[Something seems to go down the drain] Pull the right *flattened C hand,* palm facing in, downward through the left *C hand,* palm facing right, while closing the fingers and thumb of the right hand together.

---

absent-minded *adj.* See sign for BLANK[1].

---

accept *v.* Related form: **acceptance** *n.* Same sign used for: **adopt, adoption, approval, approve.**

[Bring something that is accepted toward oneself] Beginning with both *5 hands* in front of the chest, fingers pointing forward, bring both hands back toward the chest while pulling the fingers and thumbs of each hand together.

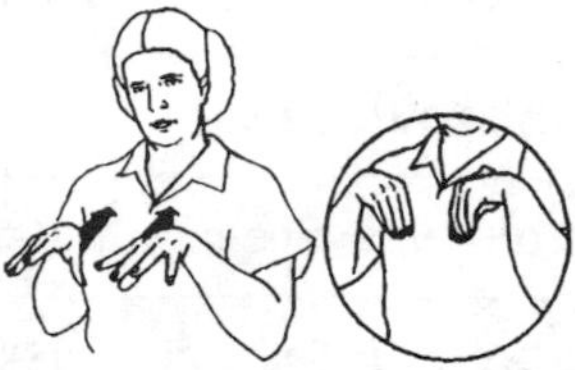

---

accident[1] *n.* Same sign used for: **collide, collision, crash.**

[Two things collide with each other] Move both *5 hands* from in front of each side of the chest, palms facing in and fingers pointing toward each other, while changing into *A hands,* ending with the knuckles of both *A hands* touching in front of the chest.

---

accident[2] *n.* See sign for HAPPEN.

---

accidentally *adv.* Alternate form: **by accident.** Related form: **accidental** *adj.* Same sign used for: **amiss.**

[Similar to sign for **mistake** except made with a twisting movement] Twist the knuckles of the right *Y hand,* palm facing in, on the chin from right to left.

acclaim *v.* See sign for ANNOUNCE.

accomplish *v.* See sign for SUCCESSFUL. Related form: **accomplishment** *n.*

accumulate[1] *v.* Related form: **accumulation** *n.* Same sign used for: **amass.**

[More and more of something being piled up on top of other things] Beginning with the right *U hand,* palm facing left, beside the left *U hand,* palm facing down, flip the right hand over with a double movement, tapping the right fingers across the left fingers each time.

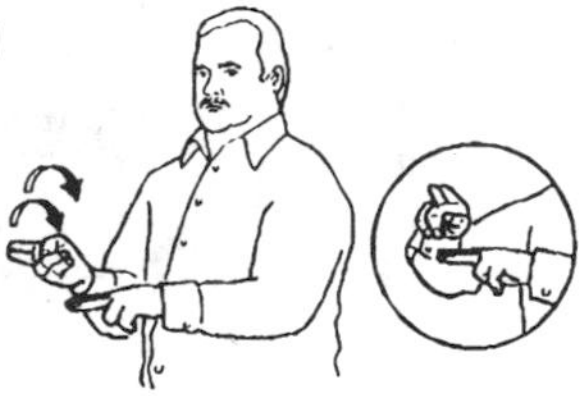

accumulate[2] *v.* See sign for COLLECT.

accurate *adj.* See signs for PERFECT, RIGHT[3].

accustomed to See sign for HABIT.

ache *v., n.* See signs for HURT, PAIN.

achieve *v.* Related form: **achievement** *n.* See also sign for SUCCESSFUL. Same sign used for: **chalk up, success.**

[An accumulation of something] Beginning with the left *bent hand* over the right *bent hand* in front of the chest, both palms facing down, move the hands with an alternating movement over each other to in front of the face.

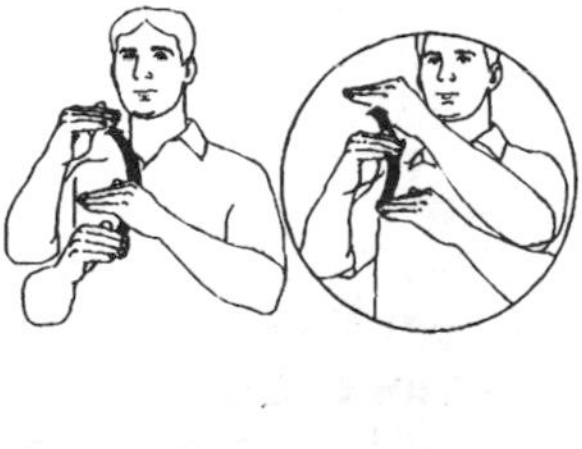

acquaint *v.* See sign for ASSOCIATE.

acquire *v.* See signs for GET, LEARN, TAKE.

across *prep., adv.* Same sign used for: **after, afterward, cross, over.**
[Movement across another thing] Push the little-finger side of the right *open hand,* palm facing left, across the back of the left *open hand,* palm facing down.

act[1] *v., n.* Related forms: **action** *n.*, **activity** *n.* Same sign used for: **deed.**
[The hands seem to be actively doing something] Move both *C hands,* palms facing down, simultaneously back and forth in front of the body with a swinging movement.

act[2] *v.* Same sign used for: **drama, perform, play, show, theater.**
[Initialized sign] Bring the thumbs of both *A hands,* palms facing each other, down each side of the chest with alternating circular movements.

active *adj.* See signs for AMBITIOUS[1], WORK.

actual *adj.* See signs for REAL, TRUE.

actually *adv.* See sign for TRUE.

adapt *v.* See sign for CHANGE[1].

add *v.* Related form: **addition** *n.* Same sign used for: **amend, bonus, extra, supplement.**
[One hand brings an additional amount to the other hand] Swing the right *5 hand* upward from the right side of the body while changing into a *flattened O hand,*

ending with the right index finger touching the little-finger side of the left *flattened O hand* in front of the chest, both palms facing in.

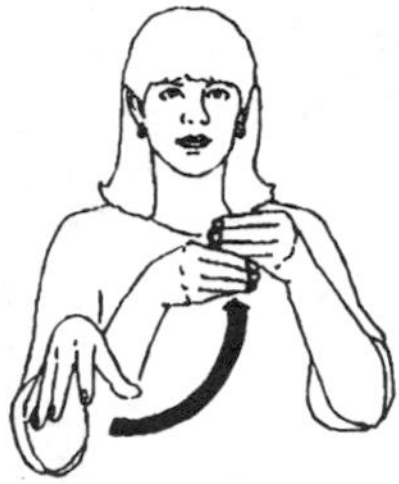

address[1] *n., v.* [Initialized sign similar to sign for **live**] Move both *A hands,* palms facing in, upward on each side of the chest with a double movement.

address[2] *v.* See sign for SPEAK[2].

adequate *adj.* See sign for ENOUGH.

adhere *v.* See signs for APPLY[3], STICK[1].

adhesive *n., adj.* See sign for STICK[1].

adjust *v.* See sign for CHANGE[1].

administer *v.* See sign for MANAGE. Alternate form: **administrate.**

admit *v.* Related form: **admission** *n.* Same sign used for: **confess, confession, submit, willing.**
[Hand seems to bring a confession from the chest] Move the right *open hand,* palm facing in, from the chest forward in an arc while turning the palm slightly upward.

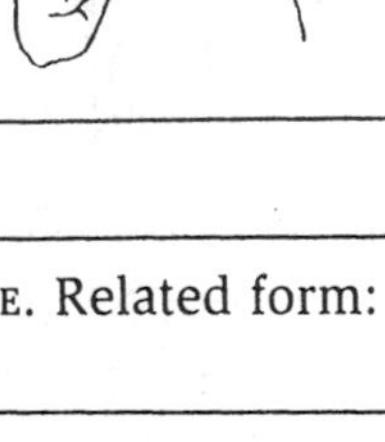

admonish *v.* See sign for SCOLD.

adopt *v.* See signs for ACCEPT, TAKE. Related form: **adoption** *n.*

adrift *adj.* See sign for ROAM.

adult *n., adj.*

[Initialized sign formed in the traditional male and female positions; can be formed with an opposite movement] Move the thumb of the right *A hand,* palm facing forward, from the side of the forehead to the lower cheek.

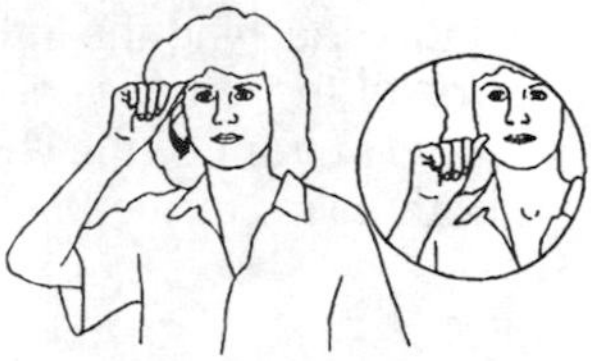

advanced *adj.* Same sign used for: **elevate, elevated, elevation, exalt, exalted, exaltation, higher, prominent, promote, promotion, supreme.**

[Moving to a more advanced position] Move both *bent hands,* palms facing each other, from near each side of the head upward a short distance in a deliberate arc.

advantage[1] *n.* Same sign used for: **take advantage of.**

[Represents "an easy touch"] Flick the bent middle finger of the right *5 hand* upward off the heel of the left *open hand.*

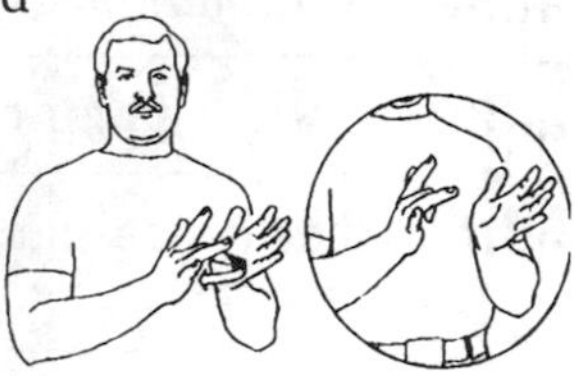

advantage[2] *n.* See sign for BENEFIT.

advertise *v.* Related form: **advertisement** *n.* Same sign used for: **broadcast, commercial, propaganda, publicity, publicize.**

[Suggests "blowing one's own horn" in order to advertise] Beginning with the thumb side of the right *S hand,* palm facing left, against the little-finger side of the left *S hand,* palm facing right, move the right hand forward and back with a double movement.

advice *n.* Same sign used for: **effect.**

[Sending information to another] Beginning with the fingertips of the right *flattened O hand* on the back of the left *open hand,* palm facing down, move the right hand forward while spreading the fingers into a *5 hand.*

advocate *v.* See sign for SUPPORT.

affect *v.* See sign for INFLUENCE.

affection *n.* See sign for HUG. Related form: **affectionate** *adj.*

affiliation *n.* See sign for COOPERATION.

affix *v.* See sign for APPLY[3].

afford *v.* Same sign used for: **debt, due, owe.**

[Indicates that money should be deposited in the palm] Tap the extended right index finger on the palm of the left *open hand* with a double movement.

affront *v.* See sign for INSULT.

afraid *adj.* Same sign used for: **fright, frightened, panic, scared, timid.**

[Hands put up a protective barrier] Beginning with both *A hands* in front of each side of the chest, spread the fingers open with a quick movement, forming *5 hands,* palms facing in and fingers pointing toward each other.

after[1] *prep., conj., adv.* Same sign used for: **afterward, beyond, from now on, rest of.**

[A time frame occurring after another thing] Beginning with the palm of the right *bent hand* touching the back of the fingers of the left *open hand,* both palms facing in, move the right hand forward a short distance.

after[2] *prep.* See sign for ACROSS.

after a while See sign for LATER.

afternoon *n.* Same sign used for: **matinee.**

[The sun going down in the afternoon] With the bottom of the right forearm resting on the back of the left *open hand,* palm facing down, move the right *open hand* downward with a double movement.

afterward *adv.* See signs for ACROSS, AFTER[1], LATER.

again *adv.* Same sign used for: **reiterate, repeat.**

[The movement indicates wanting something to be repeated] Beginning with the right *bent hand* beside the left *curved hand,* both palms facing up, bring the right hand up while turning it over, ending with the fingertips of the right hand touching the palm of the left hand.

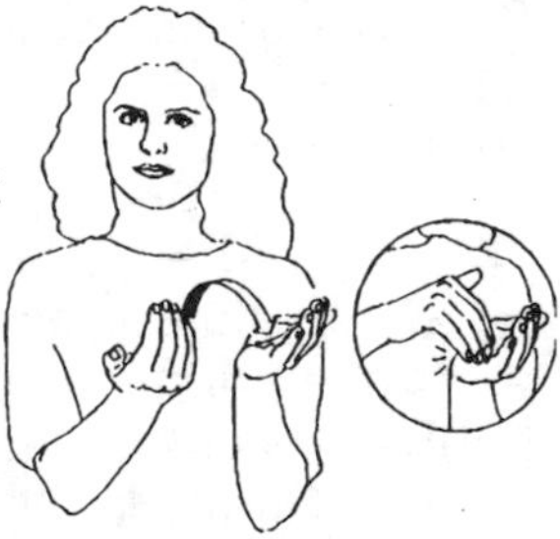

against *prep.* Same sign used for: **anti-** [prefix], **opposed to, prejudice.**

[Demonstrates making contact with a barrier] Hit the fingertips of the right *bent hand* into the left *open hand,* palm facing right.

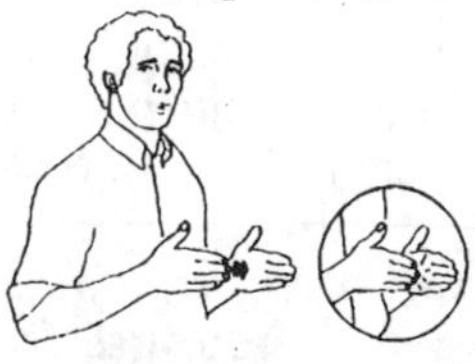

age *n.*
[An old man's beard] Move the right *O hand,* palm facing left, downward a short distance from the chin while changing into an *S hand.*

aggressive *adj.* See sign for AMBITIOUS[1].

agile *adj.* See sign for SKILL.

ago *adj.* Same sign used for: **last, past, was, were.**
[Indicates a time in the past] Move the right *bent hand* back over the right shoulder, palm facing back.

agree *v.* Same sign used for: **compromise, in accord, in agreement, suit.**
[**think**[1] + lining up two things to show they agree with each other] Move the extended right index finger from touching the right side of the forehead downward to beside the extended left index finger, ending with both fingers pointing forward in front of the body, palms facing down.

aid *n.* See sign for HELP.

aide *n.* See sign for ASSISTANT.

aim *v.* See sign for GOAL.

airplane *n.* Same sign used for: **airport, jet, plane.**

[Shape and movement of an airplane] Move the right hand with the thumb, index finger, and little finger extended, palm facing down, forward with a short repeated movement in front of the right shoulder.

---

airport *n.* See sign for AIRPLANE.

---

alarm *n.* Same sign used for: **alert, drill.**

[Action of clapper on alarm bell] Tap the extended index finger of the right hand, palm facing forward, against the left *open hand,* palm facing right, with a repeated movement.

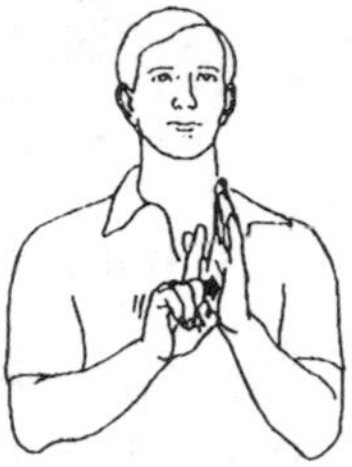

---

alert *n.* See sign for ALARM.

---

align *v.* See sign for LINE UP.

---

alike *adj., adv.* See also signs for LIKE[3], SAME. Same sign used for: **also, identical, look alike, same, similar.**

[Sign moves between two people or things that are similar] Move the right *Y hand,* palm facing down, from side to side with a short repeated movement in front of the body.

---

alive *adj.* See sign for LIVE.

---

all *pron.* Same sign used for: **entire, whole.**

[The hand encompasses the whole thing] Move the right *open hand* from near the left shoulder in a large circle in front of the chest, ending with the back of the right hand in the left *open hand* held in front of the body, palms facing in.

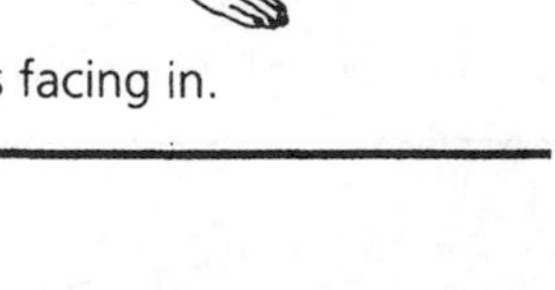

all along *adv.* See sign for GO ON.

all gone *adj.* See sign for RUN OUT OF.

all right *adv.* See sign for RIGHT[2].

allegiance *n.* See sign for SUPPORT.

allow *v.* See sign for LET.

allowance *n.* See sign for PENSION.

ally *n.* See sign for RELATIONSHIP.

almost *adv.* Same sign used for: **about, barely, nearly.**

[The fingers almost touch the other hand] Brush the fingertips of the right *open hand* upward off the back of the left fingers, both palms facing up.

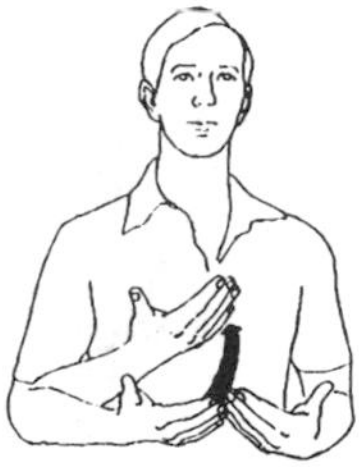

alone *adv., adj.* Same sign used for: **isolated, lone, only, solely.**

[Shows one thing alone] With the right index finger extended up, move the right hand, palm facing back, in a small repeated circle in front of the right shoulder.

a lot *adv.* See signs for MANY, MUCH.

aloud *adv.* See sign for NOISE.

already *adv.* See sign for FINISH[1].

also *adv.* See sign for ALIKE.

alter *v.* See sign for CHANGE[1].

alternate *v.* See sign for TURN[1].

alternative *n.* See sign for EITHER[1].

altitude *n.* See sign for HIGH.

always *adv.* Same sign used for: **ever.**

[A continuous circle signifying duration] Move the extended right index finger, palm facing in and finger angled up, in a repeated circle in front of the right side of the chest.

amass *v.* See sign for ACCUMULATE[1].

amaze *v.* See signs for SURPRISE, WONDERFUL. Related form: **amazement** *adj.*

ambiguous *adj.* See sign for VAGUE.

ambitious[1] *adj.* Related form: **ambition** *n.* Same sign used for: **active, aggressive.**

[Initialized sign] Move both *A hands,* palms facing in, in large alternating circles upward on each side of the chest.

ambitious[2] *adj.* See sign for GOAL.

amen *interj.* Same sign used for: **pray, prayer.**

[Natural gesture for folding one's hands to pray] Bring the palms of both *open hands* together, fingers angled upward, while moving the hands down and in toward the chest.

amend *v.* See sign for ADD.

America *n.* Related form: **American** *adj., n.*

[The rail fences built by settlers] With the fingers of both hands loosely entwined, palms facing in, move the hands in circle in front of the chest.

amid or **amidst** *prep.* See sign for AMONG.

amiss *adj.* See sign for ACCIDENTALLY.

among *prep.* Same sign used for: **amid, amidst, midst.**

[Shows one moving among others] Move the extended right index finger in and out between the fingers of the left *5 hand,* both palms facing in.

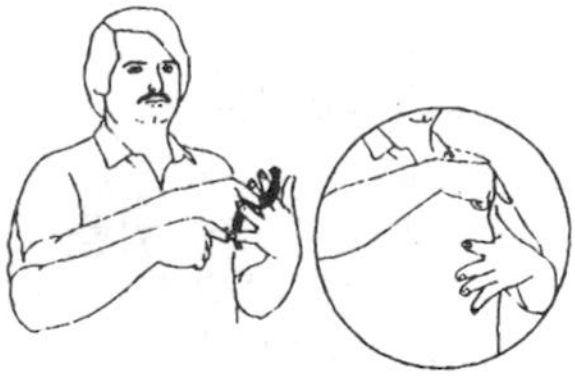

amount *n.* Same sign used for: **heap, lump, pile.**

[Shows a small amount in a pile] Move the extended right index finger, palm facing down, in an arc from near the heel to the fingers of the upturned left *open hand,* ending with the right palm facing in toward the chest.

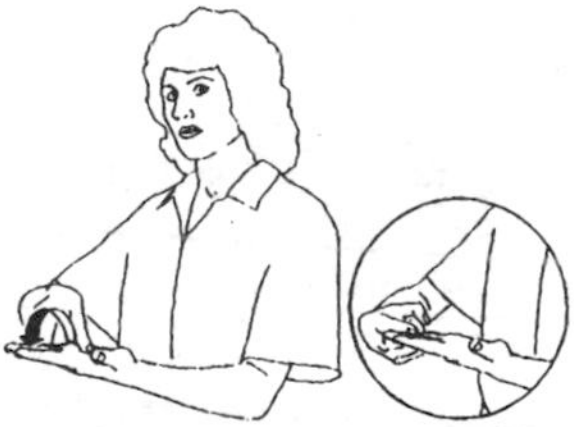

amuse *adj.* See sign for FUNNY.

analyze *v.* Related form: **analysis** *n.* Same sign used for: **diagnose, diagnosis.**

[Taking something apart to analyze it] With both *bent V hands* near each other in front of the chest, palms facing down, move the fingers apart from each other with a downward double movement.

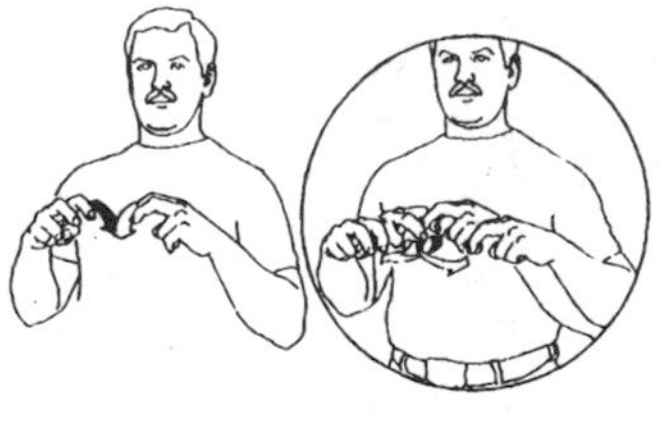

ancient *adj.* See sign for LONG TIME AGO, A.

and *conj.*

[Stretching one part of a sentence to connect it to the rest] Move the right *curved 5 hand,* palm facing left, to the right in front of the body while closing the fingers to the thumb, ending in a *flattened O hand.*

and so forth See sign for VARIETY.

anger *n.* Related form: **angry** *adj.* See also sign for CROSS[1]. Same sign used for: **enrage, fury, mad, outrage, rage.**

[Hands bring up feeling of anger in the body] Beginning with the fingertips of both *curved 5 hands* on the lower chest, bring the hands upward and apart, ending in front of each shoulder.

angry *adj.* See sign for CROSS[1].

animal *n.* Same sign used for: **beast.**

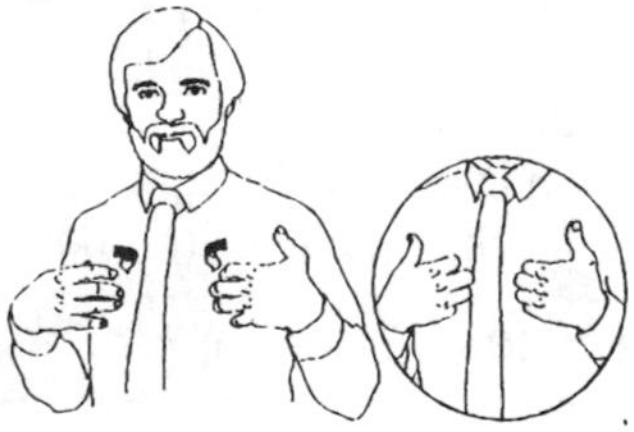

[Shows an animal breathing] Beginning with the fingertips of both *curved 5 hands* on the chest near each shoulder, roll the fingers toward each other on their knuckles with a double movement while keeping the fingers in place.

annex *v.* See sign for BELONG.

announce *v.* Related form: **announcement** *n.* Same sign used for: **acclaim, declaration, declare, proclaim, proclamation, reveal, tell.**
[**tell**[1] with a movement that shows a general announcement] Beginning with the extended index fingers of both hands pointing to each side of the mouth, palms

facing in, twist the wrists and move the fingers forward and apart from each other, ending with the palms facing forward and the index fingers pointing outward in opposite directions.

annoy *v.* Same sign used for: **bother, disturb, interfere, interrupt, irritate.**

[A gesture showing something interfering with something else] Sharply tap the little-finger side of the right *open hand,* palm facing in at an angle, at the base of the thumb and index finger of the left *open hand* with a double movement.

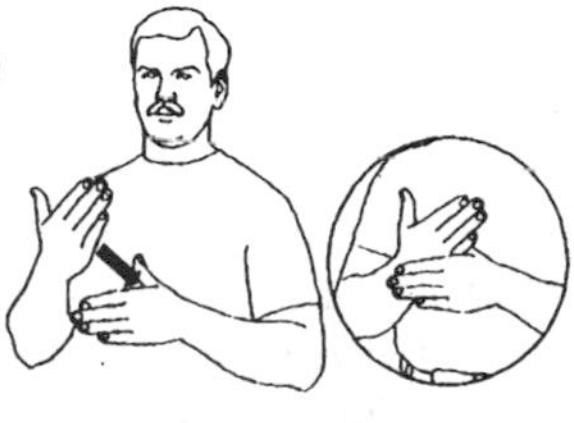

another *adj., pron.* Same sign used for: **other**.

[Points away to another] Beginning with the right *10 hand* in front of the body, palm facing down and thumb pointing left, flip the hand over to the right, ending with the palm facing up and the thumb pointing right.

answer *n., v.* Same sign used for: **react, reply, response.**

[Indicates directing words of response to another] Beginning with both extended index fingers pointing up in front of the mouth, right hand nearer the mouth than the left and both palms facing forward, bend the wrists down simultaneously, ending with fingers pointing forward and the palms facing down.

antagonism *n.* See sign for STRUGGLE.

anti- *prefix.* See signs for AGAINST, RESIST.

anxiety *n.* See sign for NERVOUS.

anxious *adj.* See signs for NERVOUS, TROUBLE[1].

any *adj., pron.*
[Initialized sign pointing to a selection of things] Beginning with the right *10 hand* in front of the chest, palm facing left, twist the wrist and move the hand down and to the right, ending with the palm facing down.

anyway *adv.* Same sign used for: **despite, doesn't matter, even though, hardly, however, nevertheless, whatever.**
[Flexible hands signify no firm position] Beginning with both *open hands* in front of the body, fingers pointing toward each other and palms facing in, move the hands forward and back from the body with a repeated alternating movement, striking and bending the fingers of each hand as they pass.

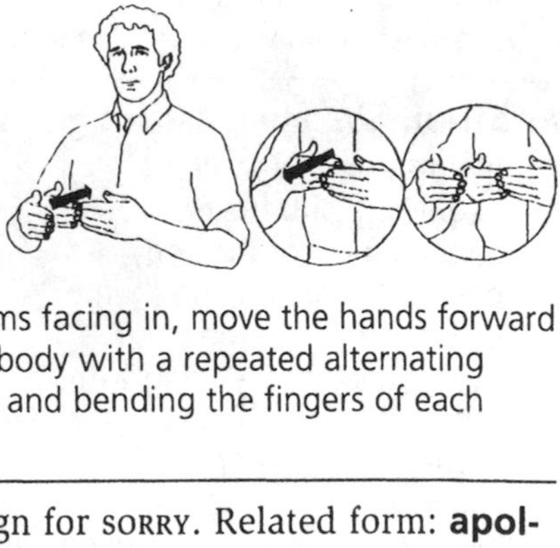

apologize *v.* See sign for SORRY. Related form: **apology** *n.*

apparently *adv.* See sign for SEEM.

appeal *v.* See sign for SUGGEST.

appear *v.* See signs for SEEM, SHOW UP.

appetite *n.* See sign for HUNGRY.

applaud *v.* Related form: **applause** *n.* Same sign used for: **clap.**
[Natural gesture for clapping] Pat the palm of the right

open hand across the palm of the left *open hand* with a double movement.

apple *n.*
[Shows action of chewing an apple] With the knuckle of the right *X hand* near the right side of the mouth, twist the wrist downward with a double movement.

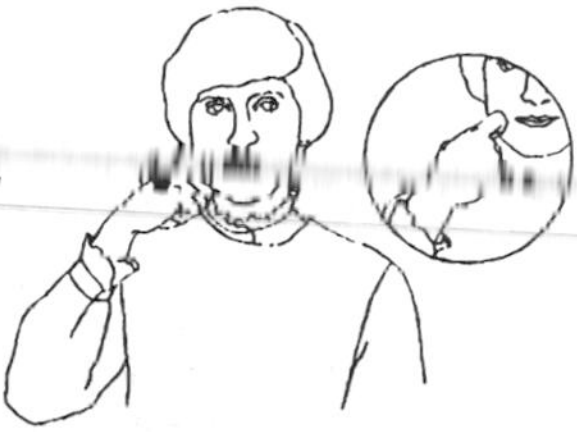

apply[1] *v.* Related form: **applicable** *adj.* Same sign used for: **charge, file, install, post.**
[Put messages on a spindle] Move the fingers of the right *V hand,* palm facing forward, downward on each side of the extended left index finger, pointing up in front of the chest.

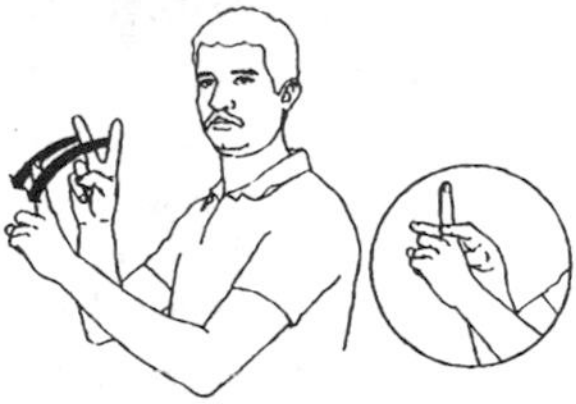

apply[2] *v.* Related form: **application** *n.* Same sign used for: **candidate, eligible, nominate, volunteer.**
[Seems to pull oneself forward to apply for something] Pinch a small amount of clothing on the right side of the chest with the fingers of the right *F hand* and pull forward with a short double movement.

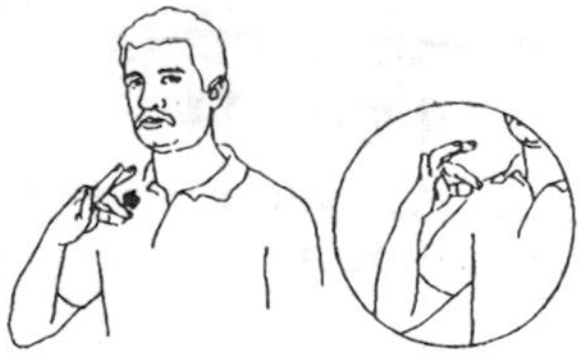

apply[3] *v.* Same sign used for: **adhere, affix.**
[Mime applying tape or a label] Tap the fingers of the right *H hand,* palm facing left, against the palm of the left *open hand,* palm facing right, first near the fingers and then near the heel.

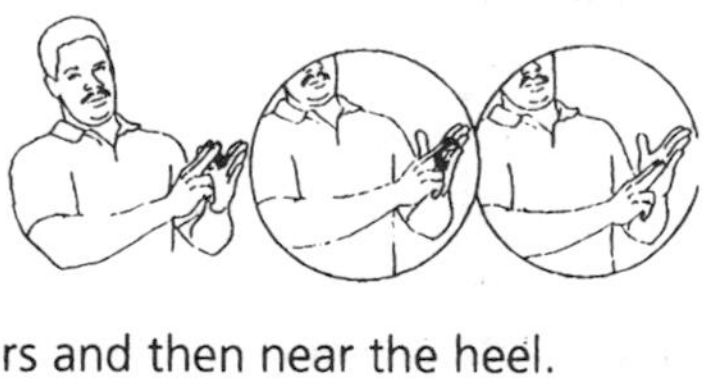

apply[4] *v.* See sign for LABEL.

---

appoint *v.* Same sign used for: **choose, elect, select.**

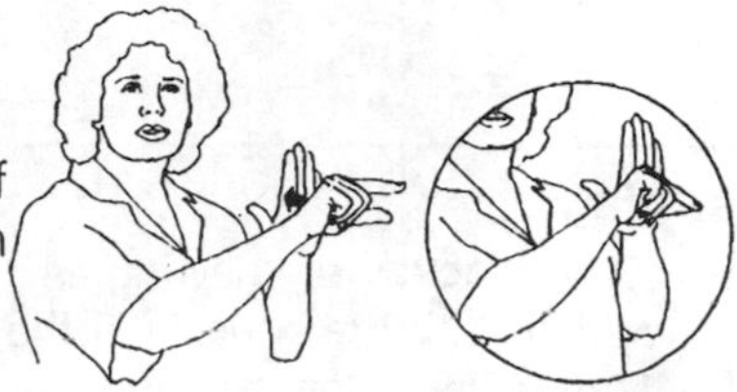

[Fingers seem to pick someone] Beginning with the thumb side of the right *G hand,* palm facing down and fingers pointing forward, against the left *open hand,* palm facing right and fingers pointing up, pull the right hand in toward the chest while pinching the index finger and thumb together.

---

appointment *n.* Same sign used for: **assignment, book, reservation.**

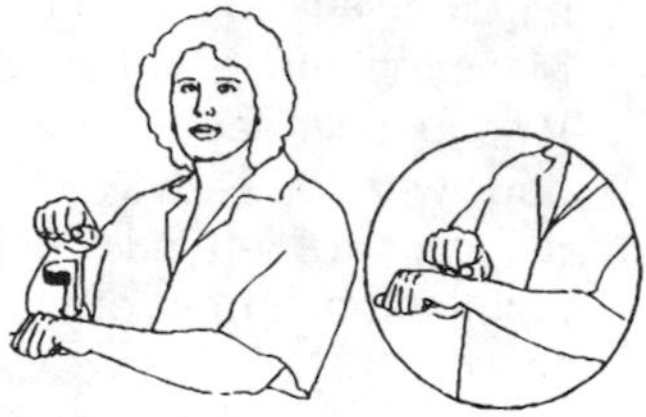

[The hands are bound by a commitment] Move the right *S hand,* palm facing down, in a small circle and then down to the back of the left *A hand,* palm facing down in front of the chest.

---

appreciate *v.* See sign for ENJOY. Related form: **appreciation** *n.*

---

apprehend *v.* See sign for UNDERSTAND.

---

approach *v.* See sign for CLOSE.

---

appropriate *adj.* See sign for REGULAR. Related form: **appropriately** *adv.*

---

approve *v.* See sign for ACCEPT. Related form: **approval** *n.*

---

approximate *adj.* See sign for ROUGH.

approximately *adv.* Related form: **approximate** *adj.* Same sign used for: **about, around.**

[Natural gesture of vagueness] Move the right *5 hand,* palm facing forward, in a circle in front of the right shoulder with a double movement.

area *n.* Same sign used for: **place, space.**

[Indicates an area] Move the right *5 hand,* palm facing down and fingers pointing forward, in a flat forward arc in front of the right side of the body.

argue *v.* Related form: **argument** *n.* Same sign used for: **fight, quarrel, squabble.**

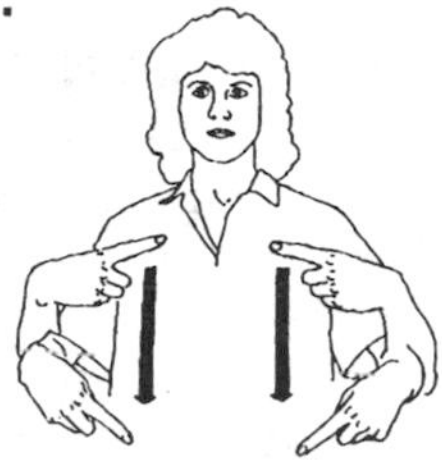

[Represents opposing points of view] Beginning with both extended index fingers pointing toward each other in front of the chest, palms facing in, shake the hands up and down with a repeated movement by bending the wrists.

argument *n.* See sign for DISCUSS.

arithmetic *n.* Same sign used for: **estimate, figure, figure out, multiplication.**

[Movement suggests combining things] Brush the back of the right *V hand* across the palm side of the left *V hand,* both palms facing up, as the hands cross with a double movement in front of the chest.

around *prep.* See sign for APPROXIMATELY.

arouse *v.* See sign for AWAKE.

arrange *v.* See sign for PLAN.

---

arrest *v.* See signs for CAPTURE, CATCH[1].

---

arrive *v.* Same sign used for: **reach.**

[Hand moves to arrive in other hand] Move the right *bent hand* from in front of the right shoulder, palm facing left, downward, landing the back of the right hand in the upturned left *curved hand.*

---

arrogant *adj.* See signs for CONCEITED, PROUD.

---

art *n.* Same sign used for: **drawing, illustration, sketch.**

[Demonstrates drawing something] Move the extended right little finger with a wiggly movement down the palm of the left *open hand* from the fingers to the heel.

---

artificial *adj.* See sign for FAKE.

---

ascend *v.* See sign for CLIMB.

---

ashamed *adj.* Same sign used for: **shame, shameful, shy.**

[Blood rising in the cheeks when ashamed] Beginning with the back of the fingers of both *curved hands* against each cheek, palms facing down, twist the hands forward, ending with the palms facing back.

ask *v.* Same sign used for: **pray, request.**
[Natural gesture used for asking] Bring the palms of both *open hands* together, fingers angled upward, while moving the hands down and in toward the chest.

asleep *adv.* See sign for FALL ASLEEP.

aspire *v.* See sign for ZEAL. Related form: **aspiration** *n.*

assemble *v.* See signs for GATHER[1].

assembly *n.* See sign for MEETING.

assign *v.* See signs for APPOINT, CHOOSE[1].

assignment *n.* See sign for APPOINTMENT.

assist *v.* See sign for HELP.

assistant *n., adj.* Same sign used for: **aide.**
[Initialized hand showing giving a boost or aid to another] Use the thumb of the right *A hand* under the little-finger side of the left *A hand* to push the left hand upward in front of the chest.

associate *v., n.* Same sign used for: **acquaint, brotherhood, each other, fellowship, fraternity, interact, mingle, one another, socialize.**
[Represents mingling with each other] With the thumb of the left *A hand* pointing up and the thumb of the right *A hand* pointing down, circle the thumbs around each other while moving the hands from left to right in front of the chest.

assume *v.* See signs for GUESS, TAKE. Related form: **assumption** *n.*

astound *v.* See sign for SURPRISE.

at fault *adj.* See sign for BLAME.

at last *adv. phrase.* See sign for FINALLY.

at odds *adj.* See sign for STRUGGLE.

attach *v.* See sign for BELONG.

attack *v.* See sign for HIT.

attain *v.* See sign for GET.

attempt *v.* See sign for TRY.

attend *v.* See also sign for GATHER[1]. Same sign used for: **go to.**

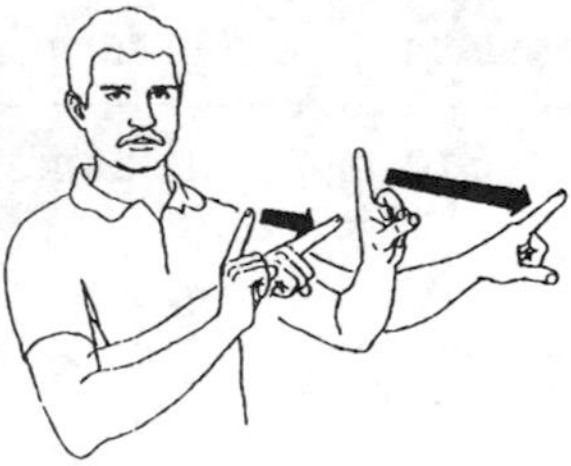

[**go** formed with a directed movement] Beginning with both extended index fingers pointing up in front of the chest, right hand closer to the chest than the left and both palms facing forward, move both hands forward simultaneously while bending the wrists so the fingers point forward.

attention *n.* Related form: **attend** *v.* Same sign used for: **concentrate, concentration, focus on, pay attention, watch.**

[Forms blinkers to direct one's attention] Move both *open hands* from near each cheek, palms facing each other, straight forward simultaneously.

attitude *n.*

[Initialized sign similar to sign for **character**] Move the thumb of the right *A hand* in a circular movement around the heart, palm facing left, ending with the thumb against the chest.

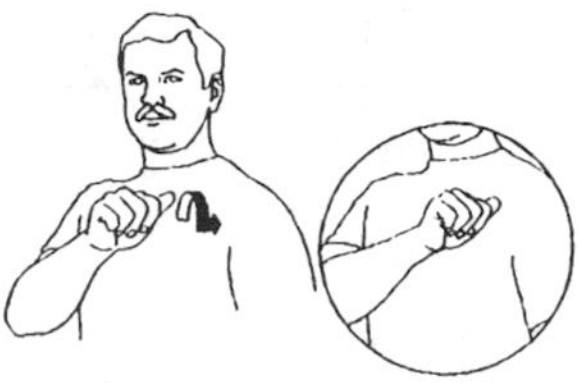

audience *n.* Same sign used for: **crowd, horde.**

[**people** + movement indicating large crowd of people] Move both *P hands,* palms facing down, in alternating forward circular movements in front of each side of the body. Then move both *curved 5 hands,* palms facing down, from in front of each side of the body forward with a simultaneous movement.

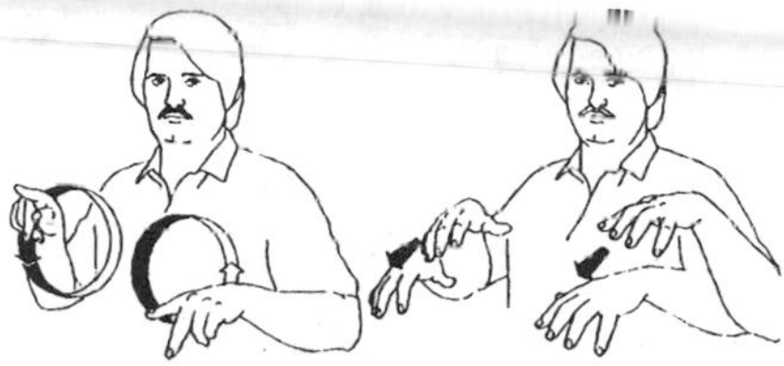

aunt *n.*

[Initialized sign formed near the right cheek] Shake the right *A hand*, palm facing forward, near the right cheek.

authority *n.*

[Shows muscle in arm symbolizing strength and authority] Beginning with the extended right thumb of *A hand,* palm facing left, near the left shoulder, move the hand down in an arc while twisting the right wrist, ending with the little-finger side of the right hand in the crook of the left arm, bent across the body.

automatic *adj.* See sign for FAST.

automobile *n.* See sign for CAR.

autumn *n.* See sign for FALL[2].

available *adj.* See sign for EMPTY.

avenge *v.* See sign for REVENGE.

average *adj.*

[Shows split down the middle] Beginning with the little-finger side of the right *open hand* across the index-finger side of the left *open hand,* palms angled down, twist the wrists down, bringing the hands apart a short distance with a double movement, palms facing down.

avoid *v., adj.* Same sign used for: **back out, elude, evade, fall behind, get away, shirk.**

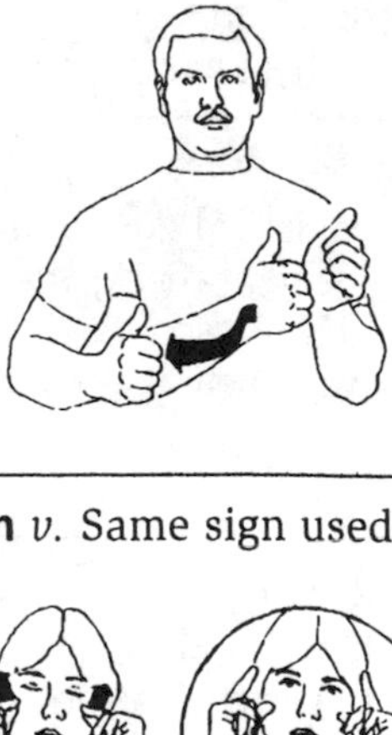

[One hand moves away from the other to avoid it] Beginning with the knuckles of the right *A hand,* palm facing left, near the base of the thumb of the left *A hand,* palm facing right, bring the right hand back toward the body with a wiggly movement.

awake *v.* Related form: **awaken** *v.* Same sign used for: **arouse, wake up.**

[Indicates eyes opening when becoming awake] Beginning with the *modified X hands* near each eye, palms facing each other, quickly flick the fingers apart while widening the eyes.

award *n.* See signs for GIFT.

aware[1] *adj.* Same sign used for: **familiar, knowledge.**

[Shows location of awareness] Tap the fingertips of the right *bent hand,* palm facing in, against the right side of the forehead with a double movement.

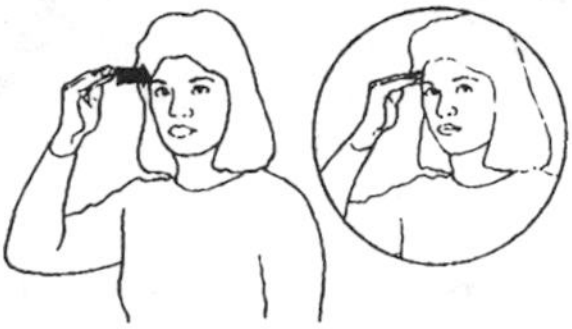

aware[2] *adj.* See sign for NOTICE[1].

awful *adj.* Same sign used for: **disastrous, dreadful, fierce, horrible, sordid, terrible.**

[Natural gesture used when indicating something terrible] Beginning with both *8 hands* near each side of the head, palms facing each other, flip the fingers open to *5 hands* while twisting the palms forward.

awkward *adj.* Same sign used for: **clumsy.**

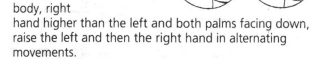

[Represents walking awkwardly] Beginning with both *3 hands* in front of the body, right hand higher than the left and both palms facing down, raise the left and then the right hand in alternating movements.

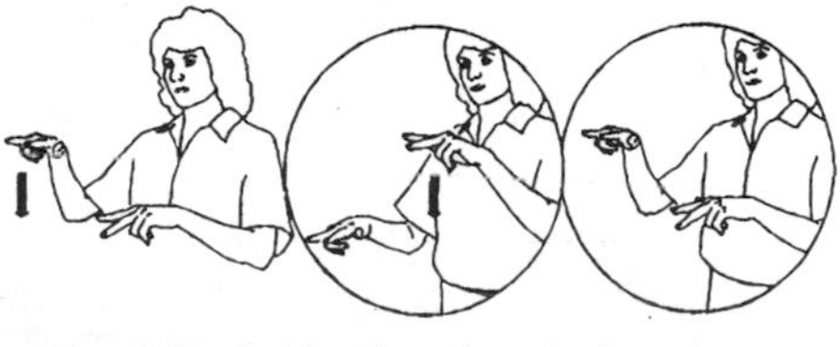

babble *v.* See sign for BLAB.

baby *n.* Same sign used for: **infant.**

[Action of rocking a baby in one's arms] With the bent right arm cradled on the bent left arm, both palms facing up, swing the arms to the right and the left in front of the body with a double movement.

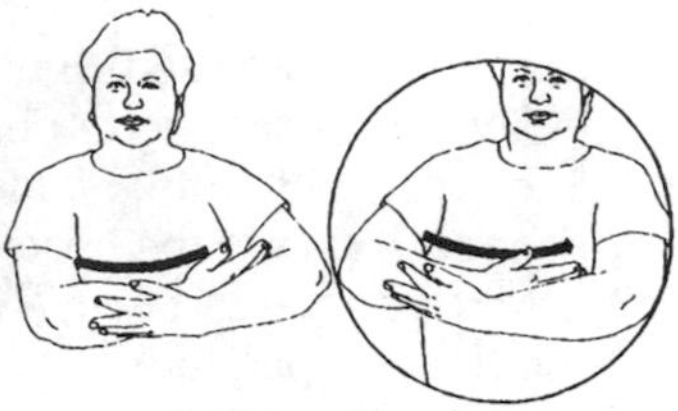

back *n.* Same sign used for: **rear.**

[Natural gesture indicating location] Pat the fingertips of the right *open hand* behind the right shoulder with a repeated movement.

back and forth *adv.* See sign for COMMUTE.

back out *v. phrase.* See signs for AVOID, RESIGN.

backslide *v.* See sign for BEHIND.

backup *n.* See sign for SUPPORT.

bad *adj.* Related form: **badly** *adv.* Same sign used for: **evil, nasty, naughty, wicked.**

[Gesture tosses away something that tastes bad] Move the fingers of the right *open hand* from the mouth, palm facing in, downward while flipping the palm quickly down as the hand moves.

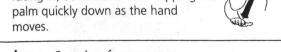

badge *n.* See sign for POLICE.

baggage *n.* Same sign used for: **luggage.**

[Shows carrying a bag in each hand] Shake both *S hands,* palms facing in, up and down with a short movement near each side of the waist with the elbows bent.

bake *v.* See sign for COOK.

balance *v., n.*

[Action shows trying to balance something] With a simultaneous movement bring the right *open hand* and the left *open hand,* both palms facing down, up and down in front of each side of the chest, shifting the entire torso slightly with each movement.

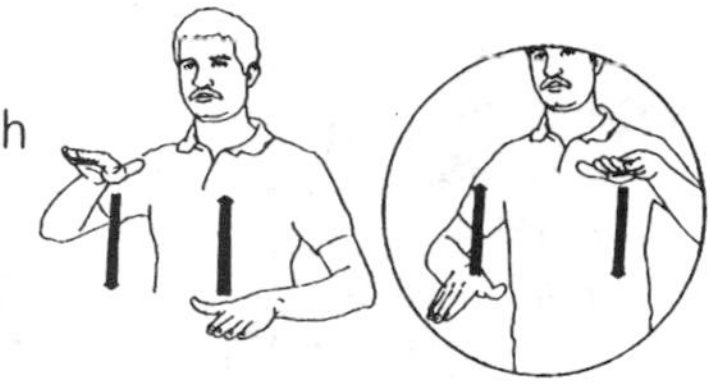

bald *adj.* Related form: **baldness** *n.* Same sign used for: **bareheaded, scalp.**

[Indicates bare area of head] Move the bent middle finger of the right *5 hand,* palm facing down, in a circle around the top of the head.

ball *n.*

[The shape of a ball] Touch the fingertips of both *curved 5 hands* together in front of the chest, palms facing each other.

balloon *n.* Same sign used for: **expand.**

[Shows shape of balloon as it expands] Beginning with the left fingers cupped over the back of the right *S hand* held in front of the mouth, move the hands apart while opening the fingers, ending with both *curved 5 hands* near each side of the face, palms facing each other.

ban *v.* See signs for FORBID, PREVENT.

banana *n.*

[Mime peeling a banana] With the extended left index finger pointing up in front of the chest, palm facing forward, bring the fingertips of the right *curved 5 hand* downward, first on the back and then on the front of the index finger, while closing the right fingers to the thumb each time.

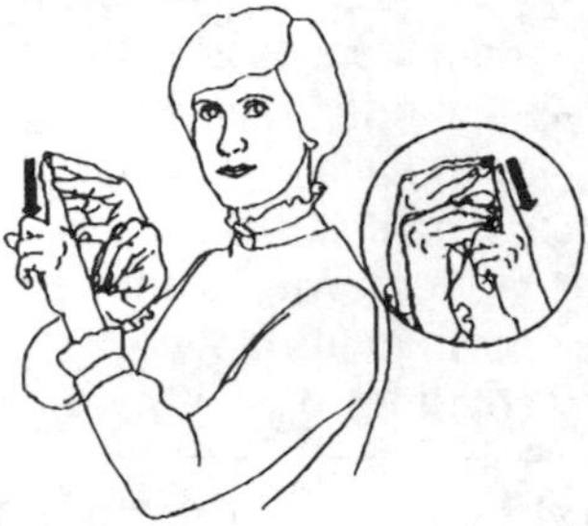

bandage *n.* Same sign used for: **Band-Aid** (*trademark*).

[Mime putting on a bandage] Pull the right *H fingers*, palm facing down, across the back of the left *open hand,* palm facing down.

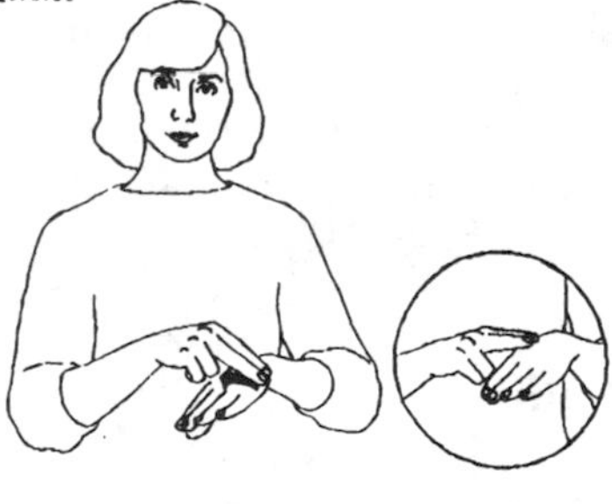

banter *v., n.* See sign for STRUGGLE.

bare *adj.* See signs for EMPTY, NUDE.

bareheaded *adj.* See sign for BALD.

barely *adv.* See sign for ALMOST.

barrier *n.* See sign for PREVENT.

base *n.* Related forms: **basic** *adj.*, **basis** *n.*

[Initialized sign] Move the right *B hand,* palm facing left, in a flat circle under the left *open hand,* palm facing down.

baseball *n.* Same sign used for: **softball.**

[Natural gesture of swinging a baseball bat] With the little finger of the right *S hand* on the index finger of the left *S hand,* palms facing in opposite directions, move the hands from near the right shoulder downward in an arc across the front of the body with a double movement.

based on *v.* See sign for ESTABLISH.

basement *n.* Same sign used for: **beneath, cellar.**

[Indicates an area beneath a house] Move the right *10 hand,* palm facing in, in a flat circle under the left *open hand* held across the chest, palm facing down.

batch *n.* See sign for PILE[1].

bath *n.* Related form: **bathe** *v.*

[Washing oneself when bathing] Rub the knuckles of both *10 hands,* palms facing in, up and down on each side of the chest with a repeated movement.

bathroom *n.* See sign for TOILET.

batter *n.* See sign for BEAT[1].

battery *n.* See sign for ELECTRIC.

battle *n., v.* Same sign used for: **war.**

[Indicates opponents in war-like maneuvers] Beginning with both *5 hands* in front of the right shoulder, palms facing down and fingers pointing toward each other, move the hands toward the left shoulder and then back toward the right shoulder.

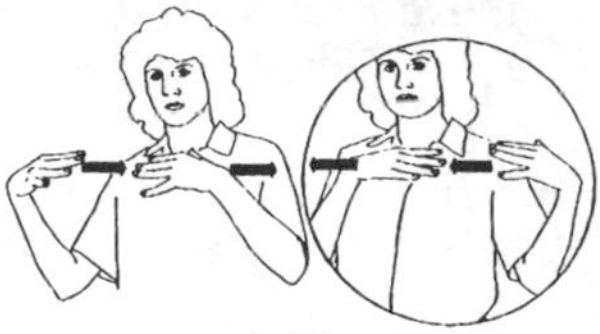

bawl out *v.* Same sign used for: **burst, burst out.**

[Represents a sudden burst of words] Beginning with the little finger of the right *S hand* on the top of the index-finger side of the left *S hand,* flick the hands forward with a deliberate double movement while opening the fingers into *5 hands* each time.

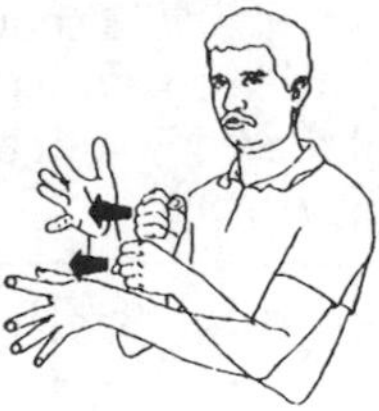

beads *pl. n.* Same sign used for: **necklace.**

[Location and shape of a necklace of beads] Move the index-finger side of the right *F hand,* palm facing left, from the left side of the neck smoothly around to the right side of the neck.

bean *n.*

[Shape of a string bean] Beginning with the extended left index finger, palm facing in and finger pointing right, held between the index finger and thumb of

the right *G hand,* palm facing left, pull the right hand outward to the right with a double movement.

bear[1] *n.*

[Action of a bear scratching itself] With the arms crossed at the wrist on the chest, scratch the fingers of both *curved hands* up and down near each shoulder with a repeated movement.

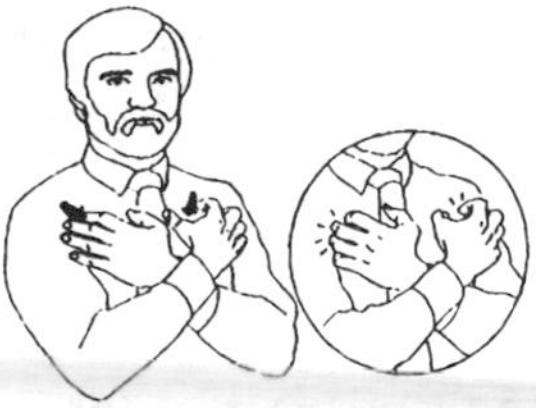

bear[2] *v.* See signs for BURDEN, PATIENT[1].

bear up *v. phrase.* See sign for ENCOURAGE.

beard *n.*

[Location and shape of beard] Beginning with the right *C hand* around the chin, palm facing in, bring the hand downward while closing the fingers to the thumb with a double movement.

beast *n.* See sign for ANIMAL.

beat[1] *v.* Same sign used for: **batter, mix, stir.**

[Mime beating using a spoon in a bowl] Move the right *A hand,* palm facing the chest, in a quick repeated circular movement near the palm side of the left *C hand,* palm facing right.

beat[2] *v.*

[Indicates beating something] Hit the back of the right *S hand,* palm facing in, against the palm of the left *open hand,* palm facing right, with a double movement.

beat[3] *v.* See also sign for DEFEAT.

[Directing a single blow] Beginning with the right *S hand* in front of the right shoulder, palm facing left, move the hand quickly forward while opening the fingers to form a *H hand.*

beau *n.* See sign for SWEETHEART.

beautiful *adj.* Related form: **beauty** *n.* See also sign for PRETTY. Same sign used for: **lovely.**

[Hand encircles a beautiful face] Move the right *5 hand* in a large circular movement in front of the face while closing the fingers to the thumb, forming a *flattened O hand.* Then move the hand forward while spreading the fingers quickly into a *5 hand.*

because *conj.* Same sign used for: **since.**

Bring the index finger of the right *L hand* with a sweeping movement across the forehead from left to right, changing to a *10 hand* near the right side of the head.

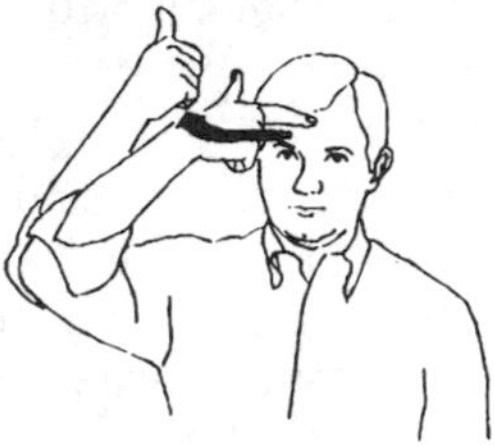

become *v.* Same sign used for: **turn into.**

[Hands reverse positions as if to change one thing into another] Beginning with the palm of the right *open hand* laying across the upturned palm of the left *open hand,* rotate the hands, exchanging positions while keeping the palms together.

bed *n.*

[Mime laying the head against a pillow] Rest the right cheek at an angle on the palm of the right *open hand.*

been *v.* See sign for SINCE[1].

been (there) Same sign used for: **finish**.

[Similar to sign for **touch** except made more quickly] Bring the bent middle finger of the right *5 hand* downward to tap quickly the back of the left *open hand* held across the chest, both palms facing down.

beer *n.*

[Initialized sign] Slide the index-finger side of the right *B hand,* palm facing forward, downward on the right cheek with a double movement.

before *adv.* Same sign used for: **last, past, previous, prior.**

[Indicates a time or place in the past] Move the fingertips of the right *open hand,* palm facing back, from near the right cheek back and down to touch the right shoulder.

beg *v.* Same sign used for: **implore, plead.**

[Mime extending a hand while begging] While holding the wrist of the upturned right *curved 5 hand* in the left palm, constrict the right fingers with double movement.

beginning *n.* See sign for START.

behind *prep.* Same sign used for: **backslide.**

[Indicates a position behind another] Move the right *10 hand,* palm facing left, from in front of the left *10 hand,* palm facing right, back toward the chest in a large arc.

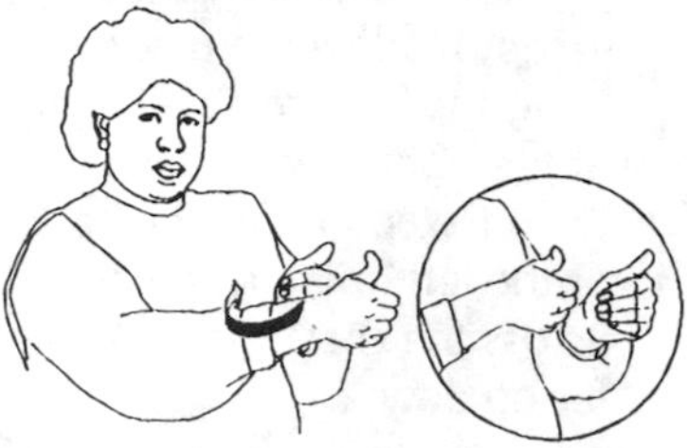

believe *v.* Related form: **belief** *n.*

[**mind** + clasping one's beliefs close] Move the extended right index finger from touching the right side of the forehead downward while opening the hand, ending with the right hand clasping the left *open hand,* palm facing up, in front of the body.

bell *n.* Same sign used for: **reverberate, ring.**

[Indicates the striking of a bell's clapper and the sound reverberating] Hit the thumb side of the right *S hand,* palm facing down, against the palm of the left *open hand.* Then move the right hand to the right while opening the fingers into a *5 hand,* wiggling the fingers as the hand moves.

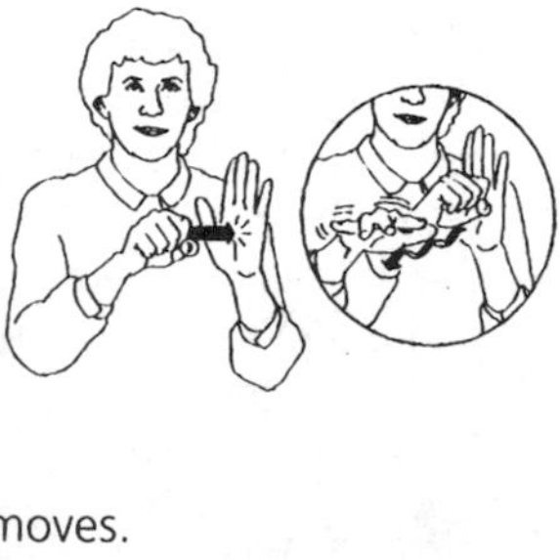

belong *v.* Same sign used for: **annex, attach, combine, connect, fasten, hook up, join, joint, link, unite.**

[Two things coming together] Beginning with both *curved 5 hands* in front of each side of the body, palms facing each other, bring the hands together while touching the thumb and index fingertips of each hand and intersecting with each other.

below *prep., adv.* Same sign used for: **beneath, bottom.**

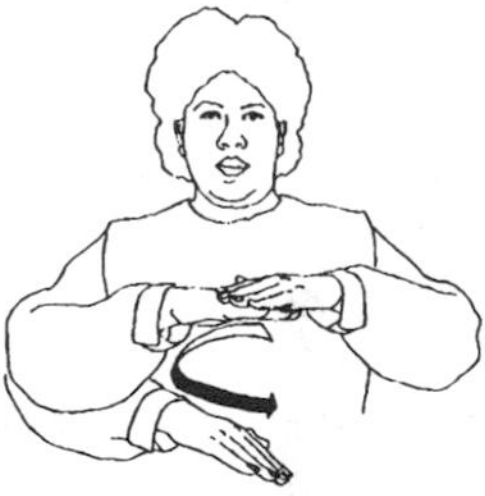

[Indicates a position below] Beginning with the left *open hand* on the back of the right *open hand,* both palms facing down, bring the right hand downward in an arc, ending several inches below the left hand.

belt *n.*

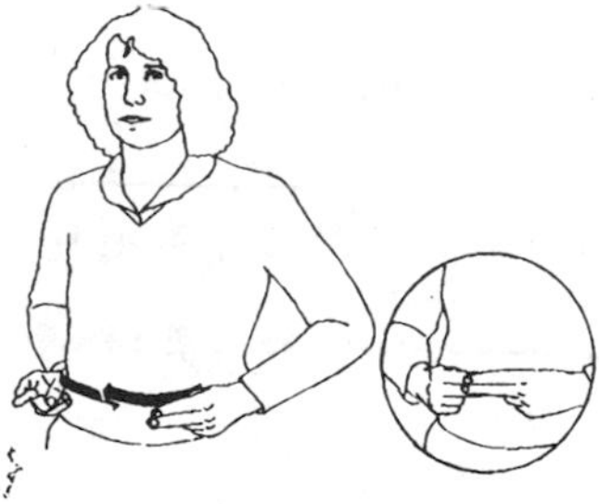

[Location of a belt] Move both *H hands* from each side of the waist around toward each other until the fingers overlap in front of the waist.

bend[1] *v.* Related form: **bent** *adj.*

[Indicates the ability to bend] Grasp the fingers of the left *open hand,* palm facing right, with the fingers of the right *flattened O hand,* and then bend the left fingers downward until both palms are facing down and hands are bent.

bend[2] *v.* See sign for BOW[1].

beneath *prep., adv.* See signs for BASEMENT, BELOW.

benefit *n.* Same sign used for: **advantage.**

[Pocketing a beneficial item] Push the thumb side of the right *F hand* downward on the right side of the chest, palm facing down, with a short double movement.

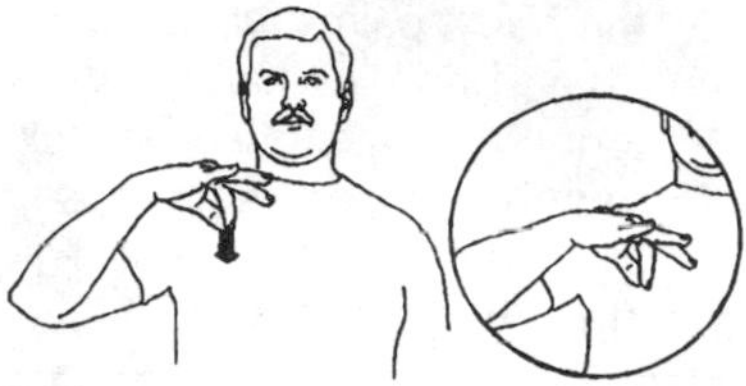

bent *adj.* See sign for DENT.

berry *n.*

[Twisting a berry to pick it from the vine] Grasp the extended little finger of the left hand, palm facing in, with the fingertips of the right *O hand* and twist the right hand outward with a double movement.

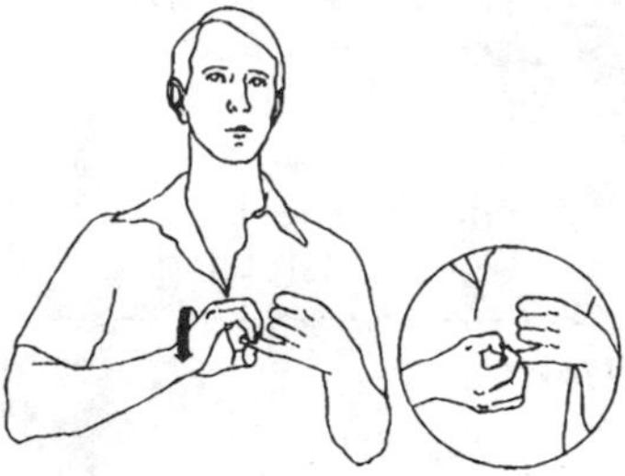

beside *prep.* Same sign used for: **next to.**

[Indicates a location beside another] Beginning with the palm of the right *bent hand,* palm facing in and fingers pointing left, touching the back of the left *bent hand,* palm facing in and fingers pointing right, move the right hand forward in a small arc.

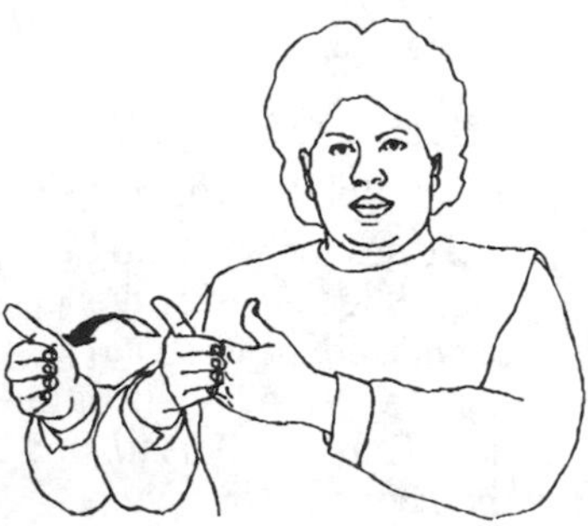

best *adj., adv.*

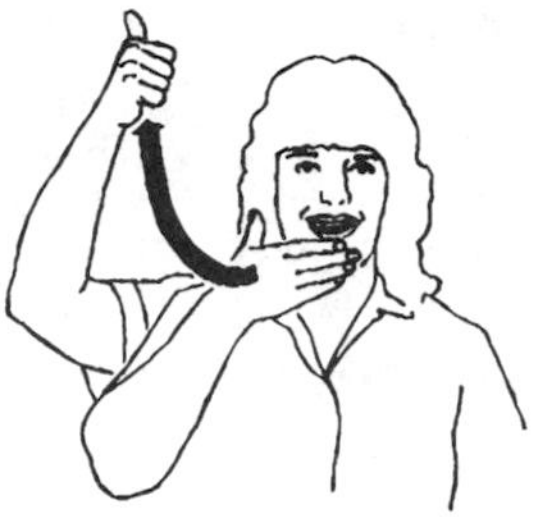

[Modification of **good,** moving the sign upward to form the superlative degree] Bring the right *open hand,* palm facing in and fingers pointing left, from in front of the mouth upward in a large arc to the right side of the head, changing to a *10 hand* as the hand moves.

bet *n., v.* Same sign used for: **bid, gamble, wager.**

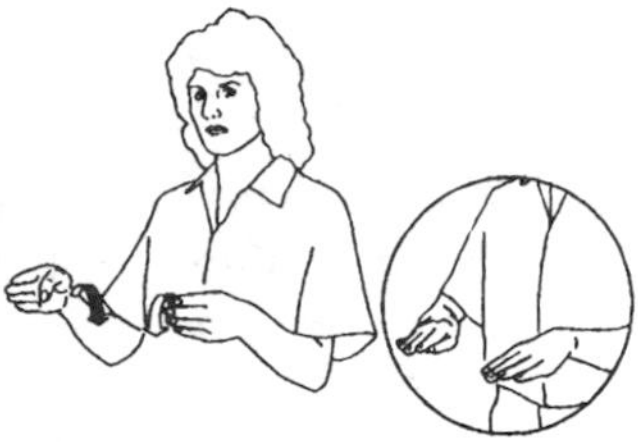

[Initialized sign showing the turning of dice] Beginning with both *B hands* in front of each side of the body, palms facing each other and fingers pointing forward, turn the hands toward each other, ending with the palms facing down.

better *adj., adv.*

[Modification of **good,** moving the sign upward to form the comparative degree] Bring the right *open hand,* palm facing in and fingers pointing left, from in front of the mouth upward in an arc to the right side of the head, changing to a *10 hand* as the hand moves.

between *prep.* Same sign used for: **gap, lapse.**

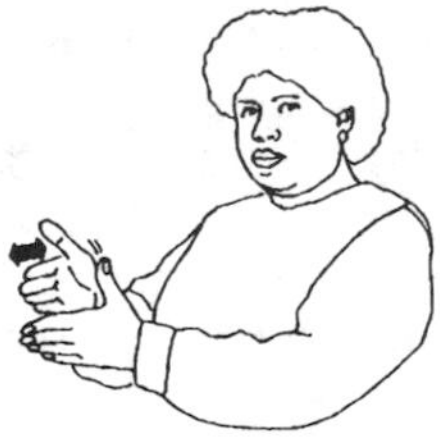

[Indicates space between two things] Brush the little-finger side of the right *open hand,* palm facing left, back and forth with a short repeated movement on the index-finger side of the left *open hand,* palm angled right.

beverage *n.* See sign for DRINK[1].

bewilder *v.* See sign for SURPRISE.

bewildered *adj.* See sign for PUZZLED.

beyond *prep., adv.* See sign for AFTER[1].

bicycle *n.*
[Shows action of pedaling a bicycle] Move both *S hands* in alternating forward circles, palms facing down, in front of each side of the body.

bid *n., v.* See signs for BET, SUGGEST.

big *adj.* See also sign for LARGE. Same sign used for: **enlarge.**
[Shows big size] Move both *L hands* from in front of the body, palms facing each other and index fingers pointing forward, apart to each side in large arcs.

big-headed *adj.* See sign for CONCEITED.

big shot *n.* See sign for CONCEITED.

bill *n.* See sign for DOLLAR.

bird *n.* Same sign used for: **chicken, coward, fowl.**
[Mime the action of a bird's beak] Close the index finger and thumb of the right *G hand,* palm facing forward, with a repeated movement in front of the mouth.

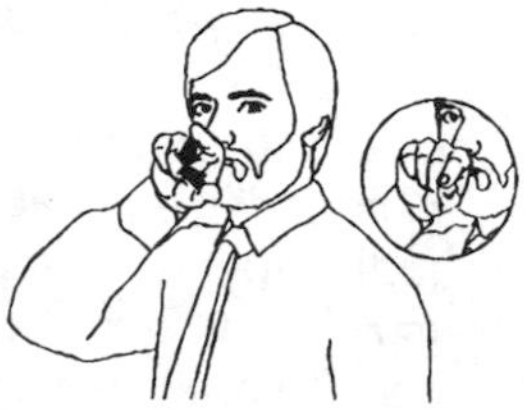

birth *n.* Same sign used for: **born.**

[Indicates the birth of a baby] Bring the right *open hand,* palm facing in, from the chest forward and down, ending with the back of the right hand in the upturned palm of the left *open hand.*

birthday *n.*

[**birth** + **day**] Bring the right *open hand,* palm facing in, from the chest forward and down, ending with the back of the right hand in the upturned palm of the left *open hand.* Then, with the right elbow resting on the back of the left hand held across the body, palm down, bring the extended right index finger downward toward the left elbow in a large sweeping arc.

biscuit *n.* See sign for COOKIE.

bizarre *adj.* See sign for STRANGE.

blab *v.* Same sign used for: **babble, chat, chatter, gab, gossip, talk, talkative.**

[Action of the mouth opening and closing] Beginning with both *flattened C hands* near each side of the face, palms facing each other, close the fingers and thumbs together simultaneously with a double movement.

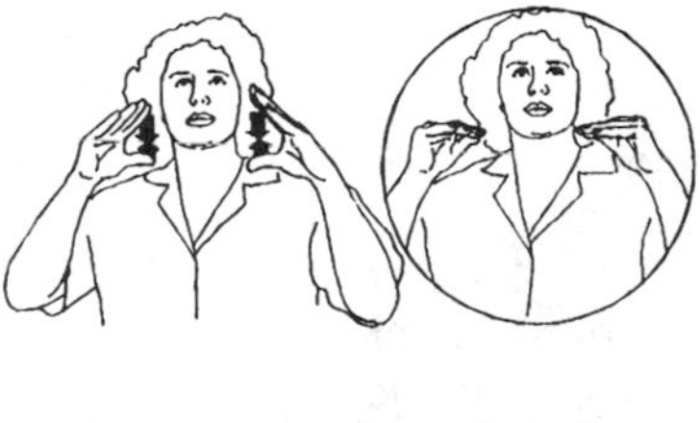

black *adj., n.*

[Shows a black eyebrow] Pull the side of the extended right index finger, palm facing down and finger pointing left, from left to right across the forehead.

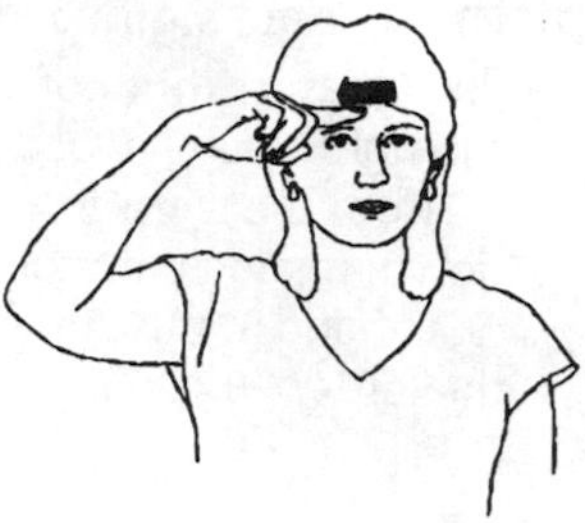

blame *v.* Same sign used for: **at fault.**

[Shoves blame at someone] Push the little-finger side of the right *A hand,* palm facing left, forward across the back of the left *A hand,* palm facing down.

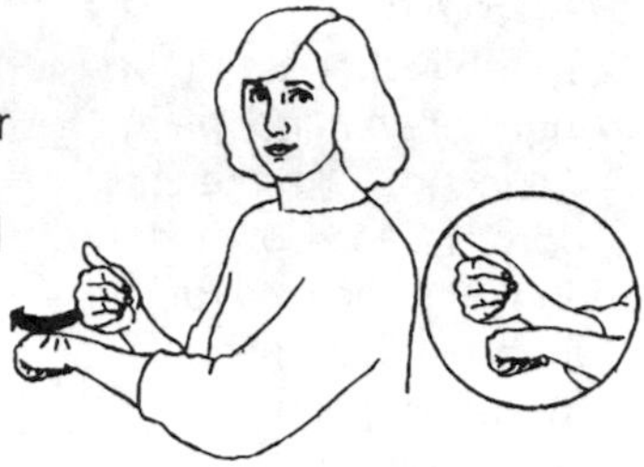

blank[1] *adj.* Same sign used for: **absent-minded.**

[Indicates a blank mind] Bring the bent middle finger of the right *5 hand,* palm facing in, from left to right across the forehead.

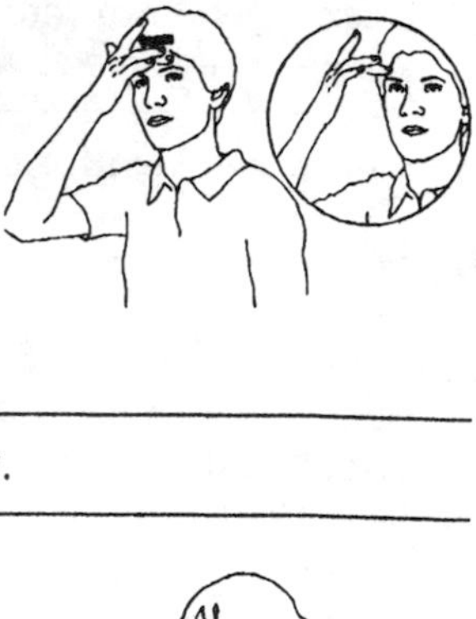

blank[2] *adj.* See sign for EMPTY.

blanket *n.*

[Initialized sign miming pulling up a blanket to the chest] Move both *B hands* from in front of the body, palms facing down and fingers pointing toward each other, upward, ending with both index fingers against the upper chest.

blend *v.* See signs for CIRCULATE, MESH, MIX[1].

block *v.* See sign for PREVENT. Related form: **blockage** *n.*

blood *n.* Related form: **bloody** *adj.*
Same sign used for: **shed.**

[**red** + a gesture representing the flow of blood from a wound] Brush the extended right index finger, palm facing in, downward on the lips. Then open the right hand into a *5 hand* and bring it downward while wiggling the fingers, palm facing in, past the open left hand held across the chest, palm facing in and fingers pointing right.

blouse *n.*

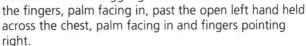

[Location and shape of woman's blouse] Touch the bent middle fingers of both *5 hands* on each side of the upper chest, and then bring the hands down in an arc, ending with the little fingers of both hands touching the waist, palms facing up and fingers pointing toward each other.

blow *v.*

[Indicates the flow of air through the mouth] Beginning with the back of the *flattened O hand* at the mouth, palm facing forward and fingers pointing forward, move the hand forward a short distance while opening the fingers into a *5 hand.*

blue *adj.*
[Initialized sign] Move the right *B hand,* fingers angled up, back and forth by twisting the wrist in front of the right side of the chest.

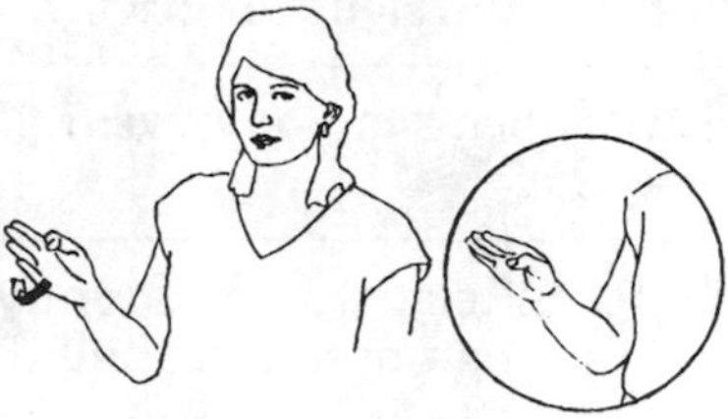

blurry *adj.* See sign for VAGUE.

board *n.*
[Initialized sign formed similar to sign for **member**] Touch the index-finger side of the right *B hand,* palm facing left, first to the left side of the chest and then to the right side of the chest.

boast *v.* See sign for BRAG.

boat *n.* Same sign used for: **cruise, sail, sailing, ship.**
[Shows the shape of a boat's hull] With the little-finger sides of both *curved hands* together, palms facing up, move the hands forward in a bouncing double arc.

body *n.*
[Location of the body] Touch the fingers of both *open hands,* palms facing in and fingers pointing toward each other, first on each side of the chest and then on each side of the waist.

bold *adj.* See signs for BRAVE, CONFIDENT, STRICT, WELL[1].

bone *n.*

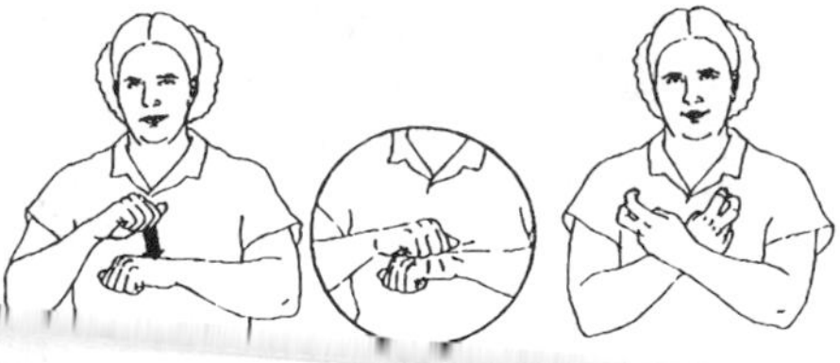

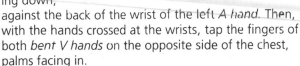

[**rock**[1] + **skeleton**] Tap the palm side of the right *A hand*, palm facing down, against the back of the wrist of the left *A hand*. Then, with the hands crossed at the wrists, tap the fingers of both *bent V hands* on the opposite side of the chest, palms facing in.

bonus *n.* See sign for ADD.

book[1] *n.*

[Represents opening a book] Beginning with the palms of both *open hands* together in front of the chest, fingers angled forward, bring the hands apart at the top while keeping the little fingers together.

book[2] *v.* See sign for APPOINTMENT.

boost *n.* See sign for SUPPORT.

boring[1] *adj.* Related forms: **bore** *v.*, **bored** *adj.* Same sign used for: **dull.**

[Boring a hole on the side of the nose] With the tip of the extended right index finger touching the side of the nose, palm facing down, twist the hand forward.

boring[2] *adj.* See sign for DRY.

born *adj.* See sign for BIRTH.

borrow *v.* Same sign used for: **lend me.**

[Bring borrowed thing toward oneself; opposite of movement for **lend**] With the little-finger side of the right *V hand* across the index-finger side of the left *V hand,* bring the hands back, ending with the right index finger against the chest.

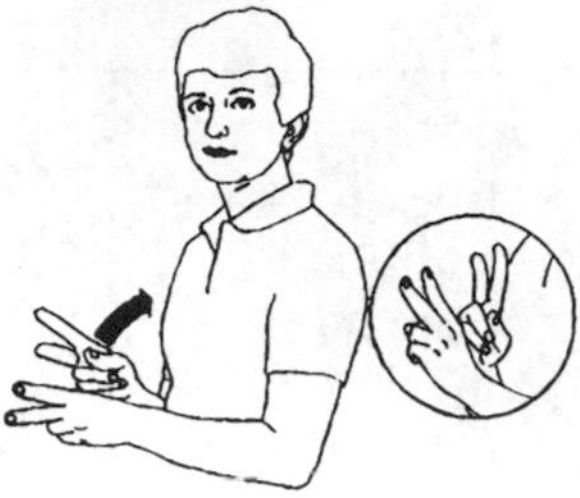

boss *n.* See signs for CAPTAIN, CHIEF[1].

both *adj., pron.* Same sign used for: **pair.**

[Two things pulled together to form a pair] Bring the right *2 hand,* palm facing in, downward in front of the chest through the left *C hand,* palm facing in and fingers pointing right, closing the left hand around the right fingers as they pass through and pulling the right fingers together.

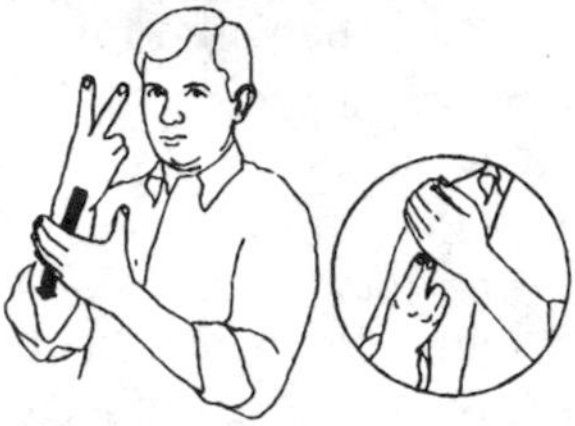

bother *v.* See sign for ANNOY.

bottle *n.* Same sign used for: **glass.**

[Shape of a bottle] Beginning with the little-finger side of the right *C hand,* palm facing left, on the upturned left *open hand,* raise the right hand.

bottom *n.* See sign for BELOW.

bow[1] *v.* Same sign used for: **bend, nod.**

[Represents bowing one's head] Beginning with the forearm of the right *S hand,* palm facing forward, against the thumb side of the left *B hand,* palm facing down and fingers pointing right, bend the right arm downward while bending the body forward.

bow² *n.* Same sign used for: **ribbon.**

[The shape of a hair bow] With both *S hands* crossed on the right side of the head, palms facing in, flip the *H fingers* of both hands outward with a deliberate movement.

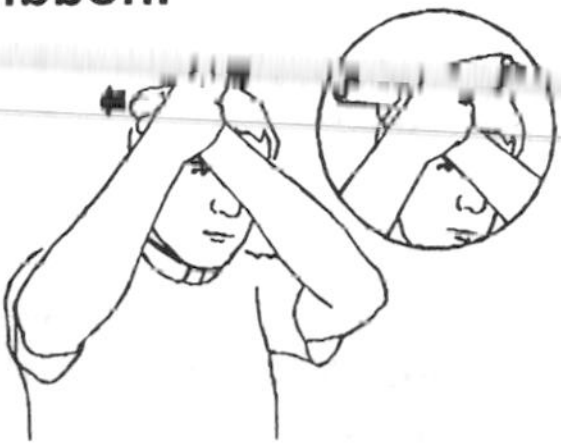

bowl *n.* Same sign used for: **pot.**

[The shape of a bowl] Beginning with the little fingers of both *C hands* touching, palms facing up, bring the hands apart and upward, ending with the palms facing each other.

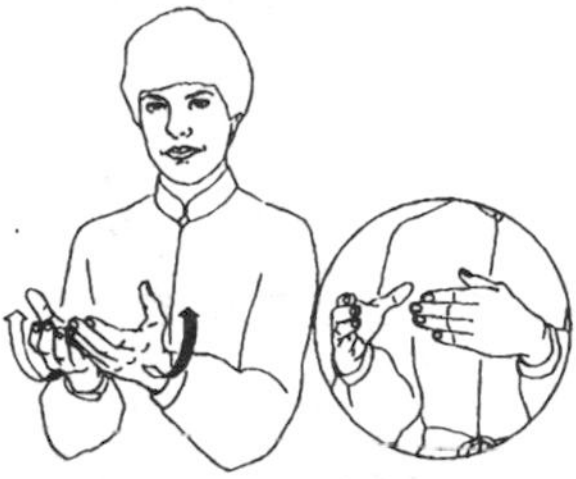

box *n.* See also sign for ROOM. Same sign used for: **package, present.**

[Shape of a box] Beginning with both *open hands* in front of each side of the chest, palms facing each other and fingers pointing forward, move the hands deliberately in opposite directions, ending with the left hand near the chest and the right hand several inches forward of the left hand, both palms facing in. (This sign may also be formed with the hands beginning in the final position and then changing to the first position.)

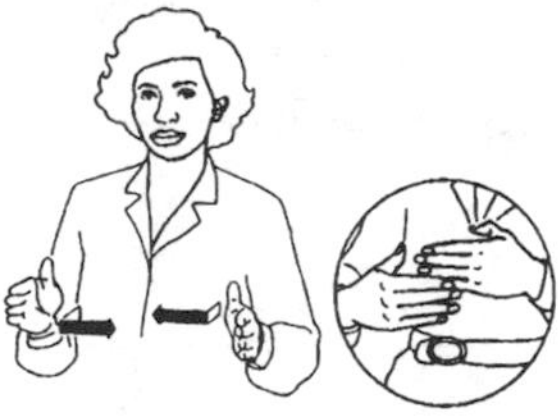

boy *n.* Same sign used for: **male.**

[Grasping the visor of a baseball cap] Beginning with the index-finger side of the right *flattened C hand* near the right side of the forehead, palm facing left, close the fingers to the thumb with a repeated movement.

boycott *v.* See sign for COMPLAIN.

bracelet *n.*
[The location of a bracelet] With the right thumb and middle finger encircling the left wrist, twist the right hand forward with a double movement.

bracket *n.* See sign for CLASS.

brag *v.* Same sign used for: **boast, show off.**
[Natural gesture while bragging] Tap the thumbs of both *10 hands,* palms facing down, against each side of the waist with a double movement.

brain *n.* See sign for MIND.

brand *n.* See signs for LABEL, STAMP^2.

brat *n.* See sign for CONCEITED.

brave *adj.* Same sign used for: **bold, courage.**
[Hands seem to take strength from the body] Beginning with the fingertips of both *5 hands* on each shoulder, palms facing in and fingers pointing back, bring the

hands deliberately forward while closing into *S hands*.

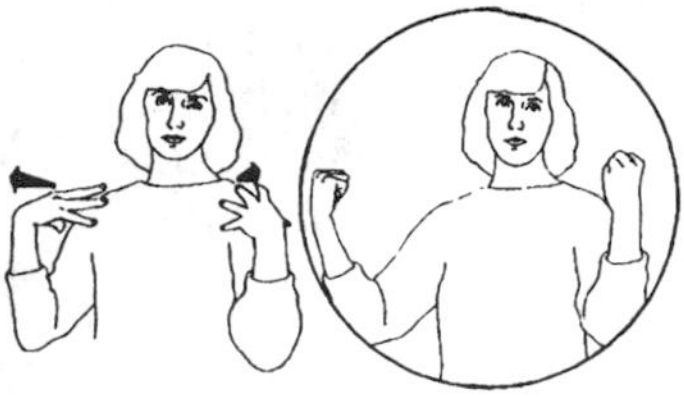

bread *n.*
[Slicing a loaf of bread] Move the fingertips of the right *bent hand* downward on the back of the left *open hand* with a repeated movement, both palms facing in.

break *v.* Same sign used for: **tear apart.**
[Mime breaking something] Beginning with both *S hands* in front of the body, index fingers touching and palms facing down, move the hands away from each other while twisting the wrists with a deliberate movement, ending with the palms facing each other.

break down *v.* Same sign used for: **collapse, destruction, fall through, tear down.**
[Indicates things crumbing down] Beginning with the fingertips of both *curved 5 hands* touching in front of the chest, palms facing each other, allow the fingers to loosely drop, ending with the palms facing down.

breakfast *n.*
[**eat** + **morning**] Bring the fingertips of the right *flattened O hand* to the lips. Then, with the left *open hand*

in the crook of the bent right arm, bring the right *open hand* upward, palm facing in.

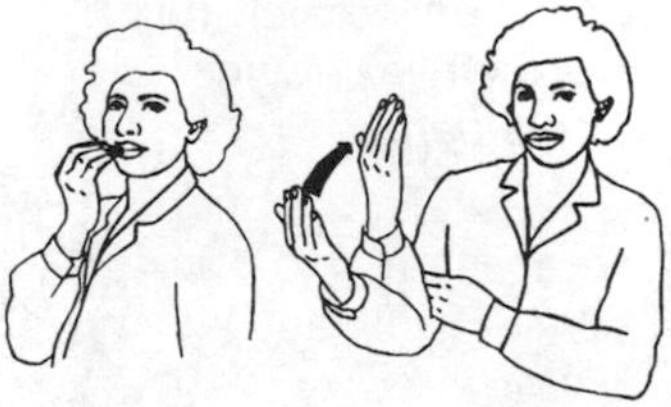

breath *n.* Related form: **breathe** *v.* Same sign used for: **expel, inhale, pant, respiration.**

[Indicates the movement of the lungs when breathing] With the right *5 hand* in front of the chest above the left *5 hand,* fingers pointing in opposite directions and palms in, move both hands forward and back toward the chest with a double movement.

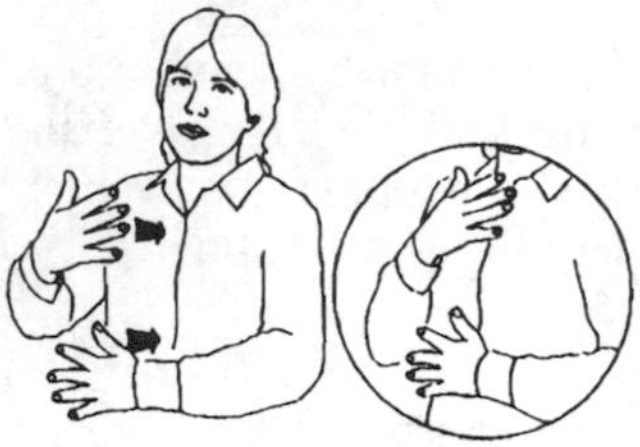

breed *v.* See signs for CONFLICT[1], PREGNANT[1].

bride *n.* Same sign used for: **bridesmaid.**

[Mime walking with a bride's bouquet] With the little-finger side of the right *S hand* on the thumbside of the left *S hand,* move the hands forward a short distance and then forward again.

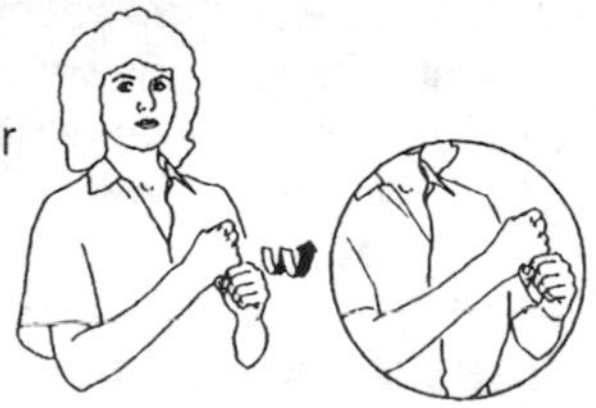

bridesmaid *n.* See sign for BRIDE.

bridge *n.*

[Shows the structure of supports for a bridge] Touch the fingertips of the right *V hand,* palm facing left, first to the bottom of the wrist and then near the elbow of the left arm held in front of the chest, palm facing down.

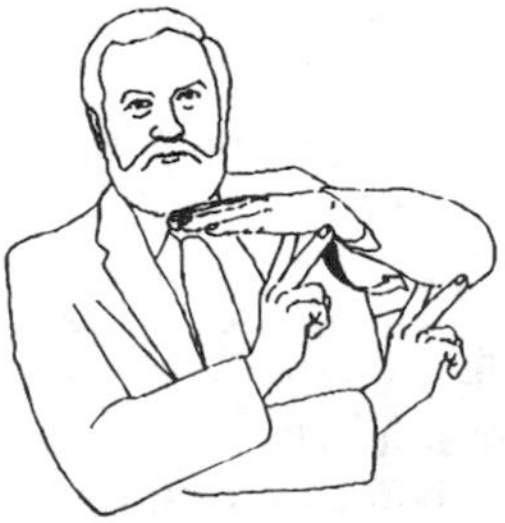

brief *adj.* See also sign for SHORT[1]. Same sign used for: **abbreviate, condense, reduce, squeeze, summarize.**

[Squeeze information together as if to condense] Beginning with both *5 hands* in front of the chest, right hand above the left hand and fingers pointing in opposite directions, bring the hands toward each other while squeezing the fingers together, ending with the little-finger side of the right *S hand* on top of the thumb side of the left *S hand.*

bright *adj.* Same sign used for: **clarify, clear, light, radiant.**

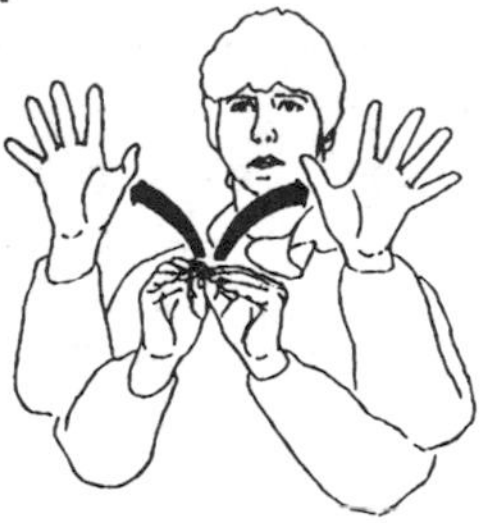

[Hands spread to reveal brightness] Beginning with the fingertips of both *flattened O hands* touching in front of the chest, palms facing each other, move the hands quickly upward in arcs to above each shoulder while opening to *5 hands.*

brilliant *adj.* See sign for SMART.

bring *v.* Same sign used for: **carry, deliver, return, transport.**

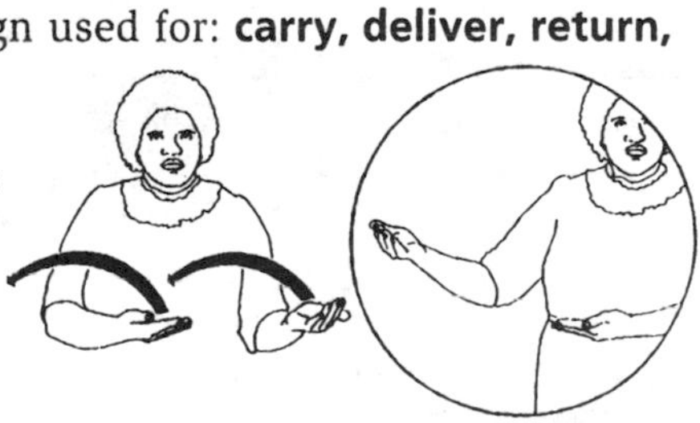

[Moving an object from one location to another] Move both *open hands,* palms facing up, from in front of the left side of the body in large arcs to the right side of the body. (This sign may be formed in the direction of the referent or its proposed new location.)

broad *adj.* See signs for GENERAL[1], WIDE.

broadcast *v., n.* See sign for ADVERTISE.

brochure *n.* See sign for MAGAZINE.

broke *adj. Informal.* See sign for PENNILESS.

broom *n.* Same sign used for: **sweep.**

[Mime sweeping] Beginning with both *S hands* in front of the right side of the body, right hand above the left hand and palms facing in, move the hands to the right with a double swinging movement.

brother *n.*

[The male area of the head plus a sign similar to **same**[1] indicating a boy in the same family] Beginning with the thumb of the right *L hand* touching the right side of the forehead, palm facing left, move the right hand downward, landing across the thumb side of the left *L hand,* palm facing right.

brotherhood *n.* See sign for ASSOCIATE.

brown *adj.*

[Initialized sign] Slide the index-finger side of the right *B hand,* palm facing left, down the right cheek.

browse *v.* See sign for LOOK OVER.

brush[1] *n., v.*
[Mime brushing one's hair] Move the palm of the right *A hand* down the right side of the head with a repeated movement.

brush[2] *n.* See sign for PAINT.

budget *n.* See sign for TRADE.

bug *n.* Same sign used for: **insect.**
[Represents a bug's antennas] With the extended thumb of the right *3 hand* on the nose, palm facing left, bend the extended index and middle fingers with a repeated movement.

build *v.* Related form: **building** *n.* Same sign used for: **construct, construction.**
[Shows putting one thing upon another to build something] Beginning with the fingers of the right *bent hand* overlapping the fingers of the left *bent hand* in front of the chest, palms facing down, reverse the position of the hands with a repeated movement as the hands move upward.

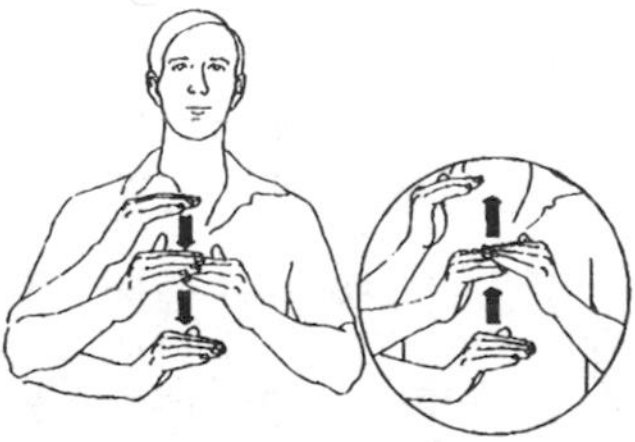

bulk *n.* See sign for PILE[1].

bully *n.* See sign for CONCEITED.

bump *n.* See sign for LUMP[1].

bunch *n.* See sign for CLASS.

burden *n.* Same sign used for: **bear, fault, liability,obligation, responsible, responsibility.**

[The weight of responsibility on the shoulder] With the fingertips of both *bent hands* on the right shoulder, push the shoulder down slightly.

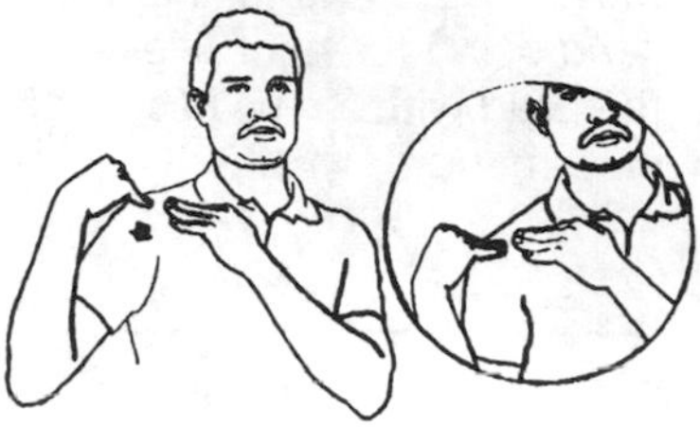

burglary *n.* See signs for ROB, STEAL.

burn *v.* See sign for FIRE[1].

burst *v.* See sign for BAWL OUT.

burst out *v. phrase.* See sign for BAWL OUT.

bury *v.* Same sign used for: **grave.**

[Shape of a mound of dirt on a grave] Move both *curved hands,* palms facing down and fingers pointing down, back toward the body in double arcs.

bus *n.*

[Initialized sign] Beginning with the little-finger side of the right *B hand* touching the index-finger side of the left *B hand,* palms facing in opposite directions, move the right hand back toward the right shoulder.

bust *v.* See sign for MEAN[1].

busy *adj.*

[Initialized sign] Brush the base of the right *B hand,* palm facing forward, with a repeated rocking movement on the back of the left *open hand,* palm facing down.

but *conj.* Same sign used for: **however.**

[Indicates opinions moving in opposite directions] Beginning with both extended index fingers crossed in front of the chest, palms facing forward, bring the hands apart with a deliberate movement.

butt in *v.* See sign for NOSY.

butter *n.* Same sign used for: **margarine.**

[Mime spreading butter] Wipe the extended fingers of the right *U hand,* palm facing down and thumb extended, across the palm of the left *open hand* with a repeated movement, drawing the right fingers back into the palm each time.

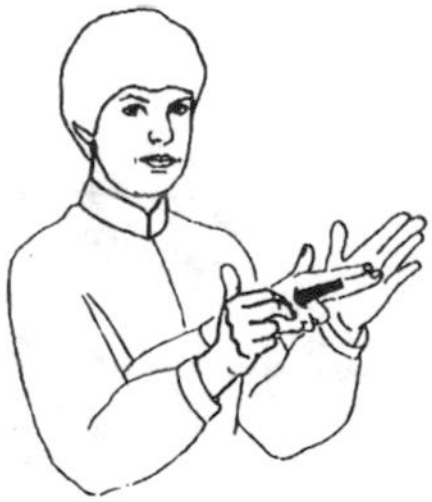

button *n.*

[Shape and location of buttons] Touch the index-finger side of the right *F hand,* palm facing left, first in the center of the chest, and then lower on the chest.

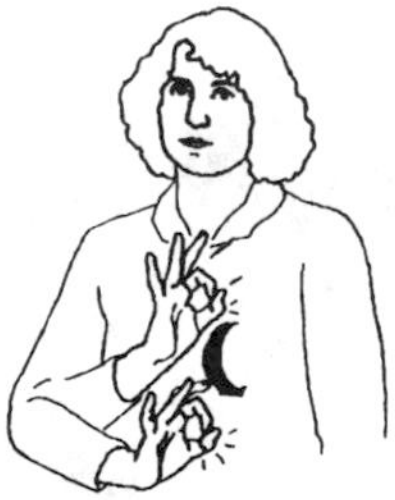

buy *v.* Same sign used for: **purchase.**

[Shows taking money from the hand to buy something] Beginning with the back of the right *flattened O hand,* palm facing up, in the upturned palm of left *open hand,* move the right hand forward in an arc.

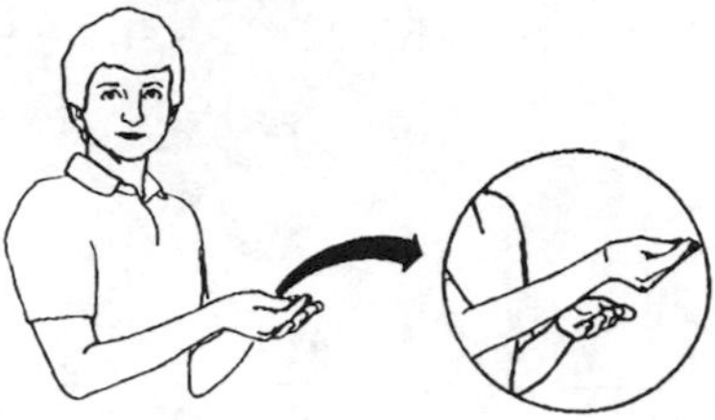

bye *interj.* See sign for GOOD-BYE.

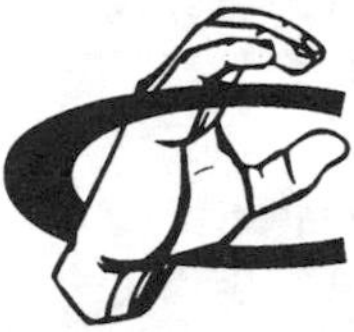

cab *n.* Same sign used for:
taxi.

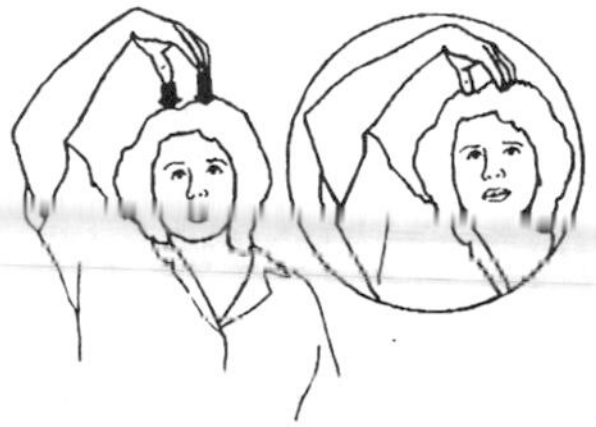

[Represents the lighted dome on top of a taxi] Tap the fingertips of the right *C hand,* palm facing down, on the top of the head with a double movement.

cafeteria *n.* Alternate form:
café.

[Initialized sign similar to sign for **restaurant**] Touch the index-finger side of the right *C hand,* palm facing left, first on the right side of the chin and then on the left side.

cage *n.*

[Shape of a wire cage] Beginning with the fingertips of both *4 hands* touching in front of the chest, palms facing in, bring the hands away from each other in a circular movement back toward the chest, ending with the palms facing forward.

cake *n.*

[Represents a cake rising] Beginning with the fingertips of the right *curved 5 hand* on the palm of the left *open hand,* raise the right hand upward in front of the chest.

calculator *n.*
[Mime using a calculator] Alternately tap each fingertip of the right *5 hand* while moving up and down the upturned left *open hand* held in front of the body.

calendar *n.*
[Initialized sign indicating turning pages on a calendar] Move the little-finger side of the right *C hand,* palm facing left, from the heel upward in an arc over the fingertips of the left *open hand,* palm facing in and fingers pointing up.

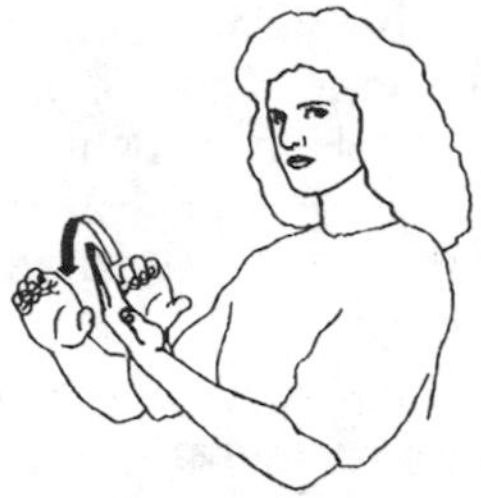

call[1] *v.* Same sign used for: **summon.**
[Tap on the hand to get one's attention] Slap the fingers of the right *open hand* on the back of the left *open hand,* palm facing down, dragging the right fingers upward and closing them into an *A hand* in front of the right shoulder.

call[2] *v.* Same sign used for: **name.**
[Similar to sign for **name**[1]] With the middle-finger side of the right *H hand* across the index-finger side of the left *H hand,* move the hands forward in an arc in front of the body.

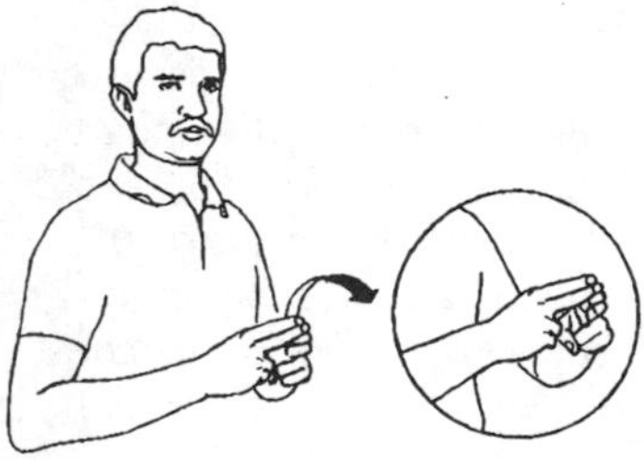

call[3] *v.* See sign for TELEPHONE.

calm *adj., v.* See signs for QUIET, SETTLE, SILENT.

calm down *v. phrase.* See signs for QUIET, SETTLE, SILENT.

camera *n.*

[Mimics taking a picture with a camera] Beginning with the *modified C hands* near the outside of each eye, palms facing each other, bend the right index finger up and down with a repeated movement.

can[1] *auxiliary v.* Same sign used for **may.**

[Both hands sign **yes**, indicating ability to do something] Move both *S hands*, palms facing down, downward simultaneously with a short double movement in front of each side of the body.

can[2] *n.* See sign for CUP.

cancel *v.* Same sign used for: **condemn, correct.**

[Finger crosses out something to cancel it] With the extended right index finger, draw a large X across the upturned left *open hand.*

candidate *n.* See sign for APPLY[2].

candle *n.* Same sign used for: **flame, glow.**

[Represents the flame on a candle] With the extended

right index finger touching the heel of the left *5 hand,* palm facing right, wiggle the left fingers.

candy *n.* Same sign used for: **sugar.**

[Similar to sign for **sweet**] Bring the fingers of the right *U hand* downward on the chin with a repeated movement, bending the fingers down each time.

can't *contraction.* Alternate form: **cannot.**

[One finger is unable to move the other finger] Bring the extended right index finger downward in front of the chest, striking the extended left index finger as it moves, both palms facing down.

cap *n.*

[Mime tipping a cap with a visor] Bring the right modified *X hand* from in front of the head, palm facing left, back to the top of the head.

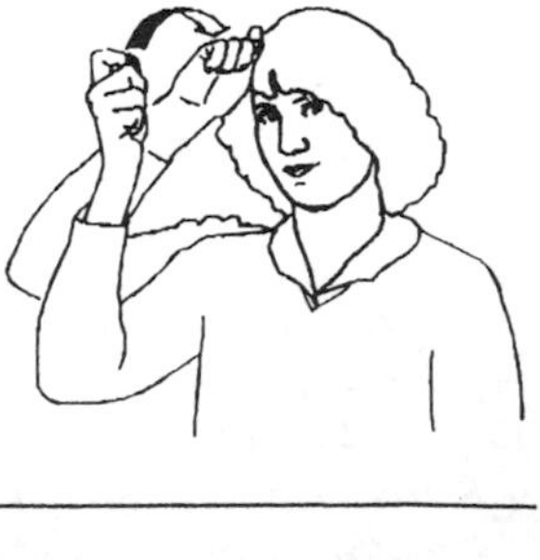

capable *adj.* See sign for SKILL.

capital *n.*

[Initialized sign] Tap the thumb of the right *C hand,* palm facing left, on the right shoulder with a double movement.

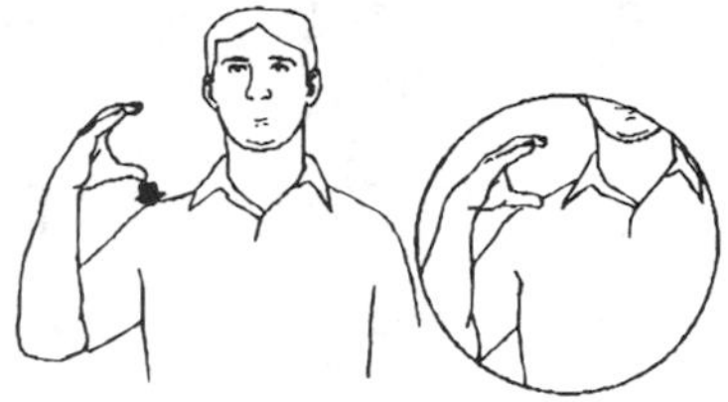

captain *n.* Same sign used for: **boss, chief, general, officer.**

[Location of epaulets on captain's uniform] Tap the fingertips of the right *curved 5 hand* on the right shoulder with a repeated movement.

capture *v.* Same sign used for: **arrest, catch, claim, conquer, nab, occupy, possess, repossess, seize, takeover.**

[Mime grabbing at something to capture it] Beginning with both *curved 5 hands* in front of each shoulder, palms facing forward, move the hands downward while closing into *S hands.*

car *n.* Same sign used for: **automobile.**

[Mime driving] Beginning with both *S hands* in front of the chest, palms facing in and the left hand higher than the right hand, move the hands in an up-and-down motion with a repeated alternating movement.

card *n.* Same sign used for: **check, envelope.**

[Shows shape of a rectangular card] Beginning with the fingertips of both *L hands* touching in front of the chest, palms facing forward, bring the hands apart to in front of each shoulder, and then pinch each thumb and index finger together.

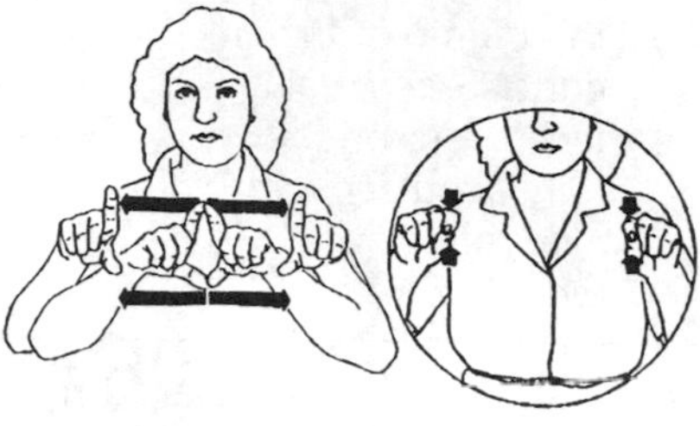

cards *n.* Same sign used for: **play cards.**

[Mime dealing cards] Beginning with both *A hands* in front of the body, palms facing each other, flick the right hand to the right with a repeated movement off the left thumb.

care[1] *n.* Same sign used for: **monitor, patrol, supervise, take care of.**

[Represents eyes watching out in different directions] With the little finger side of the right *K hand* across the index finger side of the left *K hand,* palms facing in opposite directions, move the hands in a repeated flat circle in front of the body.

care[2] *v.* See sign for TROUBLE[1].

careful *adj.* Same sign used for: **cautious.**

[Eyes looking attentively] Tap the little-finger side of the right *K hand* with a double movement across the index-finger side of the left *K hand,* palms facing in opposite directions.

carefully *adv.* Same sign used for: **cautiously.**

[Eyes looking in all directions] With the little-finger side of the right *K hand* across the index finger side of the left *K hand,* palms facing in opposite directions, move the hands upward and forward in large double circles.

careless *adj.* Related form: **carelessly** *adv.* Same sign used for: **reckless.**

[Misdirected eyes] Move the right *V hand* from near the right side of the head, palm facing left and fingers pointing up, down to the left in front of the eyes with a double movement.

carry[1] *v.* Alternate forms: **carry on** or **onto.**

[Having something in one's hands to transfer to another place] Beginning with both *curved hands* in front of the right side of the body, move the hands in a series of simultaneous arcs to the left, ending in front of the left side of the body.

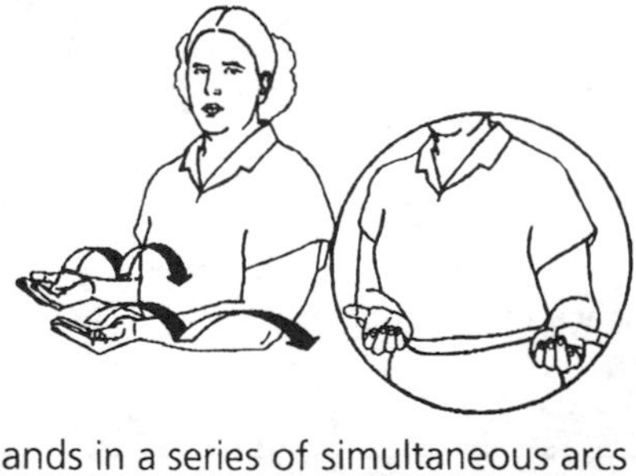

carry[2] *v.* See sign for BRING.

cast *v.* See sign for THROW.

casual *adj.* See sign for DAILY.

cat *n.*

[Cat's whiskers] Move the fingertips of both *F hands,* palms facing each other, from each side of the mouth outward with a repeated movement.

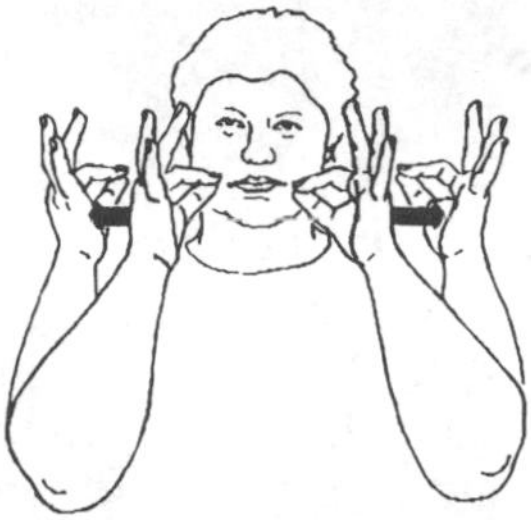

catch[1] *v.* Same sign used for **arrest, convict, nab.**

[Hand moves to "catch" the finger on the other hand] Move the right *C hand* from in front of the right shoulder, palm facing left, forward to meet the extended left index finger, palm facing right and finger pointing up, while changing into an *A hand*.

catch[2] *v.* Same sign used for: **prone.**

[One's fingers receive something and bring it to oneself] With an alternating movement, move first the right *curved 5 hand* and then the left *curved 5 hand* from in front of the chest, palms facing down and fingers pointing forward, back to the chest while changing into *flattened O* hands.

catch[3] *v.* See sign for CAPTURE.

catch up *v. phrase.*

[One hand catches up with the other hand] Bring the right *A hand* from near the right side of the chest, palm facing left, forward to the heel of the left *A hand,* palm facing right, held in front of the body.

category *n.* See sign for CLASS.

catsup *n.* See sign for KETCHUP.

cattle *n.* See sign for COW.

cause *v.*

[Something moving out from the body to affect others] Beginning with both *S hands* near the body, palms facing up and left hand nearer the body than the right hand, move both hands forward in an arc while opening into *5 hands.*

caution *v.* See sign for WARN.

cautious *adj.* See sign for CAREFUL.

cease *v.* See sign for STOP[1].

celebrate *v.* Related form: **celebration** *n.* Same sign used for: **festival, gala, rejoice.**

[Waving flags in celebration] With *modified X hands* in front of each shoulder, move both hands in large repeated outward movements, palms angled up.

cellar *n.* See sign for BASEMENT.

cent *n.* Same sign used for: **penny.**

[Symbolizes the head on a penny] With a double movement, move the extended right index finger forward at an outward angle from touching the right side of the forehead, palm facing down.

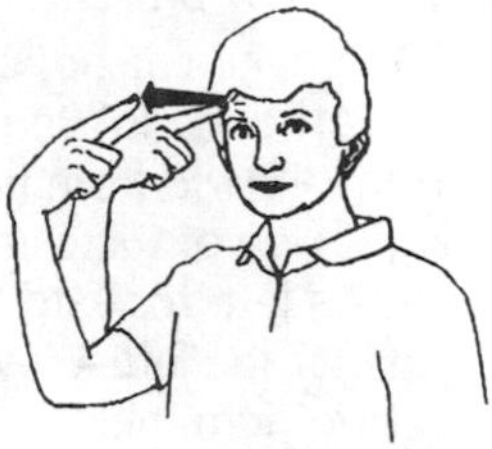

center *n.* See sign for MIDDLE.

cereal *n.*

[Action of scooping cereal from bowl to mouth] Move the right curved hand, palm facing up, from the palm of the left *open hand,* palm facing up, upward to the mouth with a double movement.

certain *adj.* See signs for SURE[1], TRUE.

certainly *adv.* See sign for TRUE.

certificate *n.* Related form: **certify** *v.*

[Initialized sign showing shape of certificate] Tap the thumbs of both *C hands* together in front of the chest with a repeated movement, palms facing each other.

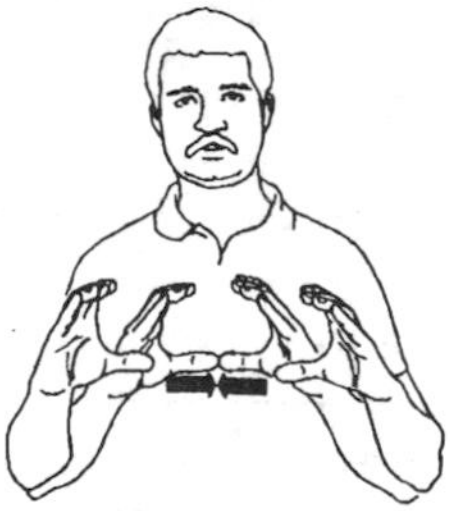

chair *n.* Same sign used for: **seat.**

[Fingers represent legs hanging down when sitting] With a double movement, tap the fingers of the right *curved U hand* across the fingers of the left *U hand,* both palms facing down.

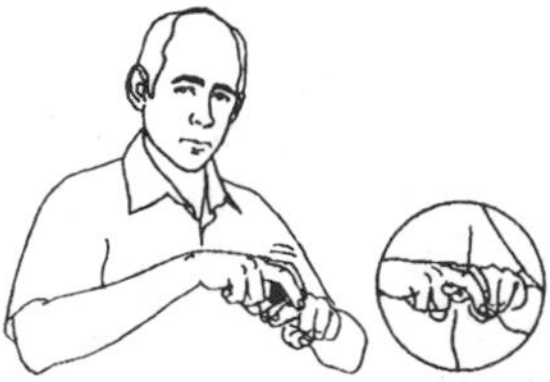

chalk up *v. phrase.* See sign for ACHIEVE.

challenge *v., n.* Same sign used for: **versus.**

[Hands seem to confront each other] Swing both *10 hands,* palms facing in, from in front of each side of the chest toward each other, ending with the knuckles touching in front of the chest, thumbs pointing up.

champagne *n.* See sign for COCKTAIL.

chance *n.*

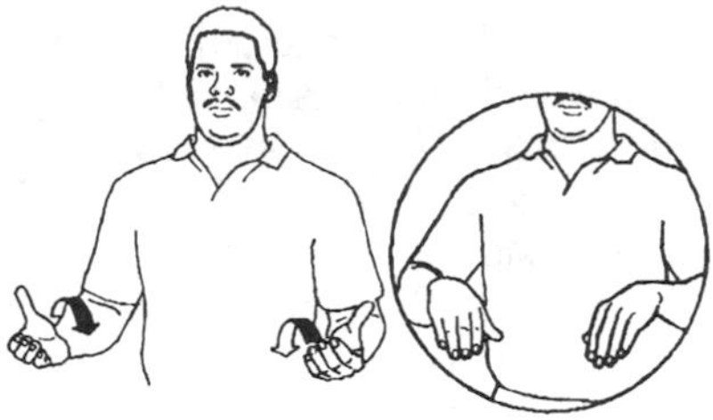

[Initialized sign formed like turning over dice] Beginning with both *C hands* in front of each side of the body, palms facing up, flip the hands over, ending with the palms facing down.

change[1] *v.* See also sign for TURN. Same sign used for: **adapt, adjust, alter, justify, modify, shift, switch.**

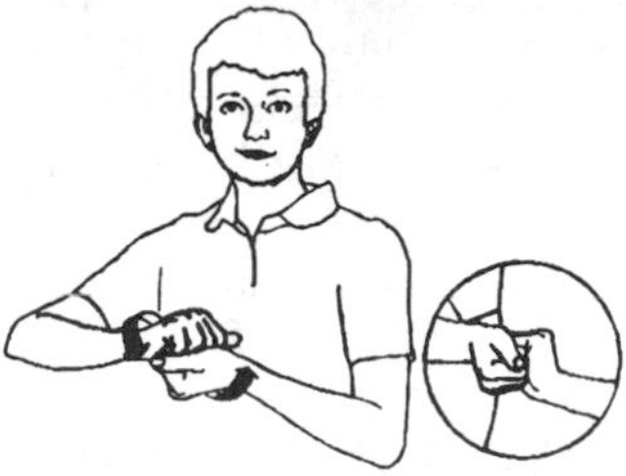

[Hands seem to twist something as if to change it] With the palm sides of both *A hands* together, right hand above left, twist the wrists in opposite directions in order to reverse positions.

change[2] *n.* See sign for SHARE. Shared idea of dividing an amount of money to be shared.

chant *n.* See sign for MUSIC.

chaos *n.* See sign for MESSY.

chapel *n.* See sign for CHURCH.

character *n.* Related form: **characteristic** *n.*

[Initialized sign similar to sign for **personality**] Move the right *C hand,* palm facing left, in a small circle and then back against the left side of the chest.

charge[1] *v.* Same sign used for: **credit card.**

[Represents getting impression of credit card charge] Rub the little-finger side of the right *S hand,* palm facing in, back and forth on the upturned left *open hand.*

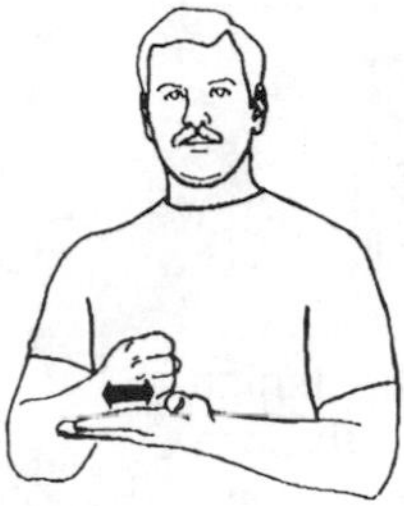

charge[2] *v.* See signs for APPLY[1], COST.

charity *n.* See sign for GIFT.

chart *n.* See sign for SCHEDULE[1].

chase *v.* Same sign used for: **pursue**.

[One hand seems to pursue the other hand] Move the right *A hand,* palm facing left, in a spiraling movement from in front of the chest forward, to behind the left *A hand* held somewhat forward of the body.

chat[1] *v.* Same sign used for: **talk.**

[Exchanging dialogue between two people] Move both *5 hands,* palms angled up, from in front of each shoulder downward at an angle toward each other with a repeated movement.

chat[2] *v.* See sign for BLAB.

chatter *v.* See sign for BLAB.

cheap *adj.*

[Pushing down the cost] Brush the index-finger side of the right *B hand* downward on the palm of the left *open hand,* bending the right wrist as it moves down.

check[1] *v.* Same sign used for: **examine, inspect.**

[Bringing one's attention to something to inspect it] Move the extended right index finger from the nose down to strike sharply off the upturned palm of the left *open hand,* and then upward again.

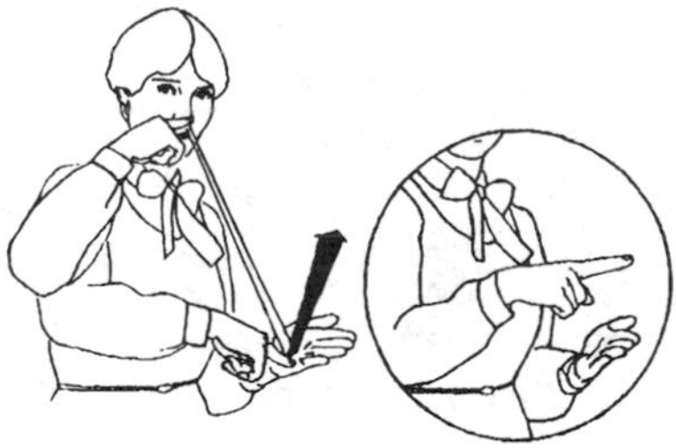

check[2] *n.* See sign for CARD.

check for *v. phrase.* See sign for LOOK FOR.

cheer *n.* See sign for HAPPY.

cheerful *adj.* See signs for FRIENDLY, HAPPY.

cheese *n.*
[Pressing cheese in a cheese press] With the heel of the right *open hand* pressed on the heel of the upturned left *open hand,* palms facing each other and perpendicular to each other, twist the right hand forward and back slightly with a repeated movement.

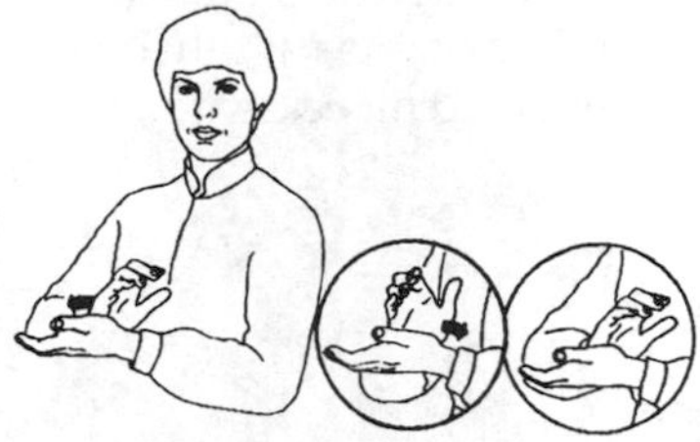

chew *v.* Same sign used for: **grind.**
[Represents grinding motion of teeth when chewing] With the palm sides of both *A hands* together, right hand on top of the left hand, move the hands in small repeated circles in opposite directions, causing the knuckles of the two hands to rub together.

chewing gum *n.* Same sign used for: **gum.**
[Action of jaw when chewing gum] With the fingertips of the right *V hand* against the right side of the chin, palm facing down, move the hand toward the face with a double movement by bending the fingers.

chicken *n.* See sign for BIRD.

chief[1] *n., adj.* Same sign used for: **boss, officer, prominent, superior.**
[Shows higher location] Move the right *10 hand* upward from in front of the right side of the chest, palm

facing in and thumb pointing up.

chief[2] *n.* See sign for CAPTAIN.

child *n.*

[Patting child on the head] Pat the right *bent hand* downward with a short repeated movement in front of the right side of the body, palm facing down.

children *pl. n.*

[Patting a number of children on their heads] Pat the right *open hand,* palm facing down, in front of the right side of the body and then to the right with a double arc.

chilly *adj.* See sign for COLD[2].

chocolate *n., adj.*

[Initialized sign] Move the thumb side of the right *C hand,* palm facing forward, in a repeated circle on the back of the left *open hand* held in front of the chest, palm facing down.

choice *n.* See sign for EITHER[1].

choose[1] *v.* Related form: **choice** *n.* See also sign for SELECT. Same sign used for: **assign, draw, pick.**

[Hand picks from alternatives] Beginning with the bent thumb and index finger of the right *5 hand* touching the index finger of the left *5 hand,* palms facing each other, pull the right hand back toward the right shoulder while pinching the thumb and index finger together.

choose[2] *v.* See sign for APPOINT.

Christmas *n.*

[Initialized sign showing the shape of a wreath] Move the right *C hand,* palm facing forward, in a large arc from in front of the left shoulder to in front of the right shoulder.

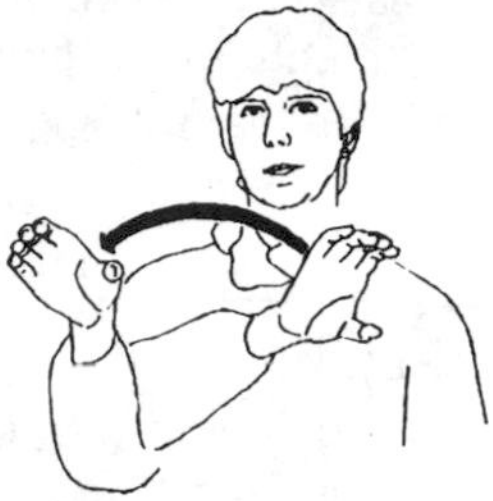

church *n.* Same sign used for: **chapel.**

[Initialized sign similar to sign for **rock**[1]] Tap the thumb of the right *C hand,* palm facing forward, on the back of the left *S hand,* palm facing down.

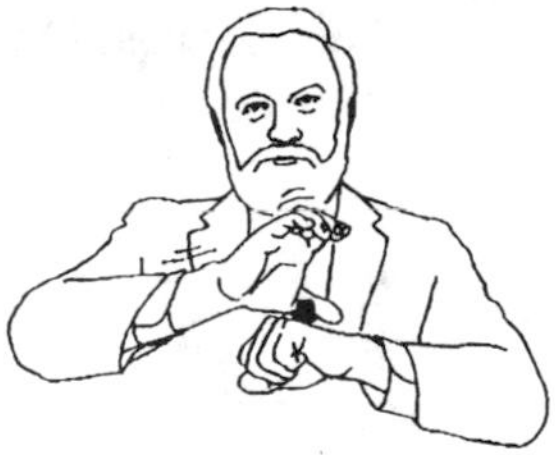

cigarette *n.*

[Tapping a cigarette to settle the tobacco] Tap the extended index finger and little finger of the right hand with a double movement on the extended left index finger, both palms facing down.

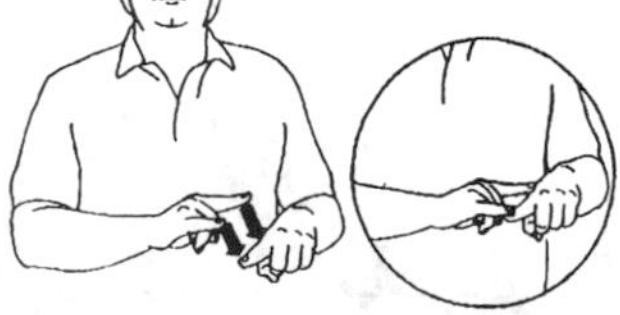

circle[1] *n.* Same sign used for: **cycle, round.**

[Shape of circle] Draw a circle in the air in front of the right side of the chest with the extended right index finger, palm facing down and finger pointing forward.

circle[2] *n.*

[Represents a number of people sitting in a circular pattern] Beginning with both *4 hands* in front of the chest, palms facing forward, bring the hands away from each other in outward arcs while turning the palms in, ending with the little fingers together.

circulate *v.* Related form: **circulation** *n.* Same sign used for: **blend, merge, mix, random.**

[Movement of circulating similar to sign for **mix**] Beginning with the right *5 hand* hanging down in front of the chest, palm facing in and fingers pointing down, and the left *5 hand* below the right hand, palm facing up and fingers pointing up, move the hands in circles around each other.

circumstance *n.* See sign for CONDITION.

city *n.* Same sign used for: **community.**

[Multiple housetops] With the palms of both *bent hands* facing in opposite directions and the fingertips touching, separate the fingertips, twist the wrists, and touch the fingertips again with a double movement.

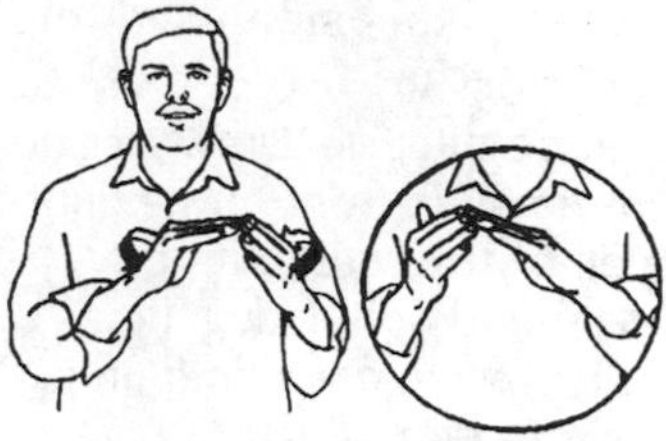

claim *v.* See sign for CAPTURE.

clap *v.* See sign for APPLAUD.

clarify *v.* See sign for BRIGHT.

class *n.* Same sign used for: **bracket, bunch, category, group, mass, section, series.**

[Initialized sign showing an identifiable group] Beginning with both *C hands* in front of the chest, palms facing each other, bring the hands away from each other in outward arcs while turning the palms in, ending with the little fingers near each other.

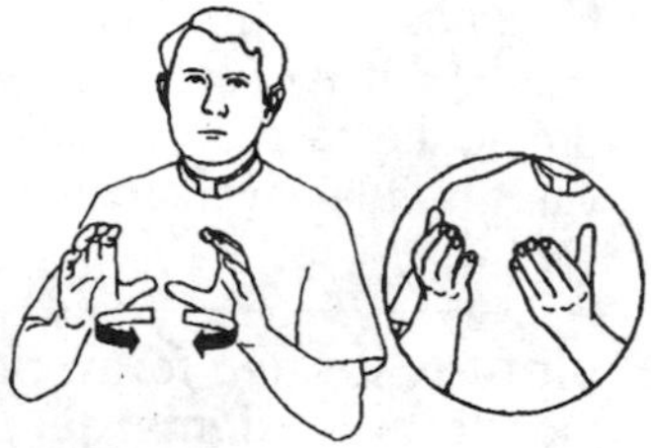

classical *adj.* See sign for FANCY.

classified *adj.* See sign for SECRET.

clean *v.* Alternate form: **clean up.**

[Wiping dirt off something to clean it] Slide the palm of the right *open hand* from the heel to the fingers of the upturned palm of the left *open hand* with a repeated movement. For the adjective, the same sign is used, but made with a double movement.

clear *adj.* See sign for BRIGHT.

clever *adj.* See sign for SMART.

climb *v.* Same sign used for: **ascend, ladder.**

[Mime climbing a ladder] Beginning with both *curved 5 hands* in front of the chest, palms facing forward and right hand higher than the left, move the hands upward one at a time with an alternating movement.

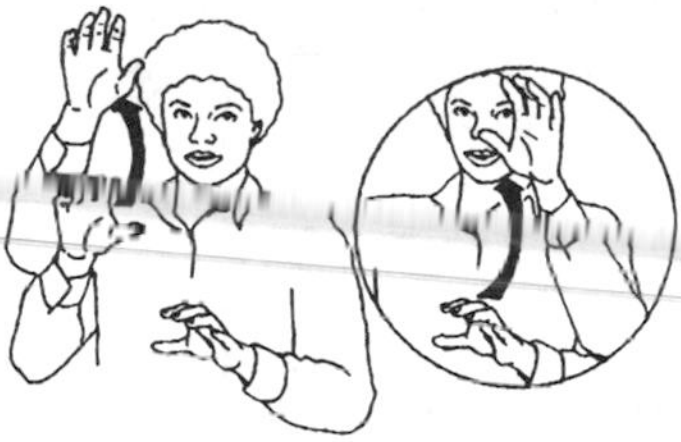

cling to *v. phrase.* See sign for DEPEND.

clock *n.*

[**time** + round shape of a clock's face] Tap the curved right index finger on the back of the left wrist. Then hold both *modified C hands* in front of each side of the face, palms facing each other.

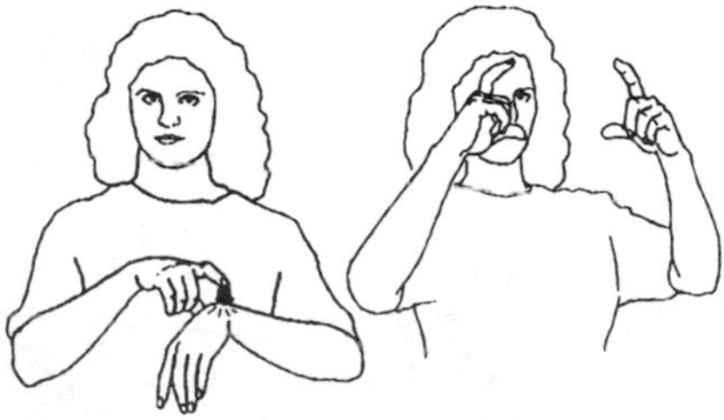

close *adv.* Same sign used for: **approach, near.**

[Moves one hand close to the other] Bring the back of the right *bent hand* from the chest forward toward the left *bent hand,* both palms facing in and fingers pointing in opposite directions.

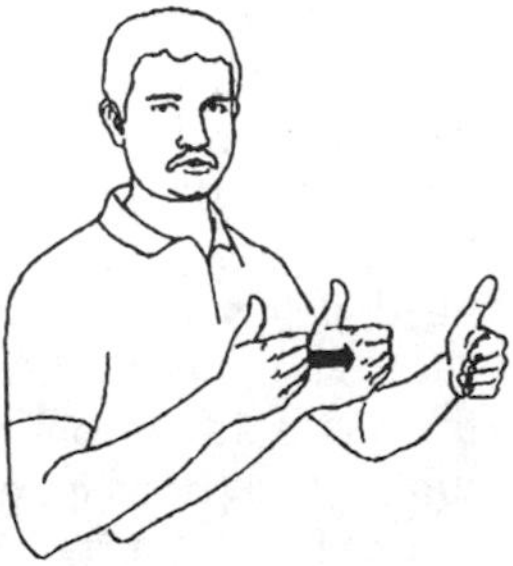

closet *n.*
[**clothes** + **door**] Brush the thumbs of both *5 hands* downward on each side of the chest with a double movement. Then, beginning with the index-finger side of both *B hands* touching in front of the chest, palms facing forward and fingers pointing up, swing the right hand back toward the right shoulder with a double movement by twisting the wrist.

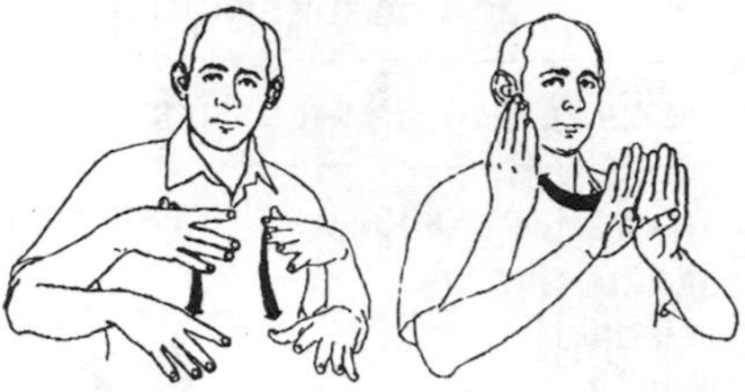

close up *adv.*
[Location of something close up to the face] Move the right *open hand,* palm facing in and fingers pointing up, back toward the face.

clothes *pl. n.* Same sign used for: **costume, dress, suit.**
[Location of clothes on body] Brush the thumbs of both *5 hands* downward on each side of the chest with a double movement.

cloud *n.*
[Shape and location of clouds] Beginning with both *C hands* near the left side of the head, palms facing each other, bring the hands away from each other in outward arcs while turning the palms in, ending with the little fingers close together. Repeat the movement near the right side of the head.

clumsy[1] *adj.* Same sign used for: **inexperienced.**

[Being held back, causing one to be clumsy] While holding the thumb of the right *5 hand* tightly in the left *S hand,* twist the right hand forward and down.

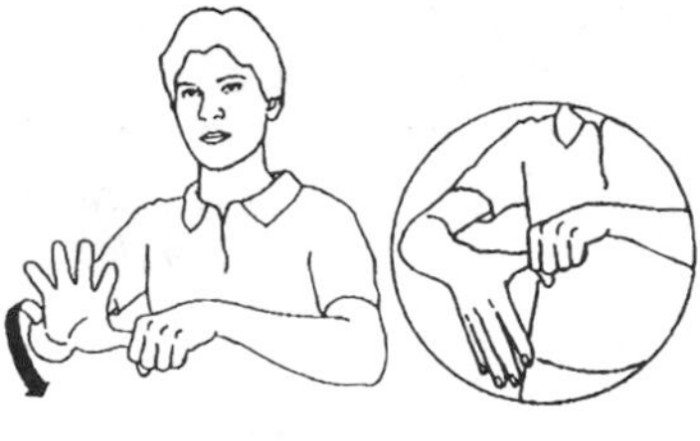

clumsy[2] *adj.* See sign for AWKWARD.

coach *n.*

[Initialized sign similar to sign for **captain**] Tap the thumb of the right *C hand,* palm facing left, against the right shoulder with a double movement.

coarse *adj.* See sign for ROUGH.

coat *n.* Same sign used for: **jacket.**

[A coat's lapels] Bring the thumbs of both *A hands* from near each shoulder, palms facing in, downward and toward each other, ending near the waist.

cocktail *n.* Same sign used for: **champagne, drink.**

[Mime drinking from a small glass] Beginning with the thumb of the right *modified C hand* near the mouth, palm facing left, tip the index finger back toward the face.

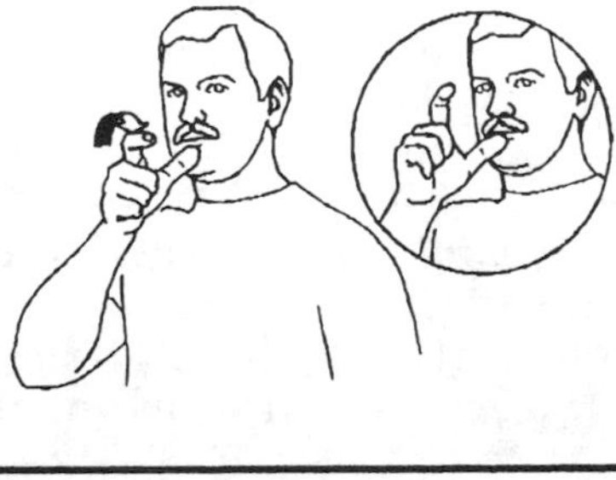

coffee *n.*
[Grind coffee beans] Move the little-finger side of the right *S hand* with a circular movement on the index-finger side of the left *S hand,* palms facing in opposite directions.

cogitate *v.* See sign for MULL.

coin *n.*
[Shape of coin held in the hand] Move the extended right index finger, palm facing in and finger pointing down, in a double circular movement on the left *open hand,* palm facing up.

Coke *n. Trademark.* Alternate form: **Coca-Cola** (*trademark*).
[Mime injecting a drug] With the index finger of the right *L hand,* palm facing in, touching the upper left arm, move the right thumb up and down with a double movement.

cold[1] *n.*
[Mime blowing one's nose] Grasp the nose with the thumb and index finger of the right *A hand,* palm facing in, and pull the hand forward off the nose with a double movement.

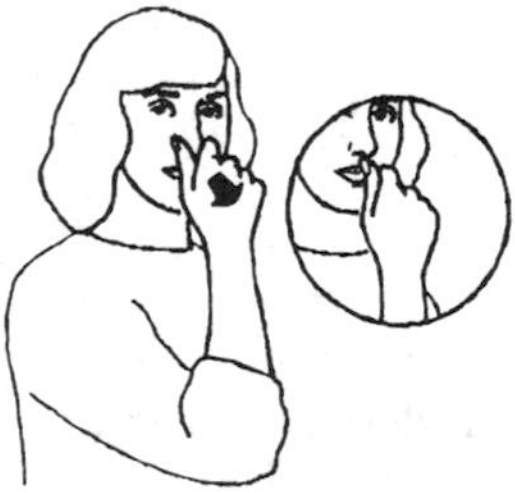

cold[2] *adj.* Same sign used for: **chilly, frigid, shiver, winter.**
[Natural gesture when shivering from cold] Shake both *S hands* with a slight movement in front of each side of

the chest, palms facing each other.

collapse *n.* See sign for BREAK DOWN.

collect *v.* Related form: **collection** *n.* Same sign used for: **accumulate, gather.**

[Pulling money to oneself] With a double movement, bring the little-finger side of the right *curved hand,* palm facing left, across the palm of the left *open hand,* palm facing up, from its fingertips to the heel while changing into an *S hand.*

college *n.*

[Similar to sign for **school** but moves upward to a higher level] Beginning with the palm of the right *open hand* across the palm of the left *open hand* in front of the chest, move the right hand upward in an arc, ending in front of the upper chest, palm angled forward and fingers angled upward toward the left.

collide *v.* See sign for ACCIDENT[1]. Related form: **collision** *n.*

color *n.*

[The fingers represent the colors of the rainbow] Wiggle the fingers of the right *5 hand* in front of the mouth, fingers pointing up and palm facing in.

comb *n.*

[Mime combing hair] Drag the fingertips of the right *curved 5 hand* through the hair on the right side of the head with a short double movement. The verb is the same sign as the noun, but made with a longer double movement.

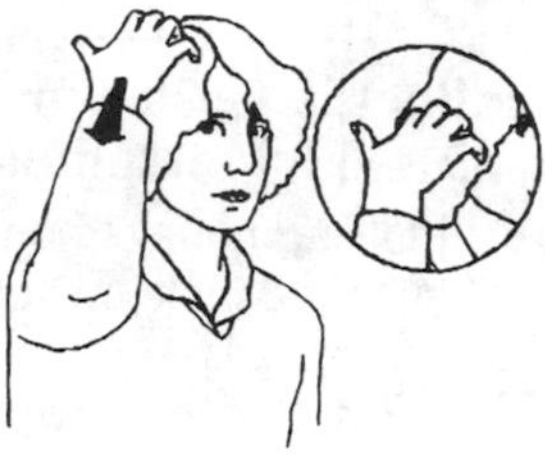

combine *v.* See signs for BELONG, MATCH, MESH.

come *v.*

[Indicates direction for another to come toward oneself] Beginning with both extended index fingers pointing up in front of the body, palms facing in, bring the fingers back to each side of the chest.

come back *v. phrase.* See sign for REFUND.

come on or **come in** *v. phrase.*

[Natural gesture beckoning someone] Move the right *open hand,* palm angled up, back toward the right shoulder.

come up *v. phrase.* See sign for SHOW UP.

command *n., v.* See sign for ORDER.

comment *v.* See sign for SAY.

commercial *n.* See sign for ADVERTISE.

commit *v.* See signs for DO, PROMISE.

committee *n.*

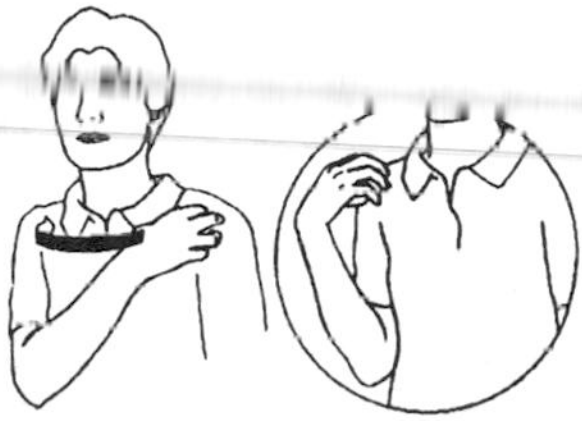

[Initialized sign similar to sign for **us**] Touch the fingertips of the right *curved 5 hand* first to the left side of the chest and then to the right side of the chest, palm facing in.

common *n, adj.* See sign for STANDARD.

communication *n.* Related form: **communicate** *v.* Same sign used for: **conversation, converse.**

[Initialized sign indicating words moving both to and from a person] Move both *C hands,* palms facing each other, forward and back from the chin with an alternating movement.

community *n.* See signs for CITY, TOWN.

commute *v.* Same sign used for: **back and forth.**

[Demonstrates movement to and from] Move the right *10 hand,* palm facing left, from in front of the right side of the body to in front of the left side of the body with a double movement.

compare *v.* Related form: **comparison** *n.*

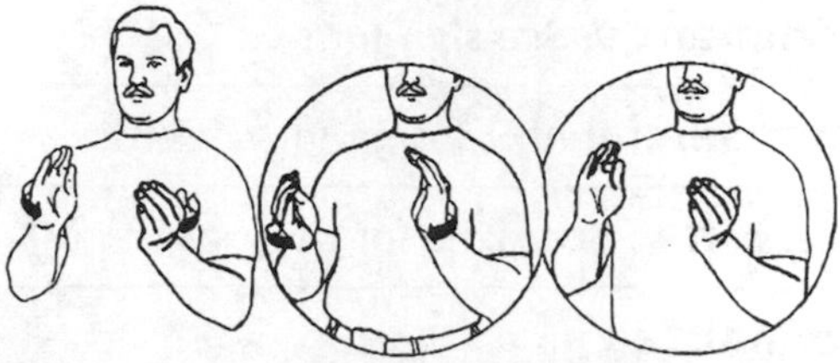

[Holding something in one hand and comparing it with something in the other hand] With both *curved hands* in front of each side of the chest, palms facing, alternately turn one hand and then the other toward the face while turning the other hand in the opposite direction, keeping the palms facing each other and the fingers pointing up.

---

complain *v.* Same sign used for: **boycott, gripe, grumble, object, protest, riot, strike.**

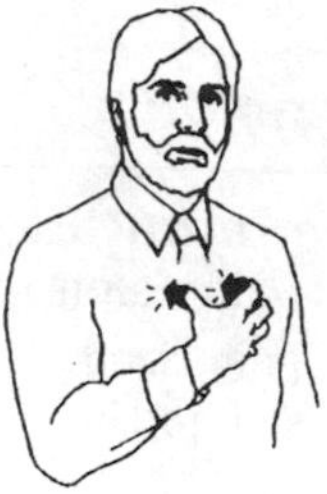

[Natural gesture used when complaining] Tap the fingertips of the right *curved 5 hand* against the center of the chest.

---

complaint *n.* See sign for PROTEST[1].

---

complete *v., adj.* See signs for END[1], FINISH[1], FULL[2].

---

complex[1] *adj.* Same sign used for: **complicated.**

[Thoughts moving through the brain in opposite directions] Beginning with both extended index fingers point toward each other in front of each side of the face, both palms facing down, continuously bend the fingers up and down as the hands move past each other in front of the face.

complex[2] *adj.* See sign for MIX[1].

comprehend *v.* See sign for UNDERSTAND.

compromise *n.* See sign for AGREE.

computer *n.*
[Initialized sign] Move the thumb side of the right *C hand,* palm facing left, from touching the lower part of extended left arm upward to touch the upper arm.

comrade *n.* See sign for FRIEND.

conceal *v.* See sign for HIDE.

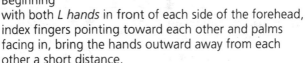

conceited *adj.* Same sign used for: **arrogant, big-headed, big shot, brat, bully.**
[**big** formed near the head, signifying a person with a "big head"] Beginning with both *L hands* in front of each side of the forehead, index fingers pointing toward each other and palms facing in, bring the hands outward away from each other a short distance.

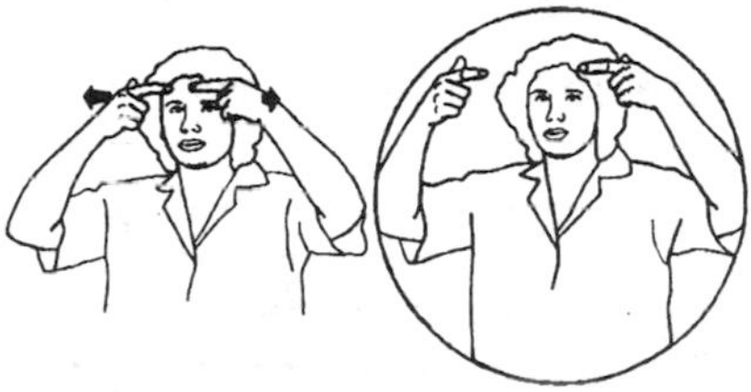

conceive *v.* See sign for PREGNANT[1].

concentrate *v.* See sign for ATTENTION. Related form: **concentration** *n.*

concept *n.* Same sign used for: **creative.**
[Initialized sign similar to sign for **invent**] Move the right *C hand,* palm facing left, from the right

side of the forehead forward and slightly upward in a double arc.

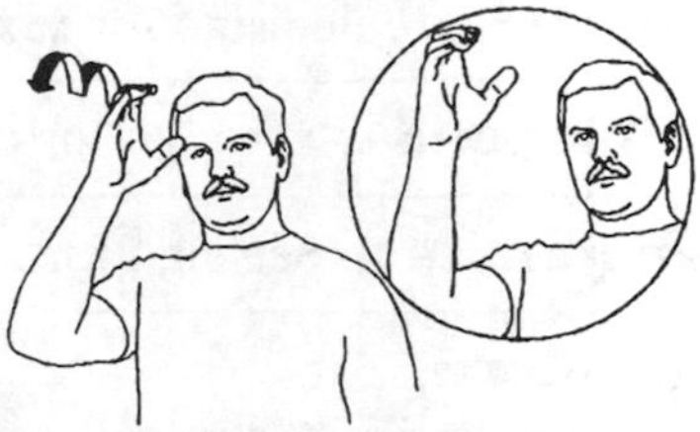

concern[1] *v.* Same sign used for: **consider, think.**

[Thoughts moving through the brain] Beginning with both extended index fingers in front of each side of the forehead, palms facing in and fingers angled up, move the fingers in repeated alternating circular movements toward each other in front of the face.

concern[2] *n.* See sign for TROUBLE[1].

concise *adj.* See sign for PRECISE.

conclude *v.* See sign for END[1].

condemn *v.* See signs for CANCEL, CURSE.

condense *v.* See sign for BRIEF.

condition *n.* Same sign used for: **circumstance, culture.**

[Initialized sign showing area around a thing] Beginning with the right *C hand,* palm facing left, near the extended left index finger, palm facing right, move the right hand in a circle forward and around the left finger.

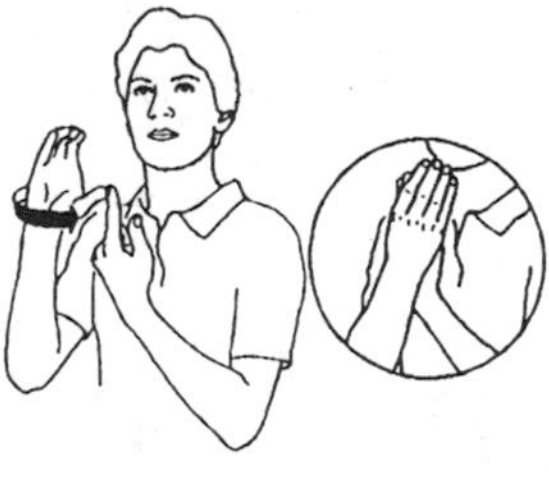

conduct *v.* See signs for DO, LEAD.

conference *n.* See sign for MEETING.

confess *v.* See sign for ADMIT. Related form: **confession** *n.*

confident *adj.* Related form: **confidence** *n.* Same sign used for: **bold, trust.**

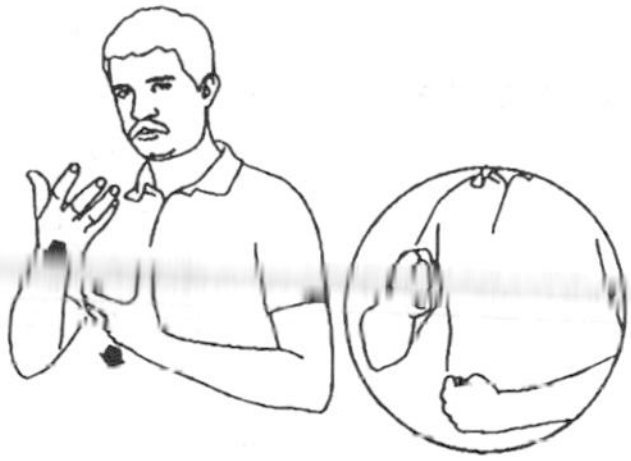

[Holding firmly to one's beliefs] Beginning with both *curved 5 hands* in front of the chest, right hand above the left and palms facing in, bring both hands downward a short distance with a deliberate movement while closing into *S hands.*

confidential *adj.* See sign for SECRET.

confined *adj.* See sign for STUCK.

conflict[1] *n., v.* Same sign used for: **breed, cross-purposes, fertilize.**

[Represents a crossing of opinions] Beginning with both extended index fingers in front of each side of the body, palms facing in and fingers angled toward each other, move the hands toward each other, ending with the fingers crossed.

conflict[2] *v., n.* See sign for STRUGGLE.

confuse[1] *v.* Related form: **confusion** *n.* Same sign used for: **mixed up.**

[**think** + **mix**[1]] Bring the extended right index finger from touching the right side of the forehead, palm facing in, down to in front of the chest, changing into a *curved 5 hand.* Then, with the right *curved 5 hand* over the left *curved 5 hand,* palms facing each other, move the hands simultaneously in repeated circles going in opposite directions.

confuse[2] *v.* See sign for MIX[1].

connect *v.* See sign for BELONG.

connection *n.* See sign for RELATIONSHIP.

conquer *v.* See signs for CAPTURE, DEFEAT.

consider *v.* See signs for CONCERN[1], WONDER.

constant *adj.* Same sign used for: **continual, persistent, steadfast, steady.**

[Indicates continuing movement] Beginning with the thumb of the right *10 hand* on the thumbnail of the left *10 hand,* both palms facing down in front of the chest, move the hands downward and forward in a series of small arcs.

construct *v.* See sign for BUILD. Related form: **construction** *n.*

contact *n., v.* Same sign used for: **in touch with.**

[Indicates two things coming into contact with each other] With the right hand above the left hand in front of the chest, touch the bent middle finger of the right *5 hand* to the bent middle finger of the left *5 hand* with a double movement, palms facing each other.

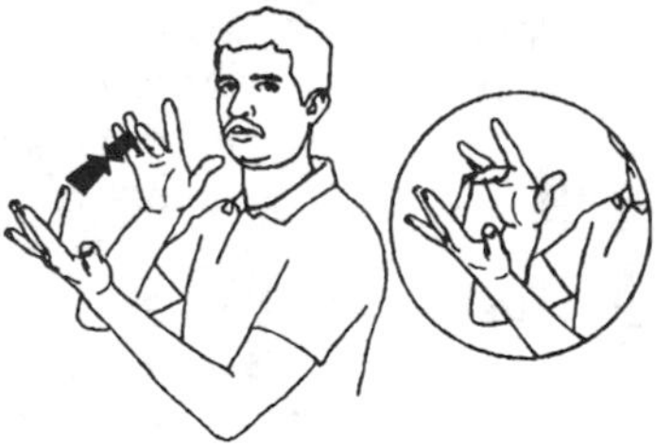

contained in See sign for INCLUDE.

contemplate *v.* See sign for WONDER.

continual *adj.* See sign for CONSTANT.

continue[1] *v.* Same sign used for: **last, remain.**
[Indicates continuous movement] Beginning with the thumb of the right *10 hand* on the thumbnail of the left *10 hand,* both palms facing down in front of the chest, move the hands downward and forward in an arc.

continue[2] *v.* See sign for GO ON.

contrary *adj.* See sign for OPPOSITE.

contrast *v.* See signs for DISAGREE, OPPOSITE.

contribute *v.* See signs for GIFT, GIVE. Related form: **contribution** *n.*

control[1] *v.* Same sign used for: **restrain, suppress, tolerate.**
[The hands seem to suppress one's feelings] Beginning with the fingertips of both *curved 5 hands* against the chest, palms facing in, bring the hands downward while forming *S hands,* palms facing up.

control[2] *v.* See sign for MANAGE.

controversy *n.* See sign for STRUGGLE.

convenient *adj.* See sign for EASY.

convention *n.* See sign for MEETING.

converse *v.* See sign for COMMUNICATION. Related form: **conversation** *n.*

convey *v.* See sign for NARROW DOWN.

convict *v.* See sign for CATCH[1].

convince *v.*

[The hands come from both sides to influence someone] Beginning with both *open hands* in front of each shoulder, palms angled upward, bring the hands down sharply at an angle toward each other.

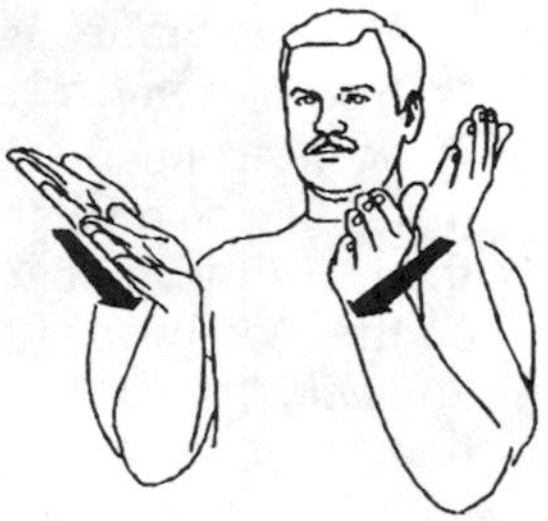

convocation *n.* See sign for MEETING.

cook *v.* Same sign used for: **bake, flip, fry, turn over.**

[As if turning food in a frying pan] Beginning with the fingers of the right *open hand,* palm facing down, across the palm of the left *open hand,* flip the right hand over, ending with the back of the right hand on the left palm.

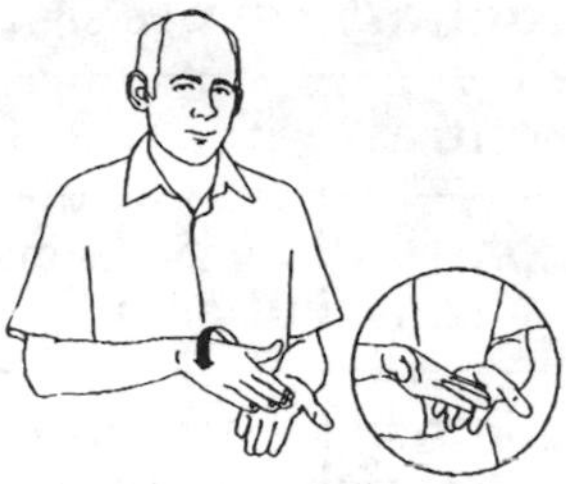

cookie *n.* Same sign used for: **biscuit.**

[Mime using a cookie cutter] Touch the fingertips of the right *C hand,* palm facing down, on the upturned palm of the left *open hand.* Then twist the right hand and touch the left palm again.

cool *adj.* Same sign used for: **pleasant, refresh.**

[As if fanning oneself] With both open hands above each shoulder, palms facing back and fingers pointing up, bend the fingers up and down with a repeated movement.

cooperation *n.* Related form: **cooperate** *v.* Same sign used for: **affiliation, union, unity, universal.**

[One thing is linked to another] With the thumbs and index fingers of both *F hands* intersecting, move the hands in a flat circle in front of the chest.

coordinate *v.* Same sign used for: **relate.**

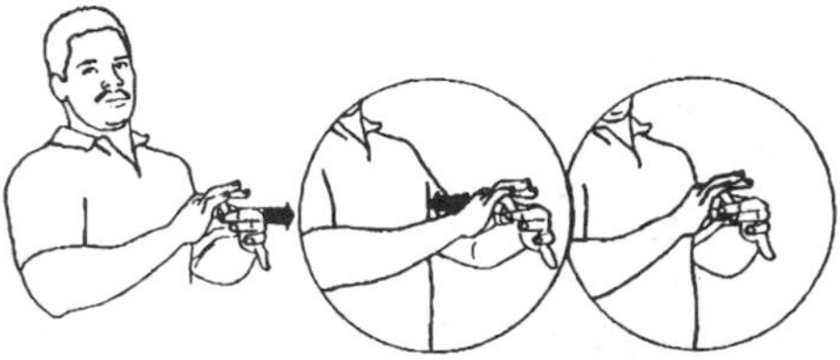

With the thumbs and index fingers of both *F hands* intersecting, move the hands forward and back with a double movement.

cop *n.* See sign for POLICE.

copy *v.* Same sign used for: **duplicate, imitate, impose.**

[Represents taking information and recording it on paper] Move the right *curved hand* in front of the chest, palm facing forward, down to touch the palm of the left *open hand* while closing the right fingers and thumb into a *flattened O hand.* The noun is formed in the same way except with a double movement.

cord *n.* Same sign used for: **thread, wire.**

[Shape of a coiled cord] Beginning with both extended little fingers pointing toward each other in front of the chest, palms facing in, move the fingers in circular movements while moving the hands away from each other.

correct *v.* See signs for CANCEL, RIGHT[3].

corridor *n.* See sign for HALL.

cosmetics *pl. n.* See sign for MAKE-UP.

cost *n., v.* Same sign used for: **charge, fare, fee, fine, price, tax.**

[Making a dent in one's finances] Strike the knuckle of the right *X hand,* palm facing in, down the palm of the left *open hand,* palm facing right and fingers pointing forward.

costly *adj.* See sign for EXPENSIVE.

costume *n.* See sign for CLOTHES.

cough *v., n.*

[Location of the origin of a cough in the chest] With the fingertips of the right *curved 5 hand* on the chest, palm facing in, lower the wrist with a repeated movement while keeping the fingertips in place.

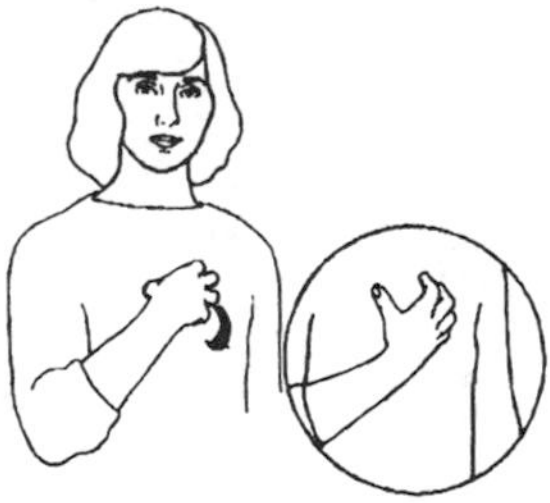

council *n.* See sign for MEETING.

count *v.*

[Counting beads on an abacus] Move the fingertips of the right *F hand*, palm facing down, across the upturned palm of the left *open hand* from the heel to the fingers.

counter *adj.* See sign for OPPOSITE.

counterfeit *n.* See sign for FAKE.

country[1] *n.*

[Similar to sign for **country**[2] but formed with a *Y hand*] Rub the bent fingers of the right *Y hand,* palm facing in, in a circle near the elbow of the bent left arm with a repeated movement.

country[2] *n.* (alternate sign)

[The tattered elbows of a farm worker] Rub the palm of the right *open hand* in a circle near the elbow of the bent left arm with a repeated movement.

couple *n.* Same sign used for: **pair.**

[Pointing to two people making up a couple] Move the right *V fingers,* palm facing up and fingers pointing forward, from side to side in front of the right side of the body with a repeated movement.

courage *n.* See sign for BRAVE.

course *n.* Same sign used for: **lesson.**

[Initialized sign similar to sign for **list**] Move the little-finger side of the right *C hand,* palm facing in, in an arc, touching first on the fingers and then near the heel of the upturned left hand.

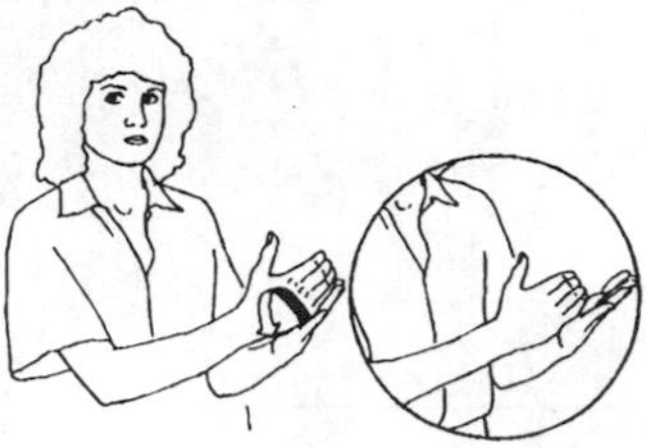

court *n.* See sign for JUDGE.

courteous *adj.* See sign for POLITE. Related form: **courtesy** *n.*

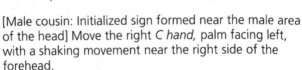

cousin *n.*

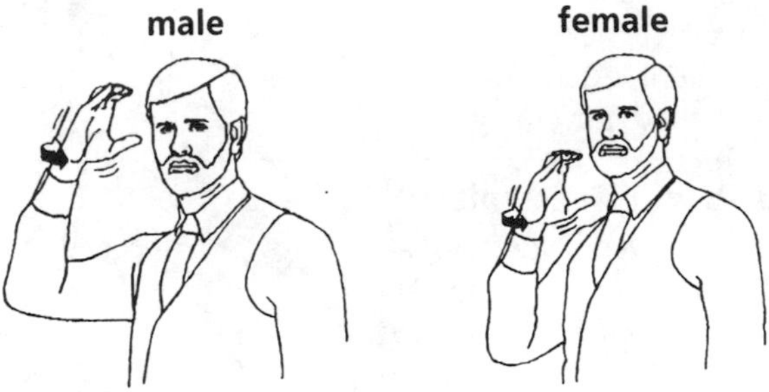

[Male cousin: Initialized sign formed near the male area of the head] Move the right *C hand,* palm facing left, with a shaking movement near the right side of the forehead.

[Female cousin: Initialized sign near the female area of the head] Move the right *C hand,* palm facing left, with a shaking movement near the right side of the chin.

cover *n.* See signs for LID.

covetous *adj.* See sign for GREEDY.

cow *n.* Same sign used for: **cattle.**

[A cow's horns] With the thumbs of both *Y hands* on

both sides of the forehead, palms facing forward, twist the hands forward.

coward *n.* See signs for BIRD, FEAR.

cracker *n.*

[The old-world custom of breaking a cracker with the elbow] Strike the palm side of the right *A hand* near the elbow of the bent left arm with a repeated movement.

cramped *adj.* See sign for CROWDED.

crash[1] *n., v.*

[Shows impact of a crash] Beginning with the right *5 hand* near the right side of the chest, palm facing down and fingers angled forward, move the hand deliberately to hit against the palm of the left *open hand,* bending the right fingers as it hits.

crash[2] *n.* See sign for ACCIDENT[1].

crave *v.* See sign for HUNGRY.

crazy *adj.* Same sign used for: **wacky** (*slang*).

[Indicates that things are confused in one's head] Twist the *curved 5 hand,* palm facing in, forward with a repeated movement near the right side of the head.

cream *n.*
[Initialized sign representing skimming cream from the top of milk] Bring the little-finger side of the right *C hand,* palm facing left, back toward the chest in a circular movement across the palm of the left *open hand.*

create *v.* See signs for INVENT, MAKE.

creative *adj.* See sign for CONCEPT.

credit card *n.* See sign for CHARGE[1].

cross[1] *adj.* See also sign for ANGER. Same sign used for: **angry, mad.**
[Hand seems to pull the face down into a scowl] With the palm of the right *5 hand* in front of the face, fingers pointing up, bring the hand slightly forward while constricting the fingers into a *curved 5 hand.*

cross[2] *prep., adv.* See sign for ACROSS.

cross-purposes *n.* See sign for CONFLICT[1].

crowd *n.* See sign for AUDIENCE.

crowded *adj.* Same sign used for: **cramped,**

crushed.
[The hands are crushed tightly together] Beginning with the palms of both *A hands* together in front of the chest, twist the hands in opposite directions.

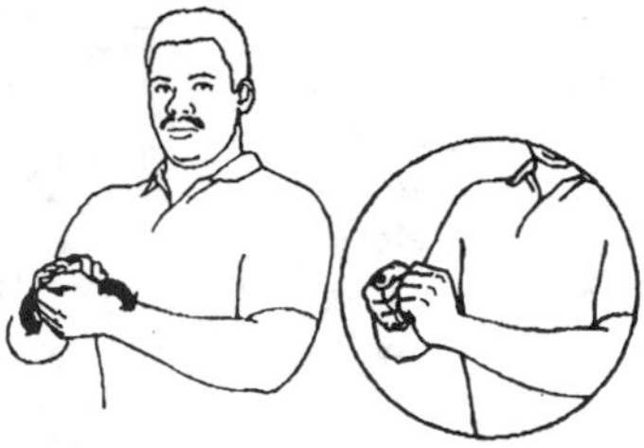

cruel *adj.* See sign for MEAN[1].

cruise *n.* See sign for BOAT.

crushed *adj.* See sign for CROWDED.

cry[1] *v.* Same sign used for: **weep.**
[Tears flowing down the cheeks] Bring both extended index fingers, palms facing in and fingers pointing up, downward from each eye with an alternating movement.

cry[2] *v.* See sign for SCREAM.

culture *n.* See sign for CONDITION.

cup *n.* Same sign used for: **can.**
[Shape of a cup] Bring the little-finger side of the right *C hand,* palm facing left, down to the upturned left *open hand* with a double movement.

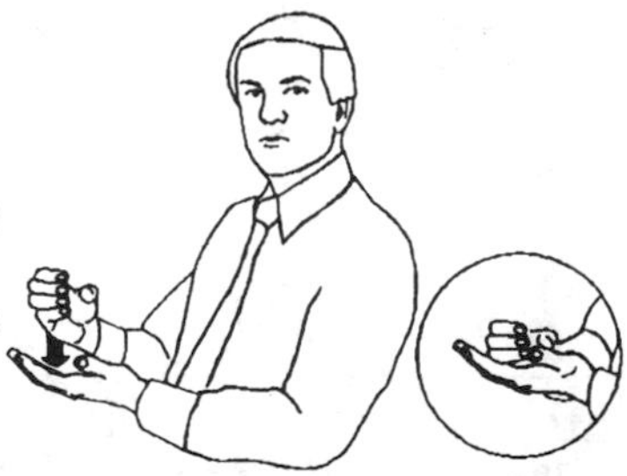

cure *n., v.* See sign for WELL[1].

curious *adj.* Related form: **curiosity** *n.*

[Pulling the neck forward out of curiosity] With the fingertips of the right *F hand* against the neck, palm facing left, twist the hand downward with a double movement.

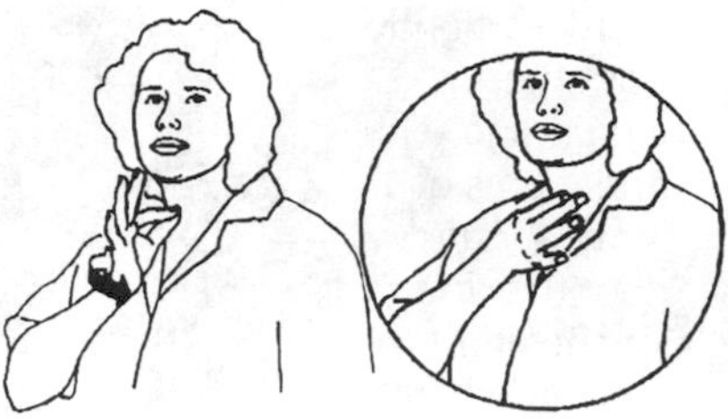

current *adj.* See sign for NOW.

curse *n., v.* Same sign used for: **condemn, swear.**

[Threatening words are directed toward God] Beginning with the right *curved 5 hand* near the mouth, palm facing in, bring the hand upward with a deliberate movement while closing into an *S hand.*

cut[1] *v.* Same sign used for: **haircut.**

[Mime cutting hair] Move both *V hands,* palms facing down, back over each shoulder while opening and closing the fingers of the *V hands* repeatedly as the hands move.

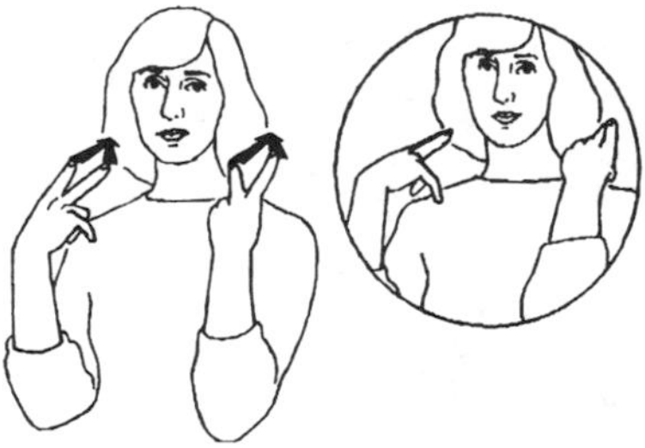

cut[2] *v.*

[Represents cutting across a piece of paper] Move the right *V hand,* fingers pointing left, across the fingertips of the left *open hand,* palm facing down, with a deliberate movement while closing the *V fingers* together.

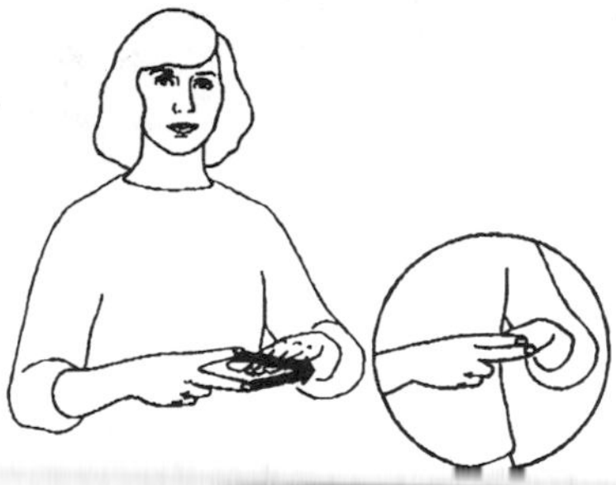

cute *adj.*

[Similar to the sign for **sweet** but formed with a *U hand*] With the right thumb extended, brush the fingers of the right *U hand,* palm facing down, downward on the chin while changing into a *10 hand.*

cycle *n.* See sign for CIRCLE[1].

dad *n.* See sign for FATHER. Related form: **daddy** *n.*

daily *adj., adv.* Same sign used for: **casual, domestic, everyday, every day, ordinary, routine, usual.**

[Similar to sign for **tomorrow,** only repeated to indicated recurrence] Move the palm side of the right *A hand* forward on the right side of the chin with a repeated movement.

damage *n., v.* Same sign used for: **abolish, demolish, destroy, ruin.**

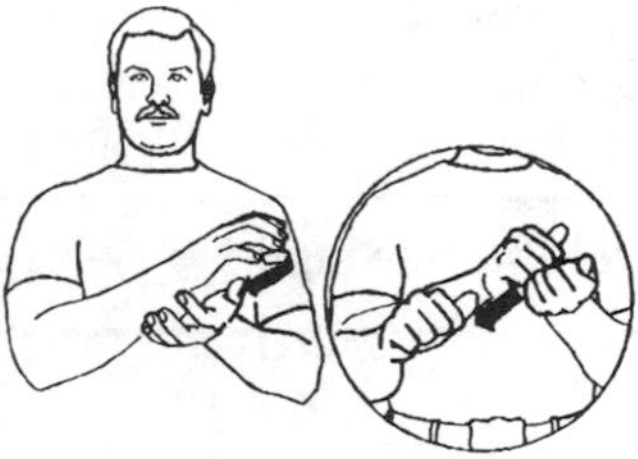

[Hands seem to take something and pull it apart] Beginning with both *curved 5 hands* in front of the chest, right hand over the left, right palm facing down and left palm facing up, bring the right hand in a circular movement over the left. Then close both hands into *A hands* and bring the knuckles of the right hand forward past the left knuckles with a deliberate movement.

damp *adj.* See sign for WET.

dance *v., n.* Same sign used for: **disco, gala.**

[Represents legs moving in rhythm to dance music] Swing the fingers of the right *V hand,* palm facing in and fingers pointing down, back and forth over the upturned left *open hand* with a double movement.

danger *n.* Related form: **dangerous** *adj.* Same sign used for: **endanger, harassment, harm, hazard, risk, threat.**

[Represents hidden danger coming at a person] Move the thumb of the right *10 hand,* palm facing left, upward on the back of the left *A hand,* palm facing in, with a repeated movement.

dark *adj.* Related form: **darkness** *n.* Same sign used for: **dim, dusk.**

[Hands shade the eyes from light] Beginning with both *open hands* in front of each shoulder, palms facing back and fingers pointing up, bring the hands past each other in front of the face, ending with the wrists crossed and the fingers pointing in opposite directions at an angle.

daughter *n.*

[Begins at the female area of the head + **baby**] Beginning with the index-finger side of the right *B hand,* palm facing left, touching the right side of the chin, swing the right hand downward, with the bent right arm cradled in the bent left arm held across the body.

dawn *n.* See sign for SUNRISE.

day *n.*

[Symbolizes the movement of the sun across the sky] Beginning with the bent right elbow resting on the back of the left hand held across the body, palm facing down, bring the extended right index finger from pointing up

in front of the right shoulder, palm facing left, downward toward the left elbow.

daydream *v., n.* See sign for DREAM.

dead *adj.* See sign for DIE.

deaf *adj.*
[Points to the ear and mouth to indicate that a person cannot hear or talk] Touch the extended right index finger first to near the right ear and then to near the right side of the mouth.

deal *v.* See sign for PASS AROUND.

death *n.* See sign for DIE.

debt *n.* See sign for AFFORD.

decal *n.* See sign for LABEL.

decay *v.* See sign for WEAR OUT.

decide *v.* Related form: **decision** *n.* Same sign used for: **determine, make up your mind, officially.**
[**think**[1] + laying one's thoughts down decisively] Move the extended right index finger from the right side of the forehead, palm facing left, down in front of the chest while changing into an *F hand,* ending with both *F hands* in front of the body, palms facing each other.

declare *v.* See sign for ANNOUNCE. Related form: **declaration** *n.*

decline *v., n.* Same sign used for: **deteriorate.**
[Hands move downward in location] Beginning with both *10 hands* in front of each shoulder, palms facing

in and thumbs pointing up, move both hands down in front of each side of the chest.

decorate *v.* Related form: **decoration** *n.*

[Hands seem to arrange ornamental items] Beginning with both *flattened O hands* in front of each side of the chest, palms facing forward, move them in alternating circles with a repeated movement.

decrease *n., v.* Same sign used for: **lessen, lose, reduce, reduction.**

[Taking some off to decrease it] Beginning with the fingers of the right *U hand* across the fingers of the left *U hand,* both palms facing down, take the right fingers off by flipping the right hand over.

deduct *v.* See sign for SUBTRACT.

deed *n.* See sign for ACT[1].

deep *adj.* Same sign used for: **depth, detail.**

[Indicates direction of bottom of something deep] Move the extended right index finger, palm facing down, downward near the fingertips of the left *5 hand,* palm facing down.

defeat *v.* See also sign for BEAT[3]. Same sign used for: **conquer, overcome, subdue, vanquish.**

[Represents forcing another down in defeat] Move the right *S hand* from in front of the right shoulder, palm facing forward, downward and forward, ending with the right wrist across the wrist of the left *S hand,* both palms facing down.

defend *v.* Related forms: **defense** *n.*, **defensive** *adj.* Same sign used for: **protect, security, shield.**

[Blocking oneself from harm] With the wrists of both *S hands* crossed in front of the chest, palms facing in opposite directions, move the hands forward with a short double movement.

defensive *adj.* See sign for RESIST.

defer[1] *v.* Same sign used for **delay, procrastinate, put off.**

[Represents taking something and putting it off several times] Beginning with both *F hands* in front of the body, palms facing each other and the left hand nearer to the body than the right hand, move both hands forward in a series of small arcs.

defer[2] *v.* See sign for POSTPONE.

define *v.* See sign for DESCRIBE. Related form: **definition** *n.*

delay *n., v.* See signs for DEFER, LATE, POSTPONE.

delete *v.* See sign for ELIMINATE[1].

deliberate *v.* See sign for MULL.

delicious *adj.* Same sign used for: **tasty.**

[Something is tasted appreciatively] Touch the bent middle finger of the right *5 hand* to the lips, palm facing in, and then twist the right hand quickly forward.

delighted *adj.* See sign for HAPPY.

deliver *v.* See sign for BRING.

deluxe *adj.* See sign for FANCY.

demand *v.* Same sign used for: **insist, require.**

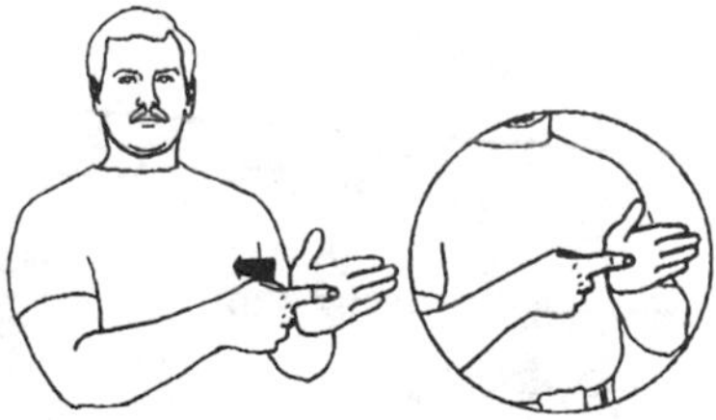

[Something is dragged in on a hook] With the extended right index finger, palm facing in, touching the palm of the left *open hand* bring both hands back toward the chest.

demolish *v.* See sign for DAMAGE.

demonstrate *v.* See sign for SHOW[1]. Related form: **demonstration** *n.*

demote *v.* See sign for LOW.

dentist *n.*

[Initialized sign showing locaton of teeth] Tap the fingers of the right *D hand,* palm facing in and index finger pointing up, against the right side of the teeth with a repeated movement.

deny *v.*

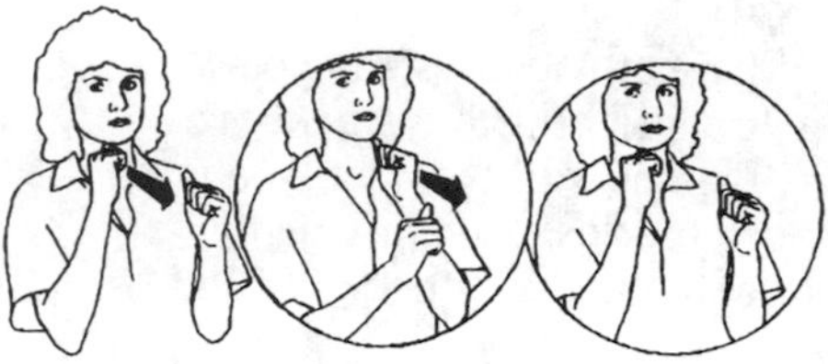

[**not** with a repeated movement] Beginning with the thumb of the right *A hand* under the chin, palm facing left, and the left *A hand* held somewhat forward, palm facing right, move the right hand forward while moving the left hand back. Repeat the movement with the left hand.

depart *v.* See signs for GO, LEAVE[1]. Related form: **departure** *n.*

department *n.*

[Initialized sign similar to sign for **class**] Beginning with the fingertips of both *D hands* touching in front of the chest, palms facing each other, bring the hands away from each other in outward arcs while turning the palms in, ending with the little fingers together.

depend or **depend on** *v.* Related forms: **dependency** *n.*, **dependent** *adj.* Same sign used for: **cling to, rely.**

[Represents resting on another] With the extended right

index finger across the extended left index finger, palms facing down, move both fingers down slightly with a double movement.

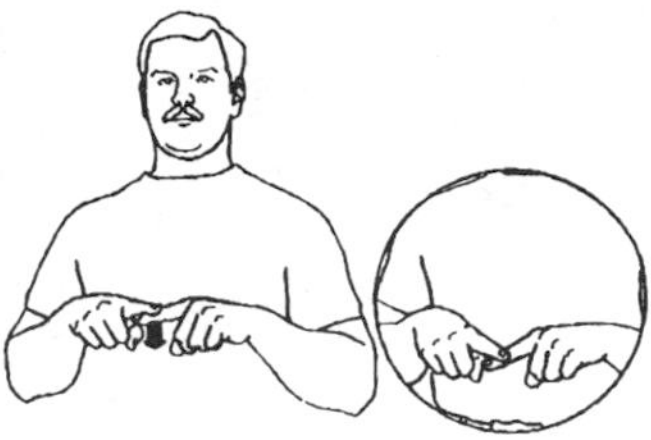

deplete *v.* See sign for RUN OUT OF.

deposit[1] *v., n.*

[Sealing a deposit envelope with the thumbs] Beginning with the thumbs of both *10 hands* touching in front of the chest, both palms facing down, bring the hands downward and apart by twisting the wrists.

deposit[2] *n., v.* See sign for INVEST.

depressed *adj.* Related forms: **depressing** *adj.*, **depression** *n.* Same sign used for: **despair, discouraged.**

[Feelings moving downward in the body] Beginning with the bent middle fingers of both *5 hands* on each side of the chest, palms facing in and fingers pointing toward each other, move the hands downward with a simultaneous movement.

depth *n.* See sign for DEEP.

describe *v.* Related form: **description** *n.* Same sign used for: **define, definition, direct, direction, explain, explanation, instruct, instruction.**

[Bringing something before one's eyes to describe it]

Beginning with the fingers of both *F hands* in front of the chest, palms facing each other and

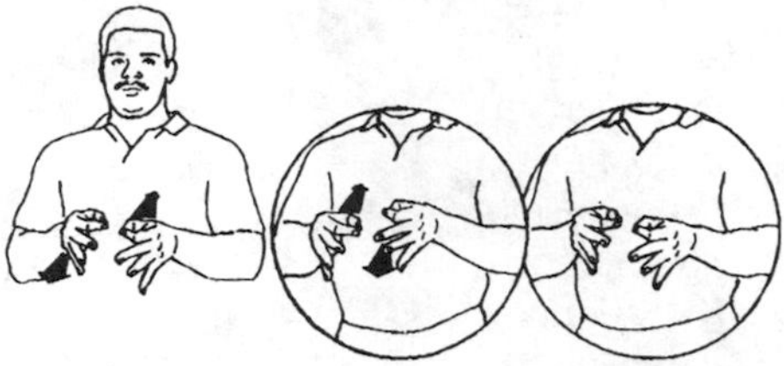

index fingers pointing forward, move the hands forward and back with an alternating movement.

desert *v.* See sign for LEAVE[1].

deserve *v.* See sign for EARN.

design *v.* Same sign used for: **draw, drawing, draft.**

[Initialized sign similar to sign for **art**] Move the fingertips of the right *D hand,* palm facing left, down the palm of the

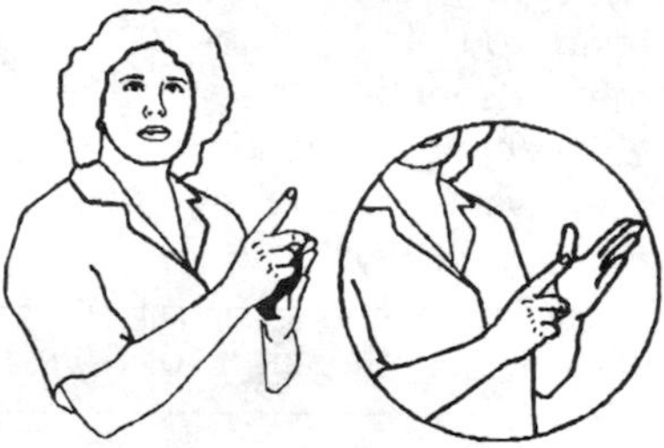

left *open hand* with a wavy movement.

desire *v.* See signs for WANT, WISH.

desist *v.* Same sign used for: **stop.**

[Natural gesture used when asking another to stop doing something] Beginning with the fingers of both *5 hands* in front of each side of the chest, palms facing in, twist the wrists to flip the hands in a quick movement, ending with the palms facing down.

desk *n.* Same sign used for: **table.**

[**table**[1] + shape of a desk] Pat the forearm of the bent right arm with a double movement on the bent left arm held across the chest. Then, beginning with the fingers of both *open hands* together in front of the chest,

palms facing down, move the hands apart to in front of each shoulder and then straight down, ending with the palms facing each other.

despair *n., v.* See sign for DEPRESSED.

despite *prep.* See sign for ANYWAY.

dessert *n.*

[Initialized sign] Tap the fingertips of both *D hands,* palms facing each other, together with a repeated movement in front of the chest.

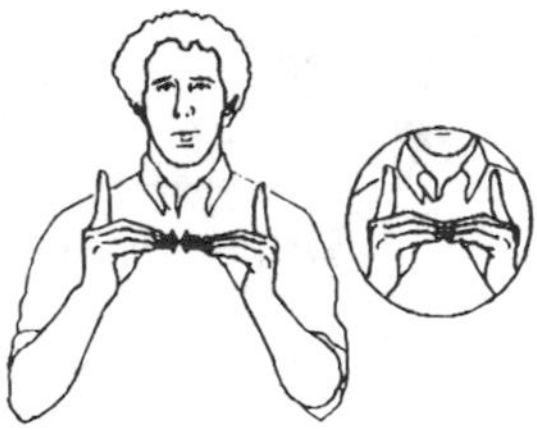

destroy *v.* See sign for DAMAGE.

destruction *n.* See sign for BREAK DOWN.

detach *v.* See sign for DISCONNECT.

detail *n.* See sign for DEEP. Shared idea of careful attention to important matters.

deteriorate *v.* See sign for DECLINE.

determine *v.* See sign for DECIDE.

develop *v.*

[Initialized sign moving upward to represent growth or development] Move the fingertips of the right *D hand,* palm facing left, upward from the heel

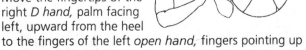

to the fingers of the left *open hand,* fingers pointing up and palm facing right.

dew *n.* See sign for WET.

diagnose *v.* See sign for ANALYZE. Related form: **diagnosis** *n.*

die *v.* Same sign used for: **dead, death, perish.**

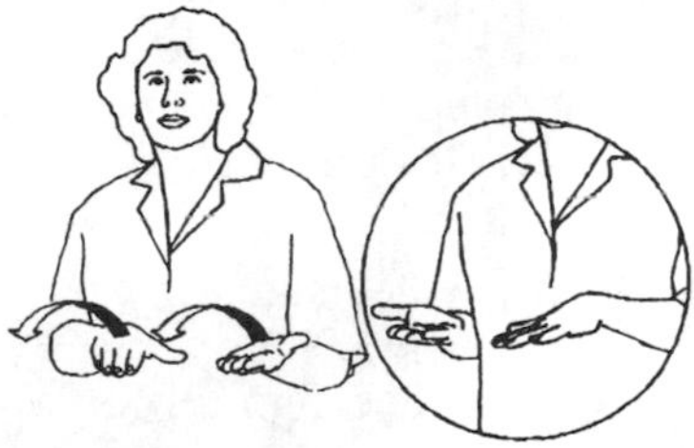

[Represents a body turning over in death] Beginning with both *open hands* in front of the body, right palm facing down and left palm facing up, flip the hands to the right, turning the right palm up and the left palm down.

diet *n.* Same sign used for: **lean, shrink, slim, thin.**

[Shows slimmer body] Beginning with both *L hands* in front of each side of the chest, palms facing in, swing the hands downward by twisting the wrists, ending with the hands in front of each side of the waist, both palms facing down.

different *adj.* Related form: **difference** *n.*

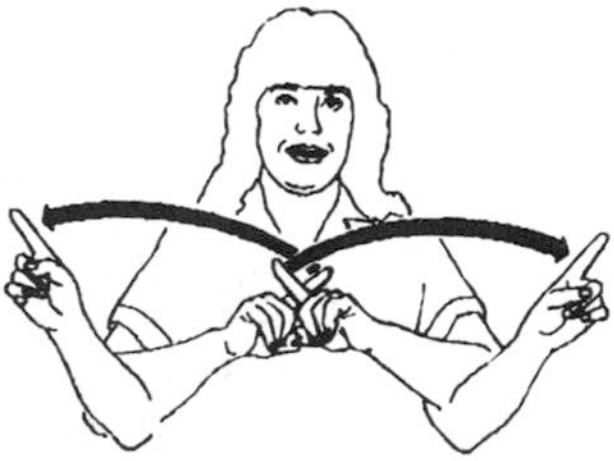

[Moving things apart that are not the same] Beginning with both extended index fingers crossed in front of the chest, palms facing forward, bring the hands apart from each other with a deliberate movement.

difficult *adj.* Same sign used for: **hard, problem, trouble.**

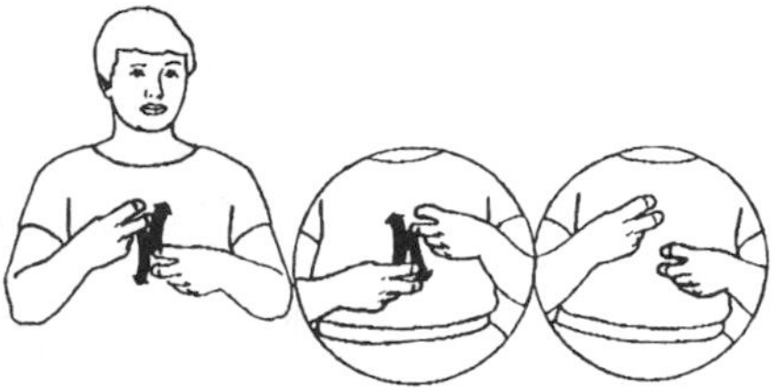

[The bent fingers impede each other, making movement difficult] Beginning with both *bent V hands* in front of the chest, right hand higher than the left hand, palms facing in, move the right hand down and the left hand upward with an alternating movement, brushing the knuckles of each hand as the hands move in the opposite direction.

---

dim *adj.* See sign for DARK.

---

dime *n.* Same sign used for: **ten cents.**

[**cent** + **ten**] Beginning with the extended right index finger touching the right side of the forehead, palm facing down, bring the right hand forward while changing into a *10 hand.* Then slightly twist the right *10 hand* with a repeated movement, palm facing in and thumb pointing up.

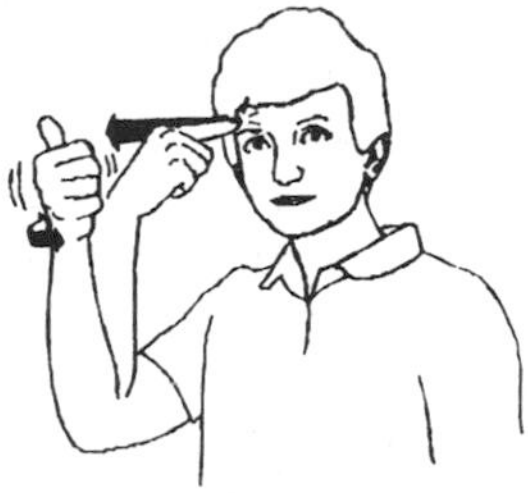

---

direct *v., adj.* See signs for DESCRIBE, MANAGE, ORDER, STRAIGHT[1]. Related form: **direction** *n.*

---

dirt *n.* Same sign used for: **ground, land, soil.**

[Feeling the texture of dirt] Beginning with both *flattened O hands* in front of each side of the body, palms facing up, move the thumb of each hand smoothly across each fingertip, starting with the little fingers and ending as *A hands.*

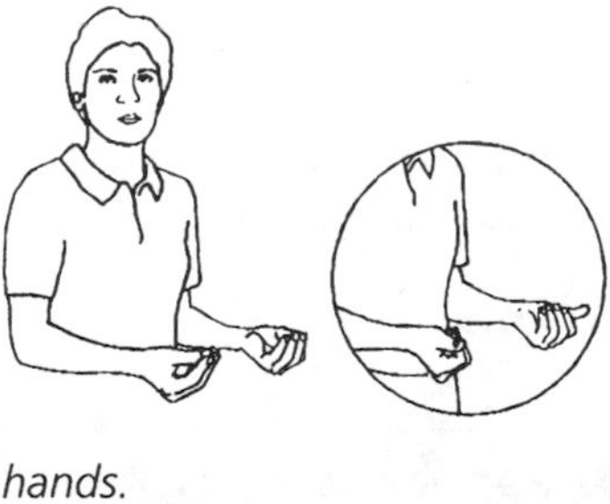

dirty *adj.* Same sign used for: **filthy, nasty, pollution, soiled.**

[Represents a pig's snout groveling in a trough] With the back of the right *curved 5 hand* under the chin, palm facing down, wiggle the fingers.

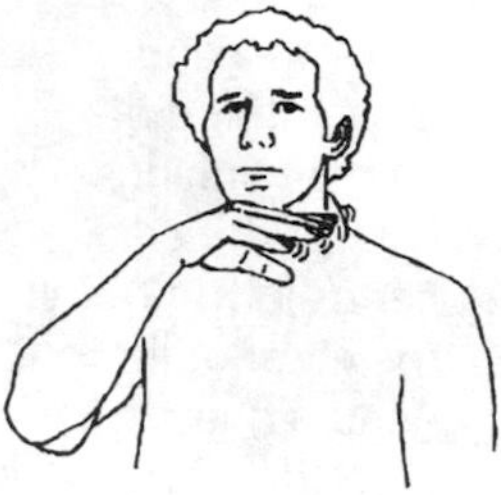

disagree *v.* Same sign used for: **contrast, object.**

[**think**[1] + **opposite**] Move the extended right index finger from touching the right side of the forehead downward to meet the extended left index finger held in front of the chest. Then, beginning with both index fingers pointing toward each other, palms facing in, bring the hands apart to each side of the chest.

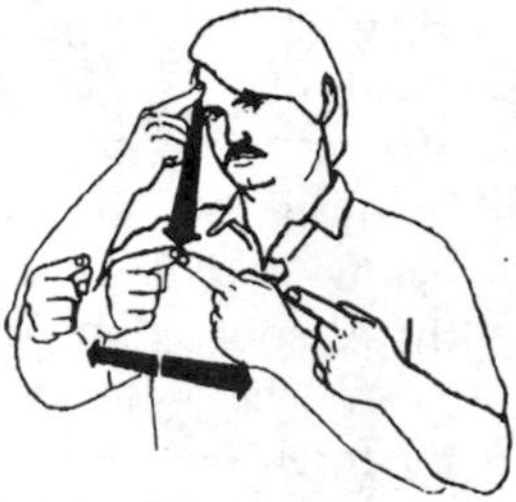

disappear[1] *v.* Related form: **disappearance** *n.* See also sign for ABSENT. Same sign used for: **vanish.**

[Moving out of sight] Beginning with the extended right index finger, palm facing left, pointing up between the index and middle fingers of the left *5 hand,* palm facing down, pull the right hand straight down a short distance.

disappear[2] *v.* See sign for DISSOLVE.

disappointed *adj.* Related form: **disappointment** *n.* Same sign used for: **miss.**

[Symbolizes "Take it on the chin," a result of disappointment] Touch the extended right index finger to the chin, palm facing down.

disastrous *adj.* See sign for AWFUL.

discard *v.* See sign for ABANDON.

discharge *v.* See sign for DISMISS.

disco *n.* See sign for DANCE.

disconnect *v.* Same sign used for: **detach, loose, part from, withdraw.**

[Demonstrates releasing of a connection] Beginning with the thumb and index fingertips of each hand intersecting with each other, palms facing each other and right hand nearer the chest than the left hand, release the fingers and pull the left hand forward and the right hand back toward the right shoulder.

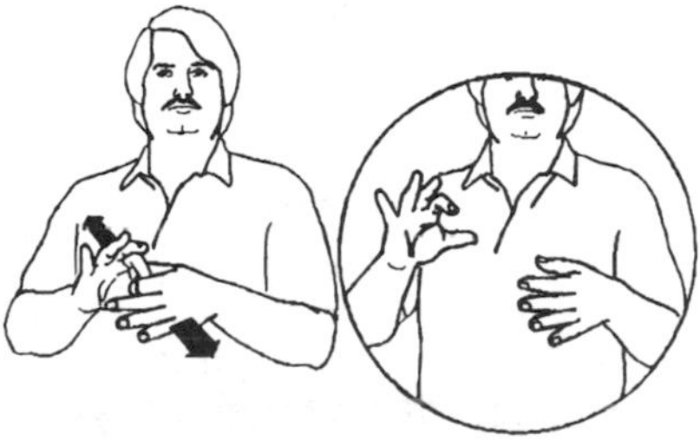

discount[1] *n.*

[Initialized sign showing reduction] Beginning with both *D hands* in front of the chest, right hand above the left hand, palms facing each other, and index fingers pointing forward, bring the hands toward each other.

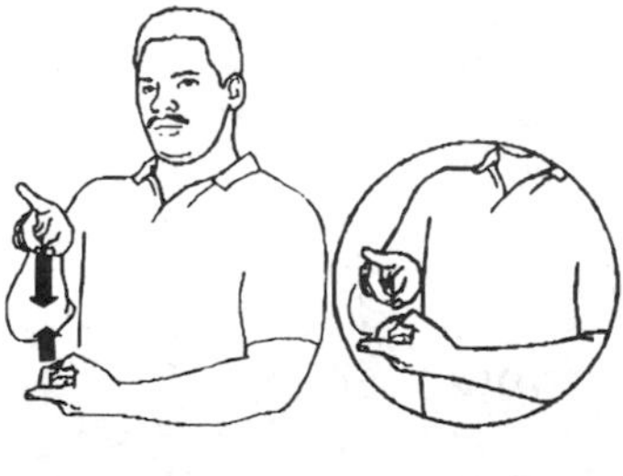

discount[2] *v.* See sign for SUBTRACT.

discouraged *adj.* See sign for DEPRESSED[1].

discover *v.* See sign for FIND.

discuss *v.* Related form: **discussion** *n.* Same sign used for: **argument, dispute.**

[Natural gesture used when making a point] Tap the side of the extended right index finger, palm facing in, on the upturned left *open hand* with a double movement.

dish *n.*

[Shape of a dish] Beginning with the fingertips of both *curved hands* touching in front of the chest, palms facing in, move the hands away from each other in a circle, ending with the heels together close to the chest.

dismiss *v.* Related form: **dismissal** *n.* Same sign used for: **discharge, lay off, pardon, parole, waive.**

[Movement seems to wipe person away] Wipe the right *open hand,* palm down, deliberately across the upturned left *open hand* from the heel off the fingertips.

disorder *n.* See signs for MESSY, MIX[1].

dispute *v.* See sign for DISCUSS.

disseminate *v.* See sign for SPREAD.

dissolve *v.* Same sign used for: **disappear, evaporate, fade away, melt, perish.**

[Something in the hands seems to melt away to nothing] Beginning with both *flattened O hands* in front of each side of the body, palms facing up, move the thumb of each [illegible] each fingertip, starting with the little fingers and ending as *10 hands* while moving the hands outward to each side.

distance *n.* See sign for FAR. Related form: **distant** *adj.*

distribute *v.* See signs for SELL, SPREAD.

disturb *v.* See sign for ANNOY.

divide *v.* Same sign used for: **split, split up.**

[Split something as if to divide it] Beginning with the little-finger side of the right *B hand* at an angle across the index-finger side of the left *B hand,* palms angled in opposite directions, move the hands downward and apart, ending with the hands in front of each side of the body, palms facing down.

divorce *v., n.*

[Initialized sign representing two people moving apart] Beginning with the fingertips of both the *D hands* touching in front of chest, palms facing each other and index fingers pointing up, swing the hands away from each other by twisting the wrists, ending with the hands in front of each side of the body, palms facing forward.

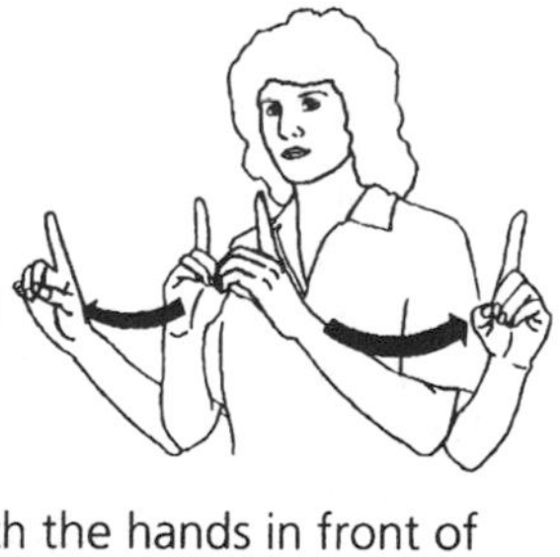

do *v.* Related form: **done** *adj.* Same sign used for: **commit, conduct.**

[Hands seem to be actively doing something] Move both *C hands,* palms facing down, from side to side in front of the body with a repeated movement.

doctor *n.* Same sign used for: **medical, physician.**

[Formed at the location where one's pulse is taken] Tap the fingertips of the right *M hand,* palm facing left, on the wrist of the upturned left *open hand* with a double movement.

document *v.* See sign for PUT DOWN.

doesn't or **does not** See sign for DON'T[1].

doesn't matter See sign for ANYWAY.

dog *n.*

[Natural gesture for signaling or calling a dog] With a double movement, snap the right thumb gently off the right middle finger, palm facing up, in front of the right side of the chest.

dollar *n.* Same sign used for: **bill.**

Beginning with the fingertips of the right *flattened C hand* holding the fingertips of the left *open hand,* both palms facing in, pull the right hand to the right with a double movement while changing to a *flattened O hand.*

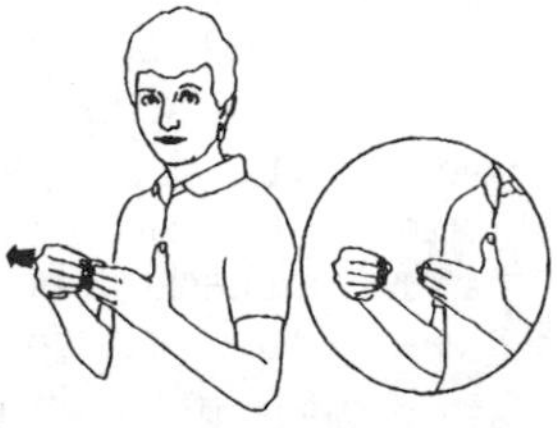

domestic *adj.* See sign for DAILY.

dominoes *n.*
[Represents moving two dominoes end to end with each other] Bring the fingertips of both *H hands,* palms facing in, together in front of the body with a double movement.

donate *v.* See signs for GIFT, GIVE. Related form: **donation** *n.*

done *adj.* See sign for FINISH[1].

donkey *n.* Same sign used for: **mule, stubborn.**
[Represents a donkey's ears] With the thumb side of the right *B hand* against the right side of the forehead, palm facing forward, bend the fingers up and down with a repeated movement.

don't[1] *contraction.* Same sign used for: **doesn't, does not.**
[Natural gesture of denial] Beginning with both *open hands* crossed in front of the chest, palms angled in opposite directions, swing the hands downward away from each other, ending at each side of the body, palms facing down.

don't[2] *contraction.* See sign for NOT.

don't believe See sign for DOUBT.

don't care Same sign used for: **don't mind, indifferent, nonchalant.**

[Outward movement indicates the negative] Beginning with the extended right index finger touching the nose, palm facing down, swing the hand forward by twisting the wrist, ending with the index finger pointing forward in front of the right shoulder.

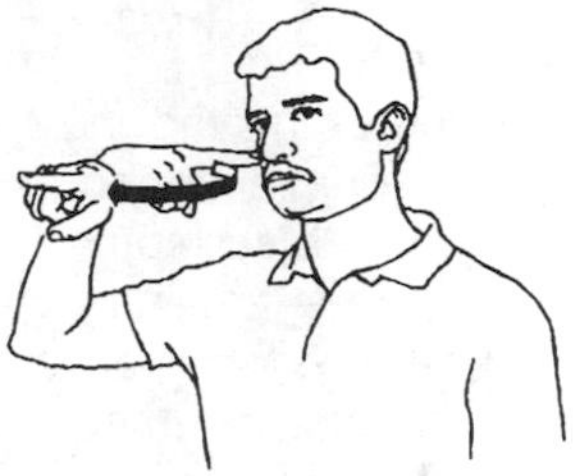

don't know Same sign used for: **unaware, unconscious, unknown.**

[**know** + an outward gesture indicating the negative] Beginning with the fingers of the right *open hand* touching the right side of the forehead, palm facing in, swing the hand forward by twisting the wrist, ending with the fingers pointing forward in front of the right shoulder.

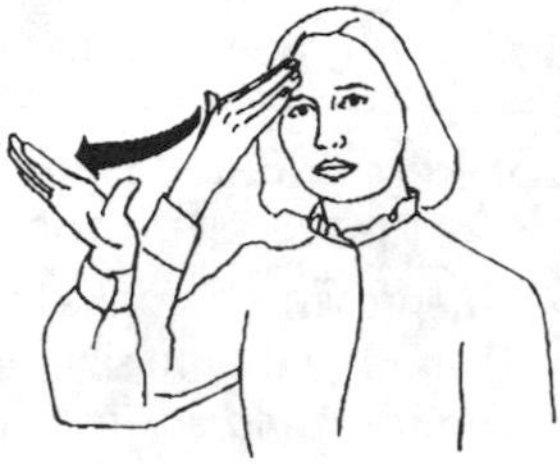

don't mind See sign for DON'T CARE.

door *n.*

[Shows movement of a door being opened] Beginning with the index-finger sides of both *B hands* touching in front of the chest, palms facing forward, swing the right hand back toward the right shoulder with a double movement by twisting the wrist.

doubt *v., n.* Same sign used for: **don't believe.**

[As if one is blind to what is doubted] Beginning with the fingers right *bent V hand* in front of the eyes, palm facing in, pull the hand downward a short distance while constricting the fingers with a single movement.

doubtful *adj.* Same sign as for DOUBT but made with a double movement.

down *adv., prep.*
[Shows direction] Move the extended right index finger downward in front of the right side of the body.

downstairs *adv.* Same sign as for DOWN but made with a double movement. Same sign used for: **downward.**

doze *v.* See signs for FALL ASLEEP, SLEEP.

draft[1] *v.* See sign for DESIGN.

draft[2] *n.* See sign for ROUGH.

drag *v.* Same sign used for: **draw, haul, pull, tow.**
[Mime pulling something] Beginning with the right *curved hand* in front of the body and the left *curved hand* somewhat forward, both palms facing up, bring the hands back toward the right side of the body while closing them into *A hands.*

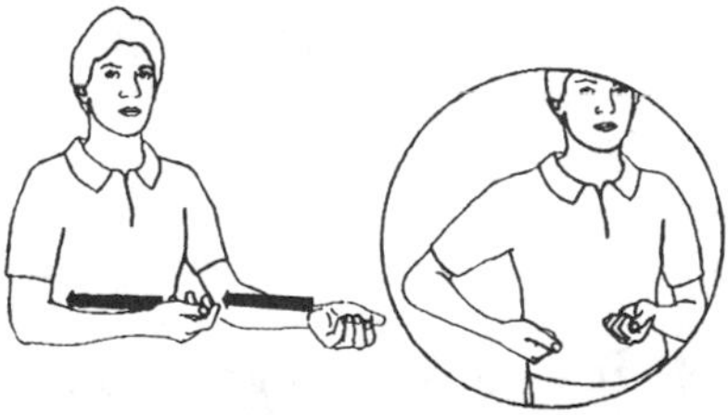

drain *adj.* See signs for ABSENT, LEAK.

drama *n.* See sign for ACT².

draw *v.* See signs for CHOOSE, DESIGN, DRAG, FIND.

draw back *v. phrase.* See sign for RESIGN.

drawing *n.* See signs for ART, DESIGN.

dreadful *adj.* See sign for AWFUL.

dream *v., n.* Same sign used for: **daydream.**

[Represents an image coming from the mind] Move the extended right index finger from touching the right side of the forehead, palm facing down, outward to the right while bending the finger up and down.

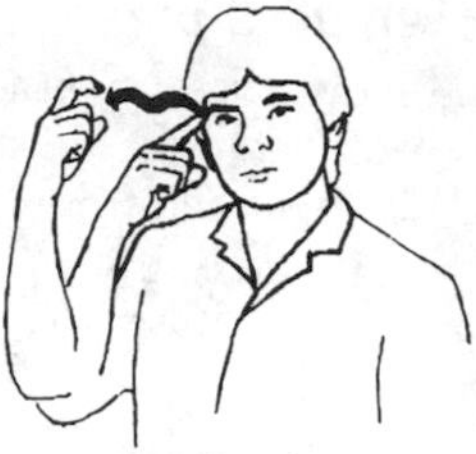

dress¹ *v.*

[Location of dress] Brush the thumbs of both *5 hands* downward on each side of the chest.

dress² *n.* See sign for CLOTHES.

dribble *v.* See sign for DRIP.

drill *n.* See sign for ALARM.

drink¹ *n., v.* Same sign used for: **beverage.**

[Mime drinking from a glass] Beginning with the thumb of the right *C hand* near the chin, palm facing left, tip the hand up toward the face, with a single movement for the noun and a double movement for the verb.

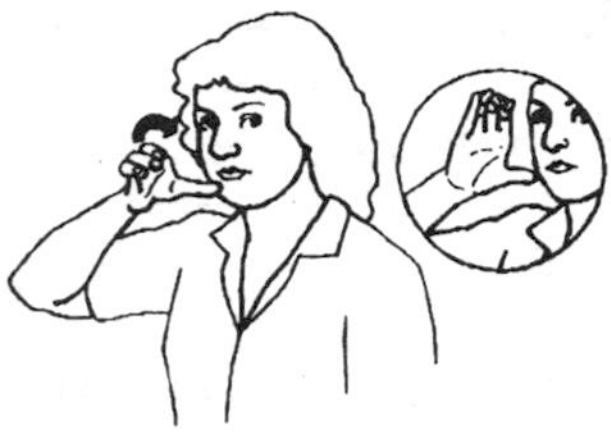

drink *n.* See sign for COCKTAIL.

drip *n., v.* Same sign used for: **dribble, drop, leak.**

[Represents action of water dripping] Beginning with the right *S hand,* palm facing down, near the fingertips of the left *open hand,* palm facing down and fingers pointing right, flick the right index finger downward with a repeated movement.

drive to *v. phrase.*

[Represents continuous driving] Beginning with both *S hands* in front of the chest, palms facing in, move the hands forward with a deliberate movement.

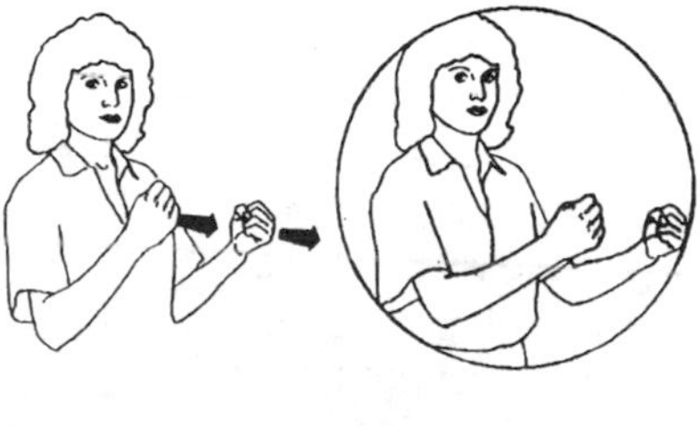

drop[1] *v.*

[Represents dropping something held in the hands] Beginning with both *flattened O hands* in front of the body, palms facing in and fingers pointing toward each other, drop the fingers of both hands downward while opening into *5 hands,* ending with both palms facing in and fingers pointing down.

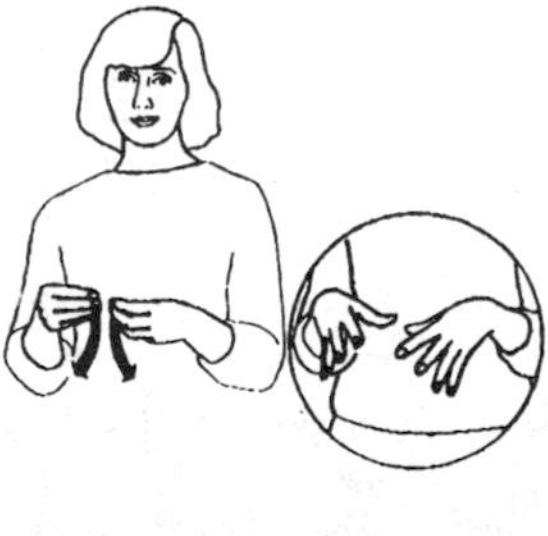

drop[2] *n.* See sign for DRIP.

drop out *v. phrase.* See sign for RESIGN.

drug *n.*
[Represents injecting a drug] Pound the little-finger side of the right *S hand,* palm facing up, with a double movement near the crook of the extended left arm.

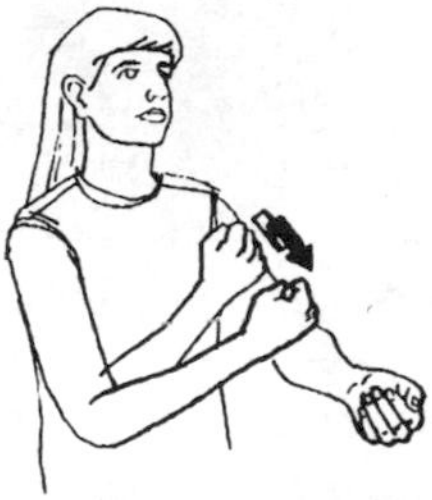

dry *adj.* Related form: **dried** *adj.* Same sign used for: **boring.**
[Wiping the chin dry] Drag the index-finger side of the right *X hand,* palm facing down, from left to right across the chin.

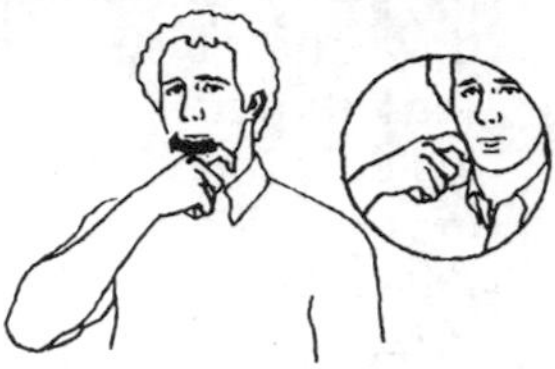

due *adj.* See sign for AFFORD.

dull *adj.* See sign for BORING[1].

dumb *adj.* Same sign used for: **stupid.**
[Natural gesture] Hit the palm side of the right *A hand* against the forehead.

dump *v.* See sign for THROW.

duplicate *v., n.* See sign for COPY.

during *prep.* Same sign used for: **meanwhile, while.**
[Shows two events occurring simultaneously] Beginning with both extended index fingers in front of each side

of the body, palms facing down, move them forward in parallel arcs, ending with the index fingers angled upward.

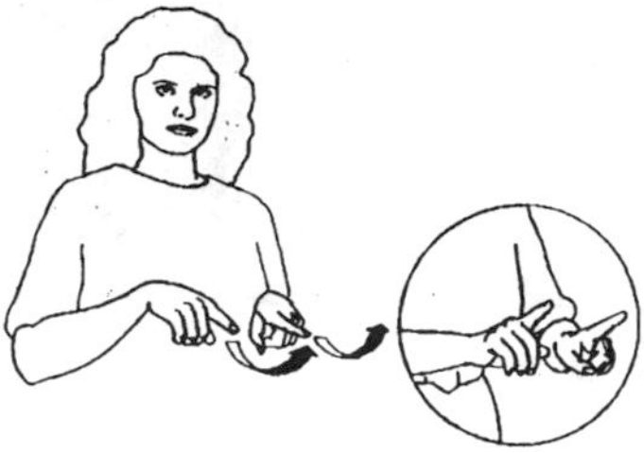

dusk *n.* See sign for DARK.

dwell *v.* See sign for LIVE.

each *adj., pron., adv.* Same sign used for: **per.**

[Emphasizes one] Bring the knuckle side of the right *10 hand* down the knuckles of the left *10 hand,* palms facing each other and thumbs pointing up.

each other *pron.* See sign for ASSOCIATE.

eager *adj.* See sign for ZEAL.

ear *n.*

[Location of an ear] Wiggle the right earlobe with the thumb and index finger of the closed right hand.

early *adv., adj.*

[Represents a bird hopping around looking for the early worm] Push the bent middle finger of the right *5 hand* across the back of the left *open hand,* both palms facing down.

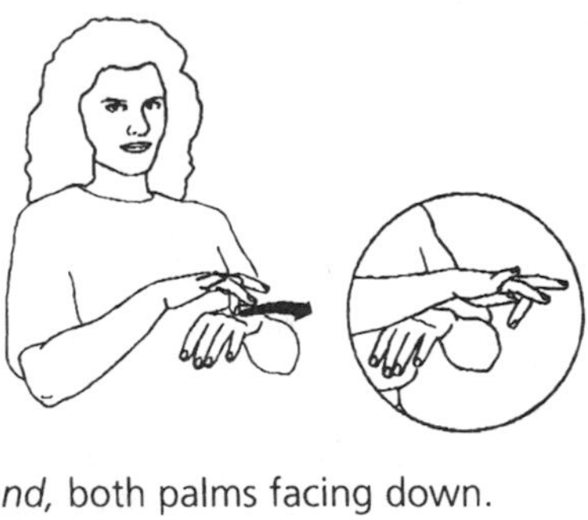

earn *v.* Same sign used for: **deserve, income, salary, wages.**

[Bringing earned money toward oneself] Bring the little-finger side of the right *curved hand,* palm facing left, across the upturned left *open hand* from fingertips to heel while changing into an *S hand.*

---

earring *n.*

[Location of earring] Shake the right earlobe with the index finger and thumb of the right *F hand* with a repeated movement. For the plural, use the same sign but made with both hands, one at each ear.

---

earth *n.* Same sign used for: **geography.**

[The earth rotating on its axis] Grasp each side of the left *S hand,* palm facing down, with the bent thumb and middle finger of the right *5 hand,* palm facing down. Then rock the right hand from side to side with a double movement.

---

easy *adj.* Same sign used for: **convenient, simple.**

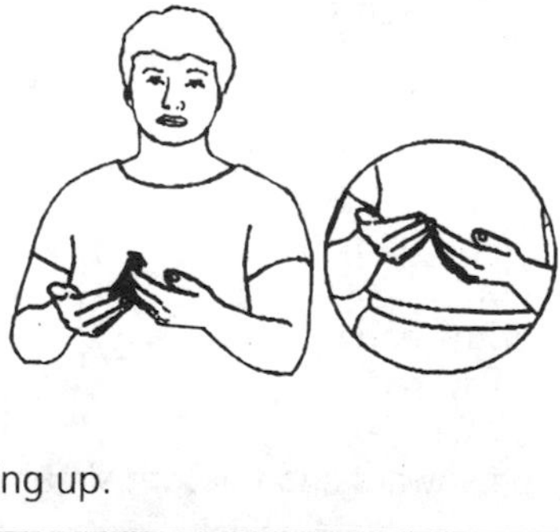

[The fingers are moved easily] Brush the fingertips of the right *curved hand* upward on the back of the fingertips of the left *curved hand* with a double movement, both palms facing up.

eat *v.*

[Putting food in the mouth] Bring the fingertips of the right *flattened O hand,* palm facing in, to the lips with a repeated movement.

eavesdrop *v.* See sign for LISTEN.

edit *v.* See sign for WRITE.

educate *v.* See signs for LEARN, TEACH. Related form: **education** *n.*

education *n.* Related form: **educate** *v.*

[Initialized sign **e-d** similar to sign for **teach**] Beginning with both *E hands* near each side of the head, palms facing each other, move the hands forward a short distance while changing into *D hands.*

effect *n.* See signs for ADVICE, INFLUENCE.

efficient *adj.* See sign for SKILL.

effort *n.*

[Initialized sign similar to sign for **try**] Move both *E hands* from in front of each side of the body, palms facing each other, downward and forward simultaneously in an arc.

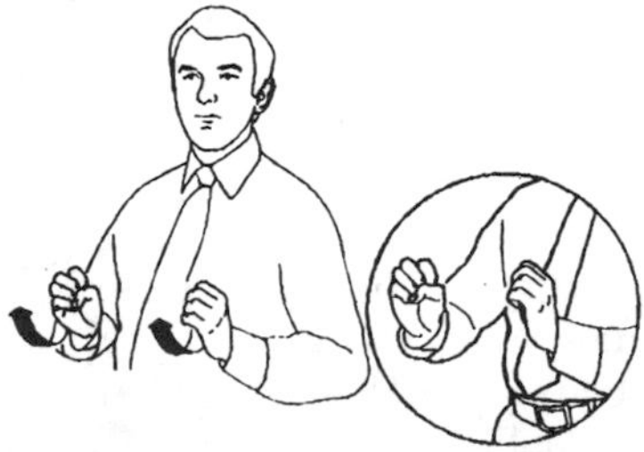

egg *n.*

[Represents cracking eggs] Beginning with the middle-finger side of the right *H hand* across the index-finger side of the left *H hand,* palms angled toward each other, bring the hands downward and away from each other with a double movement by twisting the wrists each time.

either[1] *adj., pron., conj.* See also sign for OR. Same sign used for: **alternative, choice.**

[Shows alternative choices] Tap the fingertips of the right *V hand* with a repeated alternating movement on the fingertips of the left *V hand,* palms facing each other.

either[2] *adj., pron., conj.* See sign for WHICH.

elastic *adj.* See sign for STRETCH[1].

elect *v.* See sign for APPOINT. Related form: **election** *n.*

electric or **electrical** *adj.* Related form: **electricity** *n.* Same sign used for: **battery.**

[An electrical connection] Tap the knuckles of the index fingers of both *X hands* together, palms facing in, with a double movement.

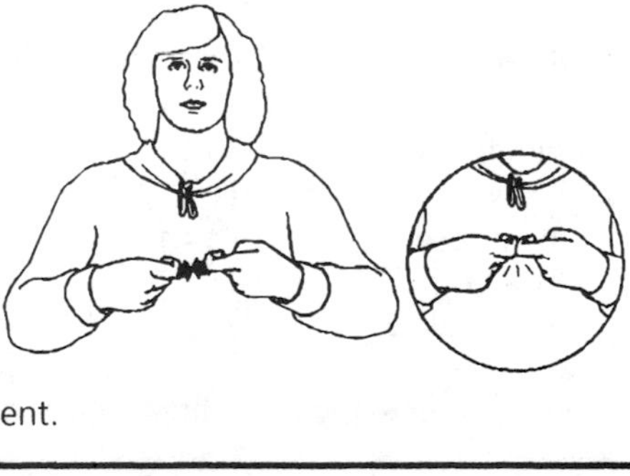

elegant *adj.* See sign for FANCY.

elevate *v.* See sign for ADVANCED. Related forms: **elevated** *adj.*, **elevation** *n.*

elevator *n.*

[Initialized sign showing movement of elevator] Move the index-finger side of the right *E hand,* palm facing forward, up and down with a repeated movement against the left *open hand,* palm facing right and fingers pointing up.

eligible *adj.* See sign for APPLY[2].

eliminate[1] *v.* Same sign used for: **abolish, abort, delete, omit, remove, repel, rid, terminate.**

[Natural gesture] Beginning with the back of the right *modified X hand,* palm facing in, touching the extended left index finger, palm facing in and finger pointing right, bring the right hand upward and outward to the right while flicking the thumb upward, forming a *10 hand.*

eliminate[2] *v.* See sign for SUBTRACT.

else *adj., adv.* See sign for OTHER[1].

elude *v.* See sign for AVOID.

embarrass *v.* Related form: **embarrassed** *adj.*

[Indicates blood rising in the face when embarrassed] Move both *5 hands,* palms facing each other, in repeated alternating circles near each cheek.

embrace *v.* See sign for HUG.

emergency *n.*

[Initialized sign] Move the right *E hand,* palm facing forward, back and forth with a double movement in front of the right shoulder.

emotional *adj.* Related form: **emotion** *n.*

[Initialized sign showing feeling welling up in the body] Move both *E hands,* palms facing in and knuckles pointing toward each other, in repeated alternating circles on each side of the chest.

emphasis *n.* See sign for IMPRESSION.

employ *v.* See sign for INVITE.

employment *n.* See sign for WORK.

empty *adj.* Same sign used for: **available, bare, blank, vacancy, vacant, void.**

[Indicates a vacant space] Move the bent middle fingertip of the right *5 hand* across the back of the left *open hand* from the wrist to off the fingertips, both palms facing down.

enable *v.* See sign for SKILL.

encourage *v.* Related form: **encouragement** *n.* Same sign used for: **bear up.**

[Hands seem to give someone a push of encouragement] Beginning with both *open hands* outside each side of the body, palms and fingers angled forward, move the hands toward each other and forward with a double pushing movement.

end[1] *v.* Same sign used for: **complete, conclude, finish, over, wind up.**

[Demonstrates going off the end] Beginning with the little-finger side of the right *open hand,* palm facing left, across the index-finger side of the left *open hand,* palm facing in, bring the right hand deliberately down off the left fingertips.

end[2] *n.* See sign for LAST[1].

endanger *v.* See sign for DANGER.

enemy *n.* Same sign used for: **foe, opponent, rival.**

[**opposite** + **person marker**] Beginning with both extended index fingers touching in front of the chest, palms facing down, pull the hands apart to in front of each side of the chest. Then move both *open hands,* palms facing each other, downward along each side of the body.

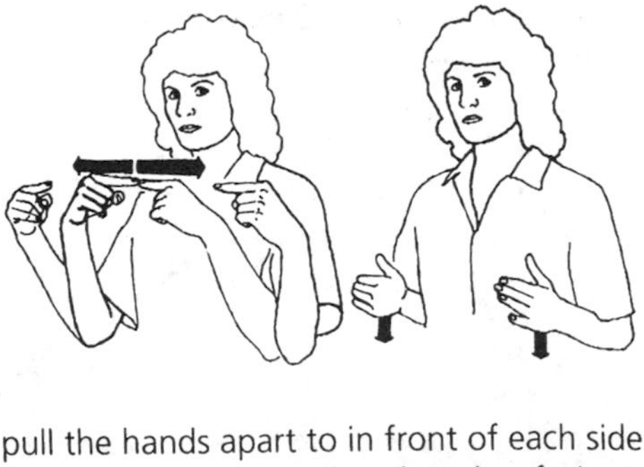

engaged *adj.* Related form: **engagement** *n.*

[Initialized sign showing the location of an engagement ring] Beginning with the right *E hand* over the left *open hand,* both palms facing down, move the right hand in a small circle and then straight down to land on the ring finger of the left hand.

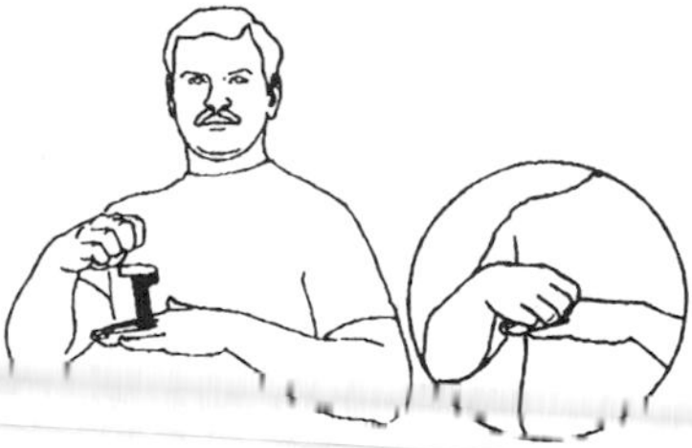

---

enjoy *v.* Related form: **enjoyment** *n.* Same sign used for: **appreciate, leisure, like, please, pleasure.**

[Hands rub the body with pleasure] Rub the palms of both *open hands* on the chest, right hand above the left hand and fingers pointing in opposite directions, in repeated circles moving in opposite directions.

---

enlarge *v.* See sign for BIG.

---

enough *adj., pron., adv.* Same sign used for: **adequate, plenty, sufficient.**

[Represents leveling off a container filled to the top] Push the palm side of the right *open hand,* palm facing down, forward across the thumb side of the left *S hand,* palm facing in.

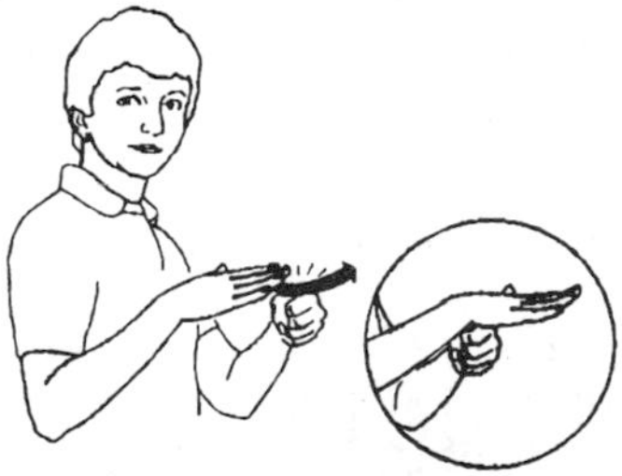

---

enrage *v.* See sign for ANGER.

---

enroll *v.* See sign for ENTER.

enter *v.* Related forms: **entrance** *n.*, **entry** *n.* Same sign used for: **enroll, immigrate, into.**

[Represents movement of entering] Move the back of the right *open hand* forward in a downward arc under the palm of the left *open hand,* both palms facing down.

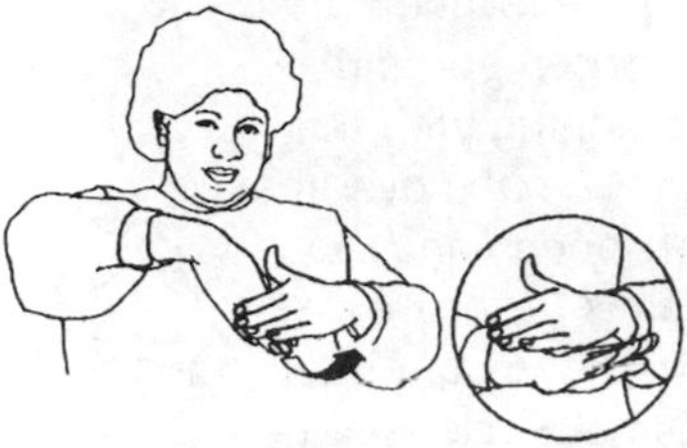

enthusiastic *adj.* See sign for ZEAL.

entire *adj.* See sign for ALL.

entitle *v.* See sign for TITLE.

envelope *n.* See sign for CARD.

envy *n.*, *v.* Related form: **envious** *adj.*

[Natural gesture used when a person envies another's possessions] Touch the teeth on the right side of the mouth with the right bent index fingertip.

equal *adj.*, *v.* Same sign used for: **even, fair, get even.**

[Demonstrates equal level] Tap the fingertips of both bent hands, palms facing down, together in front of the chest with a double movement.

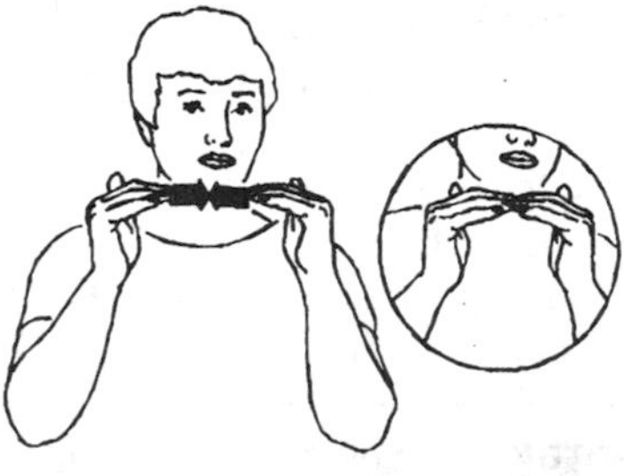

escape *v.* See sign for RUN AWAY.

especially *adv.* See sign for SPECIAL.

essential *adj.* See sign for IMPORTANT.

establish *v.* Same sign used for: **based on, founded.**

[Represents setting something up firmly] Beginning with the right *10 hand* in front of the right shoulder, palm facing down, twist the wrist upward with a circular movement and then move the right hand straight down to land the little-finger side on the back of the left *open hand,* palm facing down.

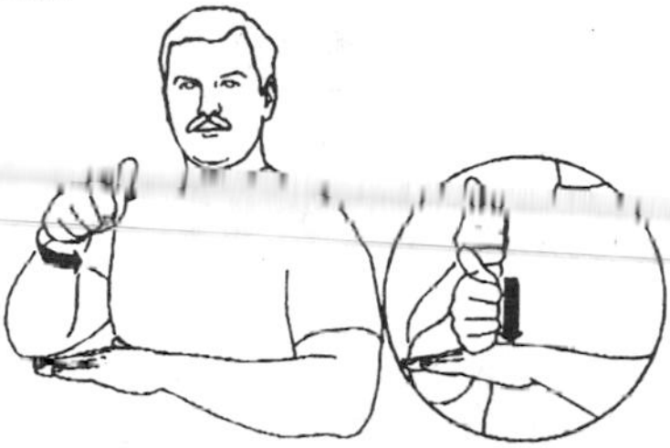

estimate *n., v.* See signs for ARITHMETIC, GUESS, MULTIPLY, ROUGH.

eternal *adj.* See sign for FOREVER.

evade *v.* See sign for AVOID.

evaporate *v.* See sign for DISSOLVE.

even[1] *adj.* Same sign used for: **fair, level.**

[Shows things of equal level] Beginning with the fingertips of both bent hands touching in front of the chest, both palms facing down, bring the hands straight apart from each other to in front of each shoulder.

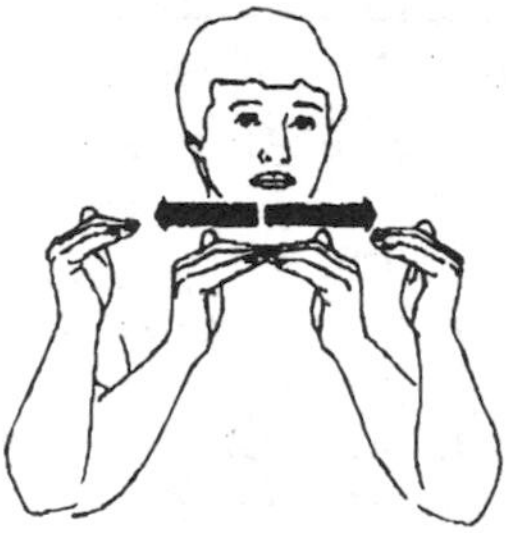

even[2] *adj., v.* See sign for EQUAL.

event *n.* See sign for HAPPEN.

even though *conj.* See sign for ANYWAY.

ever *adv.* See sign for ALWAYS.

everlasting *adj.* See sign for FOREVER.

ever since See sign for SINCE[1].

everyday *adj.* See sign for DAILY.

everything *pron.* See sign for INCLUDE.

evict *v.* See sign for ABANDON.

evidence *n.* See sign for PROOF.

evil *adj.* See sign for BAD.

exact *adj.* See sign for PRECISE.

exaggerate *v.* Same sign used for: **prolong, stretch.**

[Hands seem to stretch the truth] Beginning with the thumb side of the right *S hand,* palm facing left, against the little-finger side of the left *S hand,* palm facing right, move the right hand forward with a large wavy movement.

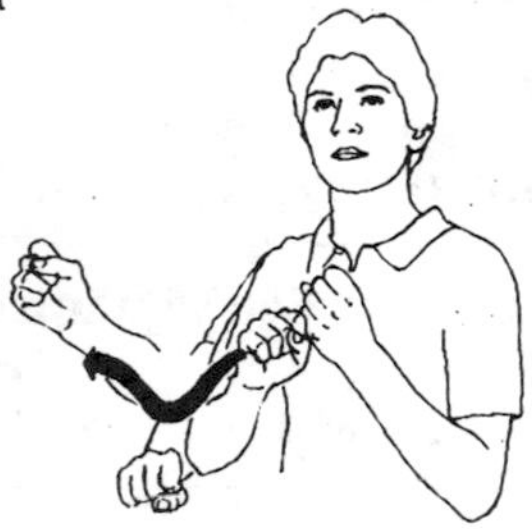

exalt *v.* See sign for ADVANCED. Related forms: **exalted** *adj.*, **exaltation** *n.*

examine *v.* See signs for CHECK[1], INVESTIGATE, LOOK FOR, TEST. Related form: **examination** *n.*

examination *n.* See signs for INVESTIGATE, TEST.

example *n.* See sign for SHOW[1].

exceed *v.* See signs for EXCESS, OVER.

excellent *adj.* See signs for SUPERB, WONDERFUL.

excess *n., adj.* Related form: **excessive** *adj.* Same sign used for: **exceed, massive, more than, too much.**

[Demonstrates an amount that is more than the base] Beginning with the right *bent hand* on the back of the left *bent hand,* both palms facing down, bring the right hand upward in an arc to the right.

exchange *n., v.* See sign for TRADE.

excite *v.* Related form: **excited** *adj.*, **exciting** *adj.*

[The finger used to show feeling brings up feeling in the body] Move the bent middle fingers of both *5 hands,* palms facing in and fingers pointing toward each other, in repeated alternating circles on each side of the chest.

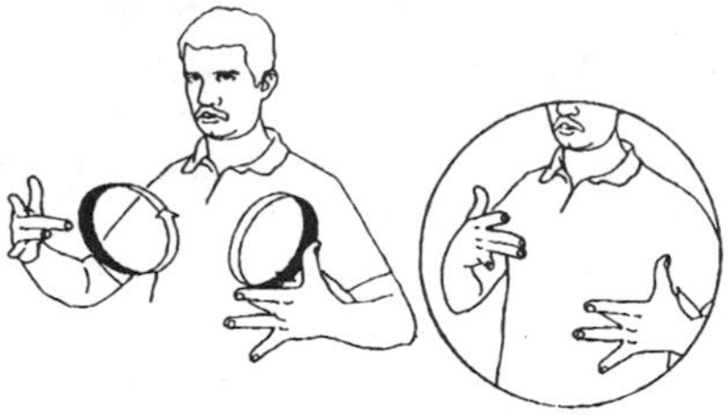

excuse[1] *n.*

[The hand seems to wipe away a mistake] Wipe the fingertips of the right *open hand* across the upturned left *open hand* from the heel off the fingertips.

excuse[2] *v.* See sign for FORGIVE.

excuse me Same sign as **excuse**[1] except made with a shorter double movement.

exempt *v.* See sign for SUBTRACT.

exercise[1] *n., v.* Same sign used for: **work out.**

[Mime exercising] Beginning with both *S hands* near each shoulder, palms facing each other, bring both arms up and down with a double movement.

exercise[2] *n., v.* See sign for PRACTICE.

exhausted *adj.* See sign for TIRED.

exhibit *n., v.* See sign for SHOW[2].

expand *v.* See sign for BALLOON.

expect *v.* See sign for HOPE. Related form: **expectation** *n.*

expel *v.* See signs for ABANDON, BREATH.

expensive *adj.* Same sign used for: **costly.**

[**money** + a gesture of throwing it away] Beginning with the back of the right *flattened O hand* on the upturned left *open hand,* bring the right hand upward to the right while opening into a *5 hand* in front of the right shoulder, palm facing down.

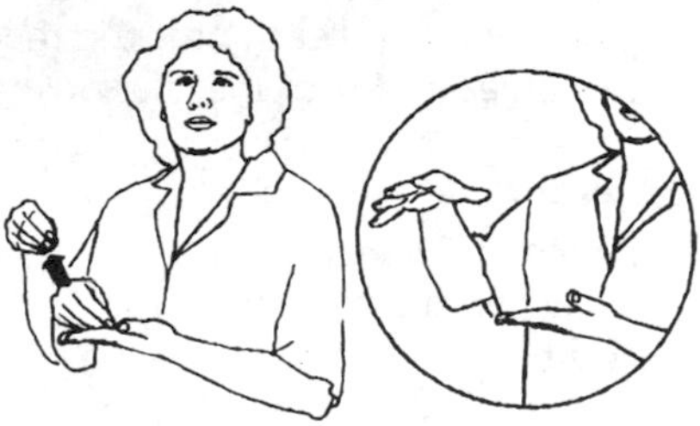

experience *n., v.* Same sign used for: **ordeal.**

[The grey sideburns of an experienced man] Beginning with the fingertips of the right *5 hand* on the right cheek, palm facing in, bring the hand outward to the right while closing the fingers into a *flattened O hand.*

expert *adj.* See signs for GOOD AT, SKILL.

explain *v.* See sign for DESCRIBE. Related form: **explanation** *n.*

expose *v.* See signs for SHOW[1], STICK[1].

expression *n.*

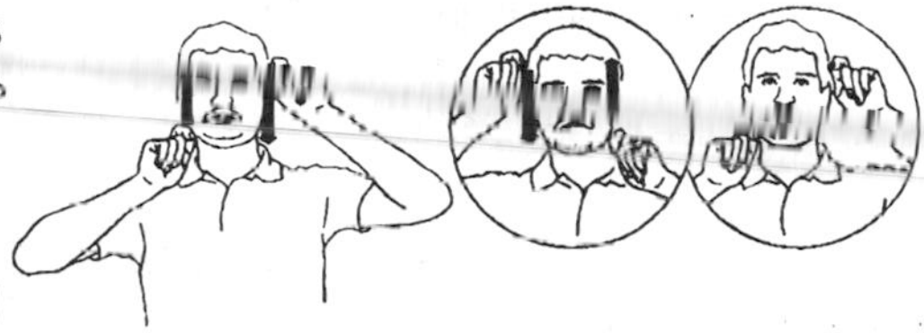

[Indicates the face's movement when changing expression] Move both *modified X hands,* palms facing forward, up and down with a repeated alternating movement in front of each side of the face.

external *n., adj.* See sign for OUTSIDE.

extinct *adj.* See sign for ABSENT.

extra *n.* See sign for ADD.

eye *n.*

[Location of the eye] Point the extended right index finger, palm facing in, toward the right eye with a double movement. For the plural, point to each eye.

eyeglasses *pl. n.* See sign for GLASSES.

face *n.*

[Location and shape of face] Draw a large circle around the face with the extended right index finger, palm facing in.

face to face See sign for IN FRONT OF.

facing *adj., v.* (*pres. participle of* FACE) See sign for IN FRONT OF.

fact *n.* See sign for TRUTH.

factory *n.* See sign for MACHINE.

fade *v.* See sign for VAGUE.

fade away *v. phrase.* See sign for DISSOLVE.

fail *v.* Related form: **failure** *n.*

[Falling off the edge] Beginning with the back of the right *V hand* on the heel of the left *open hand,* palm facing up, move the right hand across the left palm and off the fingers.

fair[1] *adj.* Same sign used for: **sort of, so-so.**

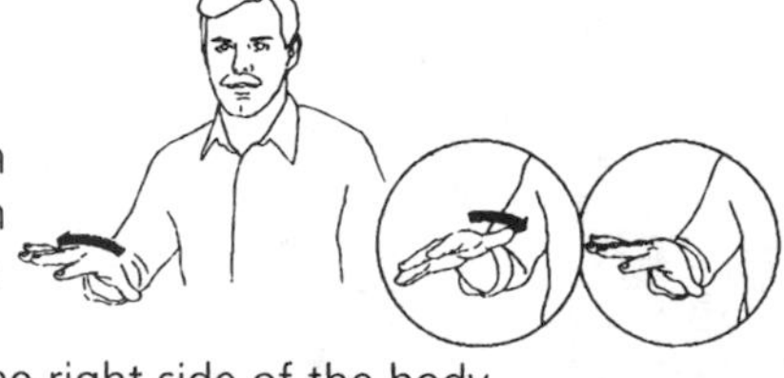

[Natural gesture showing ambivalence] Rock the right *5 hand,* palm facing down, from side to side with a repeated movement in front of the right side of the body.

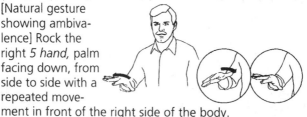

fair[2] *adj.* See signs for EQUAL, EVEN[1].

fake *adj.* Same sign used for: **artificial, counterfeit, pseudo, sham.**

[Indicates pushing the truth aside] Brush the extended right index finger, palm facing left, with a double movement against the tip of the nose from right to left by bending the wrist.

fall[1] *v., n.*

[Represents legs slipping out from under a person] Beginning with the fingertips of the right *V hand* pointing down, palm facing in, touching the upturned palm of the left *open hand,* flip the right hand over, ending with the back of the right *V hand* lying across the left palm.

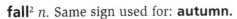

fall[2] *n.* Same sign used for: **autumn.**

[Leaves falling from a tree] Brush the index-finger side of the right *B hand,* palm facing down, downward toward the elbow of the left forearm, held bent across the chest.

fall asleep Same sign used for: **asleep, doze.**

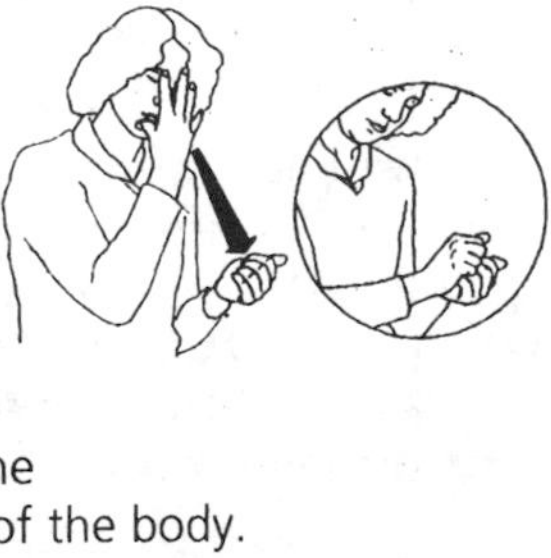

[Represents the head falling forward when dozing off] Beginning with the right *5 hand* in front of the face, palm facing in and fingers pointing up, bring the hand down while changing into an *A hand,* ending with the right hand, palm down, on top of the left *A hand,* palm up, in front of the body.

fall behind *v. phrase.* See sign for AVOID.

fall through *v. phrase.* See sign for BREAK DOWN.

familiar *adj.* See sign for AWARE[1].

family *n.*

[Initialized sign similar to sign for **class**] Beginning with the fingertips of both *F hands* touching in front of the chest, palms facing each other, bring the hands away from each other in outward arcs while turning the palms in, ending with the little fingers touching.

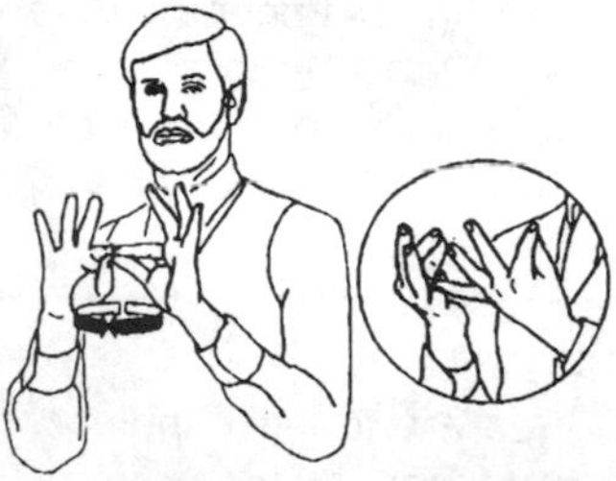

famished *adj.* See sign for HUNGRY.

famous *adj.* Related form: **fame** *n.* Same sign used for: **notorious.**

[Similar to sign for **tell**[1], except spreading the words far and wide] Beginning with both extended index fingers pointing to each side of the mouth, palms facing in, move the hands forward and outward in double arcs, ending with the index fingers pointing upward in front of each shoulder.

fancy *adj.* Same sign used for: **classical, deluxe, elegant, formal, grand, luxury.**

[The ruffles on an old-fashioned shirt] Move the thumb of the right *5 hand,* palm facing left, upward and forward in a double circular movement in the center of the chest.

fantastic *adj.* See signs for SUPERB, WONDERFUL.

far *adv., adj.* Related form: **farther** *adv., adj.* Same sign used for: **distance, distant, remote.**

[Moves to a location at a far distance] Beginning with the palm sides of both *A hands* together in front of the chest, move the right hand upward and forward in a large arc.

fare *n.* See sign for COST.

farewell *interj., n.* See sign for GOOD-BYE.

fascinating *adj.* See sign for INTEREST.

fast *adj., adv.* Same sign used for: **automatic, quick, sudden.**

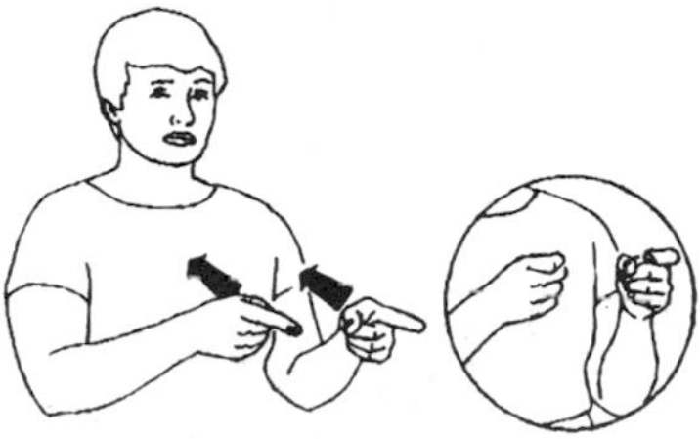

[Demonstrates quickness] Beginning with both extended index fingers pointing forward in front of the body, palms facing each other, pull the hands quickly back toward the chest while constricting the index fingers into *X hands.*

fasten *v.* See signs for BELONG, STICK[1].

fat *adj.*

[Shows shape of fat body] Move both *curved 5 hands* from in front of each side of the chest, palms facing in and fingers pointing toward each other, outward in large arcs to each side of the body.

father *n.* Same sign used for: **dad, daddy, papa.**

[Formed in the male area of the head, indicating the head of the household] Tap the thumb of the right *5 hand,* palm facing left and fingers pointing up, against the middle of the forehead with a double movement.

fatigue *n.* See signs for TIRED, WEAK.

fault[1] *n.* Same sign used for: **accuse, blame.**

[Pushes blame toward another] Push the little-finger side of the right *10 hand,* palm facing left, forward and upward in an arc across the back of the left *S hand,* palm facing down.

fault[2] *n.* See sign for BURDEN.

favorite[1] *adj., n.* Related form: **favor** *v.* Same sign used for: **flavor, prefer, preference, rather, type, typical.**

[Taste something on the finger] Touch the bent middle finger of the right *5 hand,* palm facing in, to the chin with a double movement.

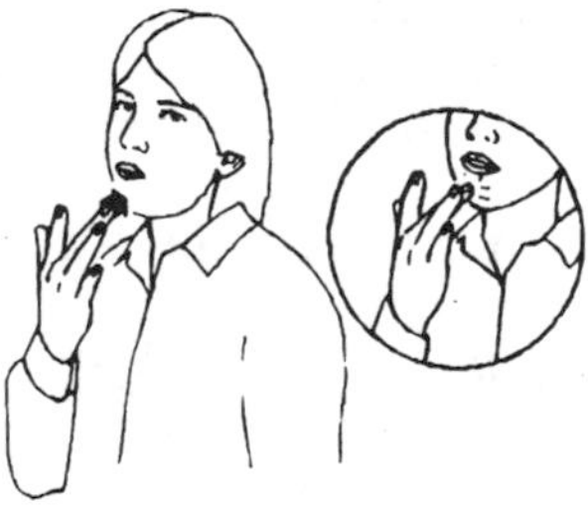

favorite[2] *adj.* See sign for PARTIAL TO.

fear *n., v.* Same sign used for: **coward, frightened, scared.**

[Natural gesture of protecting the body from the unknown] Beginning with both *5 hands* in front of each side of the chest, palms facing in and fingers pointing toward each other, move the hands toward each other with a short double movement.

federal *adj. phrase.* See sign for GOVERNMENT.

fed up *adj. phrase.* See sign for FULL[1].

fee *n.* See sign for COST[1].

feeble *adj.* See sign for WEAK.

feed *v.* Same sign used for: **supply.**

[Offering something to another] Beginning with both *flattened O hands* in front of each side of the body, palms facing up and right hand somewhat forward of the left hand, push the hands forward a short distance with a double movement.

feel *v.* Related form: **feeling** *n.* Same sign used for: **motive, sensation, sense.**

[Bent middle finger indicates feeling in sign language] Move the bent middle finger of the right *5 hand,* palm facing in, upward on the chest. Sometimes formed with a repeated movement.

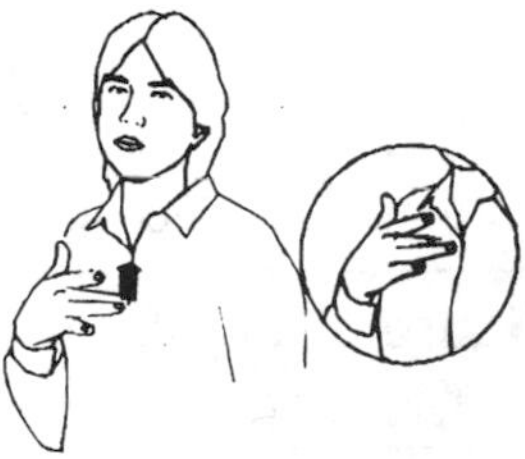

fellowship *n.* See sign for ASSOCIATE.

female *n.* See sign for LADY.

fertilize *v.* See sign for CONFLICT[1].

festival *n.* See sign for CELEBRATE.

few *adj.* Same sign used for: **several.**

[A small number of items is revealed at a time] Beginning with the right *A hand* held in front of the right side of the chest, palm facing up, slowly spread out each finger from the index finger to the little finger, ending with an upturned *4 hand.*

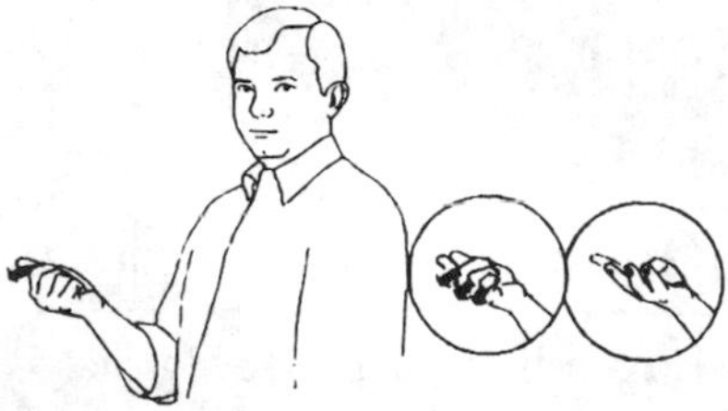

fib *v.* See sign for LIE.

field *n.* See sign for SPECIALIZE.

fierce *adj.* See sign for AWFUL.

fight[1] *n., v.*

[Mime two people striking at each other] Beginning with both *S hands* in front of each shoulder, palms facing each other, move the hands deliberately toward each other, ending with the wrists crossed in front of the chest.

fight[2] *v.* See sign for ARGUE.

figure *n., v.* See signs for ARITHMETIC, MULTIPLY.

figure out *v. phrase.* See signs for ARITHMETIC, MULTIPLY.

file[1] *v.* Same sign used for: **sort.**

[Insert something in order to file it] Slide the little-finger side of the right *B hand,* palm angled up, between the middle finger and ring finger of the left *B hand* held in front of the chest, palm facing in.

file² *v.* See signs for APPLY¹.

film *n.* Same sign used for: **movie, show.**

[Flicker of film on a screen] With the heel of the right *5 hand,* palm facing forward, on the heel of the left *open hand,* palm facing in, twist the right hand from side to side with a repeated movement.

filthy *adj.* See sign for DIRTY.

final *adj.* See sign for LAST¹. Related form: **finally** *adv.*

finally *adv.* Same sign used for: **at last, succeed.**

[Moving to higher stages] Beginning with both extended index fingers pointing up near each cheek, palms facing in, twist the wrists forward, ending with the index fingers pointing up in front of each shoulder, palms facing forward.

find *v.* Same sign used for: **discover, draw.**

[Selecting something held out in the hand] Beginning with the right *curved 5 hand* inserted in palm side of the left *curved 5 hand,* palm facing right in front of the body, bring the right hand upward while closing the thumb and index finger, forming an *F hand.*

fine[1] *adj.*

[The ruffles on the front of a fine old-fashioned shirt] Beginning with the thumb of the right *5 hand* touching the chest, palm facing left, move the hand forward a short distance.

fine[2] *n.* See sign for COST.

finish[1] *v.* Same sign used for: **already, complete, done, over, then.**

[Something shaken off the hands when finished with it] Beginning with both *5 hands* in front of the chest, palms facing in and fingers pointing up, flip the hands over with a sudden movement, ending with both palms facing down and fingers pointing forward.

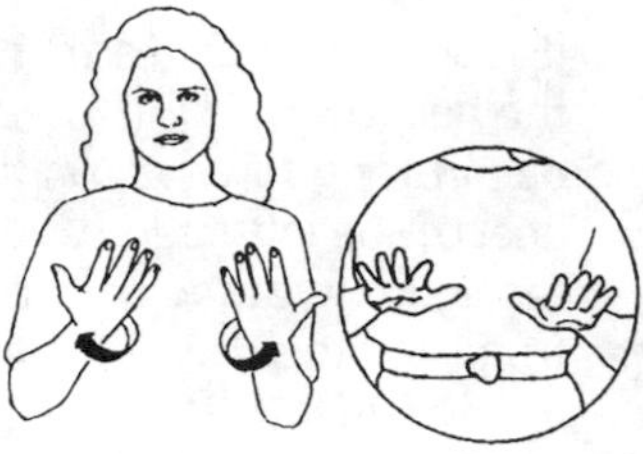

finish[2] *v.* See signs for BEEN THERE, END[1].

fire[1] *n.* Same sign used for: **burn.**

[Represents flames] Move both *5 hands,* palms facing up, from in front of the waist upward in front of the chest while wiggling the fingers.

fire[2] *v.* Same sign used for: **terminate.**

[Indicates cutting a job short] Swing the back of the right *open hand,* palm facing up, across the index-finger side of the left *B hand,* palm facing in.

firm *adj.* See sign for STRICT.

first *adj., n., adv.* Same sign used for: **one dollar.**

[**one** formed with a twisting movement used for ordinal numbers] Beginning with the extended right index finger pointing up in front of the right side of the chest, palm facing forward, twist the hand, ending with the palm facing in.

fish *n.*

[The movement of a fish in water] While touching the wrist of the right *open hand,* palm facing left, with the extended left index finger, swing the right hand back and forth with a double movement.

fit[1] *v.* Same sign used for: **suit.** *n.*

[Initialized sign showing that two things fit together] Beginning with the right *F hand* in front of the right shoulder, palm angled down, and the left *F hand* in front of the left side of the body, palm angled up, bring the fingertips together in front of the chest.

fit[2] *v., n.* See sign for MATCH.

five cents *pl. n.* See sign for NICKEL.

fix *v.* Same sign used for: **maintain, mend, repair.**

[The fingers seem to put things together] Brush the fingertips of both *flattened O hands* across each other repeatedly as the hands move up and down in opposite directions in a double movement.

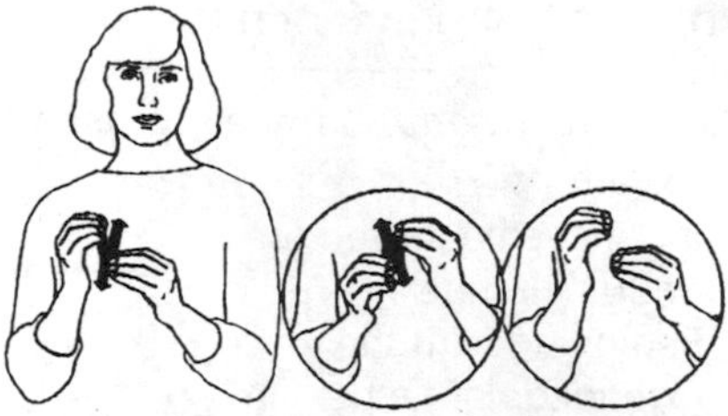

flag *n.*

[Represents a waving flag] While holding the elbow of the raised right arm in the left palm, wave the right *open hand* back and forth with a repeated movement in front of the right shoulder.

flame *n.* See sign for CANDLE.

flat *adj.*

[Shows flat surface] Beginning with the index-finger side of the right *bent hand* against the little-finger side of the left *bent hand,* both palms facing down, move the right hand forward a short distance.

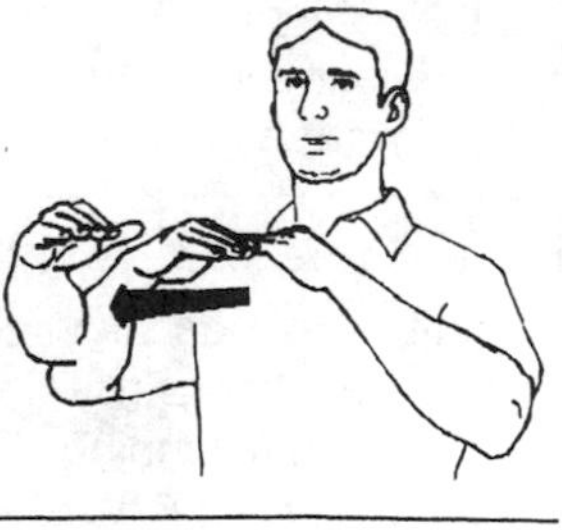

flavor *n.* See sign for FAVORITE[1].

flexible *adj.* Same sign used for: **floppy.**

[Shows something easily bent] With both *flattened O hands* in front of each side of the chest, palms facing in, bend the wrists to move the hands forward and back with an alternating repeated movement.

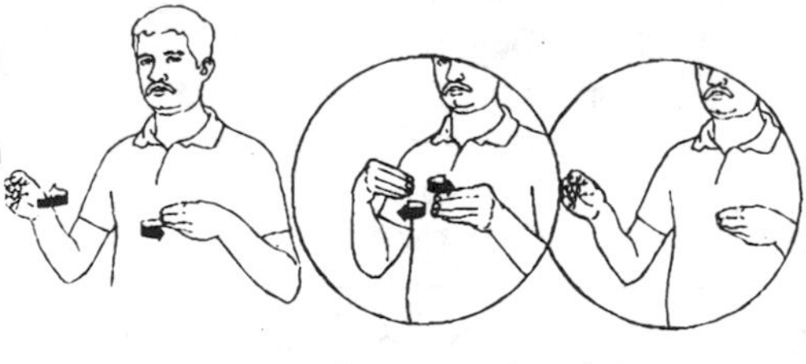

flip *v.* See sign for COOK.

floppy *adj.* See sign for FLEXIBLE.

flower *n.*

[Holding a flower to the nose to smell it] Touch the fingertips of the right *flattened O hand,* palm facing in, first to the right side of the nose and then to the left side.

fly *v.* Same sign used for: **wings.**

[Mime flapping wings to fly] Beginning with both *open hands* near each shoulder, and fingers angled outward in opposite directions, bend the wrists repeatedly, causing the hands to wave.

focus on *v. phrase.* See signs for ATTENTION, NARROW DOWN.

foe *n.* See sign for ENEMY.

folk *n.* See sign for PEOPLE.

follow *v.* Same sign used for: **trail.**

[One hand follows the other hand] With the knuckles of the right *10 hand,* palm facing left, near the wrist of the left *10 hand,* palm facing right, move both hands forward a short distance.

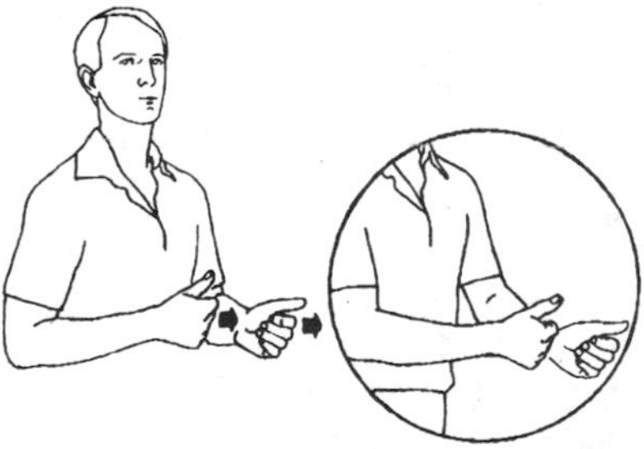

food *n.*

[Putting food in one's mouth] Bring the fingertips of the right *flattened O hand,* palm facing in, to the lips with a double movement.

fool around *v. phrase.* See sign for RUN AROUND.

foot *n.*

[Shows the length of a foot] Move the bent middle finger of the right *5 hand,* palm facing down, up and down the length of the left *open hand,* palm facing down, with a repeated movement.

football *n.*

[Represents scrimmage between two teams] Beginning with both *5 hands* in front of each side of the chest, palms facing in and fingers pointing toward each other, bring the hands together with a short double movement, interlocking the fingers of both hands each time.

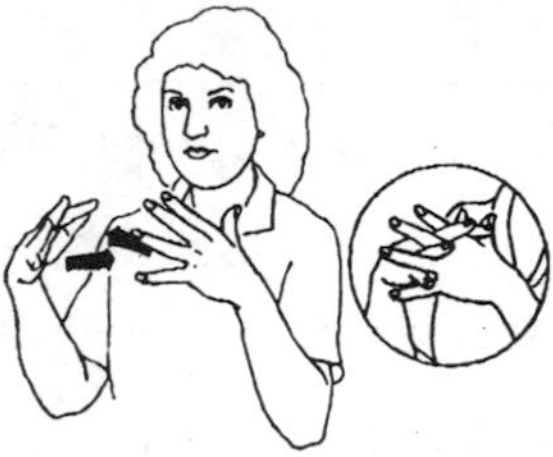

for *prep.*

[Knowledge is directed for another's use] Beginning with the extended right index finger touching the right side of the forehead, palm facing down, twist the hand forward, ending with the index finger pointing forward.

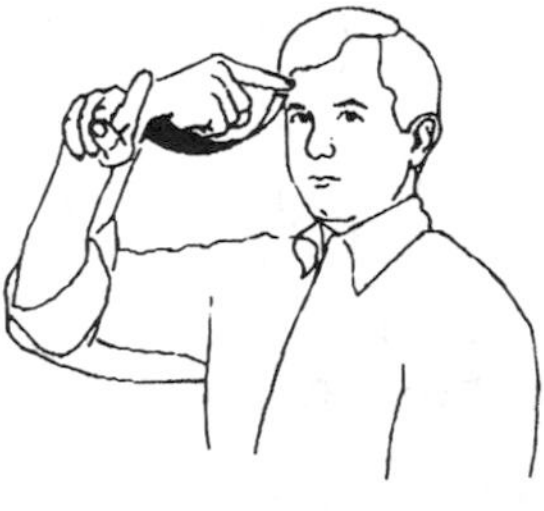

forbid *v.* Same sign used for: **ban, illegal, prohibit.**

[Similar to sign for **against** to show an opposition to something] Bring the palm side of the right *L hand,* palm facing left, sharply against the palm of the left *open hand,* palm facing right and fingers pointing up.

forecast *v.* See sign for PREDICT.

foresee *v.* See sign for PREDICT.

forever *adv.* Same sign used for: **eternal, everlasting.**

[**always** + **still**[1]] Move the right *1 hand,* palm facing up, in a circle in front of the right side of the body. Then move the right *Y hand* from in front of the right side of the body, palm facing down, forward and upward in an arc.

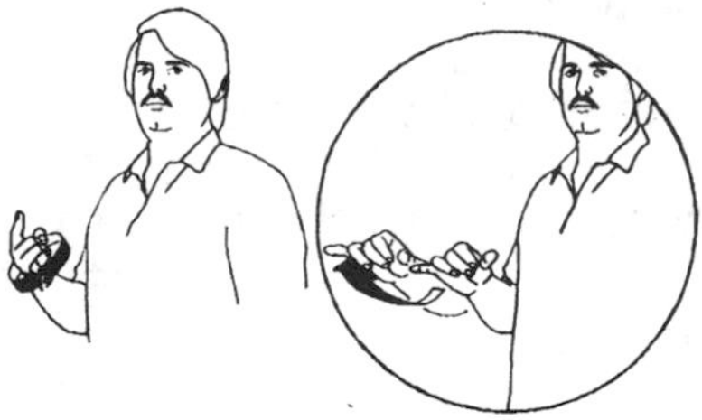

forget *v.*

[Wipes thoughts from one's memory] Wipe the fingers of the right *open hand,* fingers pointing left, across the forehead from left to right while closing into a *10 hand* near the right side of the forehead.

forgive *v.* Same sign used for: **excuse, pardon.**

[Wipes away mistake] Brush the fingertips of the right *open hand,* palm facing down, across the palm of the upturned left *open hand* from the heel off the fingertips with a double movement.

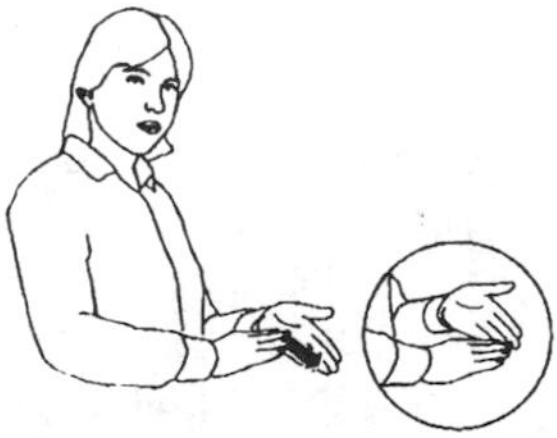

fork *n.*

[Tines of a fork] Touch the fingertips of the right *V hand,* palm facing down, on the palm of upturned left *open hand.* Then quickly turn the right hand so the palm faces the body and touch the left palm again.

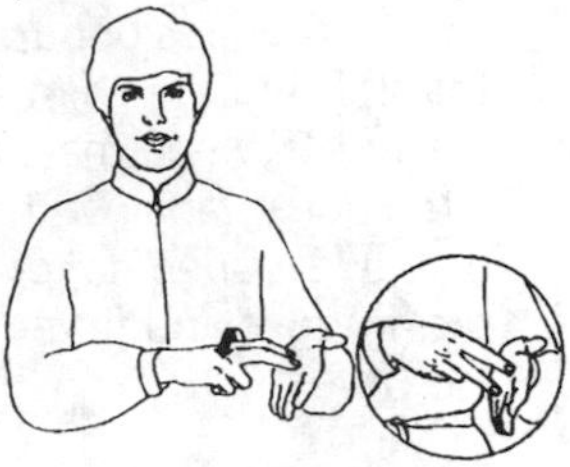

form *n., v.* See sign for SHAPE.

formal *adj.* See sign for FANCY.

forsake *v.* See signs for ABANDON, IGNORE.

fortunate *adj.* See sign for LUCK.

forward *adv.* See sign for GO ON.

founded *adj.* See sign for ESTABLISH.

fowl *n.* See sign for BIRD.

fragrance *n.* See sign for SMELL.

frank *adj.* See sign for HONEST. Related form: **frankly** *adv.*

fraternity *n.* See sign for ASSOCIATE.

freak *n., adj.* See sign for STRANGE.

free[1] *adj.* Related form: **freedom** *n.*

[Initialized sign similar to sign for **save**[1]] Beginning with both *F hands* crossed at the wrists in front of the chest, palms facing in opposite directions, twist the wrists to move the hands apart to in front of each shoulder, ending with the palms facing forward.

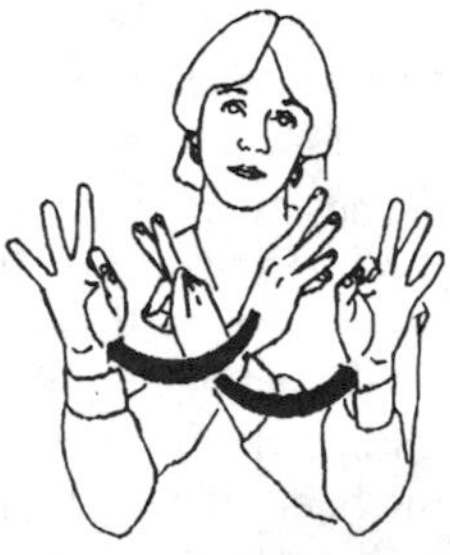

free[2] *adj.* See sign for SAVE[1]. Related form: **freedom** *n.*

freeway *n.* See sign for HIGHWAY.

freeze *v.* Same sign used for: **frost, frozen, ice, rigid, solidify.**

[Shows things hardening when frozen] Beginning with both *5 hands* in front of each side of the body, palms facing down and fingers pointing forward, pull the hands back toward the body while constricting the fingers.

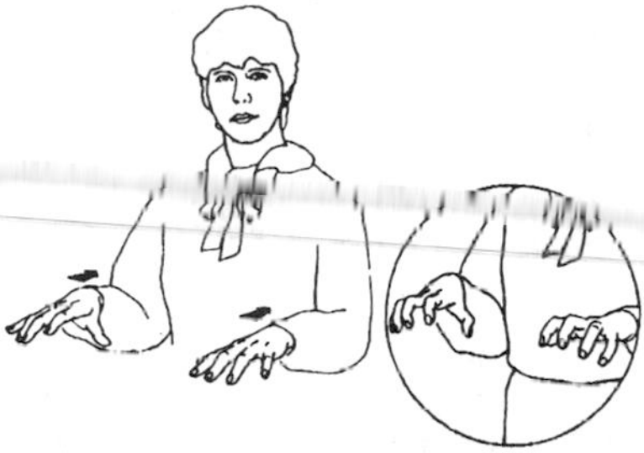

frequently *adv.* See sign for OFTEN.

friend *n.* Same sign used for: **comrade, pal.**

[Indicates the entwined lives of friends who have a close relationship] Hook the bent right index finger, palm facing down, over the bent left index finger, palm facing up. Then repeat, reversing the position of the hands.

friendly *adj.* Same sign used for: **cheerful, pleasant.**

[The face crinkling with smiles] With both *5 hands* near the cheeks, palms facing back, wiggle the fingers.

fright *n.* See sign for AFRAID. Related form: **frightened** *adj.*

frightened *adj.* See sign for FEAR.

frigid *adj.* See sign for COLD[2].

from *prep.*
[Moving from another location] Beginning with the knuckle of the right *X hand,* palm facing in, touching the extended left index finger, palm facing right and finger pointing up, pull the right hand back toward the chest.

from now on See sign for AFTER[1].

frost *v.* See sign for FREEZE.

frozen *adj.* See sign for FREEZE.

fruit *n.*
[Initialized sign] Beginning with the fingertips of the right *F hand* on the right side of the chin, palm facing left, twist the hand forward with a double movement, ending with the palm facing in.

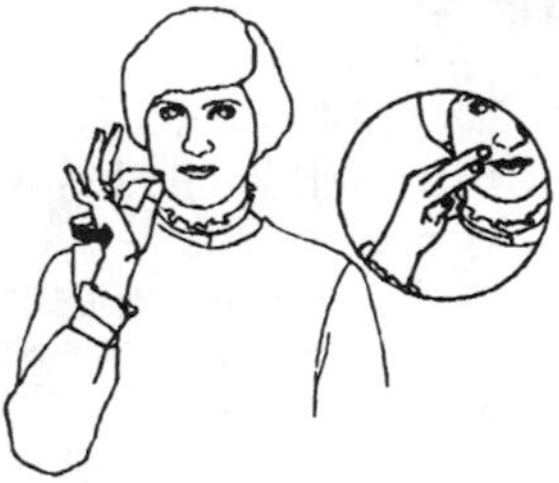

frustrate *v.* Related form: **frustration** *n.*
[Facing a wall of opposition] Bring the back of the right *B hand,* palm facing forward, back against the mouth with a double movement or, sometimes, a single movement.

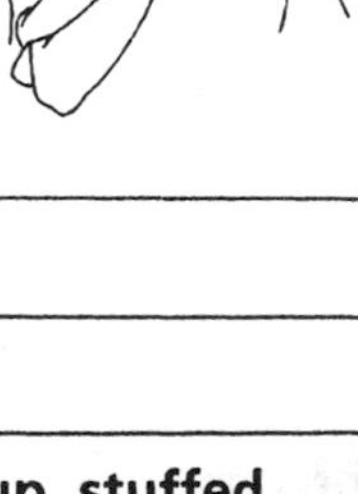

fry *v.* See sign for COOK.

fuel *n.* See sign for GAS.

full[1] *adj.* Same sign used for: **fed up, stuffed.**

[Represents feeling full] Move the right *B hand,* palm facing down, from the center of the chest upward with a deliberate movement, ending with back of the right fingers under the chin.

full^2 *adj.* Same sign used for: **complete.**

[Leveling off something that is full] Slide the palm of the right *open hand,* palm facing down, from right to left across the index-finger side of the left *S hand,* palm facing right.

fume *n., v.* See sign for SMELL.

fun *n.*

[The nose wrinkles when laughing] Bring the fingers of the right *H hand* from near the nose downward, ending with the fingers of the right *H hand* across the fingers of the left *H hand* in front the chest, both palms facing down.

fund *n.* See signs for MONEY, SUPPORT.

funny *adj.* Same sign used for: **amuse, humor.**

[The sign for **fun** moving toward something funny] With a double movement, brush the nose with the fingertips of the right *U hand,* palm facing in and thumb extended, bending the fingers of the *U hand* back toward the palm each time.

furniture *n.*
[Initialized sign] Move the right *F hand,* palm facing forward, from side to side in front of the right side of the chest with a repeated movement.

fury *adj.* See sign for ANGER.

future *n.*
[Hand moves forward into the future] Move the right *open hand,* palm facing left and fingers pointing up, from near the right cheek forward in a double arc.

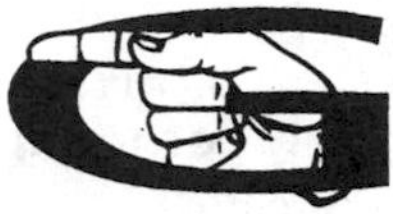

gab *v., n. Informal.* See sign for BLAB.

gain *v., n.* See sign for INCREASE.

gala *adj., n.* See signs for CELEBRATE, DANCE.

gamble *n., v.* See sign for BET.

game *n.*
[Represents opposing teams sparring] Bring the knuckles of both *10 hands,* palms facing in, against each other with a double movement in front of the chest.

gap *n.* See sign for BETWEEN.

garage *n.*
[Represents a car moving into a garage] Move the right *3 hand,* palm facing left, forward with a short repeated movement under the palm of the left *open hand,* palm facing down and fingers pointing right.

garbled *adj.* See sign for MESSY.

gas *n.* Alternate form: **gasoline.** Same sign used for: **fuel.**
[Mime pouring gas into the gas tank of a vehicle] Tap the extended thumb of the right *10 hand,* palm facing forward, downward with a repeated small movement into the thumb-side opening of the left *S hand.*

gather[1] *v.* See also sign for ATTEND. Same sign used for: **assemble, get together, go to.**

[Represents people coming together] Beginning with both *5 hands* in front of each shoulder, palms angled forward, bring the hands forward toward each other, ending with the palms facing down.

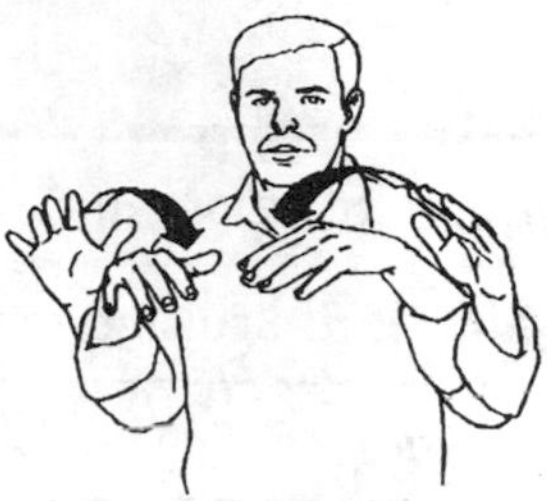

gather[2] *v.* See sign for COLLECT.

gay[1] *adj., n.* (*slang*: disparaging and offensive).

[Initialized sign] Bring the fingertips of the right *G hand,* palm facing in, back to touch the chin with a double movement.

gay[2] *adj.* See sign for HAPPY.

general[1] *adj.* Same sign used for: **broad.**

[Hands open up broadly] Beginning with both *open hands* in front of the chest, fingers angled toward each other, swing the fingers away from each other, ending with the fingers angled outward in front of each side of the body.

general[2] *adj.* See sign for WIDE.

general[3] *n.* See sign for CAPTAIN.

generous *adj.* See sign for KIND[1].

gentle *adj.* See signs for KIND[1], POLITE, SOFT, SWEET.

genuine *adj.* See sign for REAL.

geography *n.* See sign for EARTH.

get *v.* Same sign used for: **acquire, attain, obtain, receive.**

[Reaching for something and bringing it to oneself] Beginning with both *curved 5 hands* in front of the chest, right hand above the left and palms facing in opposite directions, bring the hands back toward the chest while closing into *S hands,* ending with the little-finger side of the right hand on the index-finger side of the left hand.

get along *v. phrase.* See sign for GO ON.

get away *v. phrase.* See signs for AVOID, RUN AWAY.

get even See signs for EQUAL, REVENGE.

get together See sign for GATHER[1].

get up *v. phrase.* See sign for RAISE[1].

gift *n.* Same sign used for: **award, charity, contribution, donation, grant, present, reward, tribute.**

[Presenting something to another] Move both *X hands* from in front of the body, palms facing each other, forward in simultaneous arcs.

girl *n.*

[Formed in the female area of the head] Move the thumb of the right *A hand,* palm facing left, downward on the right cheek to the right side of the chin.

give *v.* Same sign used for: **contribute, donate, grant, present, provide.**

[Presenting something to another] Move the right *X hand* from in front of the right side of the chest, palm facing left, forward in a large arc.

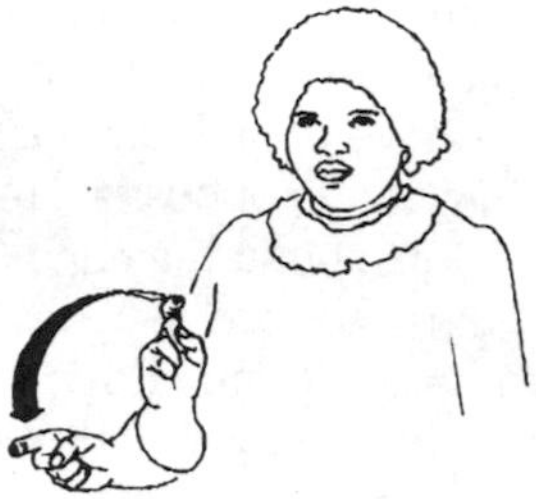

glad *adj.* See sign for HAPPY.

glass[1] *n.*

[Shows porcelain on teeth] Tap the fingertip of the right bent index finger against the front teeth with a repeated movement.

glass[2] *n.* See sign for BOTTLE.

glasses *pl. n.* Same sign used for: **eyeglasses.**

[Shape and location of eyeglasses] Tap the thumbs of both *modified C hands,* palms facing each other, near the outside corner of each eye with a repeated movement.

glitter *v., n.* See sign for SHINY.

glossy *adj.* See sign for SHINY.

glove *n.*

[Represents pulling on a glove] Pull the right *5 hand,* palm facing down, from the fingers up the length of the back of the left *5 hand,* palm facing down. To indicate the plural, repeat with the other hand.

glow *v., n.* See signs for CANDLE, SHINY.

glue *n., v.*

[Initialized sign seeming to squeeze glue on paper] Move the fingertips of the right *G hand,* palm and fingers facing down, in a circular movement over the upturned left *open hand.*

go *v.* Same sign used for: **depart, go away, leave.**

[Represents something getting smaller as it disappears into the distance] Beginning with the *flattened C hand* in front of the right shoulder, fingers pointing left, move the hand quickly to the right while closing the fingers into a *flattened O hand.*

go ahead *v. phrase.* See sign for GO ON.

goal *n.* Same sign used for: **aim, ambitious, objective, target.**

[Indicates directing something toward something else] Move the extended right index finger from touching the right side of the forehead, palm facing down, forward to point toward the extended left index finger held in front of the face, palm facing forward and finger angled up.

go by train See sign for TRAIN.

God *n.*

[Indicates the spirit of God moving down from above] Move the right *B hand,* palm facing left and fingers angled upward, from above the head downward in front of the face in an inward arc.

gold *n., adj.* Same sign used for: **golden.**

[Shows a gold earring + **yellow**] With the thumb, index finger, and little finger of the right hand extended, palm facing in, touch the index finger near the right ear. Then bring the right hand downward and forward with a shaking movement while turning the wrist forward and changing into a *Y hand.*

golden *adj.* See sign for GOLD. Shared idea of yellow color.

gone *v., adj.* See signs for ABSENT

good *adj.* Same sign used for: **well.**

[Presents something good for inspection] Beginning with the fingertips of the right *open hand* near the mouth, palm facing in and fingers pointing up, bring the hand downward, ending with the back of the right hand across the palm of the left *open hand,* both palms facing up.

good at Same sign used for: **expert, proficient.**

[Similar to sign for **adroit**] Bring the fingertips of the right *F hand,* palm facing in, back against the chin.

good-bye *interj., n.* Same sign used for: **bye, farewell.**

[Natural gesture for waving good-bye] Beginning with the right *open hand* in front of the right shoulder, palm facing forward and fingers pointing up, bend the fingers up and down with a repeated movement.

good-looking *adj.* See sign for LOOKS.

go on *v. phrase.* Same sign used for: **all along, continue, forward, get along, go ahead, onward, proceed.**

[Shows shoving something along ahead of oneself] Beginning with both *open hands* in front of the body, palms facing in and fingers pointing toward each other, move the hands forward a short distance simultaneously.

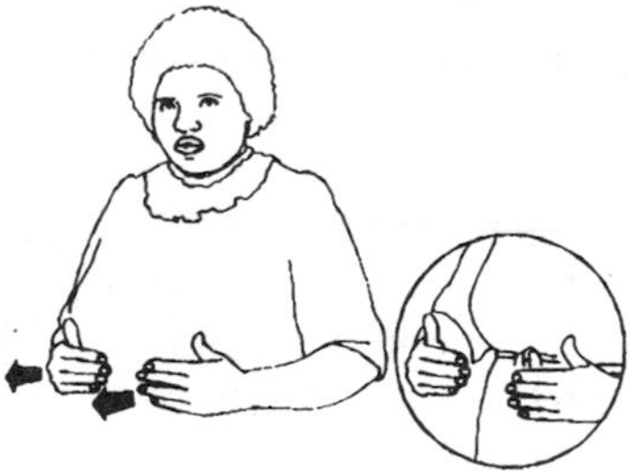

go out *v. phrase.* See sign for OUT.

gossip[1] *n., v.* Same sign used for: **rumor.**

[Represents mouths opening and closing repeatedly] Move both *G hands,* palms facing each other, in a flat circular movement in front of the chest while pinching the index finger and thumb of each hand together with a repeated movement.

gossip[2] *n., v.* See sign for BLAB.

go to *v. phrase.* See signs for ATTEND, GATHER[1].

govern *v.* See sign for MANAGE.

government *n.* Same sign for: **federal**.

[Indicates the head, one in authority] Beginning with the extended right index finger pointing upward near the right side of the head, palm facing forward, twist the wrist to touch the finger to the right temple.

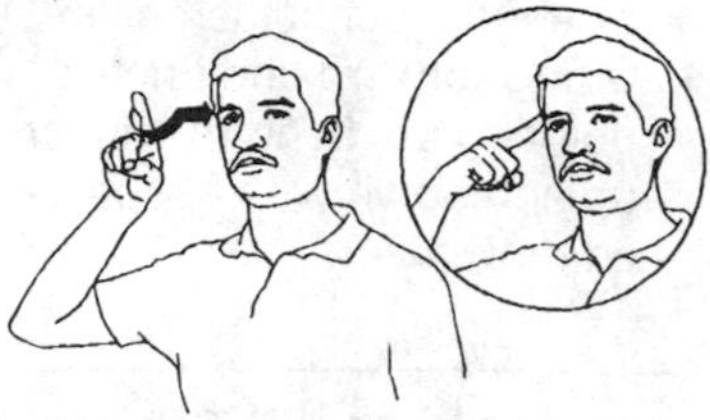

gracious *adj.* See sign for KIND[1].

grand *adj.* See signs for FANCY, LARGE.

grandfather *n.* Alternate form: **grandpa** (*informal*).

[**man** + moving forward one generation] Beginning with the thumb of the right *A hand* touching the forehead, palm facing left, bring the hand downward while opening into a *curved 5 hand* in front of the face, palm angled up.

grandma *n. Informal.* See sign for GRANDMOTHER.

grandmother *n.* Alternate form: **grandma** (*informal*).

[**girl** + moving forward one generation] Beginning with the thumb of the right *A hand* touching the chin, palm facing left, bring the hand downward while opening into a *curved 5 hand* in front of the chest, palm facing up.

grandpa *n. Informal.* See sign for GRANDFATHER.

grant *n., v.* See signs for GIFT, GIVE, LET.

graph *n.* See sign for SCHEDULE[1].

grass *n.*

[Blades of grass] Push the heel of the right *curved 5 hand,* palm facing up, upward a short distance on the chin.

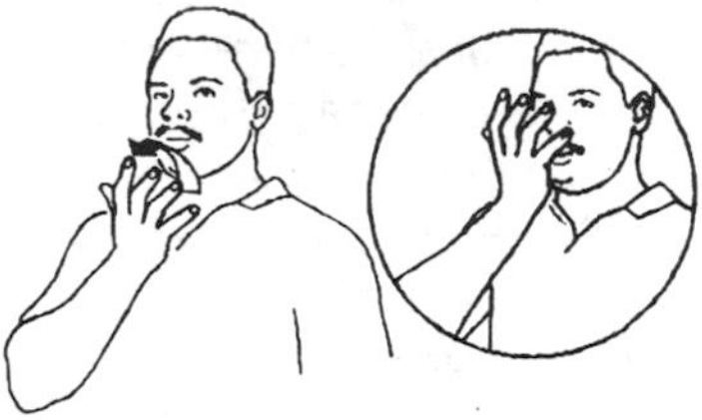

grave *n., adj.* See signs for BURY, SAD.

gravy *n.* Same sign used for: **grease, syrup.**

[Represents dripping gravy] Beginning with the extended thumb and index finger of the right *G hand* grasping the little-finger side of the left *open hand,* both palms facing in, bring the right hand downward with a double movement while closing the index finger to the thumb each time.

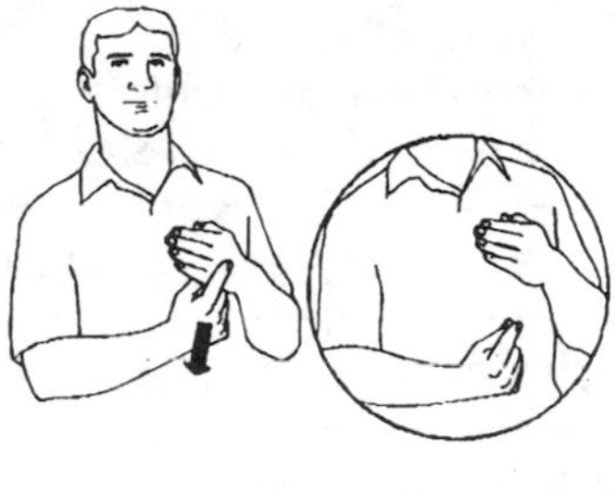

gray *adj.*

[Suggests the blending of black and white] Beginning with both *5 hands* in front of the chest, fingers pointing toward each other and palms facing in, move the hands forward and back in opposite directions, lightly brushing fingertips as the hands pass each other.

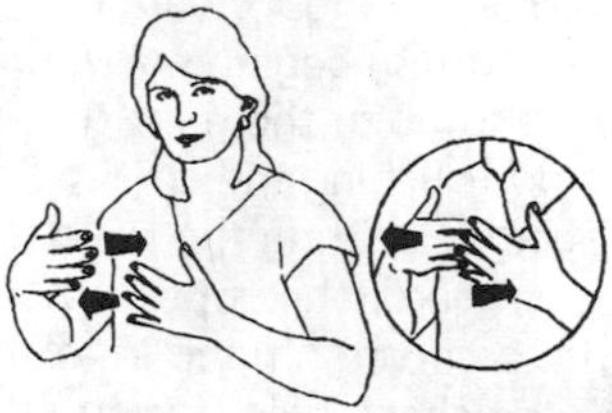

grease *n.* See sign for GRAVY. Related form: **greasy** *adj.*

great *adj.* See signs for LARGE, WONDERFUL.

greedy *adj.* Same sign used for: **covetous, niggardly, possess, selfish, thrifty, tight.**

[Clutching a prized possession] Beginning with the right *curved 5 hand* in front of the chin, palm facing in, bring the hand downward with either a single or double movement while closing the hand into an *S hand.*

green *adj.*

[Initialized sign] Twist the right *G hand,* palm facing left, back and forward with a small repeated movement in front of the right shoulder.

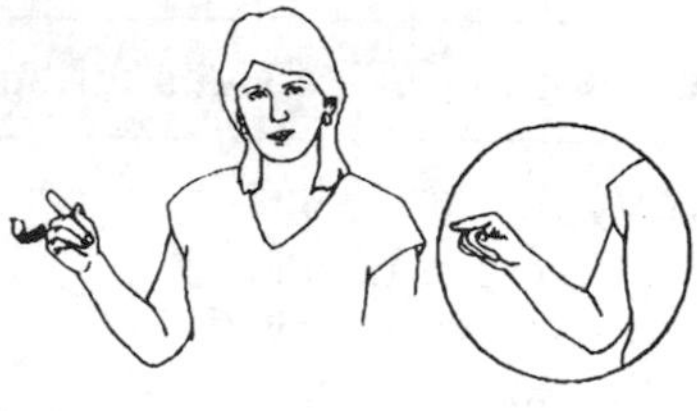

greet *v.* See signs for INVITE, MEET.

grievance *n.* See sign for PROTEST[1].

grin *v., n.* See sign for SMILE.

grind *v.* See sign for CHEW.

grip *n., v.* See sign for HOLD[1].

gripe *v.* See sign for COMPLAIN.

gross *adj.* See sign for PROFIT.

ground *n.* See sign for DIRT.

group[1] *n.*
[Initialized sign similar to sign for **class**] Beginning with both *G hands* in front of the chest, palms facing toward each other, bring the hands away from each other in outward arcs while turning the palms in, ending with the little fingers near each other.

group[2] *n.* See sign for CLASS.

grow *v.* Same sign used for: **sprout.**
[Represents a plant coming up through the soil] Bring the right *flattened O hand,* palm facing in, up through the left *C hand,* palm facing in and fingers pointing right, while spreading the right fingers into a *5 hand.*

grow up *v. phrase.* Same sign used for: **raise, rear.**
[Shows height as one grows] Bring the right *open hand,* palm facing down and fingers pointing left, from in front of the chest upward.

grumble *v.* See sign for COMPLAIN.

guarantee *n., v.* See sign for STAMP[2].

guess *v., n.* Same sign used for: **assume, estimate.**
[Hand seems to snatch at an idea as it passes the face] Move the right *C hand,* palm facing left, from near the

right side of the forehead in a quick downward arc in front of the face while closing into an *S hand,* ending with the palm facing down by the left side of the head.

guide *v.* See sign for LEAD.

guilt *n.* Related form: **guilty** *adj.* [Initialized sign formed near the heart] Bring the thumb side of the right *G hand,* palm facing left, back against the left side of the chest.

gum *n.* See sign for CHEWING GUM.

gun *n.* Same sign used for: **pistol.** [Demonstrates pulling back the hammer on a pointed gun] With the index finger of the right *L hand* pointing forward in front of the right side of the body, palm facing left, wiggle the thumb up and down with a repeated movement.

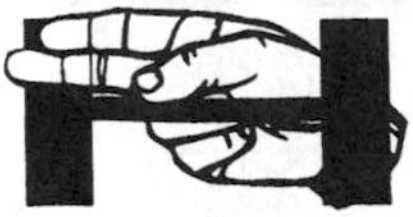

habit *n.* Same sign used for: **accustomed to.**

[Symbolizes being bound by tradition] With the heel of the right *S hand* across the wrist of the left *S hand,* both palms facing down, move the hands down simultaneously in front of the chest.

had *v.* See sign for HAVE.

hair *n.*

[Location of hair] Hold a strand of hair with the thumb and forefinger of the right *F hand,* palm facing left, and shake it with a repeated movement.

haircut[1] *n.*

[Mime cutting one's hair] Move the right *V hand,* palm facing left and fingers pointing up, from near the right cheek back to near the right ear while opening and closing the index and middle fingers with a double movement.

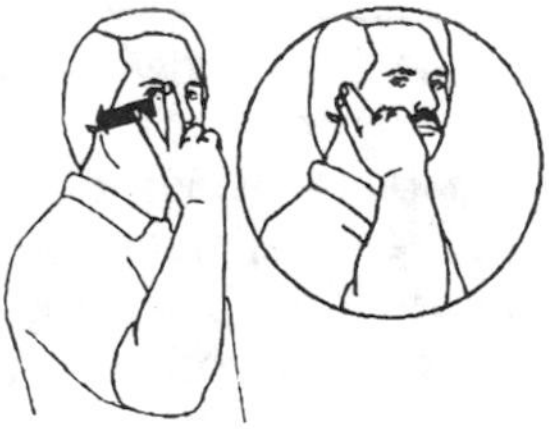

haircut[2] *n.* See sign for CUT[1].

half *adj.* See sign for ONE HALF.

hall *n.* Alternate form: **hallway.** Same sign used for: **corridor.**

[Shape of a hallway] Move both *open hands,* palms

facing each other and fingers pointing up, from in front of each shoulder straight forward.

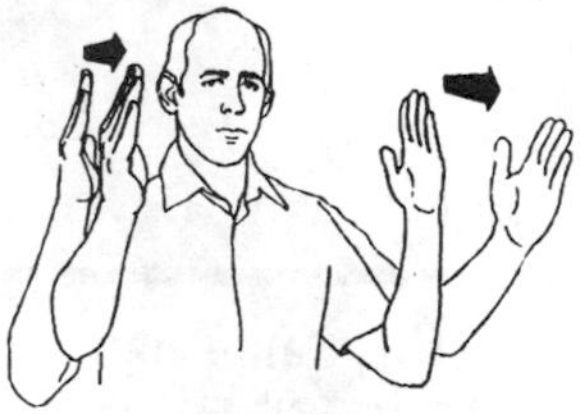

halt *v.* See signs for HOLD², STOP¹.

hamburger *n.*
[Mime making a hamburger patty] Clasp the right *curved hand,* palm facing down, across the upturned left *curved hand.* Then flip the hands over and repeat with the left hand on top.

handle *v.* See signs for MANAGE, PIPE¹.

hands *pl. n.*
[Location of one's hands] Beginning with the little-finger side of the right *B hand* at an angle on the thumb side of the left *B hand,* palms facing in opposite directions, bring the right hand down and under the left hand in order to exchange positions. Repeat the movement with the left hand.

handsome *adj.* See sign for LOOKS.

handy *adj.* See sign for SKILL.

happen *v.* Same sign used for: **accident, event, incident, occur, occurrence.**
Beginning with both extended index fingers in front of the body, palms facing up and fingers pointing forward,

flip the hands over toward each other, ending with the palms facing down.

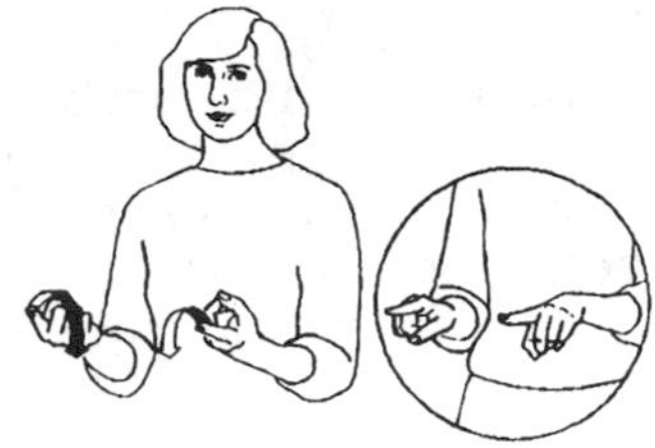

happy *adj.* Same sign used for: **cheer, cheerful, delighted, gay, glad, jolly, joy, merry.**

[Represents joy rising in the body] Brush the fingers of the right *open hand,* palm facing in and fingers pointing left, upward in a repeated circular movement on the chest.

harassment *n.* See sign for DANGER.

hard[1] *adj.* Same sign used for: **solid.**

[Indicates a hard surface] Strike the little-finger side of the right *bent V hand* sharply against the index-finger side of the left *bent V hand,* palms facing in opposite directions.

hard[2] *adj.* See sign for DIFFICULT.

hardly *adv.* See sign for ANYWAY.

harm *v.* See signs for DANGER, HURT.

has *v.* See sign for HAVE.

hassle *v.* See sign for HURRY.

haste *n.* See sign for HURRY.

hat *n.*
[Location of a hat on one's head] Pat the top of the head with the fingers of the right *open hand,* palm facing down, with a double movement.

hate *v.*
[The fingers flick away something distasteful] Beginning with both *8 hands* in front of the chest, palms facing each other, flick the middle fingers forward, changing into *5 hands.*

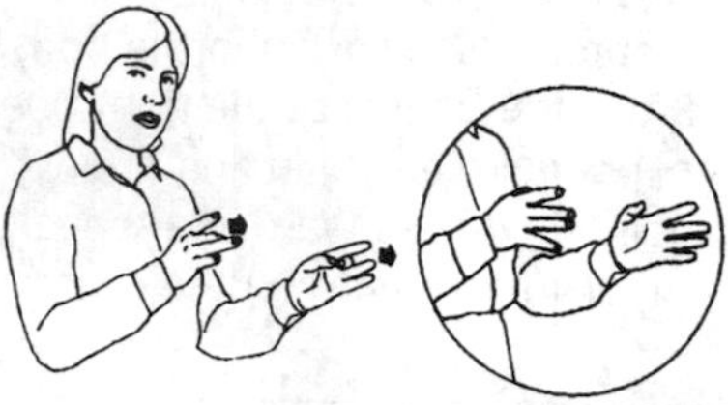

haul *v.* See sign for DRAG.

have *v.* Same sign used for: **had, has.**
[Brings something toward oneself] Bring the fingertips of both *bent hands,* palms facing in, back to touch each side of the chest.

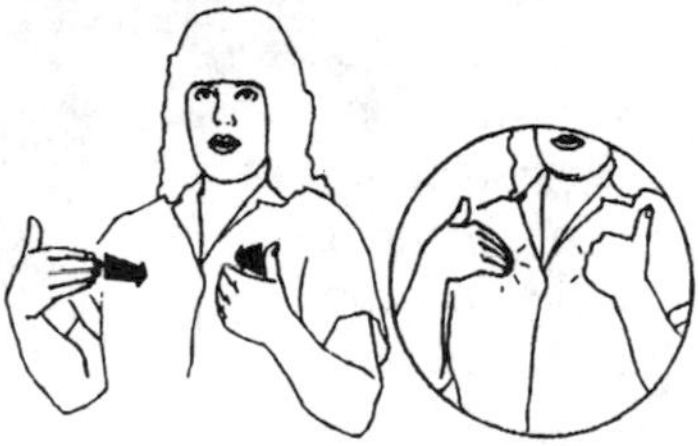

have to *auxiliary.* See sign for MUST.

hazard *n.* See sign for DANGER.

hazy *adj.* See sign for VAGUE.

he *pron.* Same sign used for: **her, him, it, she.**
[Directional sign toward another] Point the extended right index finger, palm facing down, outward to the

right or in the direction of the referent.

head[1] *n.*
[Location of the head] Touch the fingertips of the right *bent hand,* palm facing down, first to the right side of the forehead and then to the right side of the chin.

head[2] *v.* See sign for LEAD.

heal *v.* See sign for WELL[1].

healthy *adj.* See sign for WELL[1].

heap *n.* See sign for AMOUNT.

hear *v.* Related form: **hearing** *n.* Same sign used for: **sound.**
[Location of the organ of hearing] Bring the extended right index finger to the right ear.

heart *n.*
[Location and action of a heartbeat] Tap the bent middle finger of the right *5 hand,* palm facing in, with a repeated movement on the left side of the chest.

heat *adj.* See sign for HOT.

heaven *n.*

[Location of heaven] Beginning with both *open hands* in front of each shoulder, palms facing each other and fingers angled up, bring the hands upward toward each other, passing the right hand forward under the left *open hand,* both palms facing down, as the hands meet above the head.

heavy *adj.*

[The hands seem to be weighted down with something heavy] Beginning with both *curved 5 hands* in front of each side of the chest, palms facing up, move the hands downward a short distance.

height *n.*

[Indicates the top of oneself] Tap the extended right index finger, palm facing up, on the top of the head with a double movement.

hello *interj., n.*

[Natural gesture for a salute to greet someone] Beginning with the fingertips of the right *B hand* near the right side of the forehead, palm angled forward, bring the hand forward with a deliberate movement.

help *v., n.* Same sign used for: **aid, assist.**

[The lower hand seems to give assistance to the other hand] With the little-finger side of the left *A hand* in the upturned right *open hand,* move both hands upward in front of the chest.

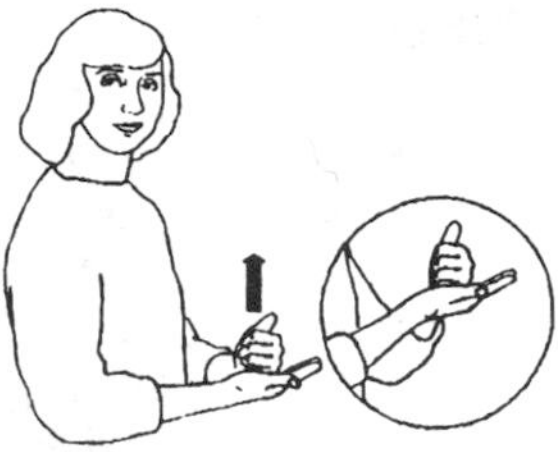

her or hers *pron.* See signs for HE, HIS.

here *adv., n.* Same sign used for: **present.**

[Indicates a location near oneself] Beginning with both *curved hands* in front of each side of the body, palms facing up, move the hands toward each other in repeated flat circles.

herself *pron.* See signs for HIMSELF, ITSELF.

hide *v.* Same sign used for: **conceal, mystery.**

[**secret** + a gesture putting something under the other hand as if to hide it] Move the thumb of the right *A hand,* palm facing left, from near the mouth downward in an arc to under the left *curved hand* held in front of the chest, palm facing down.

high *adj., adv.* Same sign used for: **altitude.**

[Initialized sign showing a location at a higher elevation] Move the right *H hand,* palm facing left and fingers pointing forward, from in front of the right side of the chest upward to near the right side of the head.

higher *adj.* See sign for ADVANCED.

highway *n.* Same sign used for: **freeway.**

[Initialized sign representing two streams of traffic going in opposite directions] Beginning with both *H hands* held in front of each side of the chest, palms facing down and fingers pointing toward each other, move the hands past each other toward the opposite sides of the chest with a repeated movement.

him *pron.* See sign for HE.

himself *pron.* See also sign for ITSELF. Same sign used for: **herself.**

[Directional sign toward the person you are referring to] Push the extended thumb of the right *10 hand,* palm facing left, forward with a short double movement in front of the right side of the body.

hinder *v.* See sign for PREVENT.

hire *v.* See sign for INVITE.

his *pron.* Same sign used for: **her, hers, its.**

[Directional sign toward the person referred to] Push the right *open hand,* palm facing forward, at an angle forward in front of the right side of the body.

hit *v.* Same sign used for: **attack, impact, strike.**

[Demonstrates action of hitting] Strike the knuckles of the right *A hand,* palm facing in, against the extended left index finger held up in front of the chest, palm facing right.

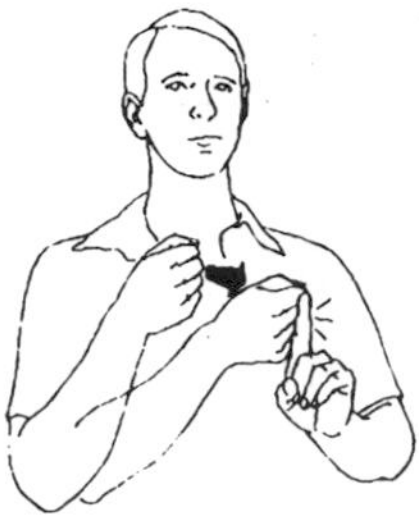

hold[1] *v.* Same sign used for: **grip.**

[The hands seem to hold something securely] Beginning with the little-finger side of the right *C hand* on the index-finger side of the left *C hand,* both palms facing in, move the hands in toward the chest while closing the fingers of both hands into *S hands.*

hold[2] or **hold on** *v.* or *v. phrase.* Same sign used for: **halt, pause, stall, suspend.**

[One hand seems to suspend the other] With the index fingers of both *X hands* hooked together, palms facing down, pull both hands upward.

hold up *v. phrase.* See sign for ROB.

hole *n.*

[Shape of a hole] Move the extended right index finger, palm facing back and fingers pointing down, in a large circle around the index-finger side of the left *C hand,* palm facing down.

holiday *n.*

[Gesture often used when one is carefree] Tap the thumbs of both *5 hands* near each armpit, palms facing each other and fingers pointing forward, with a double movement.

home *n., adv.*

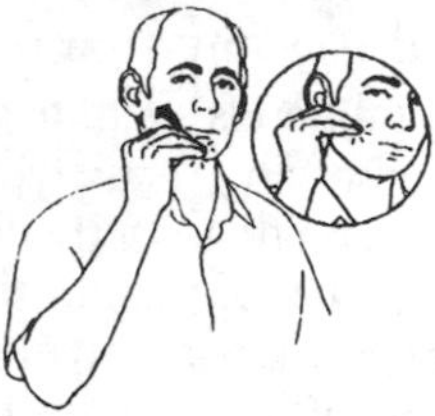

[A modification of the signs **eat** and **sleep** indicating that a home is a place where you eat and sleep] Touch the fingertips of the right *flattened O hand* first to the right side of the chin, palm facing down, and then to the right cheek.

honest *adj.* Related forms: **honestly** *adv.*, **honesty** *n.* Same sign used for: **frank, frankly, sure.**

[Initialized sign similar to sign for **clean**] Slide the extended fingers of the right *H hand,* palm facing left, forward from the heel to the fingers of the upturned left *open hand.*

hook up *v. phrase.* See sign for BELONG[1].

hope *v., n.* Same sign used for: **expect, expectation.**

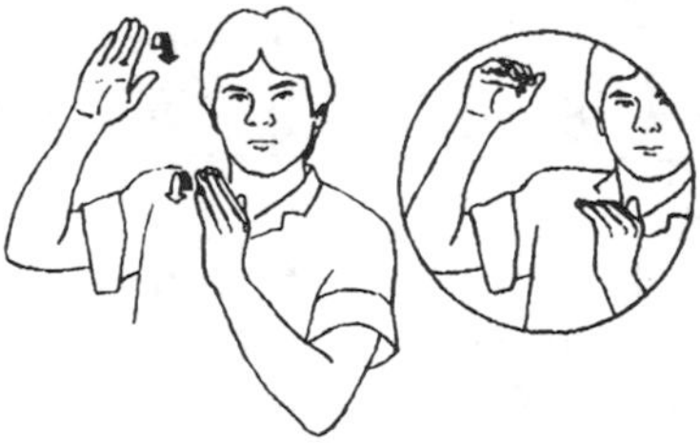

[The hands seem to compare a thought with the anticipated future] Beginning with the right *open hand* near the right side of the head, palm angled left and fingers pointed up, and the left *open hand* in front of the chest, palm facing right and fingers pointing up, bend the fingers toward each other with a double movement.

horde *n.* See sign for AUDIENCE.

horns *pl. n.* See sign for PRESIDENT.

horrible *adj.* See sign for AWFUL.

horse *n.*

[Represents a horse's ears] With the extended thumb of the right *U hand* against the right side of the forehead, palm facing forward, bend the fingers of the *U hand* up and down with a double movement.

hospital *n.*

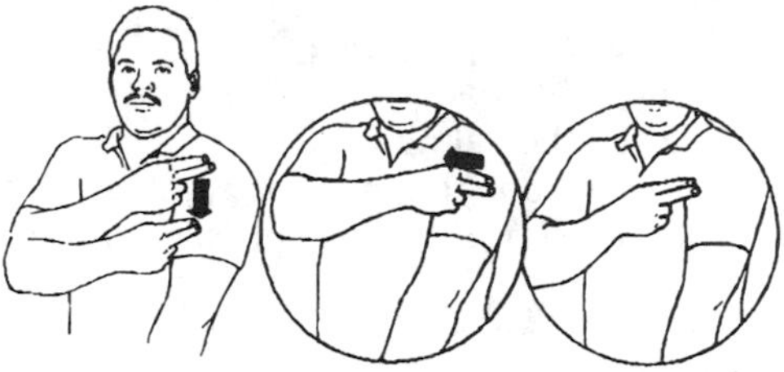

[Initialized sign following the shape of a cross, symbolic of the American Red Cross, a health-care organization] Bring the fingertips of the right *H hand,* palm facing right, first downward a short distance on the upper left arm and then across from back to front.

host *v.* See signs for LEAD, SERVE.

hot *adj.* Same sign used for: **heat.**

[Hand seems to take something hot from the mouth and throw it away] Beginning with the right *curved 5 hand* in front of the mouth, palm facing in, twist the wrist forward with a deliberate movement while moving the hand downward a short distance.

hotel *n.*

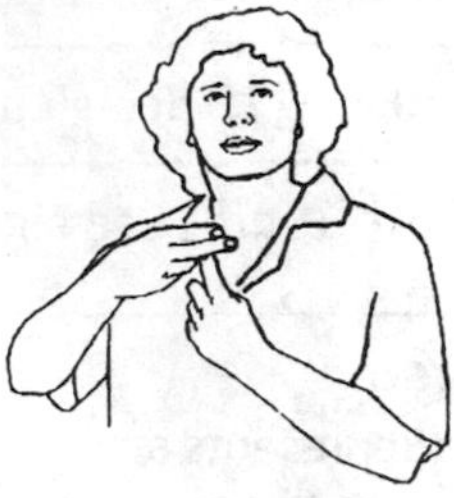

[Initialized sign] Place the fingers of the right *H hand,* palm facing in and fingers pointing left, on the back of the extended left index finger, palm facing in and index finger pointing up in front of the chest.

hour *n.*

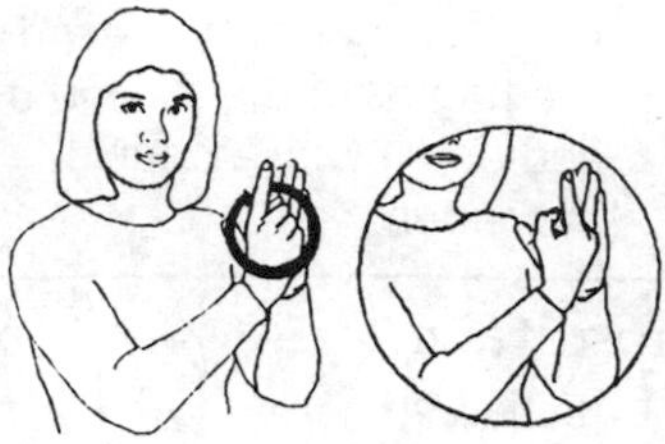

[Shows minute hand moving 60 minutes around a clock] With the right index finger extended, palm facing left, move the palm side of the right hand in a circle on the palm of the left *open hand,* palm facing right, while twisting the wrist, ending with the right palm facing in.

house *n.*

[Shape of house's roof and walls] Beginning with the fingertips of both *open hands* touching in front of the neck, palms angled toward each other, bring the hands at an downward angle outward to in front of each shoulder and then straight down, ending with the fingers pointing up and the palms facing each other.

how *adv., conj.*

[Similar to gesture used with a shrug to indicate not knowing something] Beginning with the knuckles of both *curved hands* touching in front of the chest, palms facing down, twist the hands upward and forward, ending with the fingers together pointing up and the palms facing up.

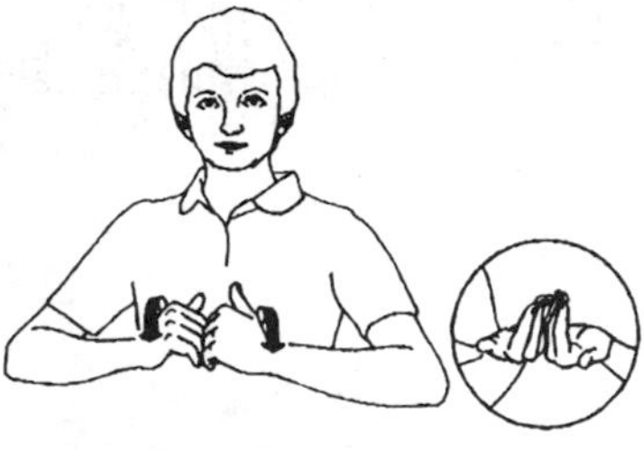

however *adv.* See signs for ANYWAY, BUT.

how many See sign for HOW MUCH.

how much Same sign used for: **how many.**

[An abbreviated form] Beginning with the right *S hand* in front of the right side of the chest, palm facing up, flick the fingers open quickly into a *5 hand.*

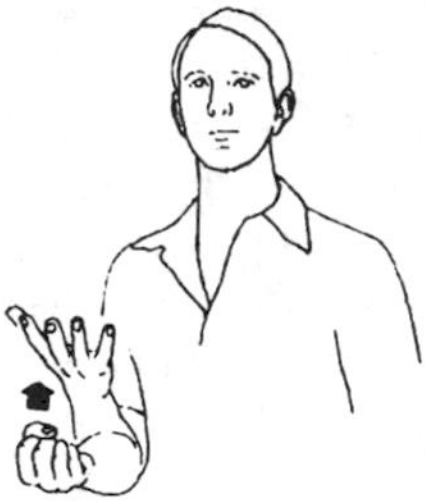

hug *v.* Same sign used for: **affection, affectionate, embrace.**

[Mime hugging someone] With the arms of both *S hands* crossed at the wrists, palms facing in, pull the arms back against the chest with a double movement.

humid *adj.* See sign for WET.

humor *n.* See sign for FUNNY.

hungry *adj.* Same sign used for: **appetite, crave, famished, starved, yearn.**

[Shows passage to an empty stomach] Beginning with the fingertips of the right *C hand* touching the center of the chest, palm facing in, move the hand downward a short distance.

hunt for *v. phrase.* See sign for LOOK FOR.

hurry *v., n.* Same sign used for: **hassle, haste, hustle, rush, urgent.**

[Initialized sign showing hurried movement] Beginning with both *H hands* in front of each side of the body, palms facing each other, move the hands up and down with a quick short repeated movement, moving the hands slightly forward each time.

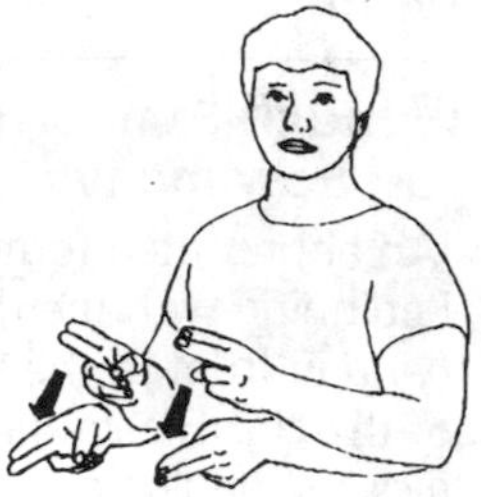

hurt *v., n.* See also signs for PAIN. Same sign used for: **ache, harm, wound.**

[Fingers indicate a stabbing pain] Beginning with both extended index fingers pointing toward each other in front of the chest, palms facing in, jab the fingers toward each other with a short repeated movement.

husband *n.*

[Hand moves from the male area of the head + **marry**] Move the right *C hand* from the right side of the forehead, palm facing left, down to clasp the left *curved hand* held in front of the chest, palm facing up.

hustle *v.* See sign for HURRY.

I *pron.* See sign for ME.

ice *n.* See sign for FREEZE.

ice cream *n.*

[Mime eating from an ice cream cone] Bring the index-finger side of the right *S hand,* palm facing left, back in an arc toward the mouth with a double movement.

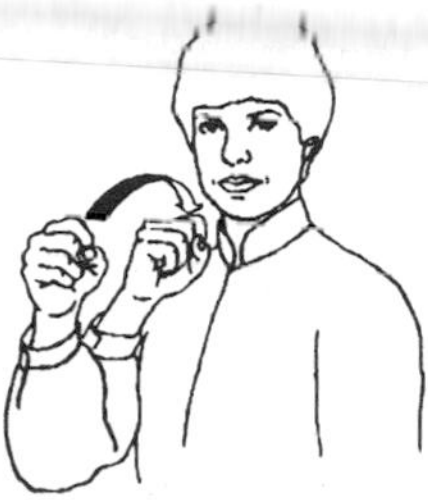

idea *n.*

[Initialized sign representing an idea coming from the head] Move the extended right little finger from near the right temple, palm facing down, upward in an arc.

ideal *n., adj.* See sign for PERFECT.

identical *adj.* See sign for ALIKE.

identify *v.*

[Initialized sign similar to sign for **show**[1]] Tap the thumb side of the right *I hand,* palm facing left, with a double movement against the left open palm held in front of the chest, palm facing forward and fingers pointing up.

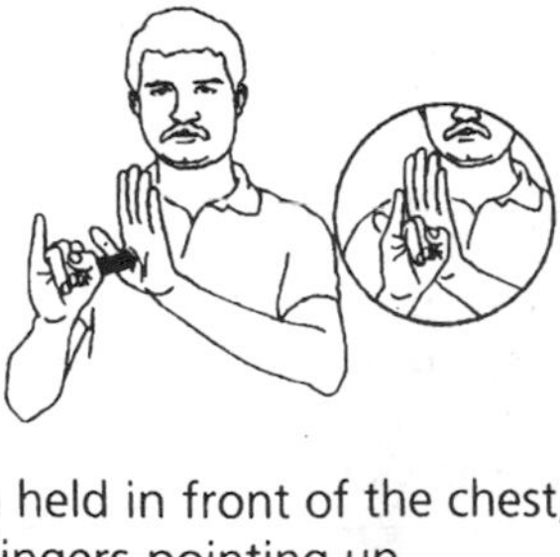

if *conj.* See sign for SUPPOSE.

ignore *v.* Same sign used for: **forsake, neglect.**

[Indicates attention moving away from object or person in view] While looking forward, place the index finger of the right *4 hand,* palm facing forward and fingers pointing up, near the right side of the face. Then move the hand outward to the right with a quick deliberate movement.

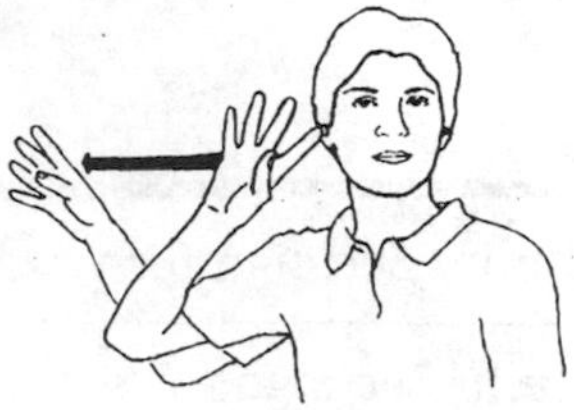

ill *adj.* See sign for SICK. Related form: **illness** *n.*

illegal *adj.* See sign for FORBID.

illegible *adj.* See sign for VAGUE.

illustration *n.* See sign for ART.

I love you (A special handshape in American Sign Language).

[Abbreviation **i-l-y** formed simultaneously in a single handshape] Hold up the right hand with the thumb, index finger, and little finger extended, palm facing forward, in front of the right shoulder.

image[1] *n.* Same sign used for: **indicate, indicator.**

[Initialized sign similar to sign for **show**[1]] Beginning with the index-finger side of the right *I hand* against the palm of the left *open hand,* palm facing right and fingers pointing up, move both hands forward simultaneously.

image[2] *n.* See sign for SHAPE.

imagine *v.* Same sign used for: **make believe.**

[Initialized sign similar to sign for **dream**] Move the extended right little finger from near the right temple, palm facing down, upward in a double circular movement.

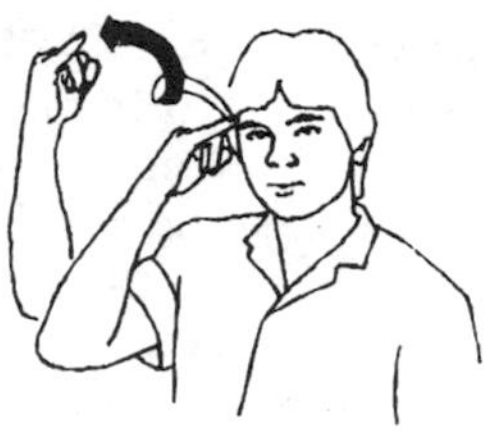

imitate *v.* See sign for COPY.

immigrate *v.* See sign for ENTER.

immune *adj.* See sign for RESIST.

impact *n.* See sign for HIT.

impair *v.* See sign for PREVENT.

implore *v.* See sign for BEG.

important *adj.* Same sign used for: **essential, main, significance, significant, value, worth.**

[The hands bring what is important to the top] Beginning with the little-finger sides of both *F hands* touching, palms facing up, bring the hands upward in a circular movement while turning the hands over, ending with the index-finger sides of the *F hands* touching in front of the chest.

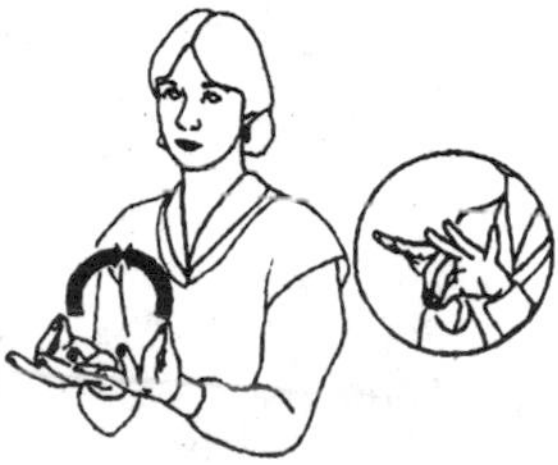

impose *v.* See sign for COPY.

impression *n.* Same sign used for: **emphasis, stress.**

[Movement seems to press something in order to make an impression] With the extended thumb of the right *10 hand,* palm facing down, pressed into the palm of the left *open hand,* palm facing right, twist the right hand downward while keeping the thumb in place.

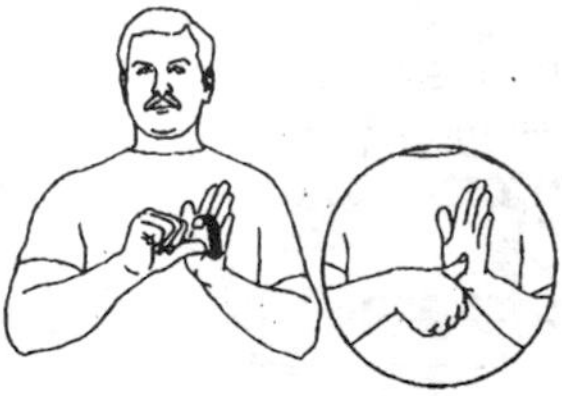

improve[1] *v.* Related form: **improvement** *n.*
[Hands seems to measure out an amount of improvement] Touch the little-finger side of the right *open hand,* palm facing back, first to the wrist and then near the crook of the extended left arm.

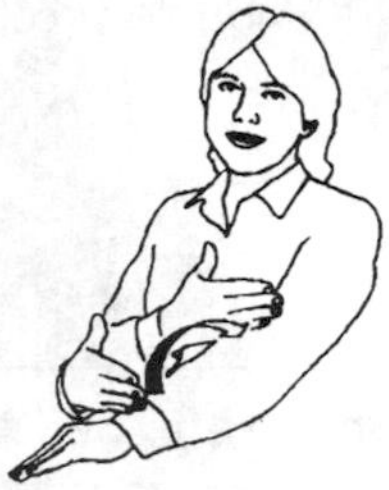

improve[2] *v.* Related form: **improvement** *n.*
Same sign used for: **remodel.** [**improve**[1] formed with a movement that indicates continued improvements] Brush the little-finger side of the right *open hand,* palm facing in and fingers pointing left, upward with a circular movement on the forearm of the bent left arm.

in *prep.* Related form: **inner** *adj.*
[Shows location in something] Insert the fingertips of the right *flattened O hand,* palm facing down, into the center of the thumb side of the left *O hand,* palm facing right in front of the chest.

in accord See sign for AGREE.

in agreement See sign for AGREE.

in behalf of See sign for SUPPORT.

incident *n.* See signs for HAPPEN, SHOW UP.

in case of See sign for SUPPOSE.

in charge of See sign for MANAGE.

include *v.* Same sign used for: **contained in, everything, involve, within.**

[The hand seems to encompass everything to gather it into one space] Swing the right *5 hand,* palm facing down, in a circular movement over the left *S hand,* palm facing in, while changing into a *flattened O hand,* ending with the fingertips of the right hand inserted in the center of the thumb side of the left hand.

income[1] *n.* Same sign used for: **revenue, salary, wages.**

[**money** + **earn**] Tap the back of the right *flattened O hand,* palm facing up, with a double movement against the left *open hand,* palm facing up. Then bring the little-finger side of the right *C hand,* palm facing left, with a double movement across the palm of the left *open hand,* closing the right hand into an *S hand* each time.

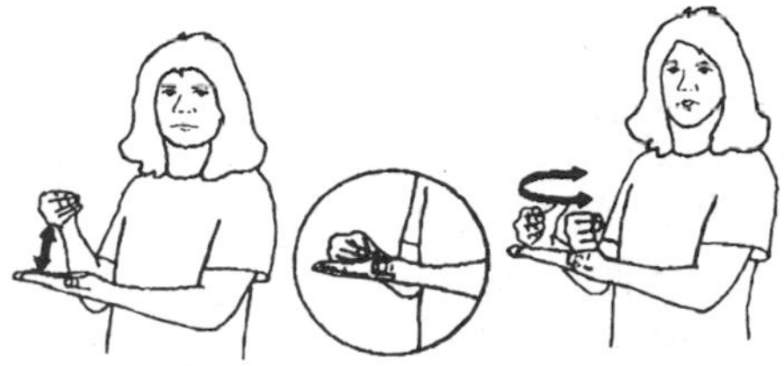

income[2] *n.* See sign for EARN.

incorrect *adj.* See sign for WRONG.

increase *n., v.* Same sign used for: **gain, raise.**

[Shows more and more things adding to a pile to increase it] Beginning with the right *U hand,* palm facing up, slightly lower than the left *U hand,* palm facing down, flip the right hand over, ending with the right fingers across the left fingers.

incredible *adj.* See sign for WONDERFUL.

indicate *v.* See signs for IMAGE, SHOW[1]. Related forms: **indicator** *n.*, **indication** *n.*

indifferent *adj.* See sign for DON'T CARE.

indoctrinate *v.* See sign for TEACH. Related form: **indoctrination** *n.*

industry *n.* See sign for MACHINE.

inexperienced *adj.* See sign for CLUMSY.

infant *n.* See sign for BABY.

in favor of See sign for SUPPORT.

infection *n.* See sign for INSURANCE.

influence *v., n.* Same sign used for: **affect, effect.**

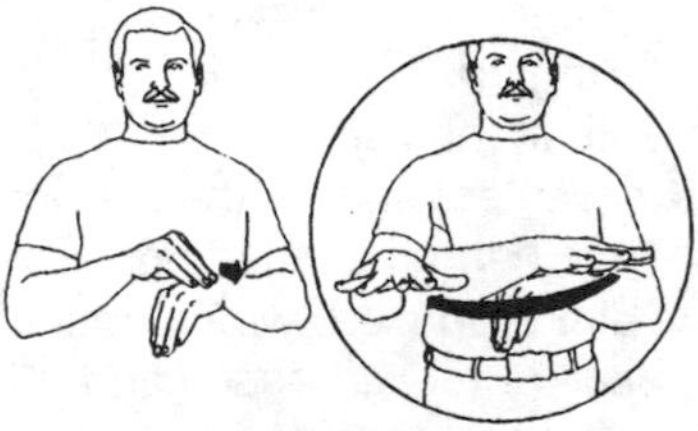

[Similar to sign for **advice** except spread outward to others] Beginning with the fingertips of the right *flattened O hand* on the back of the left *open hand,* palm facing down, move the right hand forward while opening into a *5 hand* and bringing the hand in a sweeping arc to in front of the right side of the body.

inform *v.* Same sign used for: **issue, let know, notice, notify.**

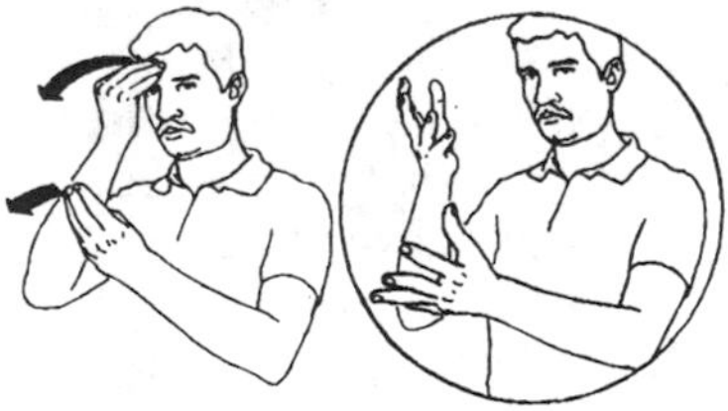

[Indicates taking information from one's head and giving it to others] Beginning with the fingertips of the right *flattened O hand* near the forehead and the left *flattened O hand* in front of the chest, move both hands forward while opening into *5 hands,* palms facing up.

information *n.* Similar to sign for **inform** except formed with a double movement.

in front of Same sign used for: **face to face, facing.**

[Shows two things facing each other] Beginning with both *open hands* in front of the chest, palms facing each other and fingers pointing up, move both hands forward simultaneously.

infuse *v.* See sign for MESH.

inhale *v.* See sign for BREATH.

injury *n.* See sign for PAIN.

inquire *v.* See sign for TEST.

insect *n.* See sign for BUG.

inside *prep., adv., n., adj.* Same sign used for: **internal.**

[Shows location inside] Insert the fingertips of the right *flattened O hand,* palm facing down, into the center of the thumb side of the left *O hand,* palm facing right in front of the chest, with a repeated movement.

insist *v.* See sign for DEMAND.

inspect *v.* See signs for CHECK[1], INVESTIGATE. Related form: **inspection** *n.*

install *v.* See signs for APPLY[1], PUT.

instruct *v.* See signs for DESCRIBE, TEACH. Related form: **instruction** *n.*

insult *v., n.* Related form: **insulting** *adj.* Same sign used for: **affront.**

[Finger seems to direct an insult at another] Move the

extended right index finger from in front of the right side of the body, palm facing left and finger pointing forward, forward and upward sharply in an arc.

insurance *n.* Related form: **insure** *v.* Same sign used for: **infection.**
[Initialized sign] Move the right *I hand,* palm facing forward, from side to side with a repeated movement near the right shoulder.

integrate *v.* See sign for MESH.

intelligent *adj.* See sign for SMART. Related form: **intelligence** *n.*

intend *v.* See sign for MEAN[2].

interact *v.* See sign for ASSOCIATE.

interest *n.* Related form: **interested** *adj.* Same sign used for: **fascinating.**
[The hands bring thoughts and feelings to the surface] Beginning with the right *modified C hand* in front of the face and the left *modified C hand* in front of the chest, both palms facing in, move the hands forward simultaneously while closing into *A hands.*

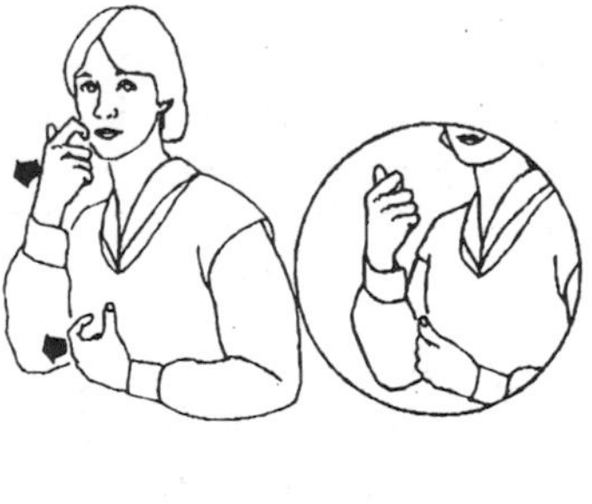

interfere *v.* See sign for ANNOY.

internal *adj.* See sign for INSIDE.

international *adj.*
[Initialized sign similar to sign for **world**] Move both *I hands* in circles around each other, palms facing each other, ending with the little-finger side of the right hand on the index-finger side of the left hand in front of the chest.

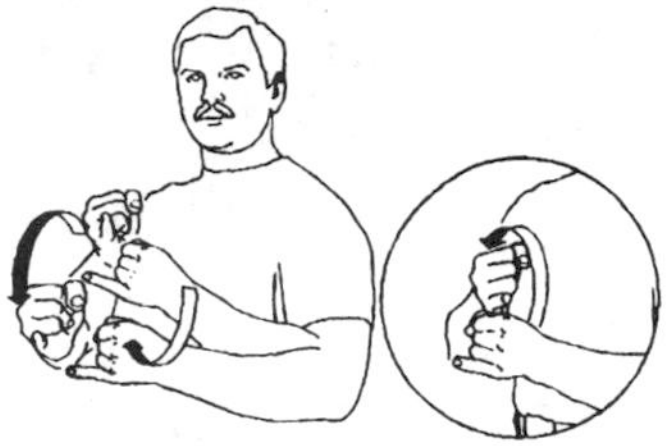

interrupt *v.* See sign for ANNOY.

interview *v., n.*
[Initialized sign similar to sign for **communication**] Move both *I hands,* palms facing each other, forward and back toward the mouth with an alternating movement.

into *prep.* See sign for ENTER.

in touch with See sign for CONTACT.

introduce *v.* Related form: **introduction** *n.*
[The hands seem to bring two people together] Bring both *bent hands* from in front of each side of the body, palms facing up and fingers pointing toward each other, toward each other in front of the waist.

invent *v.* Same sign used for: **create, make up, originate.**
[The hand seems to take ideas from the head] Move the index-finger side of the right *4 hand,* palm facing left,

from the forehead upward in an outward arc.

invest *v.* Related form: **investment** *n.* Same sign used for: **deposit, stocks.**

[Represents depositing money in a bank] Insert the fingertips of the right *flattened O hand,* palm facing left, into the center of the thumb side of the left *O hand,* palm angled forward.

investigate *v.* Related form: **investigation** *n.* Same sign used for: **examination, examine, inspect, inspection.**

[The finger seems to be paging through pages of documents] Brush the extended right index finger with a repeated movement from the heel to the fingertips of the upturned palm of the left *open hand.*

invite *v.* Related form: **invitation** *n.* Same sign used for: **employ, greet, hire, welcome.**

[The hand brings another to oneself] Bring the upturned right *curved hand* from in front of the right side of the body in toward the center of the waist.

involve *v.* See sign for INCLUDE.

irritate *v.* See signs for ANNOY, ITCH.

isolated *adj.* See sign for ALONE.

issue *v.* See signs for INFORM, NEWSPAPER.

it or **its** *pron.* See signs for HE, HIS.

itch *n., v.* Related form: **itchy** *adj.* Same sign used for: **irritate.**

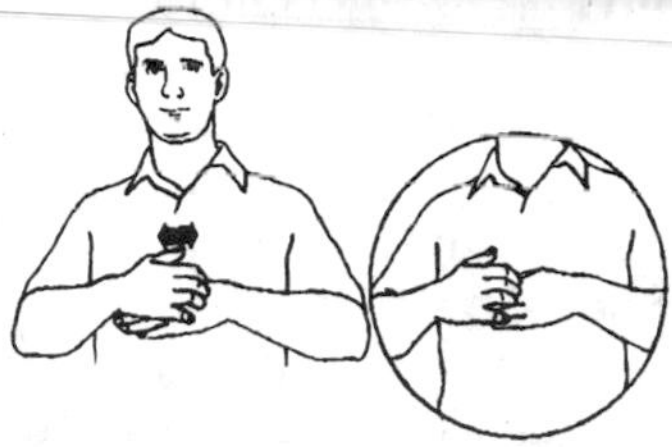

[Mime scratching an itchy place] Move the fingertips of the right *curved 5 hand,* palm facing in, back and forth with a double movement on the back of the left *open hand,* palm facing in and fingers pointing right.

itself *pron.* See also sign for HIMSELF. Same sign used for: **herself.**

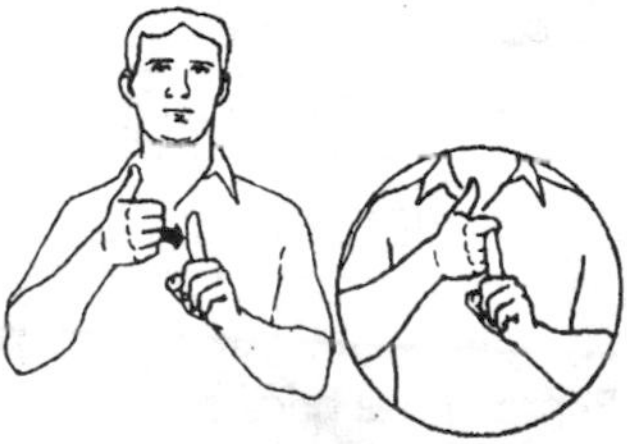

[Uses the handshape used for reflexive pronouns to emphasize another thing not in view] Bring the knuckles of the right *10 hand,* palm facing left, firmly against the side of the extended left index finger, palm facing right and finger pointing up in front of the chest.

jacket *n.* See sign for COAT.

jam *n.* See sign for JELLY.

jeans *pl. n.* See sign for PANTS.

jelly *n.* Same sign used for: **jam.**

[Initialized sign miming spreading jelly on bread] Strike the extended little finger of the right *J hand* on the upturned left *open hand* as it moves upward in an arc with a double movement.

jest *v.* See sign for TEASE.

jet *n.* See sign for AIRPLANE.

job *n.* See sign for WORK.

join[1] *v.* Same sign used for: **participate.**

[Represents a person's legs entering a place where there are other people with whom one can have social exchanges] Beginning with the right *H hand* in front of the chest, palm facing left and fingers pointing forward, and the left *C hand* in front of the lower left side of the chest, palm facing right, bring the right hand down in an arc into the palm side of the left hand while closing the left fingers around the fingers of the right *H hand.*

join[2] *v.* See sign for BELONG.

joint *n.* See sign for BELONG.

jolly *adj.* See sign for HAPPY.

journal *n.* See sign for MAGAZINE.

joy *n.* See sign for HAPPY.

judge *v.* Same sign used for: **court, justice, trial.**

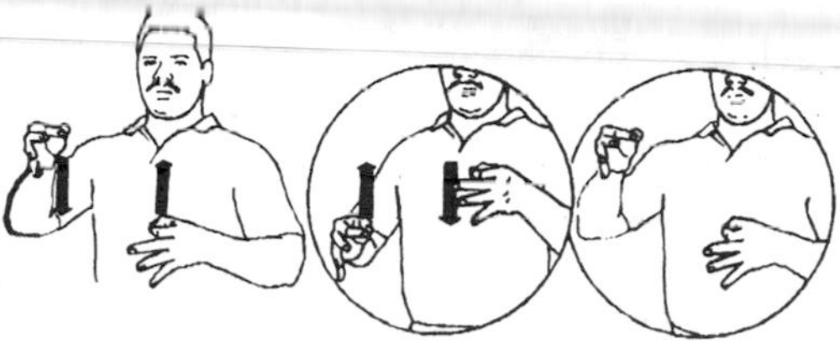

[The hands move up and down indicating weighing a decision] Move both *F hands,* palms facing each other, up and down in front of each side of the chest with a repeated alternating movement.

juice *n.*

[**drink**[1] + initialized sign] Beginning with the thumb of the right *C hand* near the chin, palm facing left, tip the hand up toward the face. Then form a *J* near the right side of the face with the right hand.

jump *v., n.*

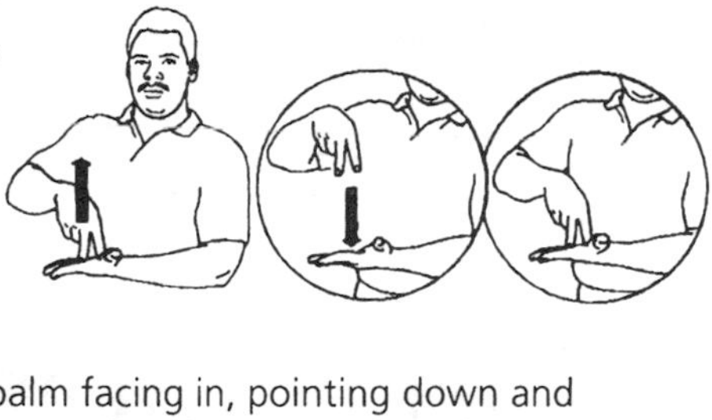

[Demonstrates the action of jumping] Beginning with the extended fingers of the right *V hand,* palm facing in, pointing down and touching the open left palm, move the right hand up and down in front of the chest with a double movement.

just *adv.* Same sign used for: **recently, while ago, a.**

[Indicates something in the recent past] Wiggle the index finger of the right *X hand,* palm facing back, up and down with a repeated movement on the lower right cheek.

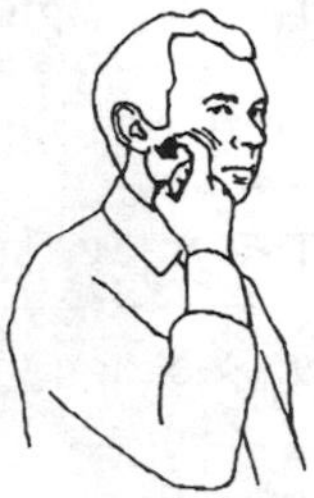

justice *n.* See sign for JUDGE.

justify *v.* See sign for CHANGE[1].

keen *adj.* See sign for SHARP.

keep *v.* Same sign used for: **maintain.**

[Eyes looking in different directions] Tap the little-finger side of the right *K hand* across the index-finger side of the left *K hand* palms facing in opposite directions.

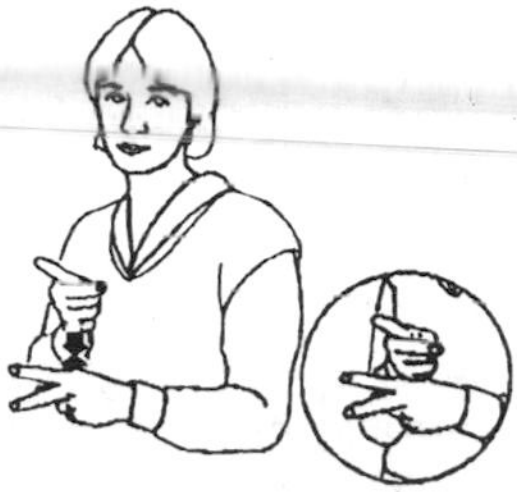

keep quiet See sign for SHUT UP (*informal*).

ketchup or **catsup** *n.*

[Initialized sign] Shake the right *K hand,* palm facing left, up and down with a short repeated movement in front of the right side of the body.

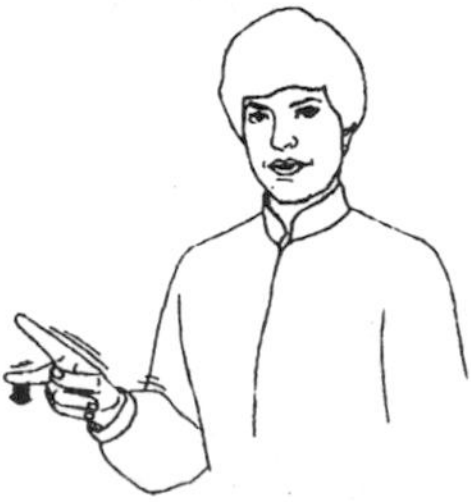

key *n.*

[Mime turning a key in a lock] Twist the knuckle of the right *X hand,* palm facing down, in the palm of the left *open hand,* palm facing right and fingers pointing forward, with a repeated movement.

kick *v.* Same sign used for: **kick off.**

[Demonstrates the action of kicking something] Bring the right *B hand* in front of the right side of the body, palm facing left and fingers angled down, upward to strike the index-finger side of the right hand against the little-finger side of the left *B hand* held in front of the body, palm facing in and fingers pointing right.

kick off *n.* See sign for KICK.

kid[1] *n.*
[Suggests a child's runny nose] With the right index finger and little finger extended, palm facing down, put the extended index finger under the nose, and twist the hand up and down with a small repeated movement.

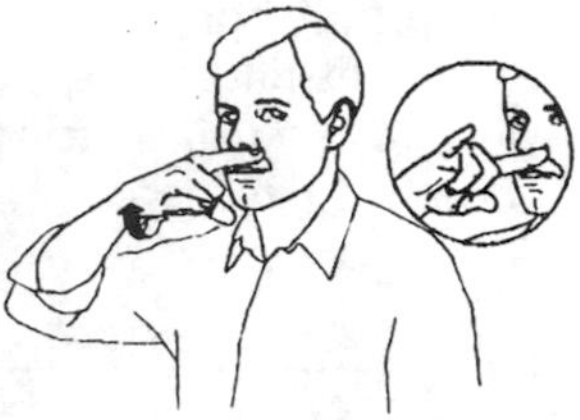

kid[2] *v.* See sign for TEASE. Related form: **kidding** *n.*

kill *v.* Same sign used for: **murder, slaughter.**
[Represents a knife being inserted] Push the side of the extended right index finger, palm facing down, across the palm of the left *open hand,* palm facing right, with a deliberate movement.

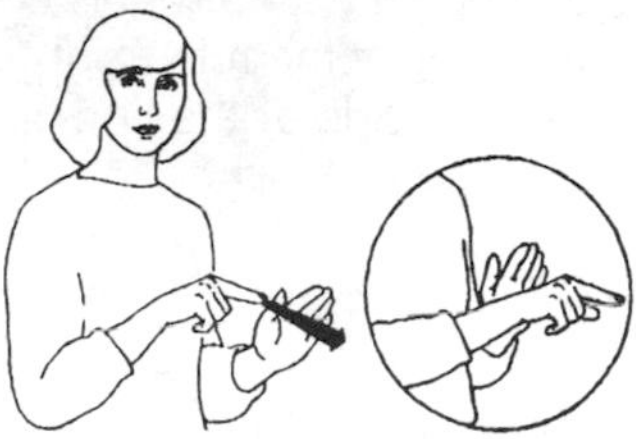

kind[1] *adj.* Same sign used for: **generous, gentle, gracious.**
[A comforting movement] Bring the right *open hand,* palm facing in near the middle of the chest, in a forward circle around the back of the left *open hand,* palm facing in, as it moves in a circle around the right hand.

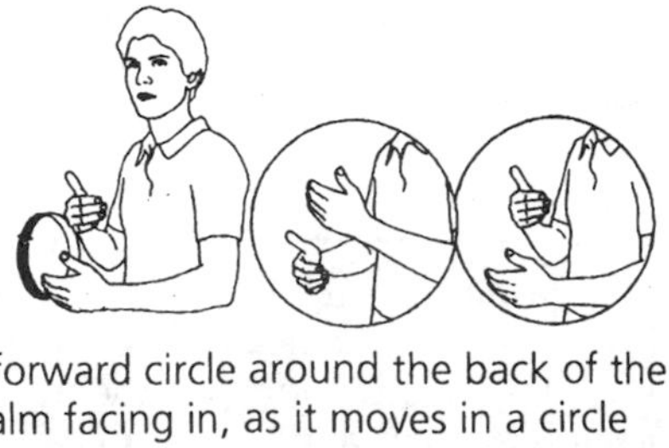

kind[2] *n.* Same sign used for: **sort, type.**

[Initialized sign similar to sign for **world**] Move the right *K hand,* palm facing left, in a forward circle around the left *K hand,* palm facing right, as it moves in a circle around the right hand, ending with the little-finger side of the right hand landing on the index-finger side of the left hand.

kiss *v., n.*

[The hand takes a kiss from the mouth and puts it on the cheek] Touch the fingertips of the right *flattened O hand,* palm facing in, to the right side of the mouth, and then open the right hand and lay the palm of the right *open hand* against the right side of the face.

kitchen *n.*

[Initialized sign similar to sign for **cook**] Beginning with the palm side of the right *K hand* on the upturned left *open hand,* flip the right hand over, ending with the back of the right hand in the left palm.

Kleenex *Trademark.* See sign for TISSUE.

knife *n.*

[Represents the slicing movement done with a knife] Slide the bottom side of the extended right index finger, palm facing in, with a double movement at an angle across the length of the extended left index finger, palm facing right, turning the right palm down each time as it moves off the end of the left index finger.

know *v.*
[Location of knowledge in the brain] Tap the fingertips of the right *bent hand,* palm facing down, on the right side of the forehead.

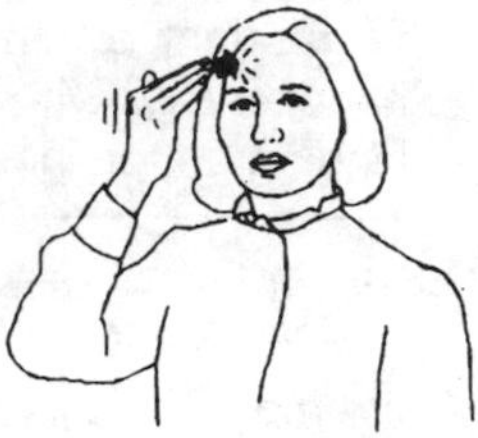

knowledge *n.* See sign for AWARE[1].

label *n., v.* Same sign used for: **apply, brand, decal, tag.**

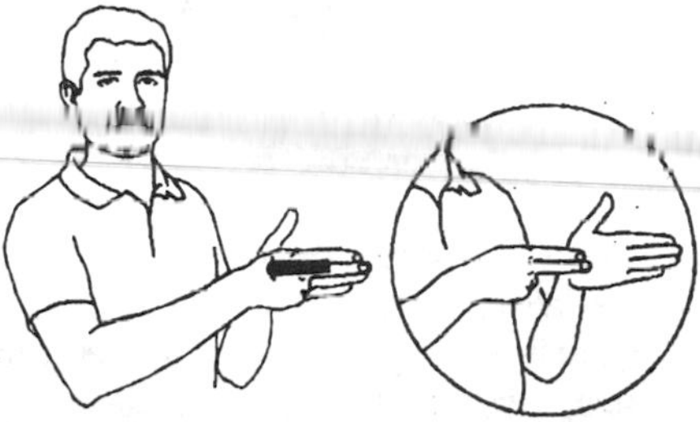

[Demonstrates applying a label] Wipe the extended fingers of the right *H hand,* palm facing left, from the fingers to the heel of the left *open hand,* palm facing right and fingers pointing forward.

labor *v.* See sign for WORK.

lack *n.* See sign for SKIP[1].

ladder *n.* See sign for CLIMB.

lady *n.* Same sign used for: **female.**

[**girl** + **polite**] Bring the thumb of the right *A hand,* palm facing left, downward from the right side of the chin while opening, ending by tapping side of the thumb of the right *open hand* in the center of the chest.

land *n.* See sign for DIRT.

language *n.*

[Initialized sign] Beginning with the thumbs of both *L hands* near each other in front of the chest, palms angled down, bring the hands outward with a wavy movement to in front of each side of the chest.

lapse *n.* See sign for BETWEEN.

large *adj.* See also sign for BIG. Same sign used for: **grand, great, massive.**

[Initialized sign showing a large size] Move both *L hands* from in front of each side of the chest, palms facing each other, in large arcs beyond each side of the body.

last[1] *adj., adv., n.* Same sign used for: **end, final, finally.**

[Indicates the last thing] Move the extended little finger of the right *I hand,* palm facing left, downward in front of the chest, striking the extended little finger of the left *I hand,* palm facing in, as it passes.

last[2] *adj., adv.* See signs for AGO, BEFORE, CONTINUE[1].

late *adj., adv.* Same sign used for: **delay, tardy.**

[Hand moves into the past] Bend the wrist of the right *open hand,* palm facing back and fingers pointing down, back near the right side of the waist with a double movement.

lately *adv.* See sign for SINCE[1].

later *adv.* Alternate form: **later on.** Same sign used for: **after a while, afterward.**

[Initialized sign representing the minute hand on a clock moving to indicate the passing of time] With the thumb of the right *L hand,* palm facing forward, on the palm of the left *open hand,* palm facing right and fingers pointing forward, twist the right hand forward, keeping the thumb in place and ending with the right palm facing down.

laugh *v.*

[Initialized sign showing the shape of the mouth when one laughs] Beginning with the extended index fingers of both *L hands* at each corner of the mouth, palms facing back, pull the hands outward to each side of the head with a double movement while closing the hands into *10 hands* each time.

lavatory *n.* See sign for TOILET.

law *n.* Same sign used for: **legal.**

[Initialized sign representing recording laws on the books] Place the palm side of the right *L hand,* palm facing left, first on the fingers and then the heel of the left *open hand,* palm facing right and fingers pointing up.

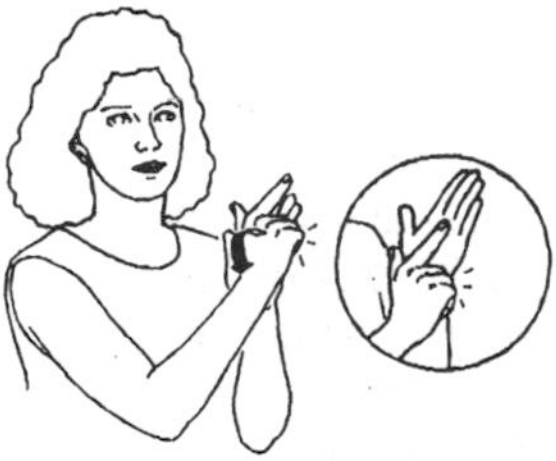

lay off *v. phrase. Informal.* See sign for DISMISS.

layer *n.* Same sign used for: **plush.**

[Shows the shape of a layer on top of something] Slide the thumb of the right *modified C hand,* palm facing left, from the heel to off the fingers of the upturned palm of the left *open hand* held in front of the chest.

lazy *adj.* Same sign used for: **slothful.**

[Initialized sign] Tap the palm side of the right *L hand* against the left side of the chest with a double movement.

lead *v.* Same sign used for: **conduct, guide, head, host, steer.**

[One hand leads the other by pulling it] With the fingers of the left *open hand,* palm facing right, being held by the fingers and thumb of the right hand, palm facing in, pull the left hand forward a short distance.

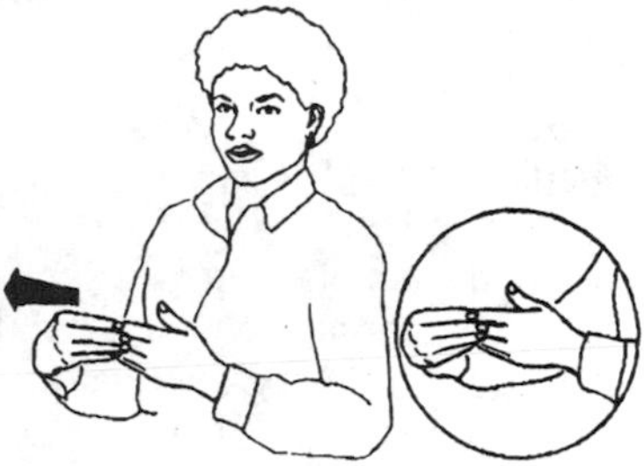

leak[1] *v., n.* Same sign used for: **drain, run.**

[Represents the flow of a leaking liquid] Beginning with the index-finger side of the right *4 hand,* palm facing in and fingers pointing left, touching the palm of the left *open hand,* palm facing down and fingers pointing right, move the right hand down with a double movement.

leak[2] *n.,v.* See sign for DRIP.

lean *adj.* See sign for DIET.

learn *v.* Same sign used for: **acquire, educate, education.**

[Represents taking information from paper and putting it in one's head] Beginning with the fingertips of the right *curved 5 hand,* palm facing down, on the palm of the upturned left *open hand,* bring the right hand up while closing the fingers and thumb into a *flattened O hand* near the forehead.

leave[1] *v.* Same sign used for: **depart, desert, withdraw.**

[The hands move from one location to another] Beginning with both *curved 5 hands* in front of each side of the chest, palms facing down, pull the hands back toward the right shoulder while closing the fingers and thumbs into *flattened O hands.*

leave[2] *v.* Same sign used for: **leftover, rest.**

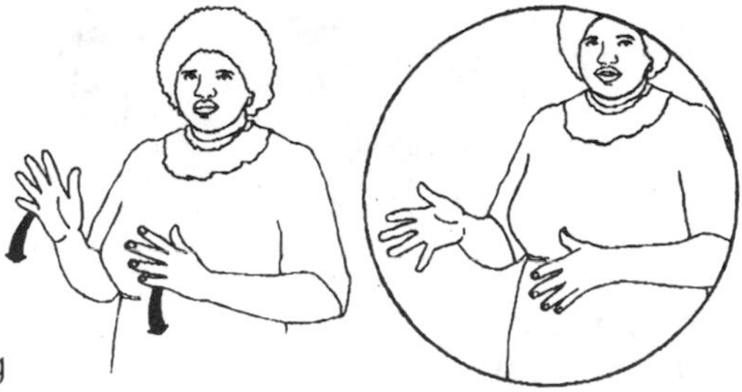

[The hands seem to leave something by thrusting it down] Beginning with both *5 hands* in front of each side of the body, palms facing each other and fingers angled up, thrust the fingers downward with a deliberate movement.

leave[3] *v.* See sign for GO.

lecture *v., n.* See sign for SPEAK[2].

left *adj., adv., n.*

[Initialized sign indicating a direction to the left] Beginning with the right *L hand* in front of the right side of the chest, palm facing forward and index finger pointing up, move the hand deliberately to the left.

leftover *n., adj.* See sign for LEAVE[2].

legal *adj.* See sign for LAW.

leisure *n.* See sign for ENJOY.

lemon *n.*

[Initialized sign pointing to puckered lips from eating a sour lemon] Tap the thumb of the right *L hand,* palm facing left, against the chin with a double movement.

lend *v.* Same sign used for: **loan.**

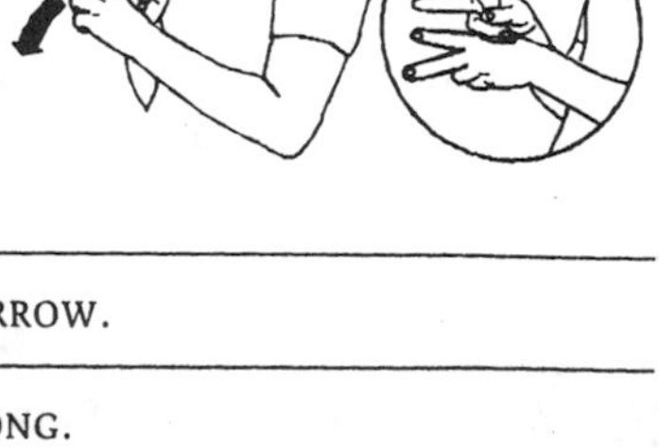

[Directional sign toward the person to whom something is lent] With the little-finger side of the right *V hand* across the index-finger side of the left *V hand,* move the hands from near the chest forward and down a short distance.

lend me See sign for BORROW.

length *n.* See sign for LONG.

lessen *v.* See signs for DECREASE.

lesson *n.* See sign for COURSE.

let *v.* Same sign used for: **allow, grant, permit.**

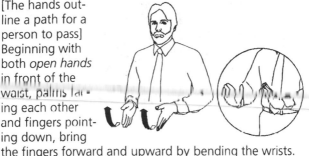

[The hands outline a path for a person to pass] Beginning with both *open hands* in front of the waist, palms facing each other and fingers pointing down, bring the fingers forward and upward by bending the wrists.

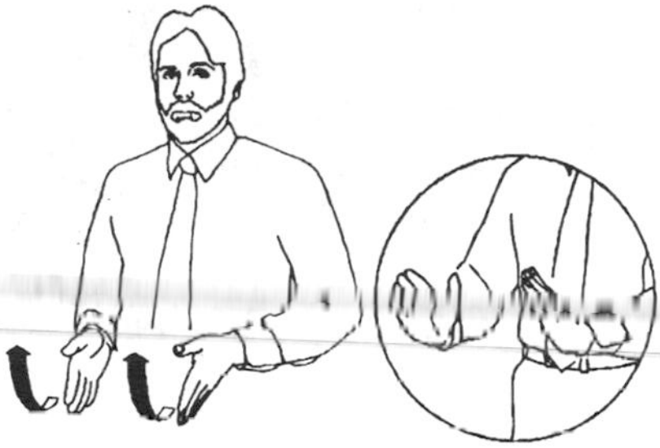

let know See sign for INFORM.

letter *n.* Same sign used for: **mail.**

[Shows licking a stamp and placing it on an envelope] Touch the extended thumb of the right *10 hand* to the lips, palm facing in, and then move the thumb downward to touch the fingertips of the left *open hand* held in front of the body, palm facing up.

lettuce *n.*

[Initialized sign formed on the head, representing a head of lettuce] Touch the thumb of the right *L hand,* palm facing forward and index finger pointing up, to the right side of the forehead.

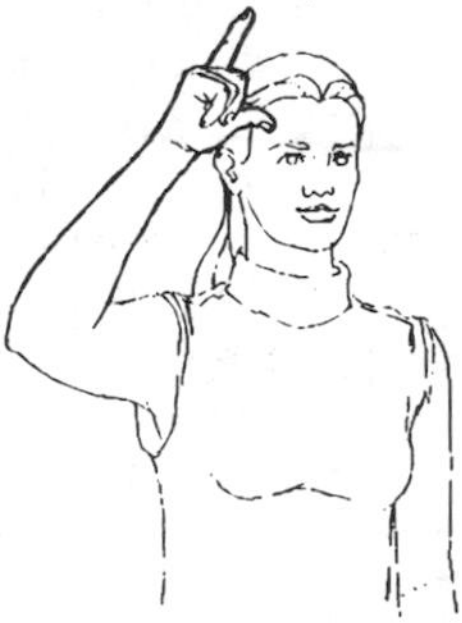

level *adj.* See sign for EVEN[1].

lever *n.* See sign for PIPE[1].

liability *n.* See sign for BURDEN.

liberate *v.* See sign for SAVE[1].

liberty *n.* See sign for SAVE[1].

library *n.*

[Initialized sign] Move the right *L hand,* palm facing forward, in a circle in front of the right shoulder.

license *n.*

[Initialized sign similar to sign for **certificate**] Tap the thumbs of both *L hands* with a double movement in front of the chest, palms facing forward.

lie *v., n.* Same sign used for: **fib.**

[The hand movement indicates that a person is speaking out of the side of the mouth when telling a lie] Slide the index-finger side of the right *bent hand,* palm facing down, with a double movement across the chin from right to left.

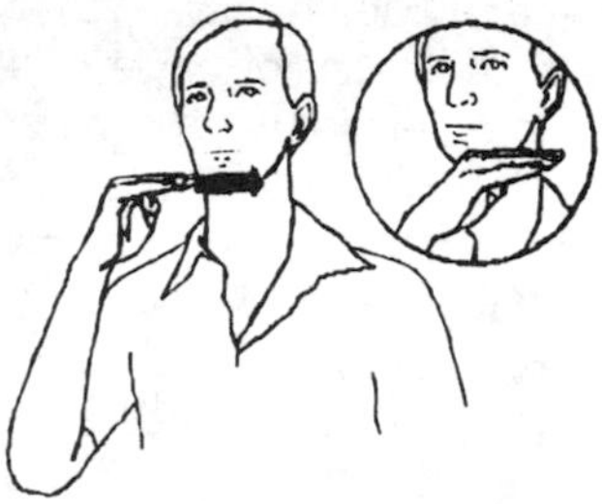

lift *v.* See sign for RAISE[1].

light[1] *adj.*

[The snap of a light being turned on] Beginning with the fingertips of the right *8 hand* near the chin, palm facing in, flick the middle finger upward and forward with a double movement while opening into a *5 hand* each time.

light[2] *adj.*

[The gesture represents something light floating upward] Beginning with both *5 hands* with bent middle fingers in front of the waist, palms facing down, twist the wrists to raise the hands quickly toward each other and upward, ending with the hands in front of each side of the chest, bent middle fingers pointing in.

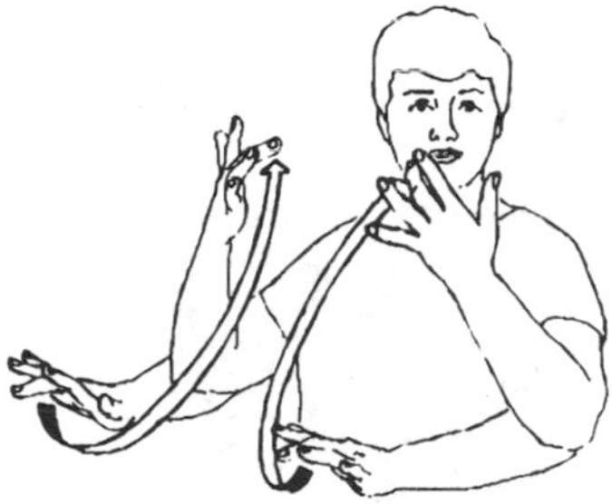

light[3] *adj.* See sign for BRIGHT.

like[1] *v.*

[Pulling out feelings] Beginning with the bent thumb and middle finger of the right *5 hand* touching the chest, palm facing in, bring the hand forward while closing the fingers to form an *8 hand.*

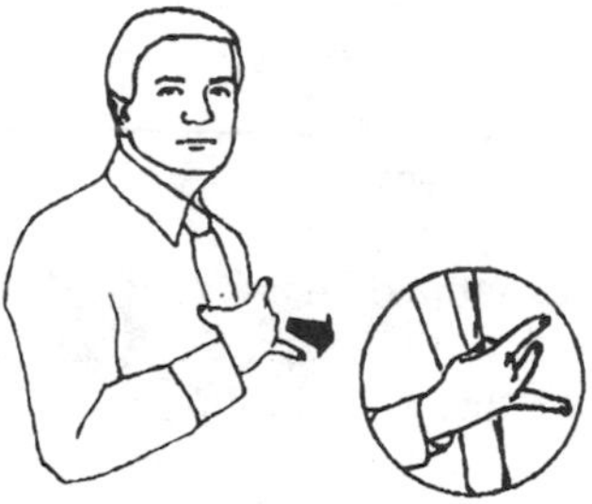

like[2] *v.* See sign for ENJOY.

line *n.* Same sign used for: **string, thread.**

[Shows shape of a line] Beginning with the extended little fingers of both *I hands* touching in front of the chest, palms facing in, move both hands outward.

line up *v. phrase.* Same sign used for: **align, queue, row.**

[Represents people lined up in a row] Beginning with the little finger of the right *4 hand,* palm facing left, touching the index finger of the right *4 hand,* palm facing right, move the right hand back toward the chest and the left hand forward.

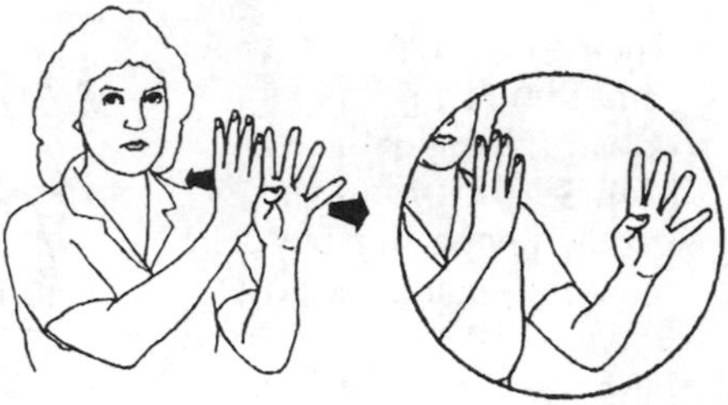

link *v.* See signs for BELONG, RELATIONSHIP.

list *n., v.* Same sign used for: **record, score.**

[The finger points out items on a list] Touch the bent middle finger of the right *5 hand,* palm facing left, several times on the palm of the left *open hand,* palm facing right and fingers pointing up, as it moves from the fingers downward to the heel.

listen *v.* Same sign used for: **eavesdrop.**

[The fingers bring sound to the ear] With the thumb of the right *curved 3 hand,* palm facing left, touching the right ear, bend the extended index and middle fingers down with a short double movement.

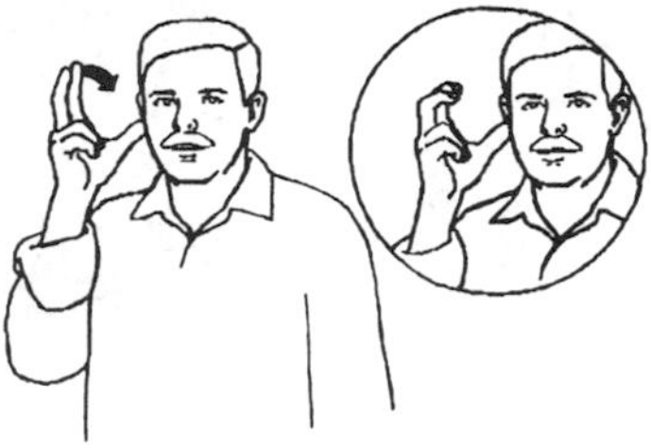

little *adj.* See also sign for SMALL[1]. Same sign used for: **short.**

[Shows someone or something short in size] Move the right *bent hand,* palm facing down, with a short double movement in front of the right side of the body.

little bit *n.* See sign for TINY.

live *v.* Same sign used for: **alive, dwell, survival, survive.**

[Outlines life within one's body] Move both *A hands,* palms facing in, upward on each side of the chest.

load *n.* See sign for PILE.

loan *v.* See sign for LEND.

local *adj.* See sign for LOCATION.

location *n.* Same sign used for: **local.**

[Initialized sign similar to sign for **area**] Beginning with the thumbs of both *L hands* touching in front of the body, palms facing down, move the hands apart and back in a circular movement until they touch again near the chest.

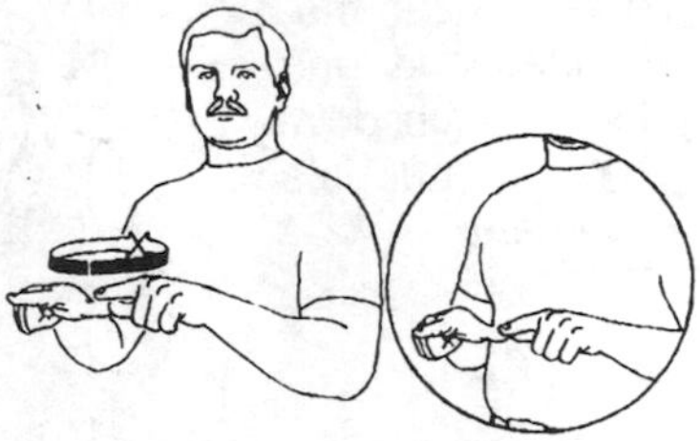

lock *n., v.*

[Represents the wrists locked together] Beginning with both *S hands* in front of the body, right hand above left and both palms facing down, turn the right hand over by twisting the wrist, ending with the back of the right *S hand,* palm facing up, on the back of the left *S hand,* palm facing down.

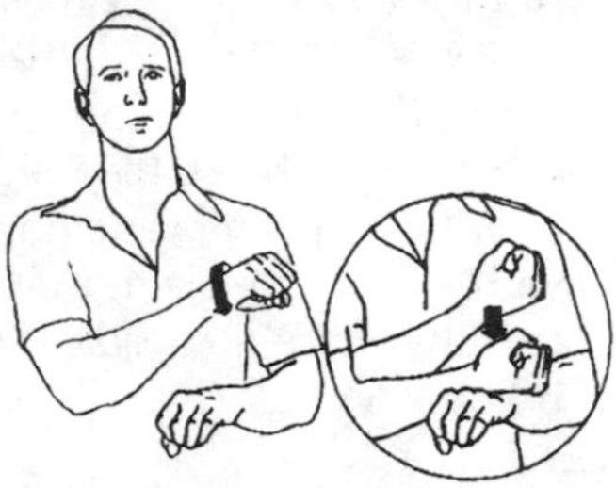

lone *adj.* See sign for ALONE. Related form: **lonely** *adj.*

lonely *adj.* Alternate form: **lonesome.**

[Suggests that someone living alone is silent] Bring the side of the extended right index finger, palm facing left, from near the nose slowly downward in front of the mouth.

long *adj.* Same sign used for: **length.**

[The finger measures out a long length] Move the extended right index finger from the wrist up the length of the extended left arm to near the shoulder.

long time ago, a Same sign used for: **ancient.**

[The hand indicates a time far in the past] Beginning with the right *5 hand* in front of the right shoulder, palm facing left, bring the hand back to behind the right shoulder.

look alike *v. phrase* See sign for ALIKE.

look at *v. phrase.*

[Represents the eyes directed toward something] Move the right *V hand,* palm facing down and extended fingers pointing forward, forward a short distance in the direction of the referent.

look for *v. phrase.* Same sign used for: **check for, examine, hunt for, search for.**

[Shows repeated searching for something] Move the right C *hand,* palm facing left, with a double movement in a circle in front of the face.

look like See sign for SEEM.

look over *v. phrase.* Same sign used for: **browse, observe, view.**

[Represents the eyes surveying something] Beginning with both *V hands* in front of each side of the chest, right hand higher than the left hand, both palms facing down, and fingers pointing forward, move the hands in double alternating circles.

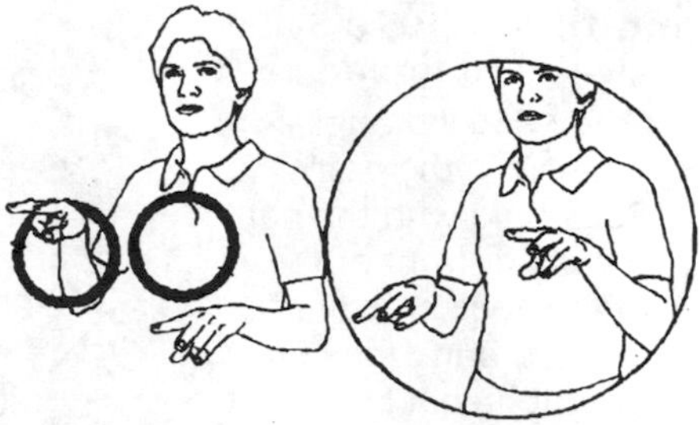

looks *n.*

Same sign used for: **good-looking, handsome.**

[The location of a person's face] Move the right extended index finger in a circle in front of the face, palm facing in.

loose *adj.* See sign for DISCONNECT.

lose[1] *v.*

[The hands seem to drop something as if to lose it] Beginning with the fingertips of both *flattened O hands* touching in front of the body, palms facing up, drop the fingers quickly downward and away from each other while opening into *5 hands,* ending with both palms and fingers angled downward.

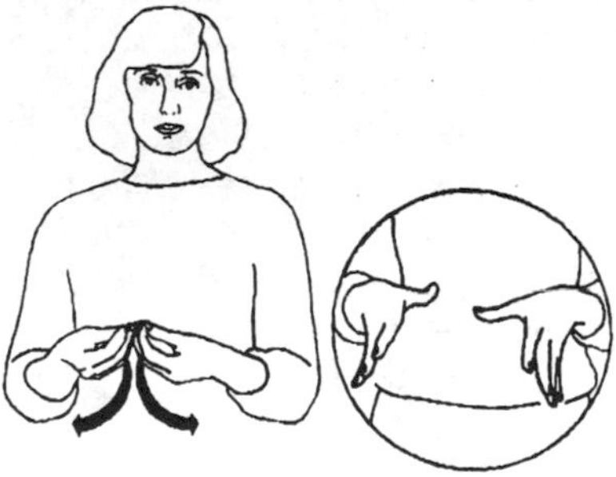

lose[2] *v.* See sign for DECREASE.

lot *n.* See sign for MUCH.

loud *adj.* See sign for NOISE.

lousy *adj. Slang.* Related form: **louse** *n.*

[Suggests that someone with a runny nose feels lousy] Beginning with the thumb of the right *3 hand* touching the nose, palm facing left, bring the hand downward in front of the chest.

love *v., n.*

[The hands bring something that is loved close to oneself] With the wrists of both *S hands* crossed in front of the chest, palms facing in, bring the arms back against the chest.

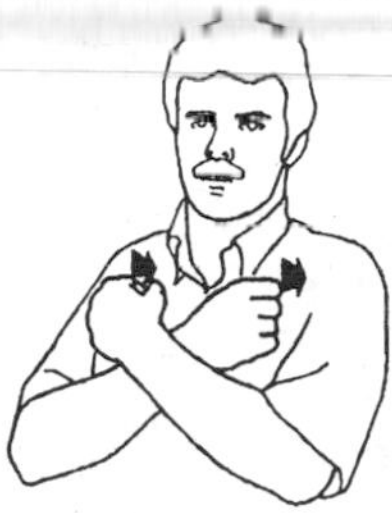

lovely *adj.* See signs for BEAUTIFUL, PRETTY.

lover *n.* See sign for SWEETHEART.

low *adj.* Related form: **lower** *adj.* Same sign used for: **demote.**

[Indicates a location lower than another location] Beginning with both *bent hands* in front of each shoulder, palms facing each other, move them downward in front of each side of the chest.

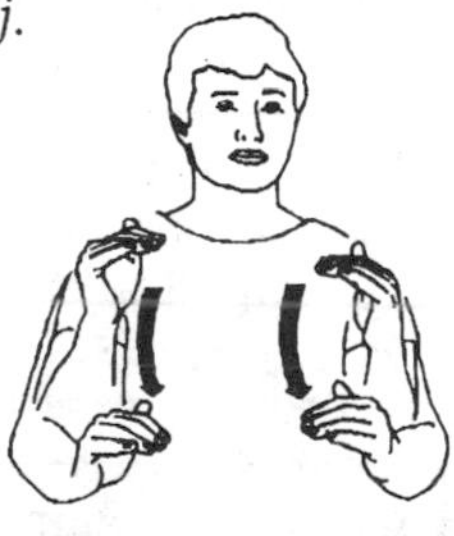

luck *n.* Related form: **lucky** *adj.* Same sign used for: **fortunate.**

[Similar to sign for **favorite**[1] but directed toward another] Beginning with the bent middle finger of the right *5 hand,* palm facing in, touching the chin, twist the wrist to swing the hand forward with a quick movement, ending with the palm angled forward.

luggage *n.* See sign for BAGGAGE.

lump[1] *n.* Same sign used for: **bump.**

[Shows the size of a small amount or swelling] Beginning with the side of the extended right index finger, palm facing left and finger pointing forward, on the back of the left *open hand,* palm facing down and fingers pointing right, bring the right finger upward in a small arc, ending farther back on the back of the left hand.

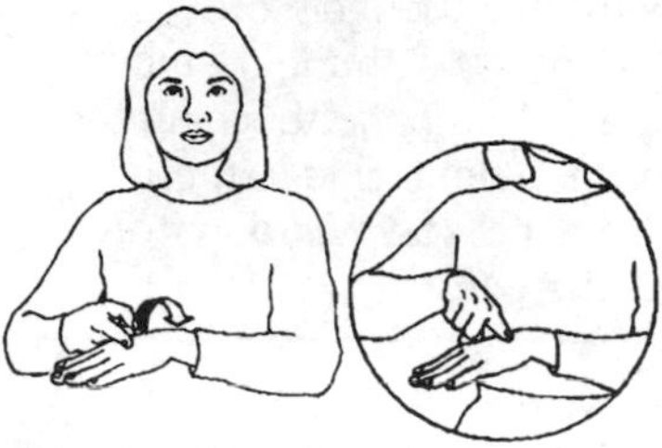

lump[2] *n.* See sign for AMOUNT.

lunch *n.*

[**eat** + **noon**] Bring the fingers of the right *flattened O hand* to the lips, palm facing in. Then place the elbow of the bent right arm, arm extended up and open right palm facing forward, on the back of the left *open hand* held in front of the body, palm facing down.

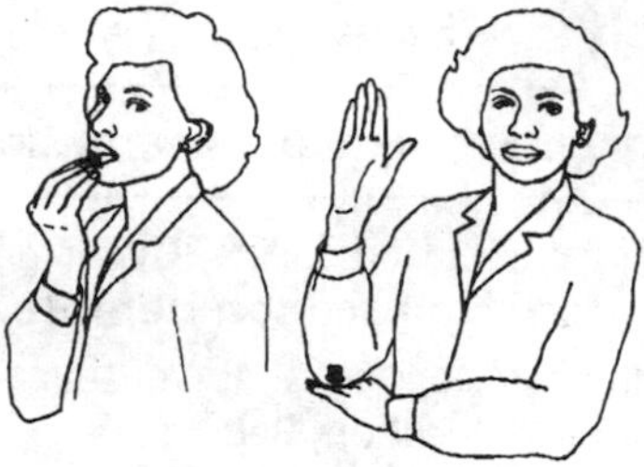

luxury *adj.* See sign for FANCY.

machine *n.* Same sign used for: **factory, industry, manufacture, mechanism, motor, run.**

[Represents movement of gears meshing together] With the fingers of both *curved 5 hands* loosely meshed together, palms facing in, move the hands up and down in front of the chest with a repeated movement.

mad *adj.* See signs for ANGER, CROSS[1].

magazine *n.* Same sign used for: **brochure, journal, pamphlet.**

[Shows the spine of a magazine] Grasp the little-finger side of the left *open hand,* palm angled up, with the index finger and thumb of the right *A hand,* and slide the right hand from heel to fingertips of the left hand with a double movement.

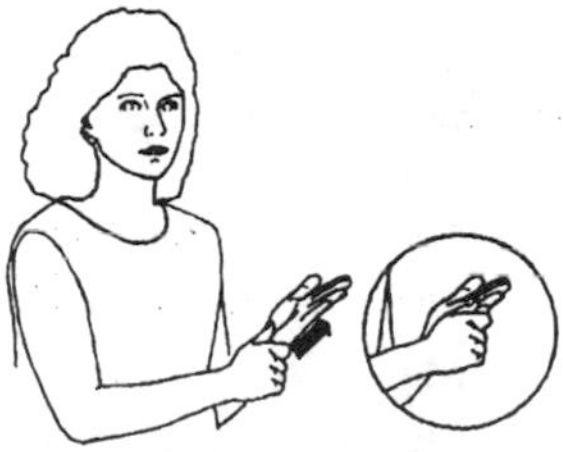

mail[1] *n., v.* Alternate form: **mail out.** Same sign used for: **send, send out.**

[Shows sending something forward] Flick the fingertips of the right *bent hand* forward across the back of the left *open hand,* both palms facing down, with a quick movement, straightening the right fingers as the right hand moves forward.

mail[2] *n.* See sign for LETTER.

main *adj.* See sign for IMPORTANT.

maintain *v.* See signs for FIX, KEEP.

major *v.* See sign for SPECIALIZE.

make *v.* Same sign used for: **create, manufacture, produce.**

[The hands seem to be molding something] Beginning with the little-finger side of the right *S hand* on the index-finger side of the left *S hand,* twist the wrists in opposite directions with a small, quick, grinding movement.

make believe See sign for IMAGINE.

make-up or **makeup** *n.* Same sign used for: **cosmetics.**

[Mime dabbing make-up on one's face] Move the fingertips of both *flattened O hands,* palms facing each other, in double alternating circles near each cheek.

make up *v. phrase.* See sign for INVENT.

make up your mind See sign for DECIDE.

malady *n.* See sign for SICK.

male *n.* See signs for BOY, MAN.

mama *n.* See sign for MOTHER.

man *n.* Same sign used for: **male.**

[A combination of **boy** and a gesture indicating the height of a man] Beginning with the thumb side of the right *flattened C hand* in front of the right side of the forehead, palm facing left, bring the hand straight forward while closing the fingers to the thumb.

manage *v.* Same sign used for: **administer, control, direct, govern, handle, in charge of, operate, preside over, reign, rule.**

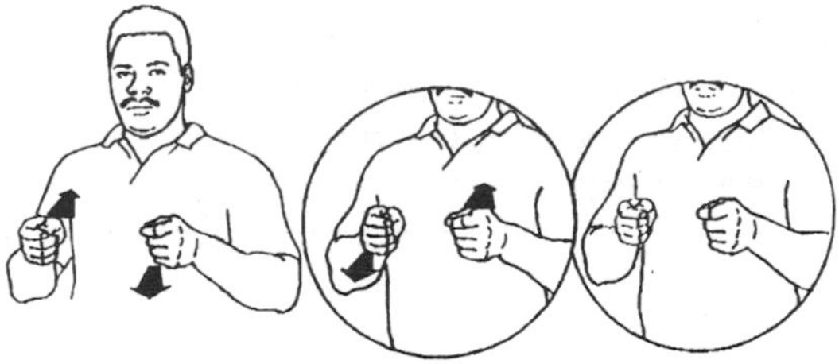

[Mime holding a horse's reigns indicating being in a position of management] Beginning with both *modified X hands* in front of each side of the body, right hand forward of the left hand and palms facing each other, move the hands forward and back with a repeated alternating movement.

manners *n.* See sign for POLITE.

manufacture *v.* See signs for MACHINE, MAKE.

many *adj., pron.* Same sign used for: **a lot, numerous.**

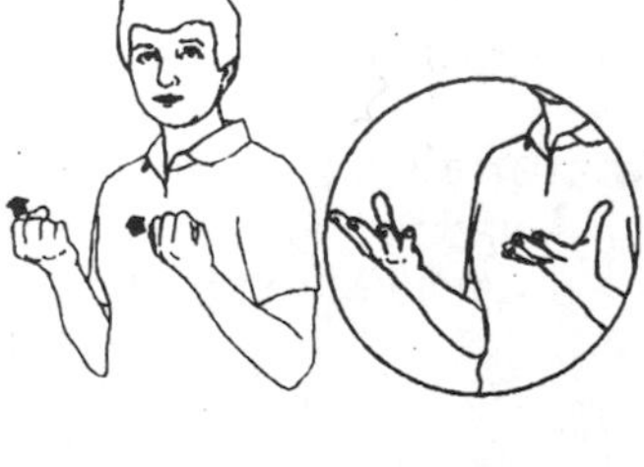

[Natural gesture for indicating many things] Beginning with both *S hands* in front of each side of the chest, palms facing up, flick the fingers open quickly with a double movement into *5 hands.*

margarine *n.* See sign for BUTTER.

market *n.* See sign for STORE[1].

marry *v.*
[Symbolizes joining hands in marriage] Bring the right *curved hand,* palm facing down, downward in front of the chest to clasp the left *curved hand,* palm facing up.

marshall *n.* See sign for POLICE.

mart *n.* See sign for STORE[1].

marvel *n.* See sign for WONDERFUL. Related form: **marvelous** *adj.*

mass *n.* See sign for CLASS.

massive *adj.* See signs for EXCESS, LARGE.

match *v., n.* Same sign used for: **combine, fit, merge, suit.**
[The fingers move together to match with each other] Beginning with both *5 hands* in front of each side of the chest, palms facing in, bring the hands together, ending with the bent fingers of both hands meshed together in front of the chest.

materialize *v.* See sign for SHOW UP.

materials *pl. n.* Same sign used for: **media.**
[Initialized sign similar to sign for **thing**] Beginning with the right *M hand* in front of the body, palm facing up,

move the hand in a double arc to the right.

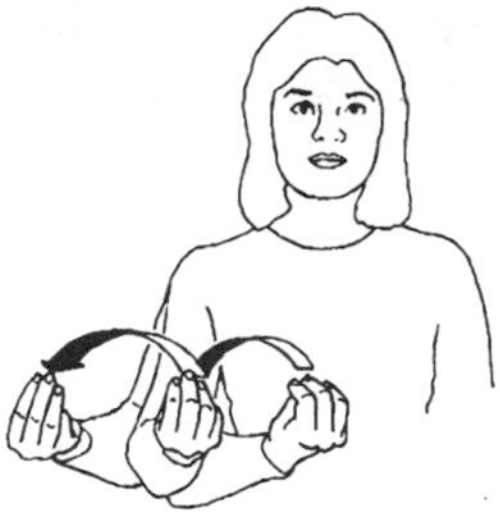

matinee *n.* See sign for AFTERNOON.

maximum *n., adj.* Same sign used for: **up to.**

[Shows reaching the top] Beginning with the right *B hand,* palm facing down and fingers pointing left, a few inches under the left *open hand,* palm facing down and fingers pointing right, bring the back of the right hand up against the left palm.

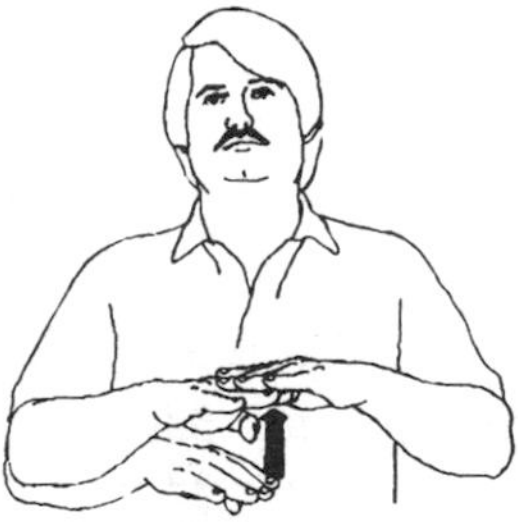

may *v.* See signs for CAN[1], MAYBE.

maybe *adv.* Same sign used for: **may, might, perhaps, probability, probable, probably.**

[Indicates weighing possibilities] Beginning with both *open hands* in front of each side of the chest, palms facing up and fingers pointing forward, alternately move the hands up and down with a double movement.

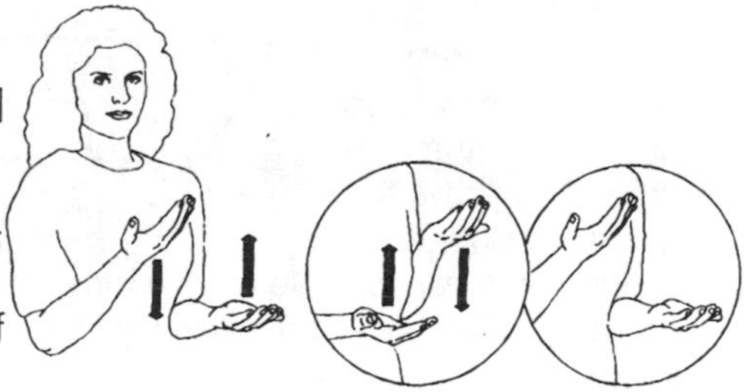

mayonnaise *n.*

[Initialized sign miming spreading mayonnaise on bread] Move the fingers of the right *M hand,* palm facing down, in a double circular movement on the palm of the left *open hand,* palm facing up.

me *pron.* Same sign used for: **I.**
[Directional sign toward self] Point the extended right index finger to the center of the chest.

meager *adj.* See sign for SMALL[1].

mean[1] *adj.* Related form: **meanness** *n.* Same sign used for: **bust, cruel, rude.**
[Shows a rough movement against another] Beginning with both *5 hands* in front of the body, palms facing in opposite directions and the right hand above the left hand, close the hands into *A hands* while quickly moving the right hand down brushing the knuckles against the left knuckles as it passes.

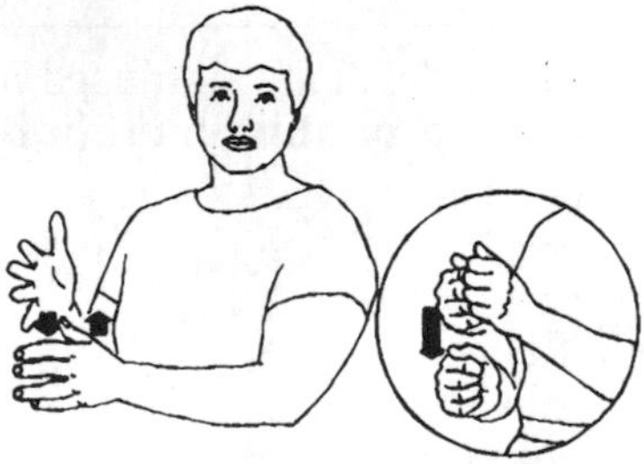

mean[2] *v.* Related form: **meaning** *n.* Same sign used for: **intend, purpose, stand for.**
[Exchanging things to look at their relative standing] Touch the fingertips of the right *V hand,* palm facing down, in the palm of the left *open hand,* palm facing up

and fingers pointing forward, and then twist the right wrist and touch the fingertips down again.

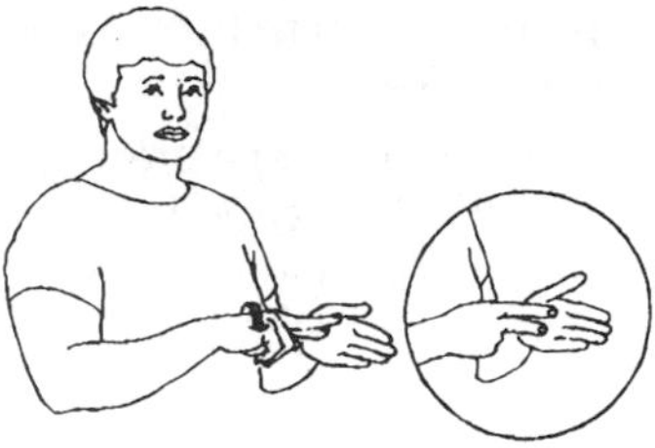

meanwhile *n.* See sign for DURING.

measure *v.* Related form: **measurement** *n.* Same sign used for: **size.**

[The fingers seem to measure something] Tap the thumbs of both *Y hands,* palms facing down, together in front of the chest with a double movement.

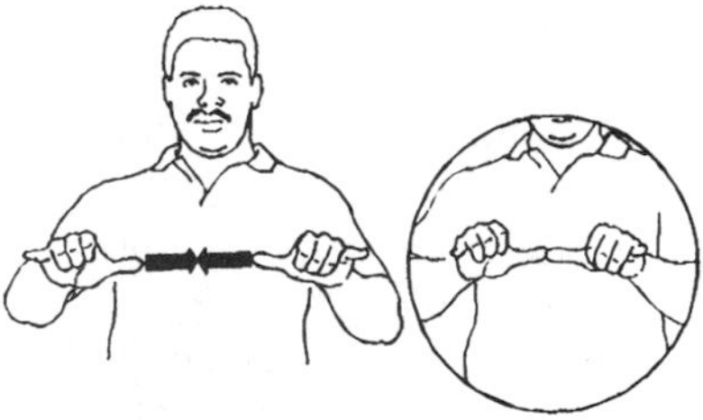

measure up *v. phrase.* See sign for MEET.

meat *n.*

[Indicates the meaty part of the hand] With the bent index finger and thumb of the right *5 hand,* palm facing down, grasp the fleshy part of left *open hand* near the thumb, palm facing right and fingers pointing forward, and shake the hands forward and back with a double movement.

mechanism *n.* See sign for MACHINE.

meddle *v.* See sign for NOSY.

media *pl. n.* See sign for MATERIALS.

medical *adj.* See sign for DOCTOR.

medicine *n.* Related forms: **medical** *adj.*, **medication** *n.*

[Represents mixing a prescription with a mortar and pestle] With the bent middle finger of the right *5 hand,* palm facing down, in the palm of the left *open hand,* rock the right hand from side to side with a double movement while keeping the middle finger in place.

meditate *v.* See sign for WONDER. Related form: **meditation**.

meet *v.* Same sign used for: **greet, measure up.**

[Represents two people approaching each other when meeting] Beginning with the extended index fingers of both hands pointing up in front of each shoulder, palms facing each other, bring the hands together in front of the chest.

meeting *n.* Related form: **meet** *v.* Same sign used for: **assembly, conference, convention, convocation, council.**

[Represents many people coming together for a meeting] Beginning with both open hands in front of the chest, palms facing each other and fingers pointing up, close the fingers with a double movement into *flattened O hands* while moving the hands together.

mellow *adj.* See sign for SOFT.

melody *n.* See sign for MUSIC.

melt *v.* See sign for DISSOLVE.

memorize *v.* Related form: **memory** *n.*

[The hand seems to take information from the brain and then hold on to it tightly, as if to keep it in the memory] Beginning with the fingertips of the right *curved hand* touching the right side of the forehead, palm facing in, bring the hand forward and down while closing the fingers into an *S hand,* palm facing in.

mend *v.* See sign for FIX.

merchandise *n.* See sign for SELL.

mercy *n.* Related form: **merciful** *adj.* Same sign used for: **poor thing**.

[The finger used to show feeling is directed toward another] Beginning with the bent middle finger of the right *5 hand* pointing forward in front of the right shoulder, move the hand forward in a repeated circular movement.

merge *v.* See signs for CIRCULATE, MATCH, MESH.

merry *adj.* See sign for HAPPY.

mesh *v.* Same sign used for: **blend, combine, infuse, integrate, merge.**

[Shows the fingers coming together to merge] Beginning with both *curved 5 hands* in front of each side of the chest, palms facing in, drop the hands down while meshing the fingers together, and then drop them apart in front of each side of the body.

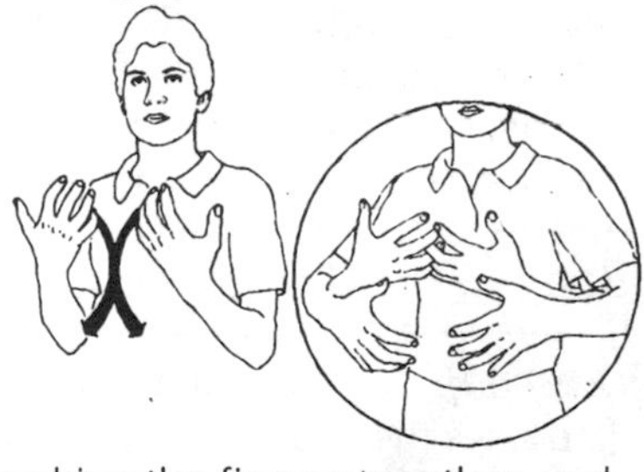

messy *adj.* Same sign used for: **chaos, disorder, garbled, riot, stir, storm.**

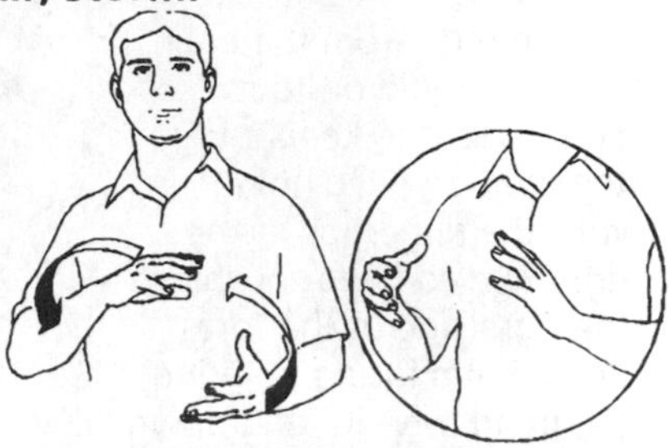

[Represents something turned upside down, causing a mess] Beginning with both *curved 5 hands* in front of the body, right hand over the left hand, twist the hands with a deliberate movement, reversing the positions.

metal *n., adj.* Same sign used for: **rock, steel.**

[Striking the chin which represents a hard substance] Bring the top of the bent index finger of the right *X hand,* palm facing left, forward from under the chin with a double movement.

microwave *n.* Alternate form: **microwave oven.**, *v.*

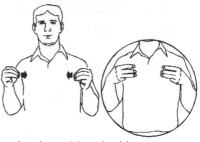

[Abbreviation **m-w**] Beginning with both *M hands* in front of each side of the chest, palms facing in, move the hands toward each other while extending the fingers toward each other with a double movement, changing into *W hands* each time.

midday *n.* See sign for NOON.

middle *adj., n.* Same sign used for: **center.**

[Indicates the middle of something] Move the bent middle finger of the right *5 hand,* palm facing down, in a circular movement and then down into the palm of the left *open hand* held in front of the chest, palm facing up.

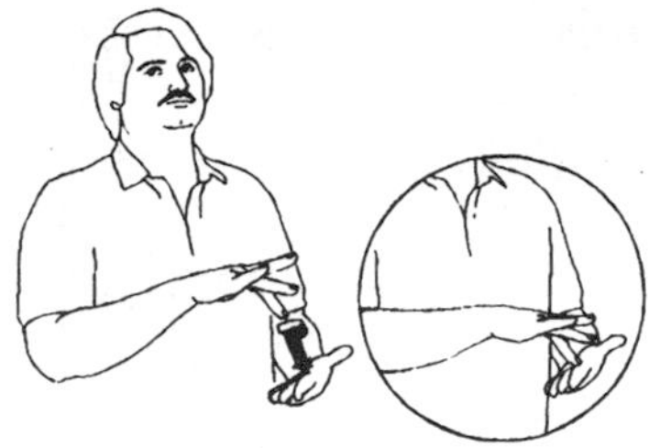

midst *prep.* See sign for AMONG.

might *v.* See sign for MAYBE.

mighty *adj.* See sign for POWER[1].

milk *n.*

[Mime squeezing a cow's udder to get milk] Beginning with the right *C hand,* palm facing left, in front of the right side of the body, squeeze the fingers together with a double movement, forming an *S hand* each time.

million *adj.*

[Initialized sign similar to sign for **thousand** except repeated] Touch the fingertips of the right *M hand,* palm facing down, first on the heel, then in the middle, and then on the fingers of the upturned left *open hand.*

mind *n.* Same sign used for: **brain, sense.**

[Location of the mind] Tap the bent extended right index finger, palm facing in, against the right side of the forehead with a double movement.

mine *pron.* See sign for MY.

mingle *v.* See sign for ASSOCIATE.

mini *adj.* See sign for SMALL[1].

minus *prep.*

[Shape of a minus sign] Touch the thumb side of the extended right index finger, palm facing down and finger pointing forward, against the palm of the left open hand, palm facing right.

minute *n.* Same sign used for: **moment, momentarily, one minute.**

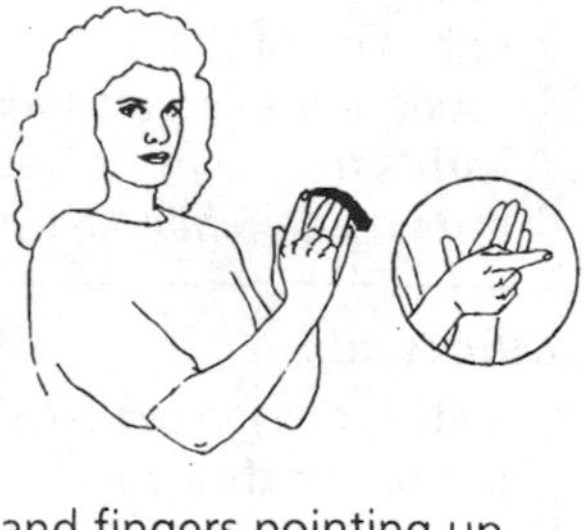

[The finger represents the movement of the minute hand on a clock] Move the extended right index finger, palm facing left, forward a short distance, pivoting the closed fingers of the right hand on the palm of the left *open hand,* palm facing right and fingers pointing up.

mirror *n.*

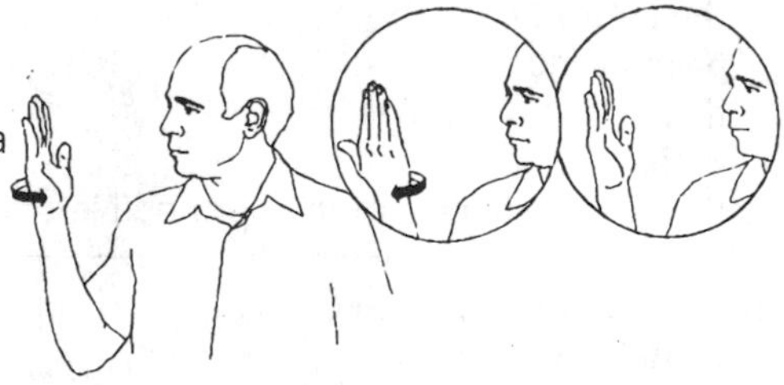

[The hand represents a mirror] Beginning with the right *open hand* held up near the right shoulder, palm facing left, twist the wrist to turn the palm in and back with a double movement.

misconception *n.* See sign for MISUNDERSTAND.

miss[1] *v.*

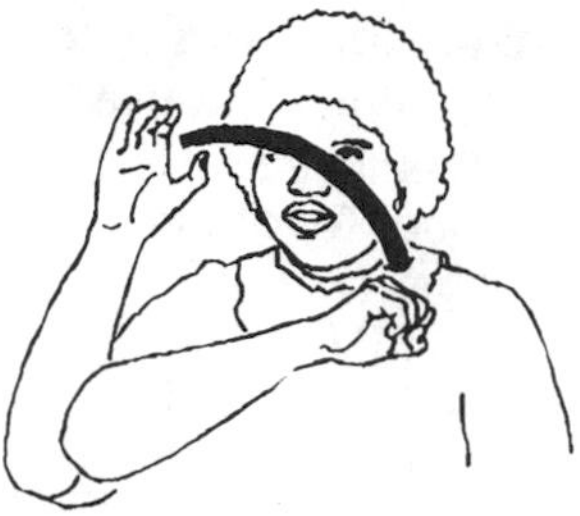

[The hand seems to snatch at something as it passes] Move the right *C hand,* palm facing left, from near the right side of the forehead in a quick downward arc in front of the face while closing into an *S hand,* ending with the palm facing down in front of the left shoulder.

miss[2] *Slang.* Same sign used for: **You're too late.**

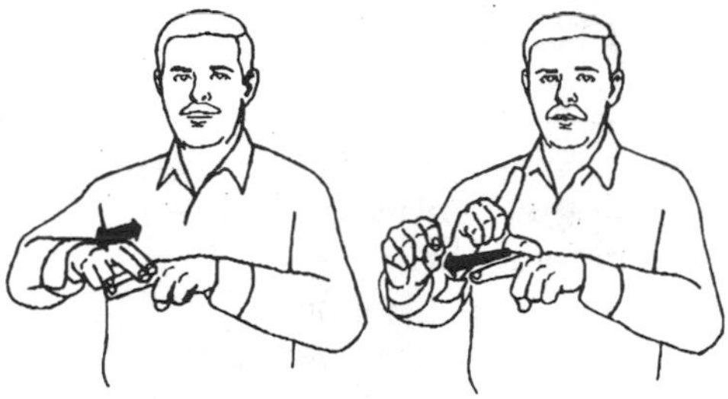

[**train** + **zoom**[1]] Rub the extended fingers of the right *H hand* across the back of the extended fingers of the left *H hand,* both palms facing down. Then beginning with the thumb of the right *L hand,* palm facing forward, on the base of the extended left index finger, palm facing down, move the right hand quickly to the right while closing the index finger to the thumb.

miss[3] *v.* See signs for ABSENT, DISAPPOINTED, SKIP[1]. Related form: **missing** *adj.*

mistake *n.* Related form: **mistaken** *adj.*

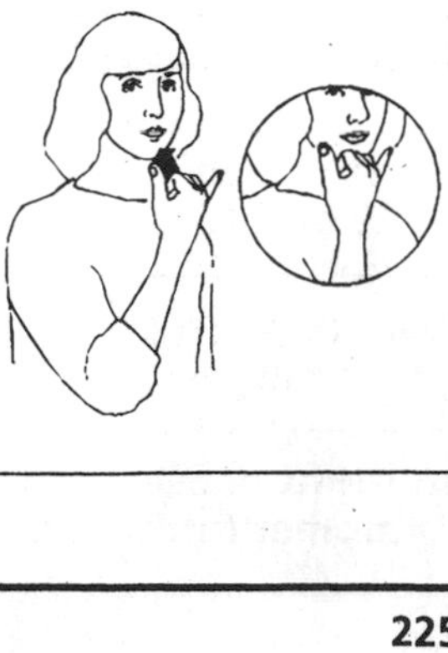

[Similar to sign for **wrong** but made with a double movement] Tap the middle fingers of the right *Y hand,* palm facing in, against the chin with a double movement.

misty *adj.* See sign for WET.

misunderstand *v.* Related form: **misunderstanding** *n.* Same sign used for: **misconception.**

[The fingers indicate something turned around in the mind] Touch the index finger of the right *V hand* to the right side of the forehead, palm facing forward, and then twist the wrist and touch the middle finger to the forehead, ending with the palm facing back.

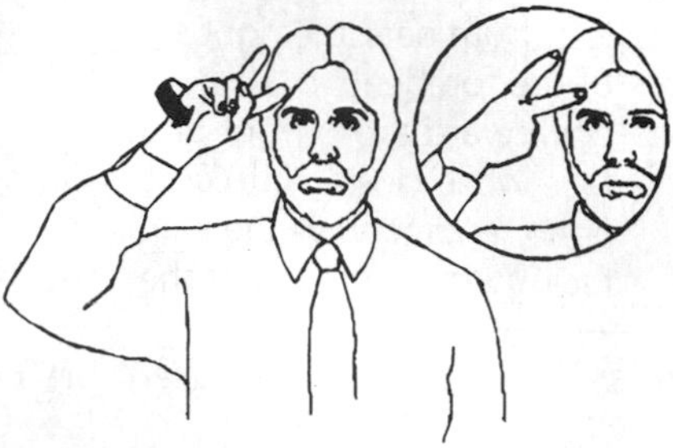

mix[1] *v.* Same sign used for: **blend, complex, confuse, disorder, scramble, stir.**

[Mime mixing things up] Beginning with the right *curved 5 hand* over the left *curved 5 hand,* palms facing each other, move the hands in repeated circles in opposite directions in front of the chest.

mix[2] *v.* See signs for BEAT[1], CIRCULATE.

mixed up *v. phrase.* See sign for CONFUSE[1].

modify *v.* See sign for CHANGE[1].

moist *adj.* See sign for WET. Related forms: **moisten** *v.*, **moisture** *n.*

mom *n.* See sign for mother. Alternate form: **mommy** *n.*

moment *n.* See sign for MINUTE. Related form: **momentarily** *adv.*

Monday *n.*

[Initialized sign] Move the right *M hand,* palm facing in, in a double circle in front of the right shoulder.

money *n.* Same sign used for: **fund.**

[Represents putting money in one's hand] Tap the back of the right *flattened O hand,* palm facing up, with a double movement against the palm of the left *open hand,* palm facing up.

monitor *v.* See sign for CARE[1].

month *n.* Same sign used for: **one month.**

[The finger moves down the weeks on a calendar] Move the extended right index finger, palm facing in and finger pointing left, from the tip to the base of the extended left index finger, palm facing right and finger pointing up in front of the chest.

moon *n.*

[The shape of the crescent moon] Tap the thumb of the right *modified C hand,* palm facing left, against the right side of the forehead with a double movement.

more *adj., adv.*

[The hands seem to add more and more things together] Tap the fingertips of both *flattened O hands,* palms facing each other, together in front of the chest with a double movement.

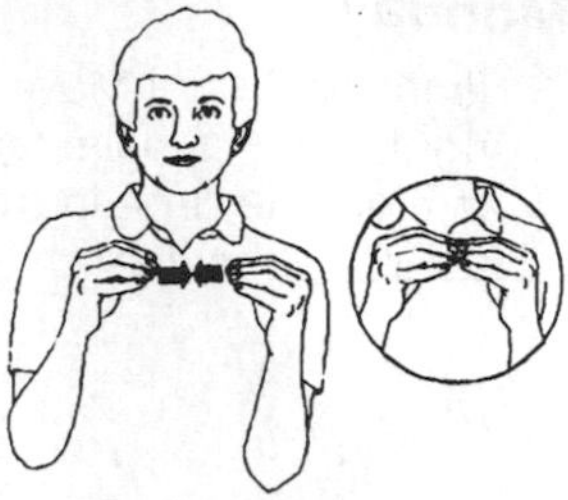

more than See sign for EXCESS.

morning *n.*

[Represents the sun coming up over the horizon] With the left *open hand* in the crook of the bent right arm, bring the right *open hand* upward, palm facing in.

most *adj., adv., n.*

[The hand rises to a higher level] Beginning with the palm sides of both *10 hands* together in front of the chest, bring the right hand upward, ending with the right hand in front of the right shoulder, palm facing left.

mother *n.* Same sign used for: **mama, mom, mommy.**

[Formed in the female area of the head] Tap the thumb of the right *5 hand,* palm facing left, against the chin with a double movement.

motion *v.* See sign for SUGGEST.

motive *n.* See signs for FEEL, ZEAL. Related form: **motivation.**

motor *n.* See sign for MACHINE.

mount *v.* See sign for PUT.

mountain *n.*

[**rock**[1] + the shape of a mountain-side] Tap the palm side of the right *S hand* on the back of the left *S hand,* both palms facing down in front of the body. Then, beginning with both *open hands* in front of each side of the waist, palms facing down and fingers angled up, move the hands upward and forward at an angle with a large wavy movement.

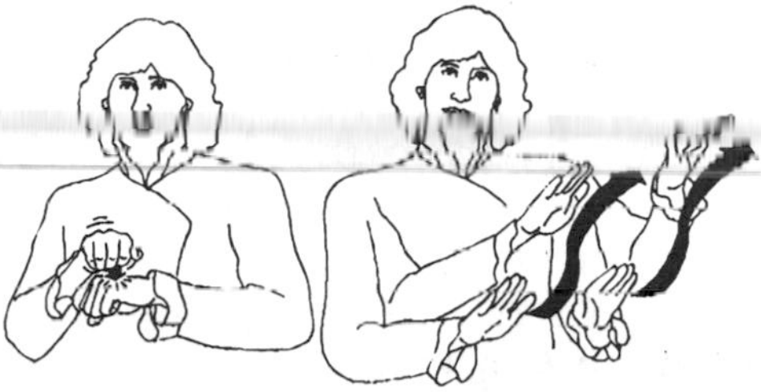

mouth *n.*

[Location of the mouth] Draw a circle around the mouth with the extended right index finger, palm facing in.

move *v.* Related form: **movement** *n.* Same sign used for: **relocate.**

[The hands seem to move something from one place to another] Beginning with both *flattened O hands* in front of the body, palms facing down, move the hands in large arcs to the right.

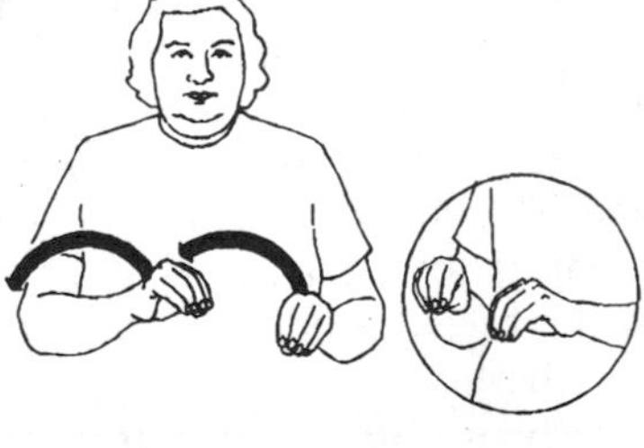

movie *n.* See sign for FILM.

much *n., adj., adv.* Same sign used for: **a lot, lot.**

[The hands expand to encompass something large] Beginning with the fingertips of both *curved 5 hands* touching each other in front of the body, palms facing each other, bring the hands outward to in front of each side of the chest.

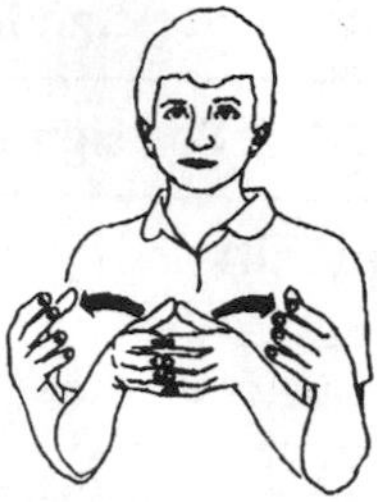

mule *n.* See sign for DONKEY.

mull or **mull over** *v.* Same sign used for: **cogitate, deliberate, ponder.**

[Represents the brain as it cogitates] Wiggle the fingers of the right *4 hand* in a small repeated circle near the forehead, palm facing in.

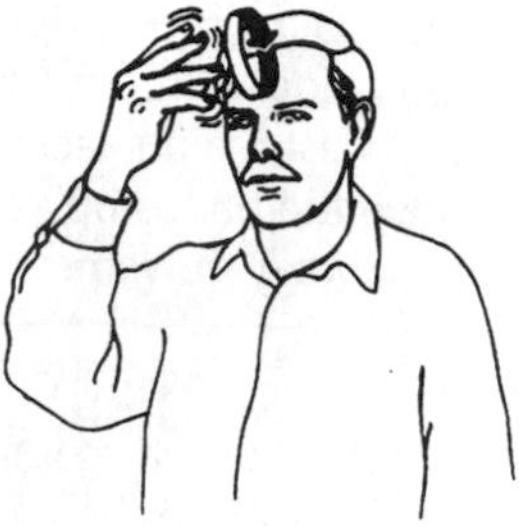

multiplication *n.* See sign for ARITHMETIC.

multiply *v.* Same sign used for: **estimate, figure, figure out.**

[The movement suggests combining things] Brush the back of the right *V hand* across the palm side of the left *V hand,* both palms facing up, as the hands cross in front of the chest.

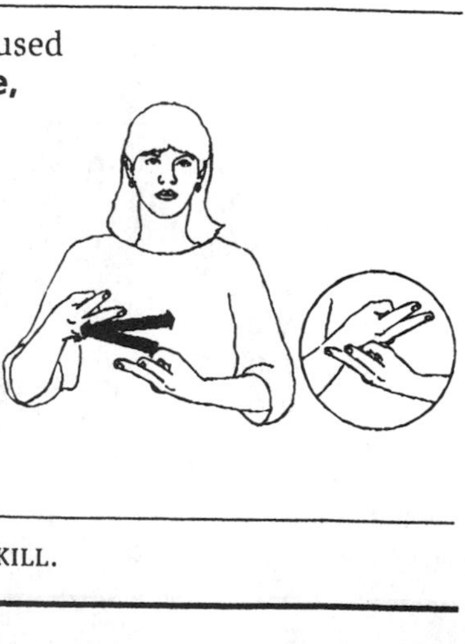

murder *v.* See sign for KILL.

music *n.* Same sign used for: **chant, melody, sing, song.**

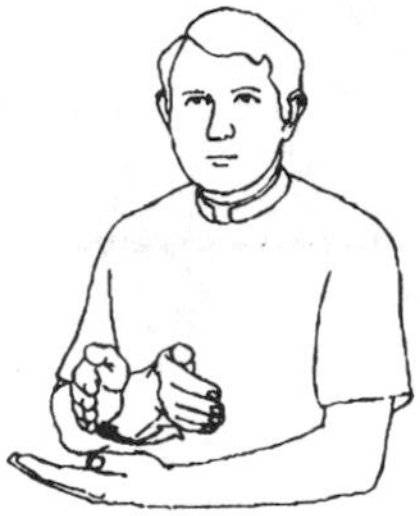

[Demonstrates the rhythm of music] Swing the little-finger side of the right *open hand,* palm facing left, back and forth with a double movement across the length of the bent left forearm held in front of the chest.

must *auxiliary v.* Same sign used for: **have to, necessary, ought to.**

[Suggests standing firm on a position] Move the bent index finger of the right *X hand,* palm facing forward, downward with a deliberate movement in front of the right side of the body by bending the wrist down.

mute *adj.* See sign for SILENT.

my *pron.* Same sign used for: **mine, own.**

[Pulling something to oneself] Place the palm of the right *open hand* on the chest, fingers pointing left.

myself *pron.*

[Sign moves toward oneself] Tap the thumb side of the right *A hand,* palm facing left, against the chest with a double movement.

mystery *n.* See sign for HIDE.

nab *v.* See signs for CAPTURE, CATCH[1].

nag *v.* See sign for PREACH.

naked *n.* See sign for NUDE.

name[1] *n., v.*

[The hands form an "X," which is used by illiterate people to sign their names] Tap the middle-finger side of the right *H hand* across the index-finger side of the left *H hand*.

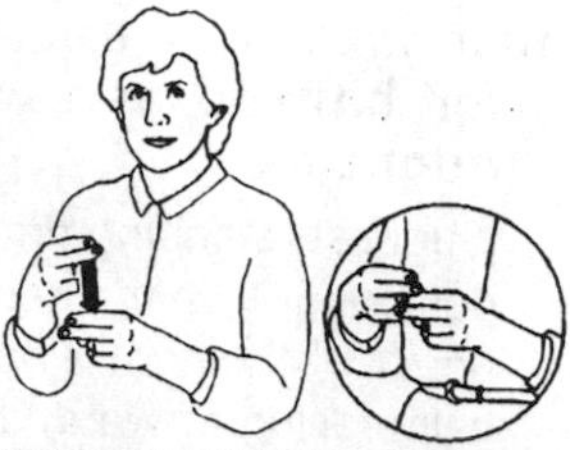

name[2] *v.* See sign for CALL[2].

napkin *n.*

[Mime wiping one's mouth with a napkin] Wipe fingertips of the right *open hand* from side to side over the lips with a double movement, palm facing in.

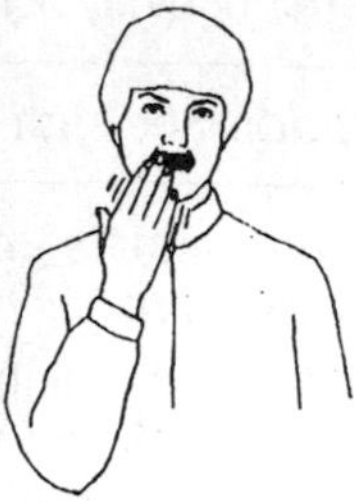

narrow *adj.*

[The hands demonstrate something getting narrower] Bring both *open hands* from in front of each side of the body, palms facing each other, toward each other in front of the waist.

narrow down *v. phrase.* Same sign used for: **convey, focus on.**

[The hands move downward from wider to narrower] Beginning with both *open hands* in front of each shoulder, palms facing each other and fingers pointing forward, bring the hands downward toward each other in front of the body.

nasty *adj.* See signs for BAD, DIRTY.

nation *n.* Same sign used for: **native, natural, nature, normal, of course.**

[Initialized sign] Beginning with the right *N hand,* palm facing down, over the left *open hand,* palm facing down, move the right hand in a small circle and then straight down to land on the back of the left *open hand.*

native *n.* See sign for NATION.

natural *n.* See sign for NATION.

nature *n.* See sign for NATION.

naughty *adj.* See sign for BAD.

near *adv.* See sign for CLOSE.

near future, in the See sign for SOON[1].

nearly *adv.* See sign for ALMOST.

neat *adj.*

[Initialized sign similar to sign for **clean**] Slide the extended fingers of the right *N hand,* palm facing down, from the heel to the fingers of the upturned left *open hand,* fingers pointing forward.

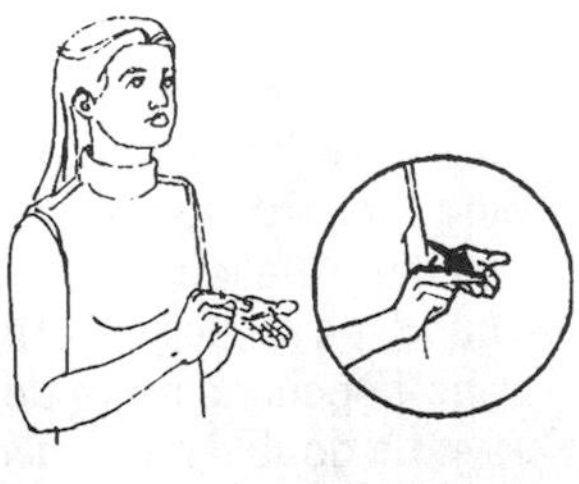

necessary *adj.* See sign for MUST, NEED.

necklace[1] *n.*

[Location of a necklace] Beginning with both extended index fingers touching near each side of the neck, bring the hands downward to touch near the middle of the chest.

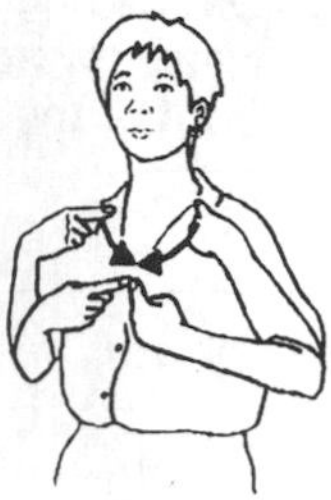

necklace[2] *n.* See sign for BEADS.

necktie *n.* Same sign used for: **tie.**

[Initialized sign showing the location of a necktie] Touch the fingertips of the right *N hand* first to near the neck and then to the lower chest, palm facing in.

need *v., n.* Same signs used for: **necessary, should.**

[A forceful movement to emphasize need] Tap the bent index finger of the right *X hand,* palm facing down, with a short, repeated downward movement in front of the right side of the body, by bending the wrist down.

negative *adj.*

[Shape of a minus sign] Tap the thumb side of the extended right index finger, palm facing down and finger pointing forward, against the palm of the left *open hand,* palm facing right and fingers pointing up, with a double movement.

neglect *v.* See sign for IGNORE. Related forms: **negligence** *n.*, **negligent** *adj.*

neighbor *n.*

[**next door + person marker**] Beginning with the palm of the right *bent hand,* palm facing in and fingers pointing left, touching the back of the left *bent hand,* palm facing in and fingers pointing right, move the right hand forward in a small arc. Then move both *open hands,* palms facing each other, downward along each side of the body.

nephew *n.*

[Initialized sign formed near the male area of the head] Beginning with the extended fingers of the right *N hand* pointing toward the right side of the forehead, palm facing left, twist the wrist to point the fingers forward with a double movement.

nervous *adj.* Related form: **nervously** *adv.* Same sign used for: **anxiety, anxious.**

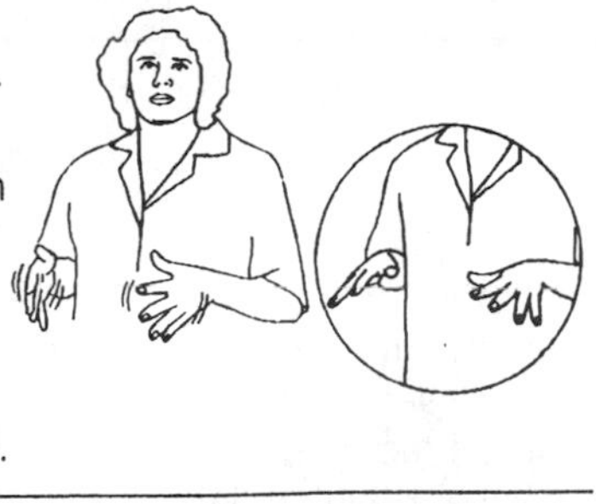

[Natural gesture of shaking when nervous] Shake both *5 hands* with a loose, repeated movement in front of each side of the body, palms facing each other and fingers pointing forward.

never *adv.*

[Natural gesture used to wave an unwanted thing away] Move the right *open hand* from near the right side of the face, palm facing left, downward with a large wavy movement to in front of the right side of the body, ending with the palm facing down.

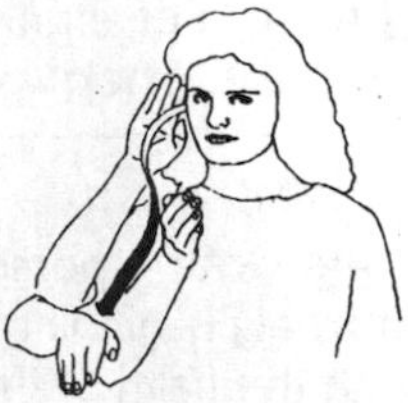

nevertheless *adv.* See sign for ANYWAY.

new *adj.*
[One hand presents the other hand with something new] Slide the back of the right *curved hand,* palm facing up, from the fingertips to the heel of the upturned left *open hand.*

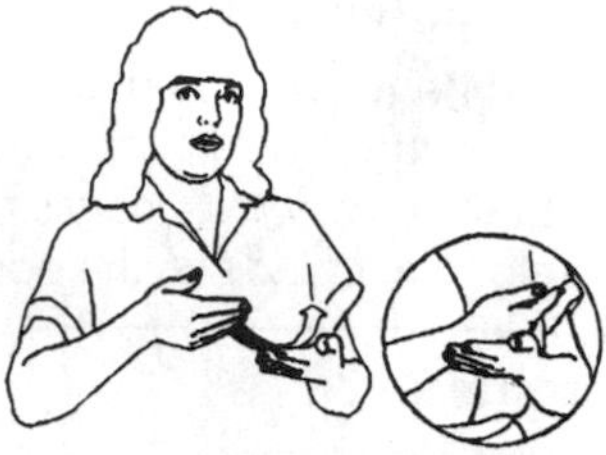

newspaper *n.* Same sign used for: **issue, press, print, publication.**
[Represents putting movable type into place to set up a newspaper] Beginning with the right *G hand,* palm facing forward, above the left *open hand,* palm facing up, pull the right hand down toward the heel of the left hand with a double movement, closing the right thumb and index finger together each time.

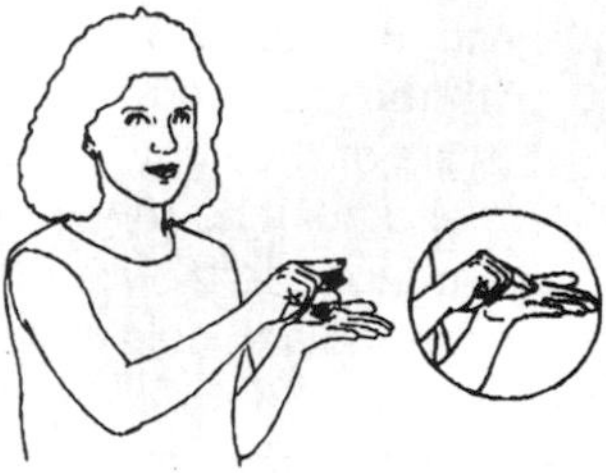

next[1] *adj., adv., prep.* Same sign used for: **next to.**
[Demonstrates one hand overcoming an obstacle to move on to the next thing] Beginning with the right *bent hand,* palm facing in and fingers pointing left, closer to the chest than the left *open hand,* palm facing in and fingers pointing right, move the right hand up and over the left hand, ending with the right palm on the back of the left hand.

next[2] *adj.* See sign for TURN.

next door or **next-door** *adv.*

[Shows a location next to another thing] Beginning with the palm of the right *bent hand,* palm facing in and fingers pointing left, touching the back of the left *curved hand,* palm facing in and fingers pointing right, move the right hand forward in a small arc.

next to *prep.* See signs for BESIDE, NEXT[1].

nickel *n.* Same sign used for: **five cents.**

[The sign **cent** is formed with a *5 hand*] Beginning with the bent index finger of the right *5 hand,* palm facing left, touching the right side of the forehead, bring the hand forward with a double movement.

niece *n.*

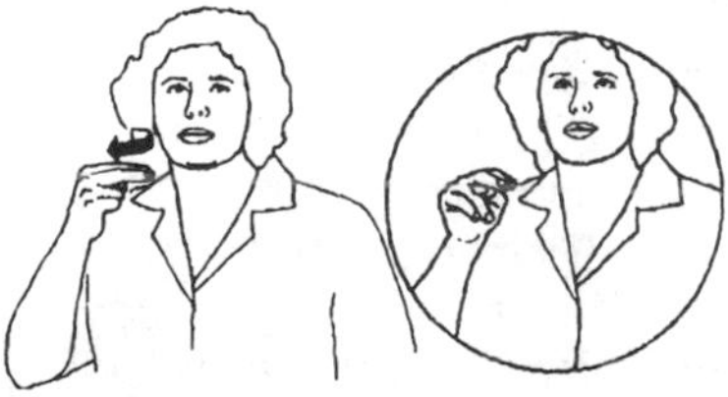

[Initialized sign formed near the female area of the head] Beginning with the extended fingers of the right *N hand* pointing toward the right cheek, palm facing left, twist the wrist to point the fingers forward with a double movement.

niggardly *adj.* See sign for GREEDY.

night *n.* Same sign used for: **tonight.**

[Represents the sun going down over the horizon] Tap the heel of the right *bent hand,* palm facing down, with a double movement on the back of the left *open hand* held across the chest, palm facing down.

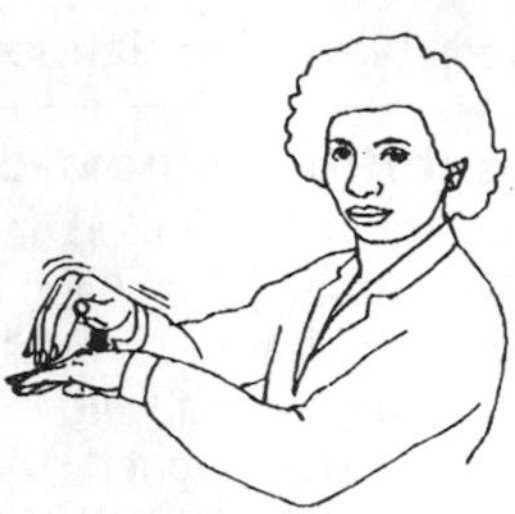

no[1] *adv.*
[Fingerspell **n-o** quickly] Snap the extended right index and middle fingers closed to the extended right thumb, palm facing down, while moving the hand down slightly.

no[2] *adv.* See sign for NONE.

nod *v.* See sign for BOW[1].

noise *n.* Same sign used for: **aloud, loud, sound.**
[Indicates the vibration of a loud sound coming from the ears] Beginning with the bent index fingers of both *5 hands* touching each ear, palms facing in, move the hands forward with a deliberate movement while shaking the hands.

nominate *v.* See signs for APPLY[2], SUGGEST.

nonchalant *adj.* See sign for DON'T CARE.

none[1] *pron.* Same sign used for: **no.**
[Indicates zero amount of something in the hand] Move both *flattened O hands,* palms facing forward, from side

to side with a repeated movement in front of each side of the chest.

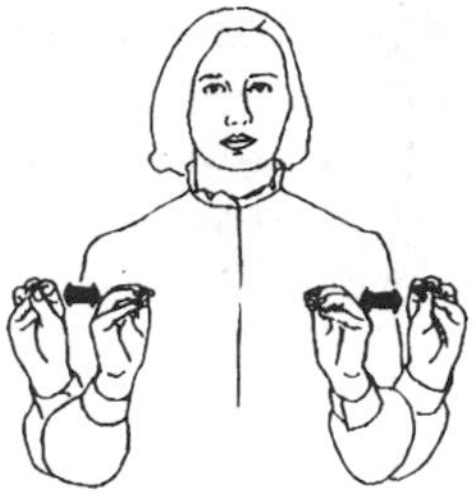

noon *n.* Alternate form: **noontime.** Same sign used for: **midday.**

[Represents the sun straight overhead at noon] Place the right elbow, arm extended up and right *open hand* facing forward, on the back of the left *open hand* held across the body, palm facing down.

normal *n., adj.* See sign for NATION.

nose *n.*

[Location of the nose] Touch the extended right index finger to the right side of the nose, palm facing down.

nosy *adj. Informal.* Same sign used for: **butt in, meddle, peek, pry, snoop.**

[Represents one's nose extending to insert it into another's business] Beginning with the bent index finger of the right *X hand* beside the nose, palm facing left, bring the right hand downward and insert the bent index finger in the thumb-side opening of the left *O hand,* palm facing right.

not *adv.* Same sign used for: **don't.**
[Flicking away something distasteful] Bring the extended thumb of the right *10 hand* from under the chin, palm facing left, forward with a deliberate movement.

notice[1] *v.* Same sign used for: **aware, recognize.**
[Brings the eye down to look at something in the hand] Bring the extended curved right index finger from touching the cheek near the right eye, palm facing left, downward to touch the palm of the left *open hand,* palm facing right in front of the chest.

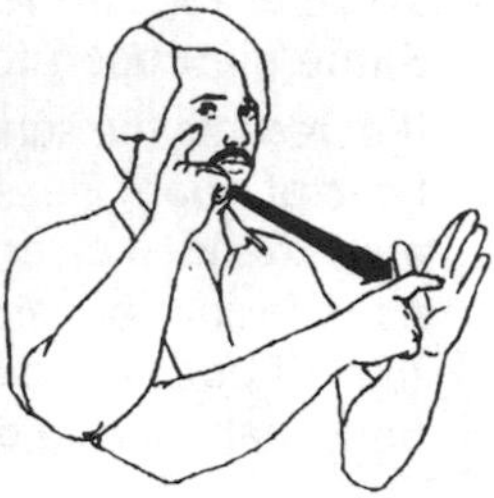

notice[2] *v.* See sign for INFORM.

notify *v.* See sign for INFORM.

notorious *adj.* See sign for FAMOUS.

now *adv.* Same sign used for: **current, present, prevailing, urgent.**
[Indicates a presence right before you] Bring both *bent hands,* palms facing up, downward in front of each side of the body.

nude *adj.* Same sign used for: **bare, naked.**
[The sign **empty** formed downward on the hand representing a person's body] Move the bent middle finger of the right *5 hand,* palm facing in, downward on the back of the left *open hand,* palm facing in and fingers pointing down, from the wrist to off the fingertips.

number *n.* Alternate form: **numeral.** Related form: **numeric** *adj.*

[Adding two quantities together] Beginning with the fingertips of both *flattened O hands* touching, left palm angled forward and right palm facing in, bring the hands apart while twisting the wrists in opposite directions and touch the fingertips again, ending with the left palm facing in and the right palm angled forward.

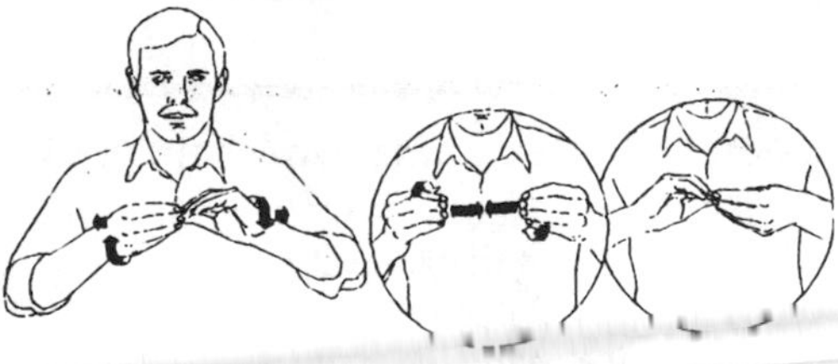

numerous *adj.* See sign for MANY.

nurse *n.*

[Initialized sign similar to sign for **doctor**] Tap the extended fingers of the right *N hand,* palm facing down, with a double movement on the wrist of the left *open hand* held in front of the body, palm facing up.

nut *n.* See sign for PEANUT.

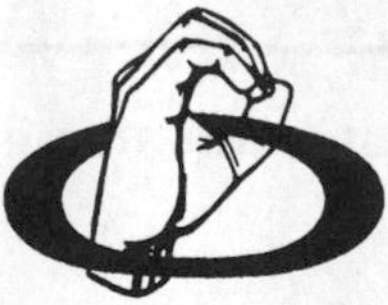

obey *v.* Related forms: **obedience, obedient.**

[Represents placing one's own ideas in a position subservient to another's] Beginning with the right *O hand* in front of the forehead and the left *O hand* in front of the left shoulder, both palms facing in, bring the hands downward simultaneously while opening the fingers, ending with both *open hands* in front of the body, palms facing up and fingers pointing forward.

object *v.* See signs for COMPLAIN, DISAGREE.

objection *n.* See sign for PROTEST[1].

objective *n.* See sign for GOAL.

obligation *n.* See sign for BURDEN.

observe *v.* See sign for LOOK OVER.

obsession *n.* Related forms: **obsess** *v.*, **obsessive** *n, adj.* Same sign for: **persevere, persistent.**

[The finger used for feeling remains on the other hand during a movement that signifies duration] With the bent middle finger of the right *5 hand* on the back of the left *open hand,* both palms facing down, move the hands forward in a repeated circular movement in front of the body.

obstruct *v.* See sign for PREVENT.

obtain *v.* See sign for GET.

occasional[1] *adj.* Related form: **occasionally** *adv.* Same sign used for: **once in a while, periodically.**

[**next-next-next**] Beginning with the right *bent hand* in front of the right side of the chest, palm facing left and fingers pointing left, move the hand forward in a deliberate double arc.

occasional[2] *adj.* See sign for SOMETIMES.

occupation *n.* See sign for WORK.

occupy *v.* See sign for CAPTURE.

occur *v.* See signs for HAPPEN, SHOW UP. Related form: **occurrence** *n.*

odd *adj.* See sign for STRANGE.

odor *n.* See sign for SMELL.

of course See sign for NATION.

off *prep., adv.*

[Shows moving one hand off the other hand] Beginning with the palm of the right *open hand* across the back of the left *open hand* at an angle, both palms facing down in front of the body, raise the right hand upward in front of the chest.

offer *v.* See sign for SUGGEST.

office *n.*

[Initialized sign similar to sign for **box**] Beginning with both *O hands* in front of each side of the body, palms facing each other, move the hands deliberately in opposite directions, ending with the left hand near the chest and the right hand several inches forward of the left hand, both palms facing in.

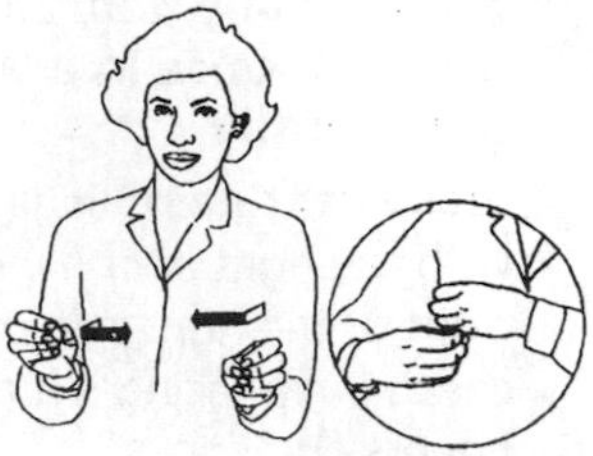

officer *n.* See signs for CAPTAIN, CHIEF.

officially *adv.* See sign for DECIDE.

often *adv.* Same sign used for: **frequently.**

[The sign **again** formed with a repeated movement to indicate frequency of occurrence] Touch the fingertips of the right *bent hand,* palm facing left, first on the heel and then on the fingers of the left *open hand,* palm angled up.

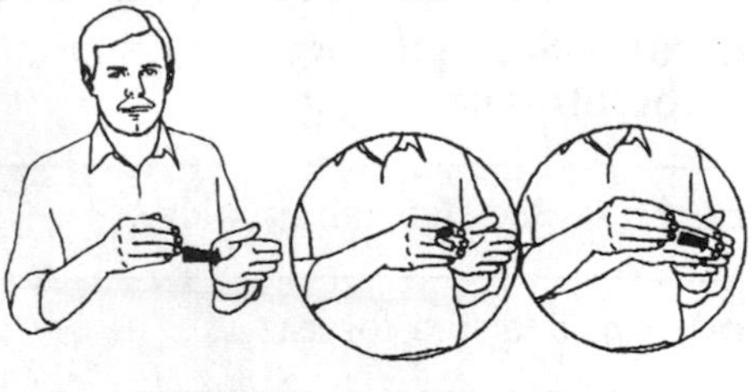

okay *adj.* See sign for SUPERB.

old *adj.*

[Shows the shape of a beard on an old man] Move the right *C hand* from near the chin, palm facing left, downward a short distance while closing into an *S hand.*

omit *v.* See sign for ELIMINATE[1].

on *prep.*

[Shows moving one hand on the other] Bring the palm of the right *open hand* downward on the back of the left *open hand* held in front of the body, both palms facing down.

once *adv.*

Beginning with the extended right index finger touching the left *open hand* held in front of the body, palm facing right and fingers pointing forward, bring the right finger upward with a quick movement while twisting the right wrist in, ending with the palm facing in and finger pointing up in front of the right side of the chest.

once in a while See sign for OCCASIONAL[1].

one another *pron.* See sign for ASSOCIATE.

one dollar *n. phrase.* See sign for FIRST.

one fourth *n.* Related form: **one-fourth** *adj.* Same sign used for: **quarter.**

[**one** + **four** formed over each other as in a fraction] Beginning with the extended right index finger pointing up in front of the right side of the chest, palm facing in, drop the hand while opening into a *4 hand*.

one half *n.* Related form: **one-half** *adj.* Same sign used for: **half**

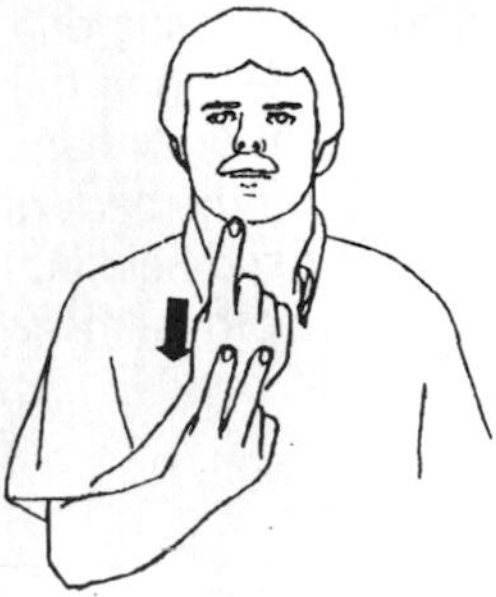

[**one** + **two** formed over each other as in a fraction] Beginning with the extended right index finger pointing up in front of the right side of the chest, palm facing in, drop the hand while opening into a *2 hand.*

one minute *n.* See sign for MINUTE.

one month *n.* See sign for MONTH.

one third *n.* Related form: **one-third** *adj.* Same sign used for: **third.**

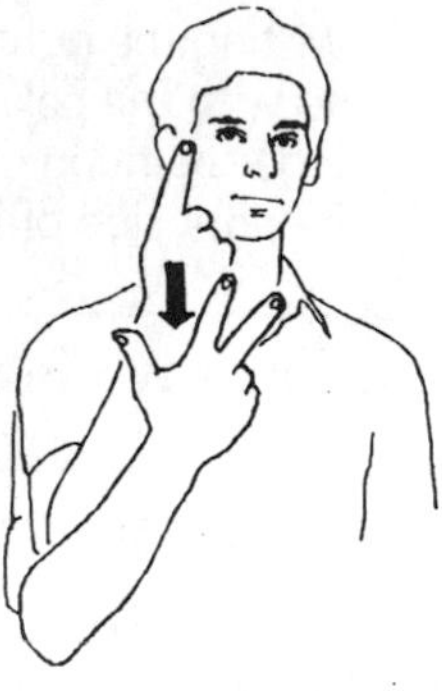

[**one** + **three** formed over each other as in a fraction] Beginning with the extended right index finger pointing up in front of the right side of the chest, palm facing in, drop the hand while opening into a *3 hand.*

one week *n.* See sign for WEEK.

onion *n.*

[As if wiping a tear away from onion fumes] Twist the knuckle of the bent index finger of the right *X hand,* palm facing forward, with a double movement near the outside corner of the right eye.

only[1] *adj., adv.*

[Emphasizes one alone] Beginning with the extended right index finger pointing up in front of the right shoulder, palm facing forward, twist the wrist in, ending with the palm facing in near the right side of the chest.

only[2] *adj., adv.* See sign for ALONE.

onward *adv.* See sign for GO ON.

open *adj., v.*

[Represents doors opening] Beginning with the index-finger sides of both *B hands* touching in front of the chest, palms facing forward, twist both wrists while bringing the hands apart to in front of each side of the chest, ending with the palms facing each other and the fingers pointing forward.

operate[1] *v.* Related form: **operation** *n.* Same sign used for: **surgery.**

[Represents the action of cutting during surgery] Move the thumb of the right *A hand,* palm facing down, from the fingers to the heel of the left *open hand,* palm facing right and fingers pointing forward.

operate[2] *v.* See signs for MANAGE, RUN[2].

opinion *n.*
[Initialized sign] Move the right *O hand,* palm facing left in front of the forehead, toward the head with a double movement.

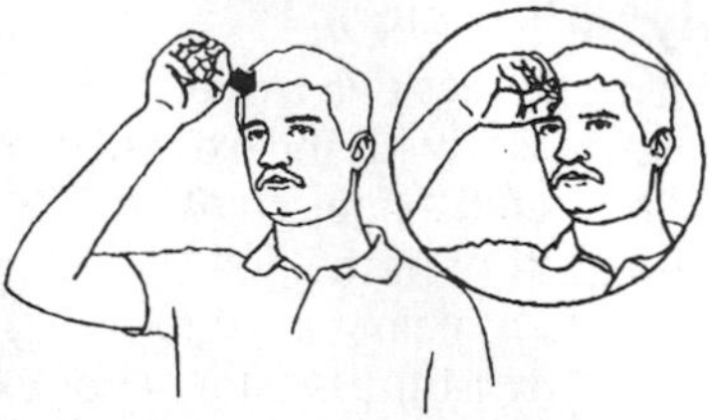

opponent *n.* See sign for ENEMY.

opportunity *n.*
[Abbreviation **o-p** formed in a way that is similar to the sign for **let**] Beginning with both *O hands* in front of the chest, palms facing down, move the hands forward and upward in an arc while changing into *P hands.*

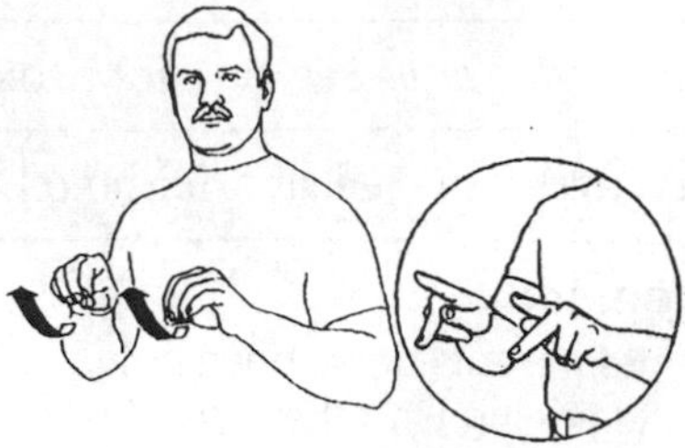

opposed to See sign for AGAINST.

opposite *adj.* Related form: **oppose** *v.* Same sign used for: **contrary, contrast, counter.**
[Shows two things repelled by each other] Beginning with the fingertips of both extended index fingers touching in front of the chest, palms facing in, bring the hands straight apart to in front of each side of the chest.

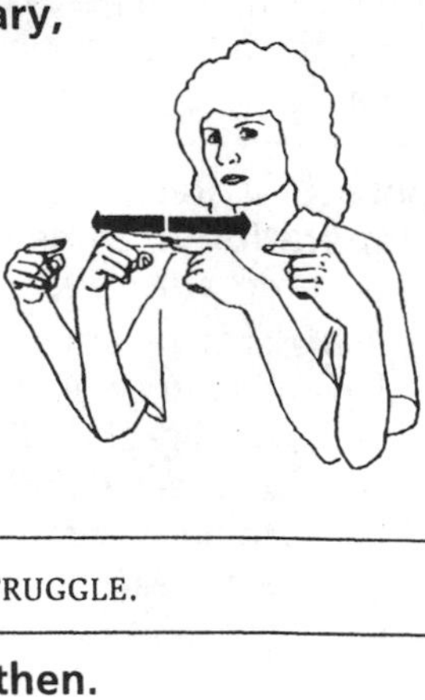

opposition *n.* See sign for STRUGGLE.

or[1] *conj.* Same sign used for: **then.**
[Touches two choices] Tap the extended right index finger, palm facing in, first to the thumb tip and then to the end of the index finger of the left *L hand,*

palm facing right and index finger pointing forward.

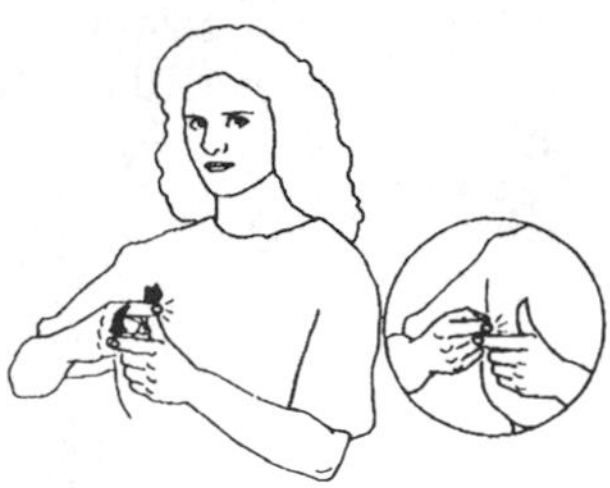

or[2] *conj.* Same sign used for: EITHER.

orange *n., adj.*

[The hand seems to squeeze an orange] Beginning with the right *C hand* in front of the mouth, palm facing left, squeeze the fingers open and closed with a repeated movement, forming an *S hand* each time.

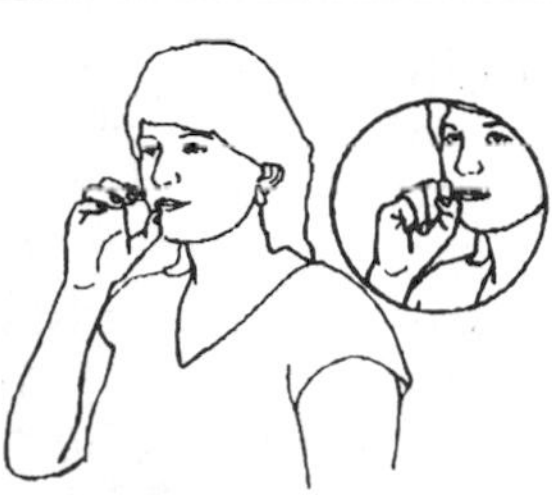

ordeal *n.* See sign for EXPERIENCE.

order *n., v.* Same sign used for: **command, direct.**

[Represents taking words from the mouth and directing them at another] Move the extended right index finger, palm facing left and finger pointing up, from in front of the mouth straight forward while turning the palm down, ending with the finger pointing forward.

ordinary *adj.* See sign for DAILY.

origin *n.* See sign for START. Related form: **origination** *n.*

originate *v.* See sign for INVENT.

other[1] *adj., n.* Same sign used for: **else.**

[The thumb points over to another person, object, etc.] Beginning with the right *10 hand* in front of the chest, palm facing down, twist the hand upward to the right, ending with the palm facing up and the extended thumb pointing right.

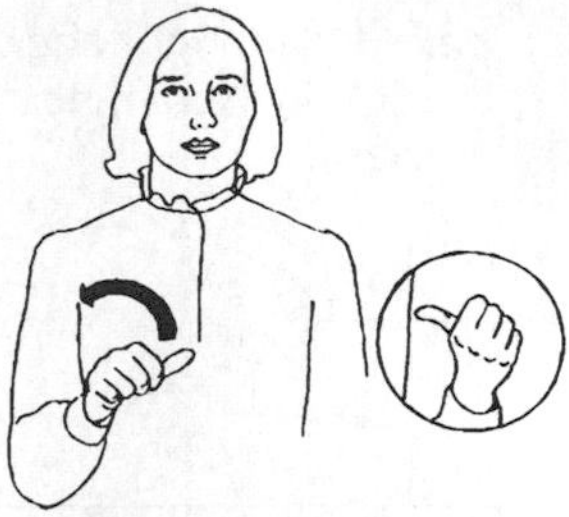

other[2] *adj.* See sign for ANOTHER.

ought to See sign for MUST.

our *adj.* Related form: **ours** *pron.*

[The hand seems to draw a possession to oneself] Beginning with the thumb side of the right *C hand* on the right side of the chest, palm facing left, bring the hand forward in an arc across the chest, ending with the little-finger side of the left hand on the left side of the chest, palm facing right.

ourselves *pl. pron.*

[Uses the handshape used for reflexive pronouns] Beginning with the thumb of the right *A hand* touching the right side of the chest, palm facing left, bring the hand in an arc across the chest and touch again on the left side of the chest.

out *adv.* Same sign used for: **go out.**

[Demonstrates a movement out of something] Beginning with the right *5 hand,* palm facing down, inserted in the thumb side opening of the left *C hand,* palm facing right, bring the right hand upward, closing the fingers and thumb together into a *flattened O hand.*

outdoors *adv.* See sign for OUTSIDE.

outrage *n.* See sign for ANGER.

outside *n., adj., adv., prep.* Same sign used for: **external, outdoors.**

[An exaggerated form of the sign for **out**] Beginning with the right *5 hand,* palm facing down, inserted in the thumb side opening of the left *C hand,* palm facing right, bring the right hand upward and forward in an arc while closing the fingers and thumb together into a *flattened O hand* in front of the chest, fingers pointing in.

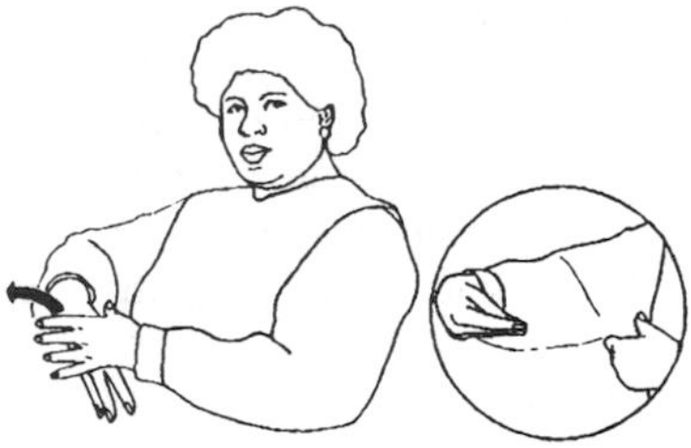

over[1] *prep.* Same sign used for: **exceed, too much.**

[Shows a location higher than another] Beginning with the fingertips of the right *bent hand* on the fingertips of the left *bent hand,* palms facing each other and fingers pointing in opposite directions, bring the right hand upward a short distance in a small arc.

over[2] *prep., adv.* See signs for ABOVE, ACROSS, END[1], FINISH[1].

overcome *v.* See sign for DEFEAT.

overflow *v.* Same sign used for: **plenty, run over.**

[Demonstrates a substance flowing over the sides of a container] Slide the fingers of the right *open hand,* palm facing forward, over the index-finger side of the left *open hand,* palm facing in, while opening into a *5 hand* as it goes over to the back of the left hand.

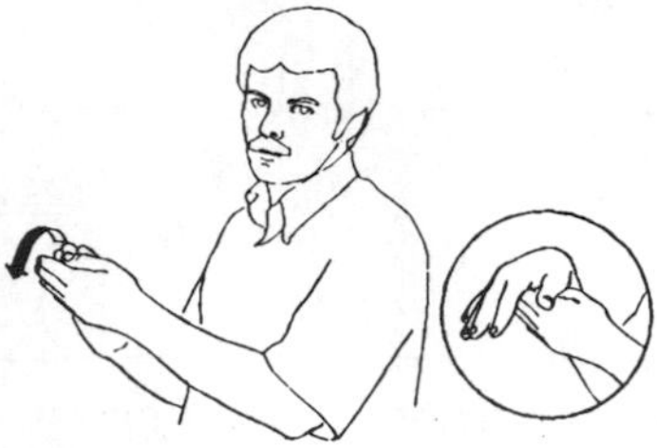

overlook *v.* Same sign used for: **oversight.**

[Represents something passing in front of the eyes without notice] Beginning with the right *open hand* near the right side of the head, palm facing left and fingers pointing up, move the hand in an arc in front of the face to the left while turning the fingers down, ending with the fingers pointing left and the palm facing in, in front of the left side of the chest.

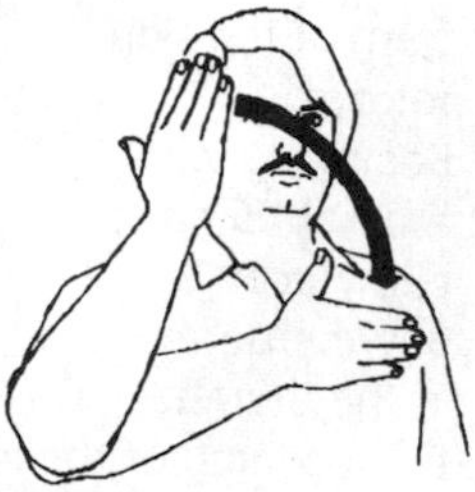

owe *v.* See sign for AFFORD.

own[1] *adj., pron.* Same sign used for: **self.**

[The hand moves back toward oneself] Bring the knuckles of the right *10 hand,* palm facing right, back against the center of the chest.

own[2] *adj., pron.* See sign for MY.

pace *n.* See sign for PROCEDURE. Shared idea of taking orderly steps.

pack *v.*

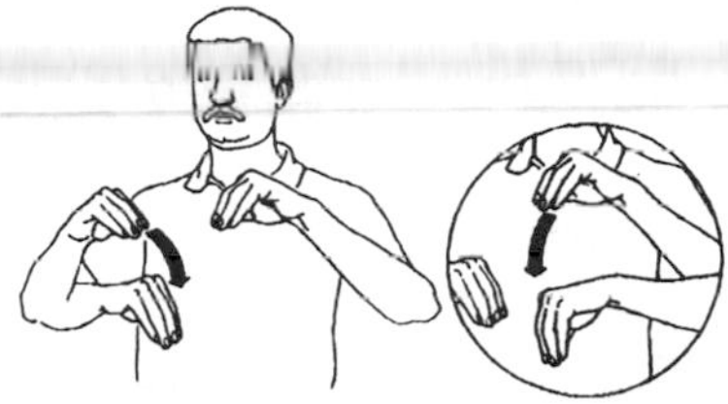

[Mime putting things into a suitcase] Beginning with both *flattened O hands* in front of each side of the chest, palms facing down, move the hands downward with an alternating double movement.

package *n.* See signs for BOX, ROOM.

pain *n.* See also sign for HURT. Same sign used for: **ache, injury.**

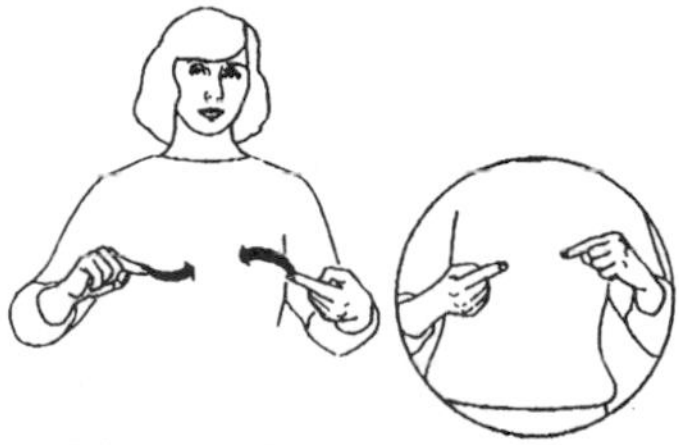

[Similar to sign for **hurt** except with a twisting movement] Beginning with both extended index fingers pointing toward each other in front of the chest, right palm facing down and left palm facing up, twist the wrist in opposite directions, ending with right palm facing up and the left palm facing down.

paint *n., v.* Same sign used for: **brush.**

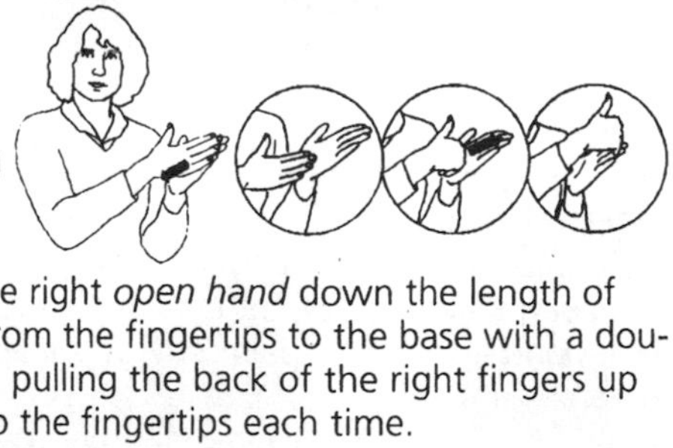

[Mime the action of a paintbrush's bristles moving when painting] Bring the fingertips of the right *open hand* down the length of the left palm from the fingertips to the base with a double movement, pulling the back of the right fingers up the left palm to the fingertips each time.

pair *n.* See signs for BOTH, COUPLE.

pal *n.* See sign for FRIEND.

pamphlet *n.* See sign for MAGAZINE.

panic *n.,v.* See sign for AFRAID.

panties *n.*

[Mime pulling up panties] Beginning with the fingertips of both *F hands,* palms facing in, touching each hip, move the hands up to touch the fingertips again at the waist.

pants *n.* Same sign used for: **jeans, slacks, trousers.**

[Shows location of pants on both legs] Beginning with the fingertips of both *open hands* touching each hip, palms facing in, move the hands upward toward the waist with a double movement.

papa *n.* See sign for FATHER.

paper *n., adj.*

[The pressing of pulp to make paper] Brush the heel of the right *open hand,* palm facing down, on the heel of the left *open hand,* palm facing up, in front of the body with a double movement.

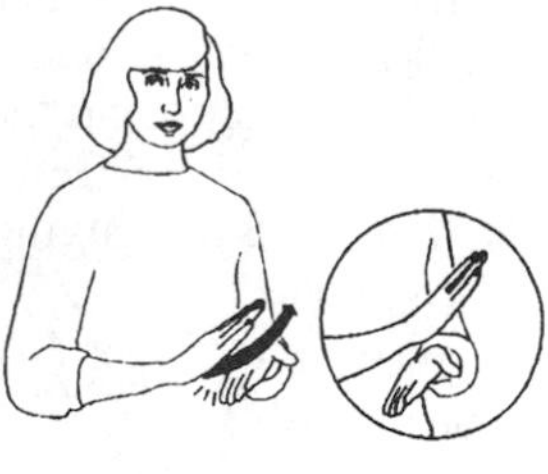

paper clip *n.*

[Demonstrates clipping a paper clip on the edge of paper] Beginning with the extended thumb of the right *U hand* against the palm side of the left *B hand,* palm facing down, close the extended right middle and index fingers down against the back of the left hand.

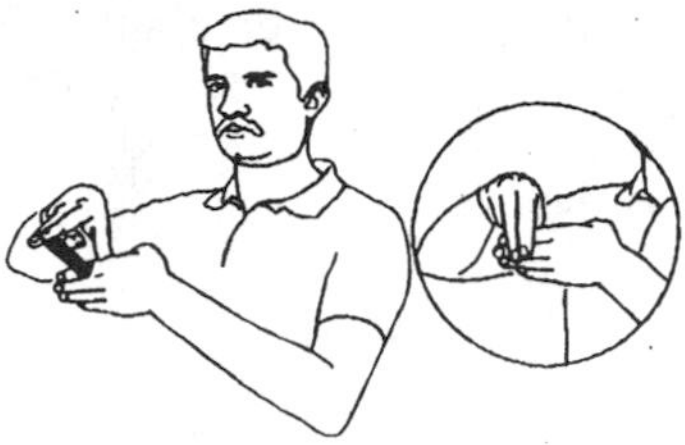

parable *n.* See sign for STORY.

paradox *n.* See sign for PUZZLED.

parched *adj.* See sign for THIRSTY.

pardon *v.* See signs for DISMISS, FORGIVE.

parents *n. pl.*
[**mother + father**] Touch the thumb of the right *5 hand,* palm facing left, first to the chin, then to the forehead.

park *v.*
[The handshape represents a vehicle that is set on the other hand as if to park] Tap the little-finger side of the right *3 hand,* palm facing left and fingers pointing forward, on the palm of the left *open hand,* palm facing up, with a repeated movement.

parole *n.,v.* See sign for DISMISS.

part[1] *n.* Related form: **partial** *adj.* Same sign used for: **piece, section, segment.**
[The hand seems to divide what is in the other hand into parts] Slide the little-finger side of the right *open hand,*

palm facing left, across the palm of left *open hand,* palm facing up, with a curved movement.

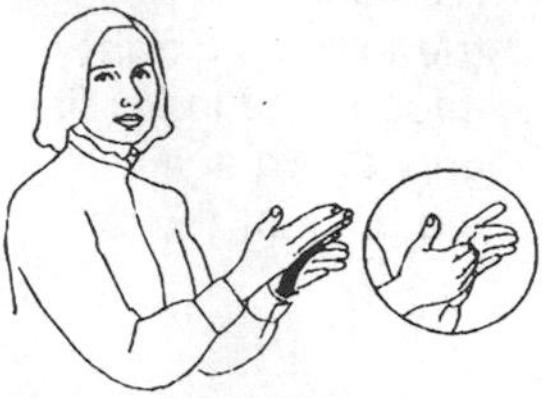

part[2] *n., adj.* See sign for SOME.

part from *v. phrase.* See sign for DISCONNECT.

partial to *adj.* Same sign used for: **favorite.**

[Pointing out a favorite] Tap the fingertips of the right *B hand*, palm facing left, with a double movement against the index finger of the left *B hand* held up in front of the chest, palm facing right.

participate *v.* See sign for JOIN[1].

particular *adj.* See sign for POINT[2].

party *n.*

[Initialized sign] Beginning with both *P hands* in front of the right side of the body, palms facing down, swing the hands from side to side in front of the body with a large double arc.

pass *v.* Same sign used for: **by, past.**

[One hand moves past the other hand] Beginning with both *A hands* in front of the body, palms facing in opposite directions and left hand somewhat forward of the right hand, move the right hand forward, striking the knuckles of the left hand as it passes.

pass around *v. phrase.* Same sign used for: **deal, pass out.**

[Mime passing something around] Beginning with the fingers of both *flattened O hands* together in front of the body, palms facing up, move the right hand forward and then twist it around to the right, ending with the palm facing left.

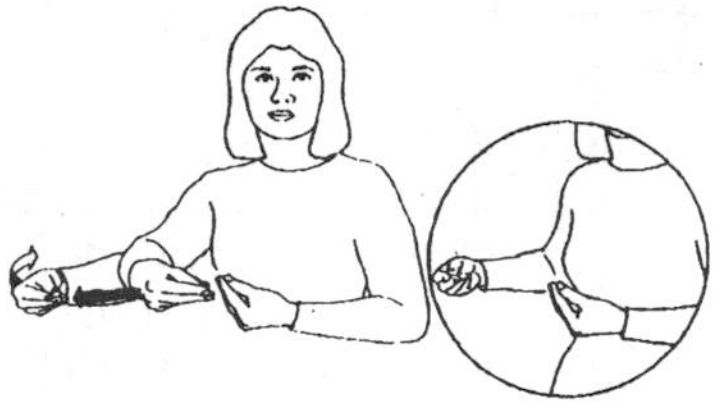

---

passion *n.* See sign for WANT.

---

passive *adj.* See sign for QUIET.

---

pass out *v. phrase* See sign for PASS AROUND.

---

past *adv.* See signs for AGO, BEFORE, PASS.

---

path *n.* See sign for ROAD. Related form: **pathway** *n.*

---

patient[1] *adj.* Related form: **patience** *n.* Same sign used for: **bear, tolerant, tolerate.**

[The thumb seems to seal the lips as a person tolerates something] Move the right *A hand,* palm facing left, downward in front of the chin.

---

patient[2] *n.*

[Initialized sign similar to sign for **hospital**] Move the extended middle finger of the right *P hand,* palm facing in, first down and then forward on the left upper arm.

---

patrol *v.* See sign for CARE[1].

---

pauper *n.* See sign for POOR.

pause *v.* See sign for HOLD[2].

pay *v.*

[Represents directing money from the hand to pay another person] Beginning with the extended right index finger touching the palm of the left *open hand,* palms facing each other, move the right finger forward and off the left fingertips.

pay attention See sign for ATTENTION.

peace *n.* Related form: **peaceful** *adj.*

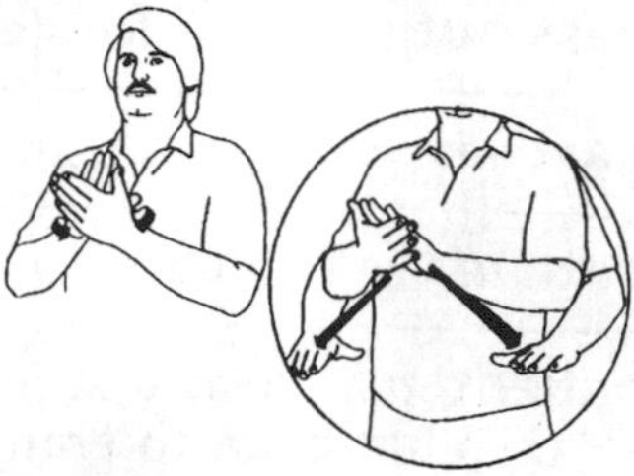

[The hands seem to calm down what is before them] Beginning with the palms of both *open hands* together in front of the chest, right palm facing forward and left palm facing in, twist the wrist to reverse positions. Then move the hands downward, ending with both *open hands* in front of each side of the waist, palms facing down and fingers pointing forward.

peach *n.*

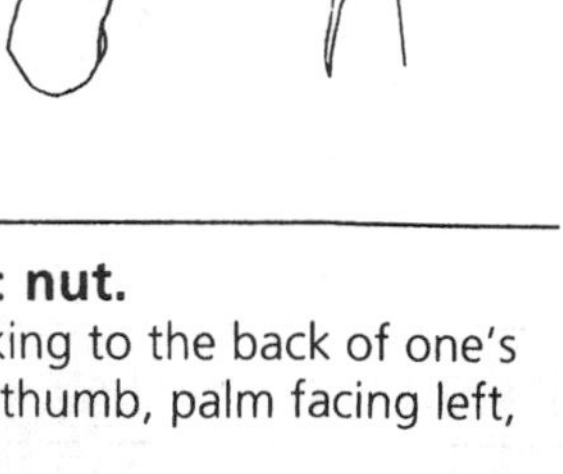

[The fingers seem to feel peach fuzz] Beginning with the fingertips of the right *curved 5 hand* on the right cheek, palm facing left, bring the fingers down with a double movement, forming a *flattened O hand* near the right side of the chin.

peanut *n.* Same sign used for: **nut.**

[Represents peanut butter sticking to the back of one's teeth] Flick the extended right thumb, palm facing left, forward off the edge of the top front teeth with an upward double movement.

peculiar *adj.* See sign for STRANGE.

peddle *v.* See sign for SELL.

peek *v.* See sign for NOSY.

penalty *n.* See sign for PUNISH. Related form: **penalize** *v.*

pencil *n.*
[Indicates wetting the tip of a pencil and then writing with it] Touch the fingertips of the right *modified X hand,* palm facing in, near the mouth. Then move the right hand smoothly down and across the upturned left *open hand* from the heel to off the fingertips.

penitent *adj.* See sign for SORRY. Related form: **pentitence** *n.*

penniless *adj.* Same sign used for: **broke** (*informal*).
[Gesture indicates a broken neck to signify being broke] Bring the little-finger side of the right *bent hand,* palm facing down and fingers pointing back, against the right side of the neck with a deliberate movement while bending the head down to the left.

penny *n.* See sign for CENT.

pension *n.* Same sign used for: **allowance, royalty, subscribe, welfare.**

[Collecting money out of nowhere] With right *curved hand* in front of the right shoulder, palm facing back, bring the hand downward and inward toward the right side of the chest with a double movement, closing the fingers to form an *A hand* each time.

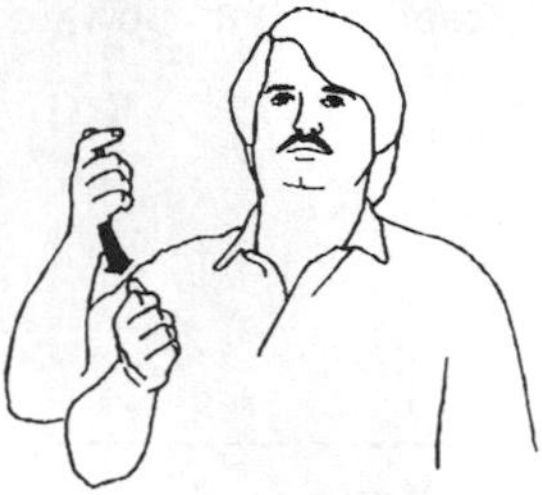

people *n.* Same sign used for: **folk, public.**

[Initialized sign] Move both *P hands,* palms facing down, in alternating forward circles in front of each side of the body.

pepper *n.*

[The hand seems to drop pepper on food] Shake the right *F hand,* palm facing down, up and down in front of the right side of the body with a repeated movement.

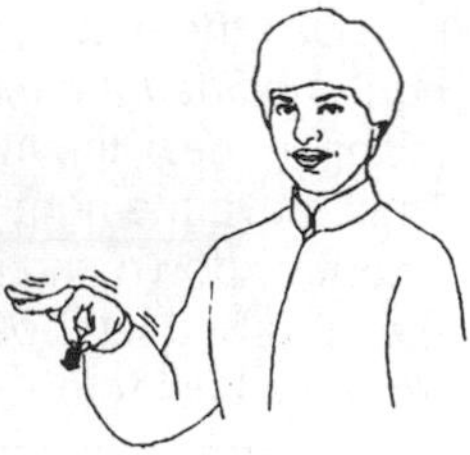

per *prep.* See sign for EACH.

perceive *v.* See signs for PREDICT, UNDERSTAND. Related form: **perception** *n.*

percent *n.* Related form: **percentage** *n.*

[Draw the shape of a percent sign in the air] Move the right *O hand* from near the right side of the face, palm facing forward, a short distance to the right, then down at an angle to in front of the right side of the chest.

perfect *adj.* Related form: **perfection** *n.* Same sign used for: **accurate, ideal.**

[Initialized sign showing things matching perfectly] Move the right *P hand,* palm facing left, in a small circle above the left *P hand,* palm facing up. Then move the right hand downward to touch both middle fingers together in front of the chest.

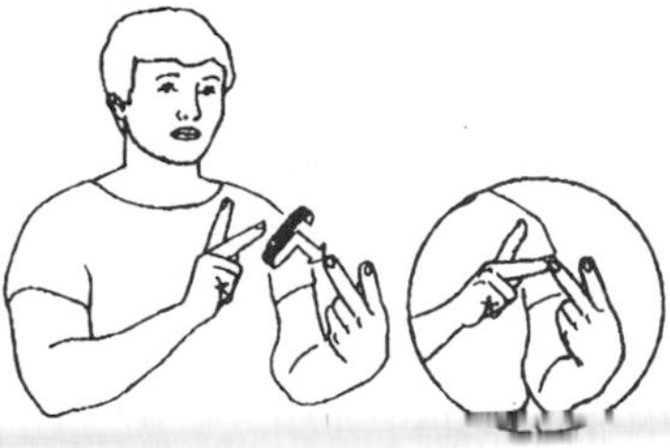

perform *n.* See sign for ACT[2]. Related form: **performance** *n.*

perhaps *adv.* See sign for MAYBE.

period *n.*

[Draw a period in the air] With the right index finger and thumb pinched together, palm facing forward in front of the right side of the chest, push the right hand forward a short distance.

periodically *adv.* See sign for OCCASIONAL[1].

perish *v.* See signs for DIE, DISSOLVE.

permit *v.* See sign for LET.

perplexed *adj.* See sign for PUZZLED.

perservere *v.* See sign for OBSESSION.

persistent *adj.* See signs for CONSTANT, OBSESSION. Related form: **persistence** *n.*

person *n.*

[Initialized sign following the shape of a person] Bring both *P hands,* palms facing each other, downward along the sides of the body with a parallel movement.

personal *adj.* Same sign used for: **personnel.**
[Initialized sign] Move the right *P hand,* palm facing down, in a small double circle on the left side of the chest with a double movement.

personality *n.*
[Initialized sign similar to sign for **character**[1]] Move the right *P hand,* palm facing down, in a small circle in front of the left side of the chest. Then bring the thumb side of the right *P hand* back against the left side of the chest.

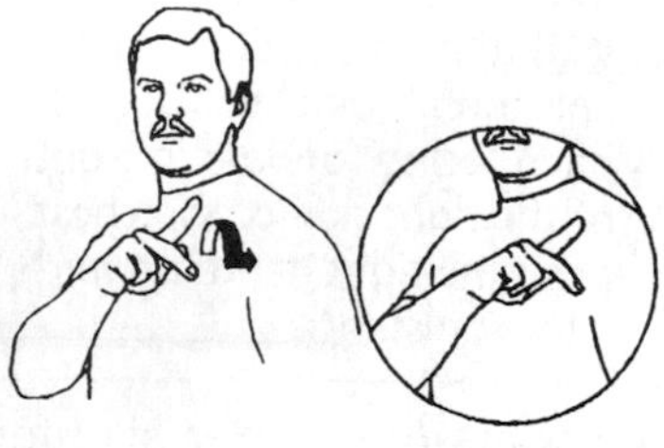

person marker *n.*
[The hands follow the shape of a person] Move both *open hands,* palms facing each other, downward along each side of the body.

personnel *n.* See sign for PERSONAL.

perspire *v.* See sign for SWEAT. Related form: **perspiration** *n.*

petition *n.* See sign for SUGGEST.

phone *n.*, *v.* See sign for TELEPHONE.

photo *n.* See sign for PICTURE. Alternate form: **photograph.**

photograph *v.* See sign for TAKE PICTURES.

phrase *n.* See sign for STORY.

physician *n.* See sign for DOCTOR.

pick *v.* See sign for CHOOSE.

picture *n.* Same sign used for: **photo, photograph.**

[The hand seems to focus the eyes on an image and then record it on paper] Move the right *C hand,* palm facing forward, from near the right side of the face downward, ending with the index-finger side of the right *C hand* against the palm of the left *open hand,* palm facing right.

pie *n.*

[Demonstrates cutting a pie into slices] Slide the fingertips of the right *open hand,* palm facing left, from the fingers to the heel of the upturned left hand, fingers pointing forward, and then perpendicularly across the left palm.

piece *n.* See sign for PART[1].

pile[1] *n.* Same sign used for: **batch, bulk, load.**

[The shape and size of a pile] Move the right *5 hand*

from in front of the left side of the chest, palm facing right and fingers pointing forward, upward in an arc in front of the right shoulder, ending near the right side of the body, palm facing left.

pile[2] *n.* See sign for AMOUNT.

pill *n.*

[Represents flicking a pill into the mouth] Beginning with the index finger of the right *A hand* tucked under the thumb, palm facing in, flick the right index finger open toward the mouth with a double movement.

pillage *v.* See sign for STEAL.

pillow *n.*

[The hands seem to squeeze a soft pillow] With the fingers of both *flattened C hands* pointing toward each other near the right ear, palms facing each other, close the fingers to the thumbs of each hand with a repeated movement.

pin *n.*

[Represents clipping on a pin] Beginning with the thumb of the right *modified C hand* against the left side of the chest, palm facing left, pinch the right index finger to the thumb.

pinpoint *n.* See sign for POINT[1].

pipe[1] *n.* Same sign used for: **handle, lever, pole, rod.**

[The shape of a pipe] Beginning with the index-finger sides of both *O hands* touching in front of the chest, palms facing forward, move the hands apart to in front of each side of the chest.

pipe[2] *n.* See sign for STICK[2].

pistol *n.* See sign for GUN.

pitch *v.* See sign for THROW.

pizza *n.*

[**z** formed with *P hand*] Form a *Z* with the right *P hand,* palm facing left, in front of the right side of the chest.

place[1] *n.* Same sign used for: **position.**

[Initialized sign outlining an area] Beginning with the middle fingers of both *P hands* touching in front of the body, palms facing each other, move the hands apart in a circular movement back until they touch again near the chest.

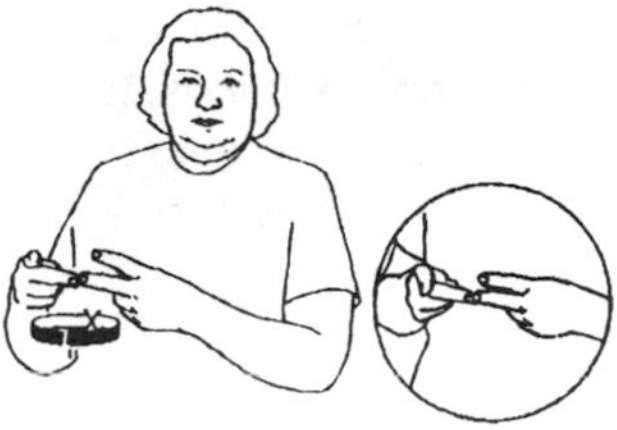

place[2] *v.* See sign for PUT.

place[3] *n.* See sign for AREA.

plan *n., v.* Same sign used for: **arrange, prepare, schedule.**

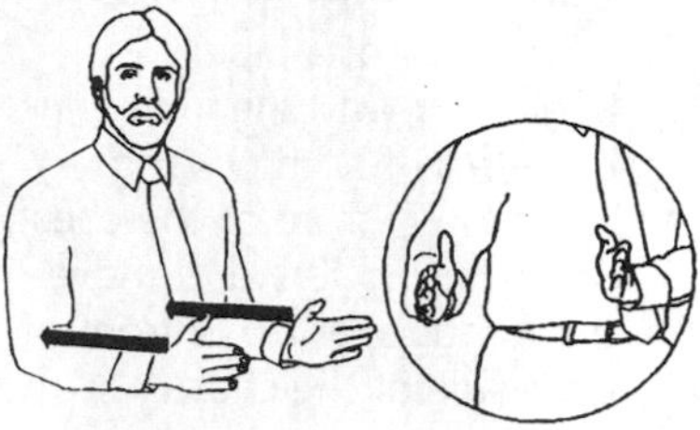

[The hands show a smooth and orderly flow of events] Move both *open hands* from in front of the left side of the body, palms facing each other and fingers pointing forward, in a long smooth movement to in front of the right side of the body.

plane *n.* See sign for AIRPLANE.

plant *n.*

[Represents a seed sprouting and growing as it emerges from the ground] Bring the right *flattened O hand,* palm facing in, with a repeated movement upward through the left *C hand,* palm facing in and fingers pointing right, while spreading the right fingers into a *5 hand* each time.

play[1] *v., n.* Same sign used for: **romp.**

[The movement is loose and playful] Swing both *Y hands* up and down by twisting the wrists in front of each side of the body with a repeated movement.

play[2] *n.* See sign for ACT[2].

play cards See sign for CARDS.

plead *v.* See sign for BEG.

pleasant *adj.* See signs for COOL, FRIENDLY.

please[1] *adv.*
[Rubbing the heart, indicating a feeling of well-being] Rub the palm of the right *open hand* in a large circle on the chest.

please[2] *v.* See sign for ENJOY. Related form: **pleasure** *n.*

plenty *n.* See signs for ENOUGH, OVERFLOW.

plush *adj.* See sign for LAYER.

pocketbook *n.* See sign for PURSE.

point[1] *n.* Same sign used for: **particular, pinpoint, specific, target.**
[Demonstrates pointing at a specific thing] Bring the right extended index finger from in front of the right shoulder, palm facing left and finger pointing up, downward to touch the left extended index finger held in front of the left side of the chest, palm facing right and finger pointing up.

point[2] *v.* See sign for THERE.

pole *n.* See signs for PIPE[1], STICK[2].

police *n.* Same sign used for: **badge, cop, marshall, security, sheriff.**
[Shows the location of a police badge] Tap the thumb side of the right *modified C hand,* palm facing left, against the left side of the chest with a double movement.

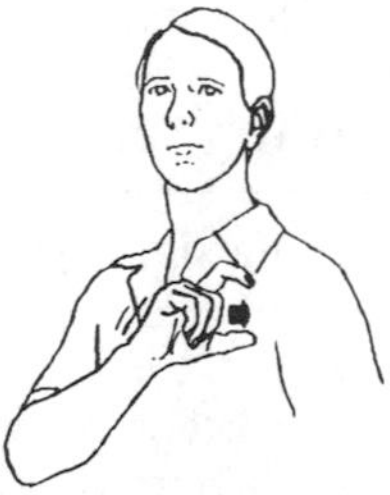

polite *adj.* Same sign used for: **courteous, courtesy, gentle, manners, prim.**

[The ruffles on an old-fashioned shirt worn in polite society] Tap the thumb of the right *5 hand,* palm facing left, with a double movement against the center of the chest.

politics *n.* Related form: **political** *adj.*

[Initialized sign similar to sign for **government**] Beginning with the right *P hand* near the right side of the head, palm facing forward, twist the wrist to turn the palm back and touch the middle finger of the right *P hand* against the right side of the forehead.

pollution *n.* See sign for DIRTY.

ponder *v.* See signs for MULL, WONDER.

poor *adj.* Same sign used for: **pauper, poverty.**

[Represents the tattered sleeves on the elbows of poor people] Beginning with the fingertips of the right *curved 5 hand,* palm facing up, touching the elbow of the bent left arm, pull the right hand downward while closing the fingers to the thumb with a double movement, forming a *flattened O hand* each time.

poor thing See sign for MERCY.

pop *v.* See sign for SODA POP.

popcorn *n.*

[Shows action of popcorn popping] Beginning with both *S hands* in front of each side of the body, palms facing up, alternately move each hand upward while flicking out each index finger with a repeated movement.

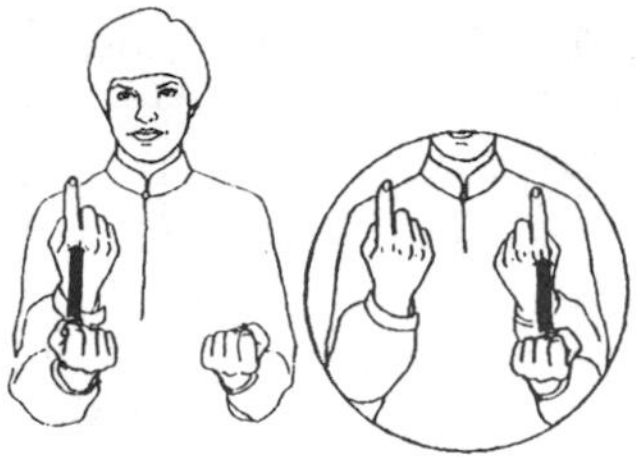

popular *adj.* [Represents many people surrounding a popular person] With the extended left index finger against the palm of the right *5 hand,* palm facing forward, twist the right hand around the index finger with a double movement, ending with the palm facing in.

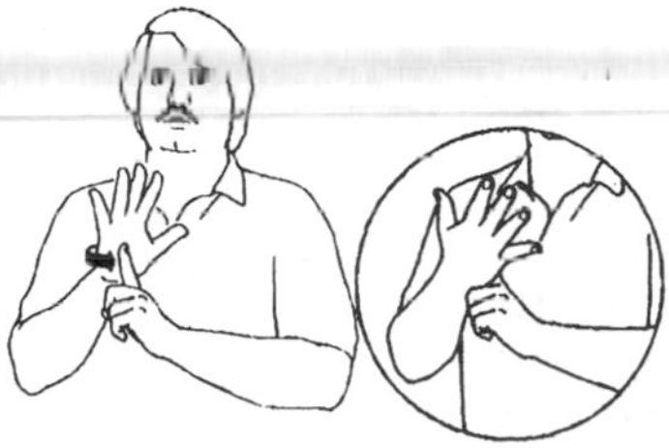

pop up *v. phrase.* See sign for SHOW UP.

portray *v.* See sign for SHOW[1].

position *n.* See sign for PLACE.

possess *v.* See signs for CAPTURE, GREEDY.

post *v.* See sign for APPLY[1].

postage *n.* See sign for STAMP[1].

postage stamp *n.* See sign for STAMP[1].

postpone *v.* Same sign used for: **defer, delay, put off.**

[Represents taking something and putting it off until the future] Beginning with both *F hands* in front of the body, palms facing each other and the left hand nearer to the body than the right hand, move both hands forward in small arcs.

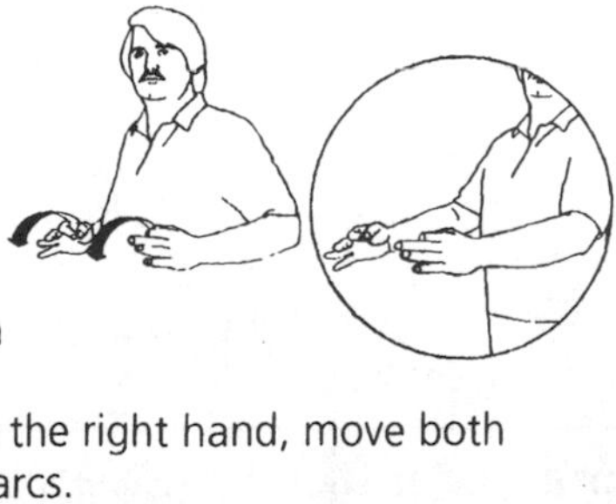

pot *n.* See sign for BOWL.

potato *n.*

[Represents putting fork tines into a baked potato to see if it is done] Tap the fingertips of the right *bent V hand,* palm facing down, with a double movement on the back of the left *open hand,* palm facing down.

potent *adj.* See sign for POWER[1].

pound *n.* See sign for WEIGH.

poverty *n.* See sign for POOR.

power[1] *n.* Related form: **powerful** *adj.* Same sign used for: **mighty, potent, strength, sturdy.**

[Demonstrate power in one's arms] Move both S hands, palms facing in, forward with a short deliberate movement from in front of each shoulder.

power[2] *n.* See sign for STRONG[1].

practice *n., v.* Same sign used for: **exercise, rehearse, training.**

[The repetitive action symbolizes doing something again and again] Rub the knuckles of the right *A hand,* palm facing down, back and forth on the extended left index finger held in front of the chest, palm facing down and finger pointing right, with a repeated movement.

pray *v.* See signs for AMEN, ASK. Related form: **prayer** *n.*

preach *v.* Same sign used for: **nag.**

[Information is directed emphatically toward another] Move the right *F hand,* palm facing forward, with a short double movement forward in front of the right shoulder.

precise *adj.* Same sign used for: **concise, exact.**

[Demonstrates something coming together precisely] Beginning with the right *modified X hand* near the left *modified X hand,* move the right hand in a small circle and then forward to touch the hands together in front of the chest.

predict *v.* Same sign used for: **forecast, foresee, perceive, perception, prophecy.**

[Represents the eyes looking forward into the future] Beginning with the fingers of the right *V hand* pointing to each eye, move the right hand forward under the palm of the left *open hand.*

prefer[1] *v.* Same sign used for: **rather.**

[**favorite**[1] + **better**] Beginning with the bent middle finger of the right *5 hand* touching the chin, palm facing in, bring the hand forward to the right while closing into a *10 hand.*

prefer[2] *v.* See sign for FAVORITE[1]. Related form: **preference** *n.*

pregnant[1] *adj.* Same sign used for: **breed, conceive.**

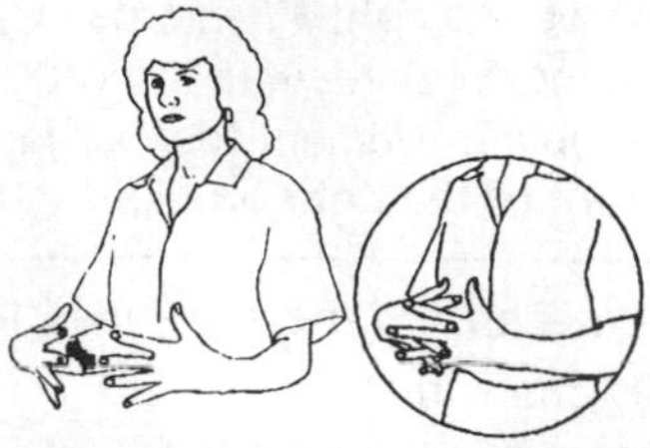

[The shape of a pregnant woman's stomach] Bring both *5 hands* from in front of each side of the body, palms facing in, toward each other, entwining the fingers in front of the stomach.

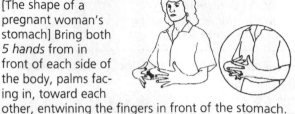

pregnant[2] *adj.* See sign for STUCK. This sign is used only when referring to an unwanted pregnancy.

prejudice *n.* See sign for AGAINST.

prepare *v.* See sign for PLAN.

present[1] *n.* See signs for BOX, GIFT, ROOM.

present[2] *adv.* See signs for HERE, NOW.

present[3] *v.* See sign for GIVE.

presentation *n.* See sign for SPEAK[2].

preserve *v.* See sign for SAVE[2]. Related form: **preservation** *n.*

preside over *v. phrase.* See sign for MANAGE.

president *n.* Same sign used for: **horns, superintendent.**

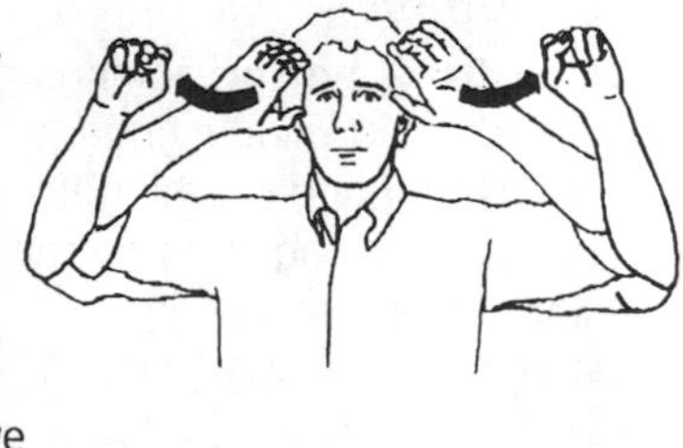

[The horns of authority, as on a stag] Beginning with the index-finger sides of both *C hands* near each side of the forehead, palms facing forward, move the hands outward to above each shoulder while closing into *S hands.*

press *n.* See sign for NEWSPAPER.

pretty *adj.* See also sign for BEAUTIFUL. Same sign used for: **lovely.**

[The hand encircles the beauty of the face] Beginning with the right *5 hand* in front of the face, palm facing in, move it in a circular movement, closing the fingers to the thumb in front of the chin, forming a *flattened O hand.*

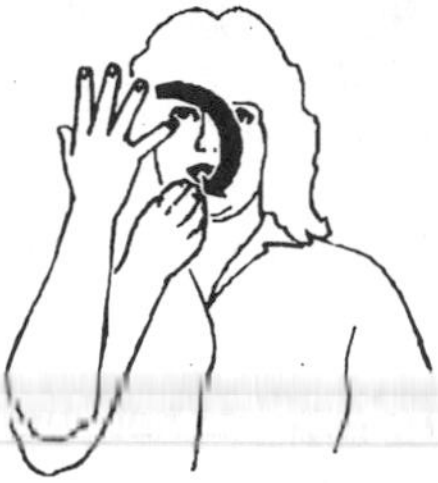

prevailing *adj.* See sign for NOW.

prevent *v.* Same sign used for: **ban, barrier, block, blockage, hinder, impair, obstruct.**

[The hands seem to shield the body with a barrier] With the little-finger side of the right *B hand,* palm facing down, against the index-finger side of the left *B hand,* palm facing right, move the hands forward a short distance.

previous *adj.* See sign for BEFORE.

price *n.* See sign for COST.

prim *adj.* See sign for POLITE.

print *v., n.* See sign for NEWSPAPER.

prior *adj.* See sign for BEFORE.

private *adj.* See sign for SECRET. Related form: **privacy** *n.*

privilege *v.* See sign for RIGHT².

probably *adv.* See sign for MAYBE. Related forms: **probability** *n.*, **probable** *adj.*

problem[1] *n.*
[The knuckles rub together with friction] Beginning with the knuckles of both *bent V hands* touching in front of the chest, twist the hands in opposite directions with a deliberate movement, rubbing the knuckles against each other.

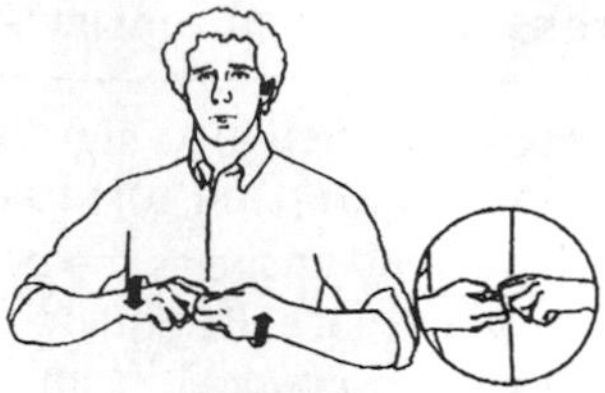

problem[2] *n.* See sign for DIFFICULT.

procedure *n.* Related form: **procedural** *adj.* Same sign used for: **pace, process, progress, take steps.**
[Represents the progression of activities in a procedure] Beginning with both *open hands* in front of the body, palms facing in, left fingers pointing right and right fingers pointing left, and the right hand closer to the chest than the left hand, move the right hand over the left hand and then the left hand over the right hand in an alternating movement.

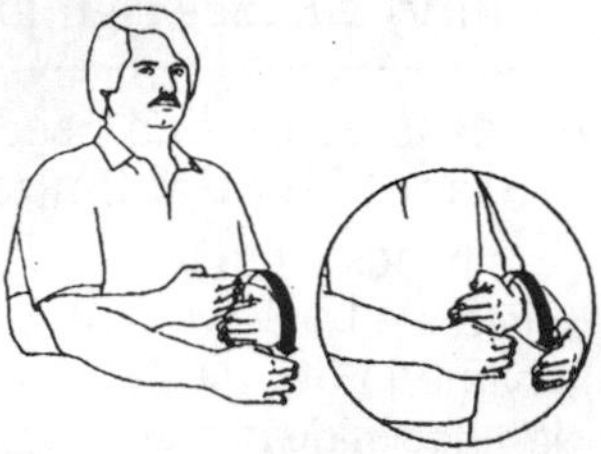

proceed *v.* See sign for GO ON.

process *n.* See sign for PROCEDURE.

proclaim *v.* See sign for ANNOUNCE. Related form: **proclamation** *n.*

produce *v.* See sign for MAKE.

proficient *adj.* See signs for GOOD AT, SKILL.

profit *n.* Same sign used for: **gross.**
[The hand seems to put a profit into one's pocket] Move the right *F hand,* palm facing down, downward with a double movement near the right side of the chest.

program *n.*
[Initialized sign] Move the middle finger of the right *P hand,* palm facing left, from the fingertips to the base of the left *open hand,* palm facing right and fingers pointing up. Repeat the movement on the back side of the left hand.

progress *n.* See sign for PROCEDURE.

prohibit *v.* See sign for FORBID.

prolong *v.* See sign for EXAGGERATE.

prominent *adj.* See signs for ADVANCED, CHIEF[1].

promise *n., v.* Same sign used for: **commit.**
[**true** + a gesture seeming to seal a promise in the hand] Bring the extended right index finger, palm facing left and finger pointing up, from in front of the lips downward, changing into an *open hand* and placing the palm of the right hand on the index-finger side of the left *S hand* held in front of the body, palm facing right.

promote[1] *v.* Related form: **promotion** *n.* Same sign used for: **rank.**
[**advanced** formed with a repeated movement to indicate levels of promotion] Move both *bent hands,* palms facing each other, from near each side of the head upward in a series of deliberate arcs.

promote[2] *v.* See sign for ADVANCED. Related form: **promotion** *n.*

promptly *adv.* See sign for REGULAR.

prone *v.* See sign for CATCH[2].

proof *n.* Related form: **prove** *v.* Same sign used for: **evidence.**

[The hand seems to bring something forward to present to another as proof] Move the fingertips of the right *open hand,* palm facing in, from in front of the mouth downward, ending with the back of the right hand on the palm of the left *open hand,* both palms facing up in front of the chest.

propaganda *n.* See sign for ADVERTISE.

proper *adj.* See sign for REGULAR. Related form: **properly** *adv.*

prophecy *n.* See sign for PREDICT.

proposal *n.* See sign for SUGGEST. Related form: **propose** *v.*

prose *n.* See sign for STORY.

prosper *v.* See sign for SUCCESSFUL.

protect *v.* See sign for DEFEND.

protest[1] *n.* Same sign used for: **complaint, grievance, objection.**

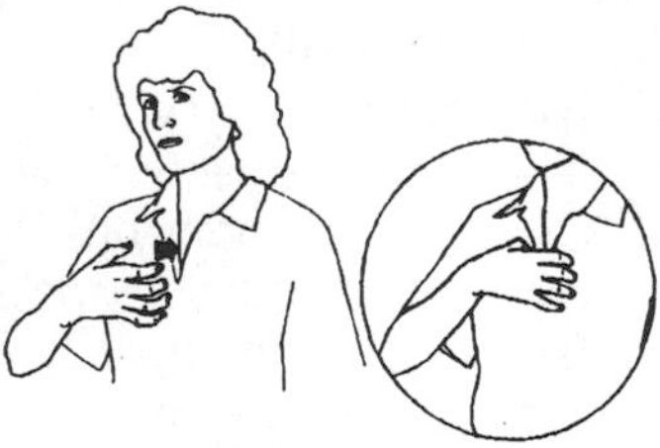

[Similar to sign for **complain** but formed with a single movement] Strike the fingertips of the right *curved 5 hand* against the center of the chest with a double movement.

protest[2] *v.* See sign for COMPLAIN.

proud *adj.* Related form: **pride** *n.* Same sign used for: **arrogant.**

[Feelings of self-worth welling up in the body] Move the thumb of the right *10 hand,* palm facing down, from the center of the lower chest upward with a smooth movement.

provide *v.* See signs for GIVE, SUGGEST.

pry *v.* See sign for NOSY.

pseudo *adj.* See sign for FAKE.

public *n.* See sign for PEOPLE.

publication *v.* See sign for NEWSPAPER.

publicize *v.* See sign for ADVERTISE. Related form: **publicity** *n.*

pull *v.* See sign for DRAG.

punish *v.* Same sign used for: **penalize, penalty.**

[The arm is struck] Strike the extended right index finger, palm facing left, downward across the elbow of the left bent arm.

puny *adj.* See sign for TINY[1].

pupil[1] *n.* Same sign used for: **student.**

[**learn + person marker**] Beginning with the fingertips of the right *flattened C hand,* palm facing down, on the upturned palm of the left open hand, bring the right hand up while

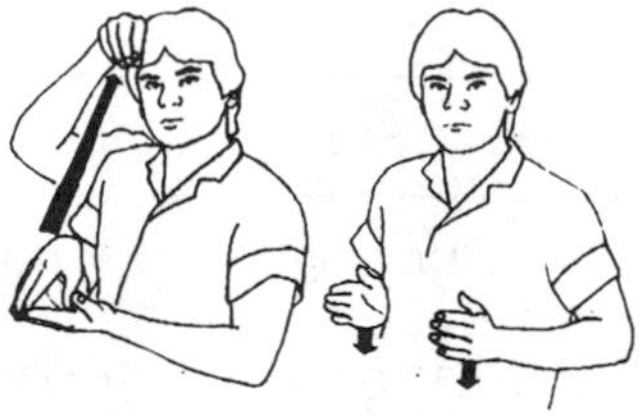

closing the fingers and thumb into a *flattened O hand* near the forehead. Then move both open hands, palms facing each other, downward along each side of the body.

pupil[2] *n.*
[**eye**[1] + the shape of one's pupil in the eye] Point the extended right index finger to the right eye, palm facing in. Then place the thumb side of the right *F hand*, palm facing left, in front of the right eye.

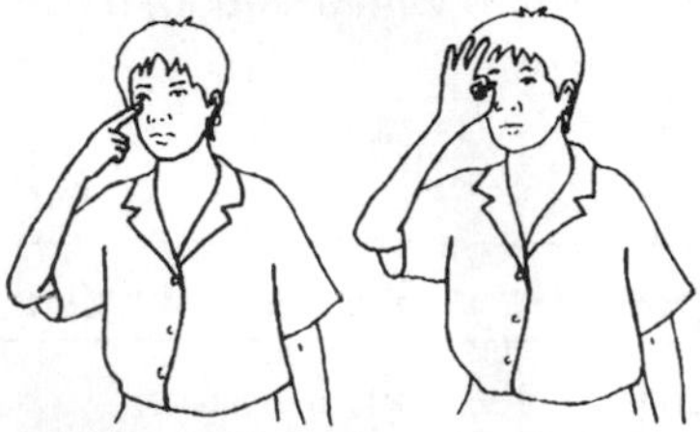

purchase *v.* See sign for BUY.

purple *n., adj.*
[Initialized sign] Shake the right *P hand,* palm facing down, back and forth in front of the right side of the body with a double movement.

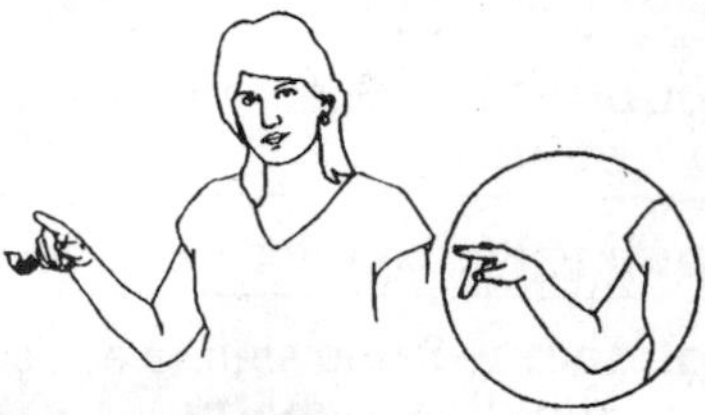

purpose *n.* See sign for MEAN[2].

purse *n.* Same sign used for: **pocketbook, suitcase.**
[Mime holding a purse] Shake the right *S hand,* palm facing left, up and down near the right side of the waist with the elbow bent.

pursue *v.* See sign for CHASE.

put *v.* Same sign used for: **install, mount, place, set.**
[The hands seem to take an object and put it in another location] Beginning with both *flattened O hands* in front

of the body, palms facing down, move the hands upward and forward in a small arc.

put down *v. phrase.* Same sign used for: **document, record**.

[The hand seems to put something on a list] Touch the fingertips of the right *flattened O hand,* palm facing down, to the palm of the left *open hand,* palm facing up. Then slap the palm of the right *open hand* against the left palm.

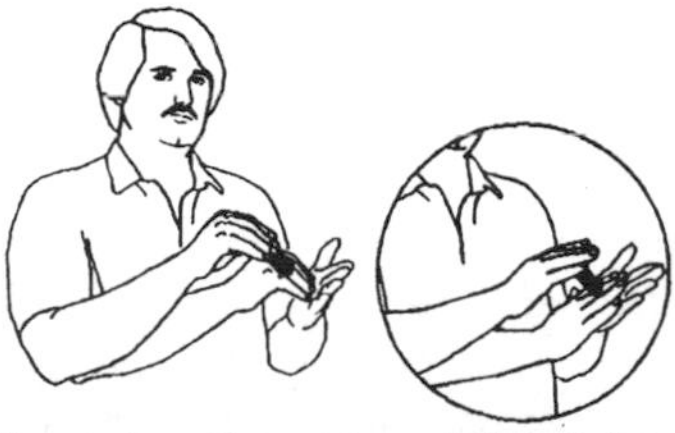

put off *v. phrase.* See sign for POSTPONE.

puzzled *adj.* Same sign used for: **bewildered, paradox, perplexed.**

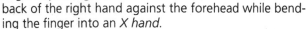

[Indicates a question in the mind] Beginning with the extended right index finger in front of the forehead, palm facing forward and finger angled up, bring the back of the right hand against the forehead while bending the finger into an *X hand.*

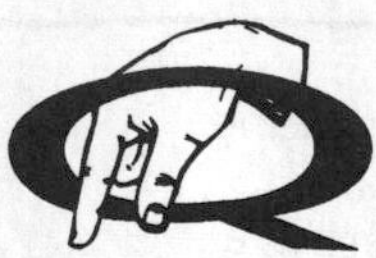

qualification *n.* Related form: **qualify.**

[Initialized sign similar to sign for **character**] Move the right *Q hand* in a small circle and then back against the right side of the chest, palm facing down.

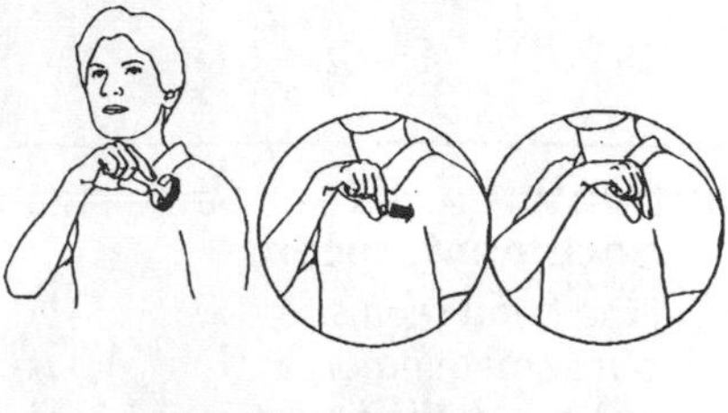

quarrel *v.* See sign for ARGUE.

quarter[1] *n.* Same sign used for: **twenty-five cents.**

[**cent** + **twenty-five**] Beginning with the extended right index finger touching the right side of the forehead, palm facing left and finger pointing up, twist the hand forward while changing into a *5 hand* with a wiggling bent middle finger, palm facing forward.

quarter[2] *n.* See sign for ONE FOURTH.

queer *adj.* See sign for STRANGE.

question *n., v.* See also sign for QUERY.

[Draw a question mark in the air] Move the extended right index finger from pointing forward in front of the right shoulder, palm facing down, downward with a curving movement while retracting the index finger and then pointing it straight forward again at the bottom of the curve.

queue *v.* See sign for LINE UP.

quick *adj., adv.* See sign for FAST. Related form: **quickly** *adv.*

quick-witted *adj.* See sign for SMART.

quiet *adj.* Same sign used for: **calm, calm down, passive, silence, silent, still, tranquil.**

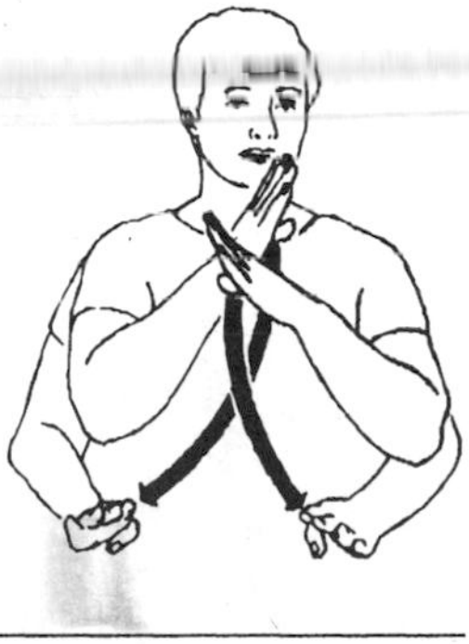

[Natural gesture requesting others to be quiet] Beginning with both *B hands* crossed in front of the upper chest, palms angled outward in either direction, bring the hands downward and outward, ending with both *B hands* in front of each side of the waist, palms facing down.

quiet down *v. phrase.* See sign for SETTLE.

quit[1] *v.*

[Formed with the opposite movement as **join**[1] and indicates withdrawing involvement with others] Beginning with the extended fingers of the right *H hand* inside the opening of the left *O hand* held in front of the body, palm facing right, bring the right hand upward, ending in front of the right shoulder, palm facing left and fingers pointing up.

quit[2] *v.* See signs for RESIGN, STOP[1].

quiz *n., v.* See sign for TEST.

quotation *n.* Related form: **quote** *n., v.* Same sign used for: **theme.**

[Natural gesture forming quotation marks in the air] Beginning with both *V hands* held near each side of the

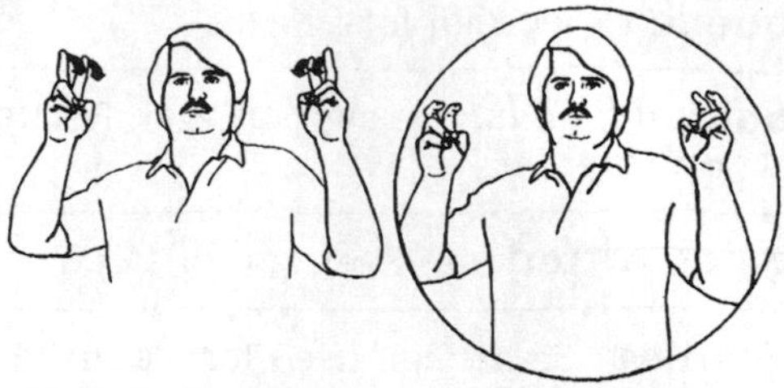

head, palms angled forward and fingers pointing up, bend the fingers downward with a double movement.

quotes *pl. n.* See sign for TITLE.

race *v.*
[The hands move back and forth as if in contention with each other in a race] With an alternating movement, move both *A hands* forward and back past each other quickly, palms facing each other in front of the body.

radiant *adj.* See sign for BRIGHT.

radio *n.*
[Represents radio headphones on the ears] With the fingers of the right *curved 5 hand* near the right ear, twist the hand forward with a double movement.

rage *n.* See sign for ANGER.

raid *v.* See sign for ROB.

railroad *n.* See sign for TRAIN.

rain *n., v.*
[Represents raindrops falling] Bring both *curved 5 hands,* palms facing down, from near each side of the head downward to in front of each shoulder with a double movement.

raise[1] *v.* Same sign used for: **get up, lift, rise.**

[Natural gesture of raising something] Beginning with both *open hands* in front of each side of the body, palms facing up, lift the hands upward to in front of each shoulder.

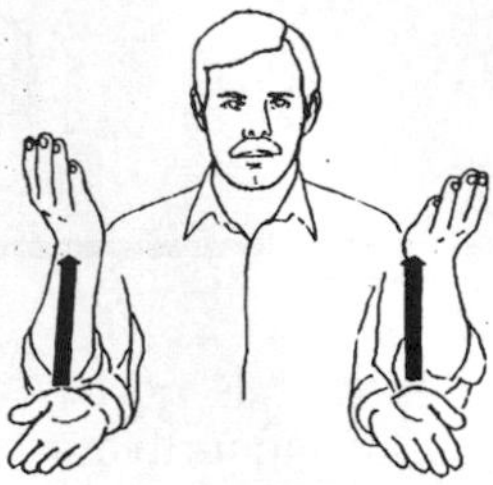

raise[2] *v.* See sign for GROW UP.

raise[3] *n.* See sign for INCREASE.

random *adj.* See signs for CIRCULATE, VARIETY.

range *n.* See sign for VARIETY.

rank *n.* See sign for PROMOTE.

rape *v.* See sign for STUCK.

rather *adv.* See signs for FAVORITE, PREFER[1].

rational *adj.* See sign for REASON.

rationale *n.* See sign for REASON.

razor *n.* See sign for SHAVE.

reach *v.* See sign for ARRIVE.

react *v.* See signs for ANSWER, REPORT. Related form: **reaction** *n.*

read *v.*

[Represents the movement of the eyes down a page to read it] Move the fingertips of the right *V hand,* palm facing down, from the fingertips to the heel of the left *open hand,* palm facing right.

ready *adj.* Related form: **readiness.**

[Initialized sign] Move both *R hands* from in front of the left side of the body, palms facing each other and fingers pointing forward, in a smooth movement to in front of the right side of the body.

real *adj.* Same sign used for: **actual, genuine.**

[Movement emphasizes validity of one's statement] Move the side of the extended right index finger from in front of the mouth, palm facing left and finger pointing up, upward and forward in an arc.

realize *v.* See sign for REASON. Related form: **realization** *n.*

really *adj.* See sign for TRUTH.

rear[1] *v.* See sign for GROW UP.

rear[2] *n.* See sign for BACK.

reason *n.* Related form: **reasonable** *adj.* Same sign used for: **rational, rationale, realization, realize.**

[Initialized sign similar to sign for **think**[1]] Move the fingertips of the right *R hand,* palm facing in, in a double circular movement in front of the right side of the forehead.

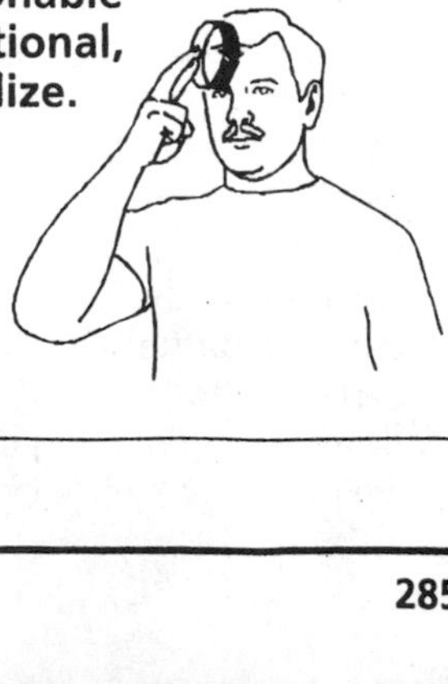

rebuke *v.* See sign for WARN.

receive *v.* See sign for GET.

recently[1] *adv.* Related form: **recent** *adj.* Same sign used for: **a while ago**.

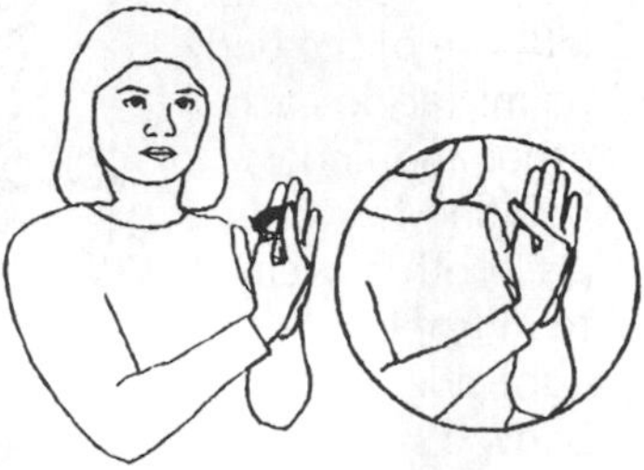

[Represents the minute hand on a clock moving a short distance into the past] With the little-finger side of the right *1 hand,* palm facing in and finger pointing up, against the palm of the left *open hand,* palm facing right and fingers pointing up, bend the extended right index finger back toward the chest with a double movement.

recently[2] *adv.* See sign for JUST.

recess *n.* See sign for REST[1].

reckless *adj.* See sign for CARELESS.

recognize *v.* See sign for NOTICE.

record[1] *n., v.* See sign for LIST.

record[2] *v.* See sign for PUT DOWN.

recover *v.*

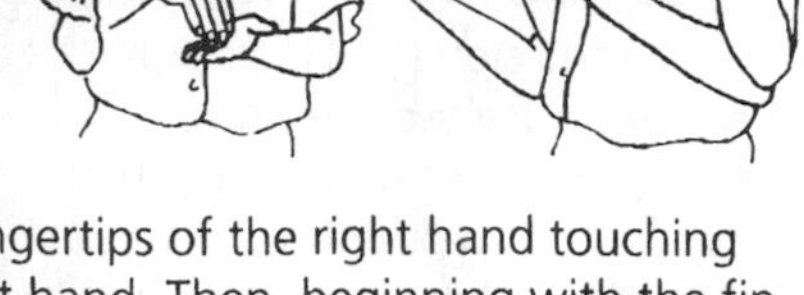

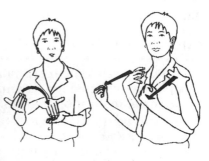

[**again** + **well**[1]] Beginning with the bent right hand beside the left *curved hand,* both palms facing up, bring the right hand up while turning it over, ending with the fingertips of the right hand touching the palm of the left hand. Then, beginning with the fingertips of both *curved 5 hands* touching each shoulder, palms facing in, bring the hands forward with a deliberate movement while closing into *S hands.*

red *adj.*

[Shows the redness of the lips] Bring the extended right index finger, palm facing in, from the lips downward with a short double movement.

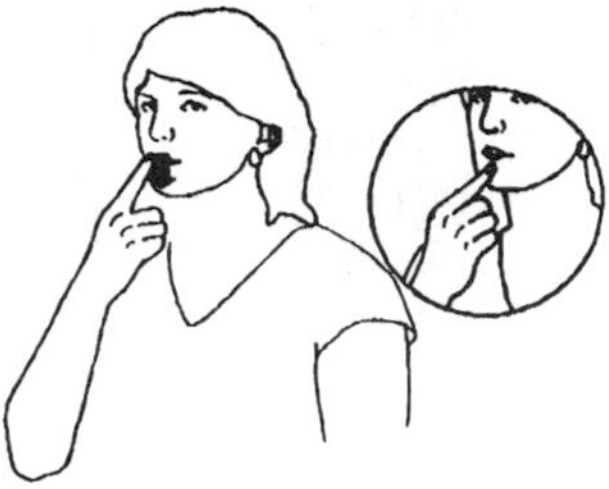

reduce *v.* See signs for BRIEF, DECREASE. Related form: **reduction** *n.*

refer *v.*

[Initialized sign] Beginning with the fingers of the right *R hand,* palm facing in, on the back of the left *open hand,* palm facing in, twist the right hand forward, ending with the right palm facing down.

reflect *v.* See sign for WONDER.

refresh *v.* See sign for COOL.

refrigerator *n.*

[Initialized sign similar to sign for **door**] Beginning with the thumb side of the right *R hand*, palm facing forward and fingers pointing up, against the palm side of the left *open hand*, palm facing right and fingers pointing up, move the right hand to the right in an arc while twisting the palm back in front of the right side of the chest.

refund *v., n.* Same sign used for: **come back, return.**

[Shows the direction that something takes in coming back to oneself] Beginning with both extended index fingers pointing up in front of the chest, palms facing in, bring the fingers back to point at each side of the chest, palms facing down.

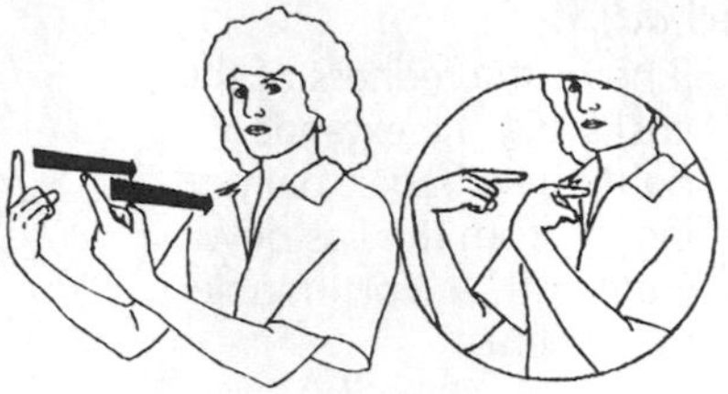

refuse *v.* See sign for WON'T.

register[1] *v.* Related form: **registration** *n.*

[Initialized sign similar to sign for **sign**[2]] Touch the fingertips of the right *R hand,* palm facing down, first to the heel and then to the fingertips of the palm of the left *open hand.*

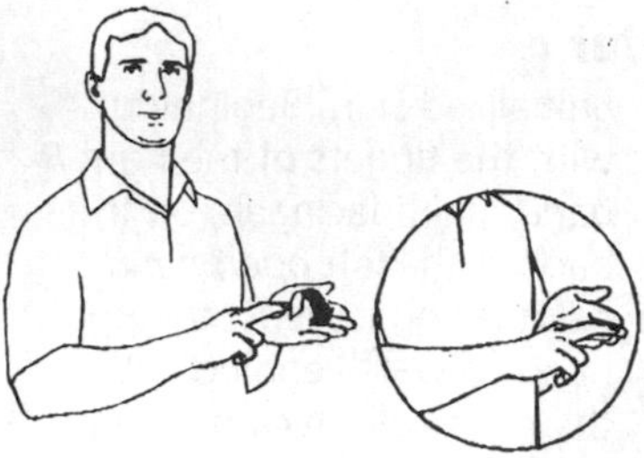

register[2] *v.* See sign for SIGN[2].

regret *n.* See sign for SORRY.

regular *adj.* Related form: **regularly** *adv.* Same sign used for: **appropriate, appropriately, promptly, proper, properly.**

[The fingers hit with regularity] With the right index finger extended, brush the little-finger side of the right hand, palm facing in, across the extended left index finger, palm facing in, as the right hand moves toward the chest in a double circular movement.

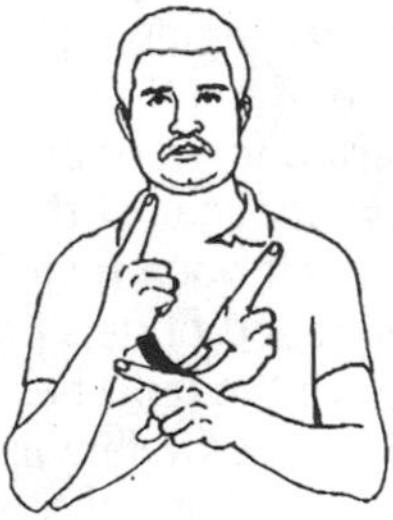

rehearse *v.* See sign for PRACTICE.

reign *v.* See sign for MANAGE.

reindeer *n.* See sign for DEER.

reiterate *v.* See sign for AGAIN.

reject *v.* Same sign used for: **turn down, veto.**

[Natural gesture indicating turning down something] Beginning with the right *10 hand* in front of the right shoulder, elbow extended and palm facing down, twist the wrist downward, ending with the thumb pointing down and the palm facing right.

rejoice *v.* See sign for CELEBRATE.

relate *v.* See sign for COORDINATE.

relationship *n.* Related form: **relate** *v.* Same sign used for: **ally, connection, link, tie.**

[Represents a link between two persons or things] With the thumbs and index fingers of both *F hands* intersecting, move the hands forward and back toward the chest with a double movement.

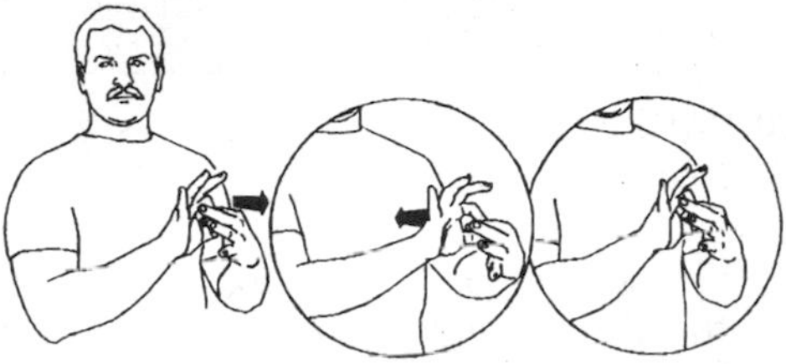

relax *v.* See signs for REST[1], SETTLE.

relief *n.* Related form: **relieved** *v.*

[Shows feeling being calmed in the body] With the index-finger sides of both *B hands* against the chest, left hand above the right hand, move the hands downward simultaneously.

relocate *v.* See sign for MOVE.

rely *v.* See sign for DEPEND.

remain *v.* See signs for CONTINUE[1], STAY.

remark *v.* See sign for SAY.

remarkable *adj.* See sign for WONDERFUL.

remarks *pl. n.* See sign for STORY.

remember *v.*

[Bringing a thought from the mind forward to examine it] Move the thumb of the right *10 hand* from the right side of the forehead, palm facing left, smoothly down to touch the thumb of the left *10 hand* held in front of the body, palm facing down.

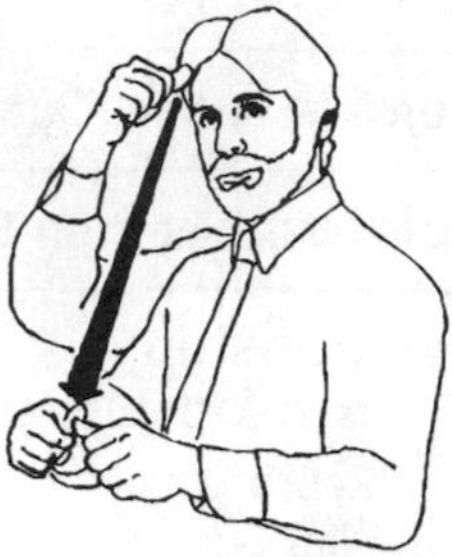

remind *v.*

[Natural gesture to tap someone to remind them of something] Tap the fingertips of the right *bent hand* with a double movement on the right shoulder, palm facing down.

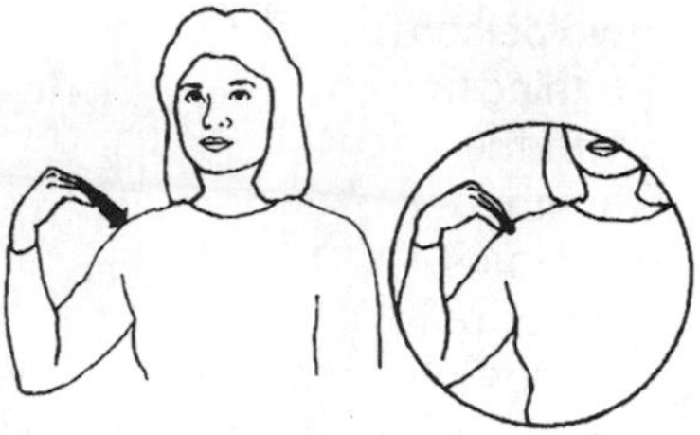

remodel *v.* See sign for IMPROVE[2].

remote *adj.* See sign for FAR.

remote control *n.*

[Mime operating a remote control with one's thumb] Bend the extended thumb of the right *10 hand,* palm facing in, up and down with a repeated movement in front of the right shoulder.

remove[1] *v.* Related form: **removal** *n.* Same sign used for: **abolish, abort, abortion.**

[Demonstrates picking something up and tossing it away to remove it] Bring the fingertips of the right *curved hand* against the palm of the left *open hand* while changing into an *A hand*, palms facing each other. Then move the right hand downward off the left fingertips while opening into a *curved 5 hand* in front of the right side of the body.

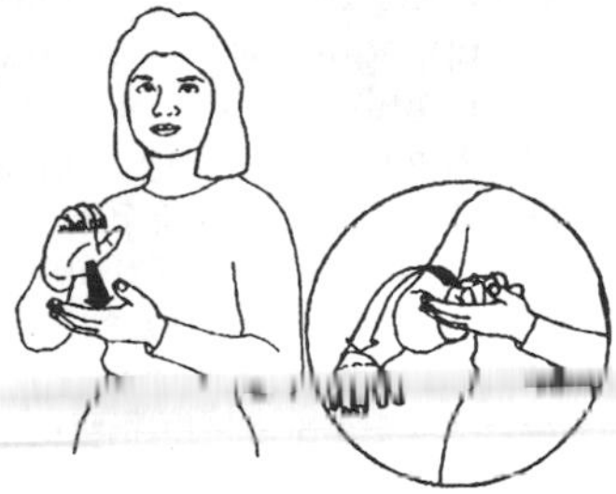

remove[2] *v.* See signs for ELIMINATE[1], TAKE OFF.

rent *v., n.*

[Initialized sign similar to sign for **month**] Move the middle finger side of the right *R hand,* palm facing down and fingers pointing left, downward with a double movement from the tip to the base of the extended left index finger, palm facing right and finger pointing up in front of the chest.

repair *v.* See sign for FIX.

repeat *v.* See sign for AGAIN.

repel *v.* See sign for ELIMINATE[1].

repent *v.* See sign for SORRY.

replace *v.* See sign for TRADE.

reply *n., v.* See signs for ANSWER, REPORT.

report *n., v.* Same sign used for: **react, reaction, reply, respond, response.**

[Initialized sign similar to sign for **answer**] Beginning with fingers of both *R hands* pointing up, right hand closer to the mouth than the left hand and the palms facing in opposite directions, move the hands forward and downward with a deliberate movement, ending with the palms facing down and fingers pointing forward.

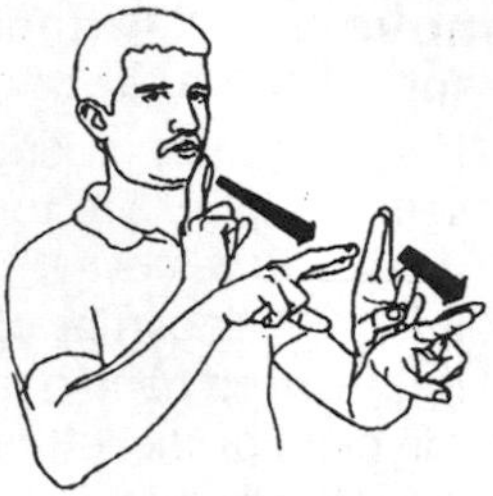

repossess *v.* See sign for CAPTURE.

request *v.* See sign for ASK.

require *v.* See sign for DEMAND.

reservation *n.* See sign for APPOINTMENT.

resign *v.* Same sign used for: **back out, draw back, drop out, quit.**

[Represents pulling one's legs out of a situation] Beginning with the fingers of the right *bent U hand,* palm facing down, in the opening of the left *O hand,* palm facing right, pull the right fingers out to the right.

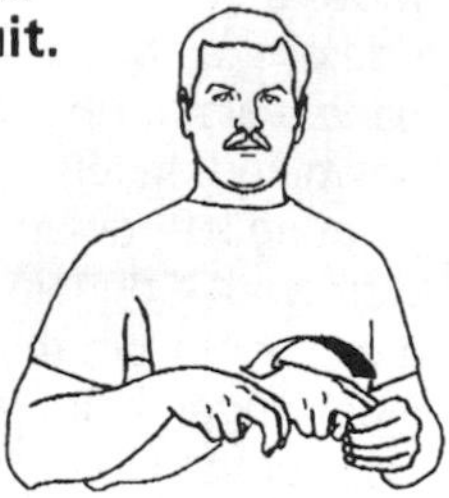

resist *v.* Same sign used for: **anti-, defensive, immune, uncertain.**

[Natural gesture for resisting something] Move the right *S hand,* palm facing down, from in front of the right side of the body outward to the right with a deliberate movement.

respiration *n.* See sign for BREATH.

respond *v.* See sign for REPORT. Related form: **response** *n.*

response *n.* See sign for ANSWER.

responsibility *n.* See sign for BURDEN. Related form: **responsible** *adj.*

rest[1] *v., n.* Same sign used for: **recess, relax.**

[Shows laying one's hands on one's chest as if in repose] With the arms crossed at the wrists, lay the palm of each open hand on the chest near the opposite shoulder.

rest[2] See sign for LEAVE[2].

restaurant *n.*

[Initialized sign similar to sign for **cafeteria**] Touch the fingers of the right *R hand,* palm facing in, first to the right and then to the left side of the chin.

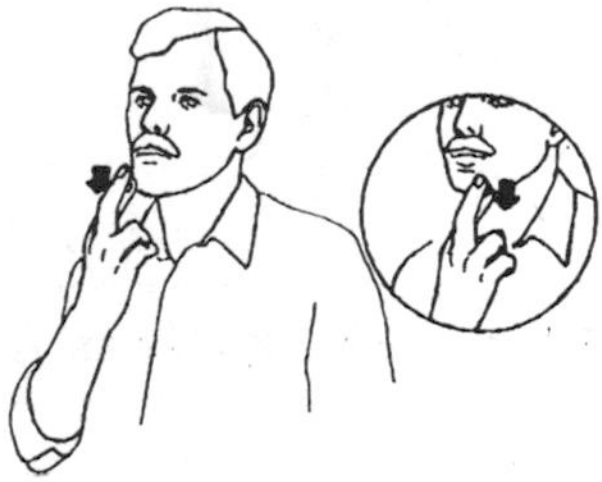

restless *adj.*

[Represents one's legs turning over restlessly during a sleepless night] With the back of the right *bent V hand* laying across the open left palm, both palms facing up, turn the right hand over and back with a double movement.

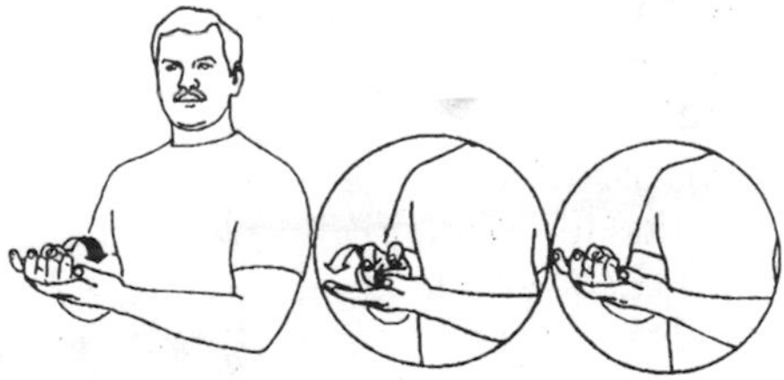

rest of See sign for AFTER[1].

restore *v.* See sign for SAVE[2].

restrain *v.* See sign for CONTROL[1]. Related form: **restraint** *n.*

rest room[1] *n.*
[Abbreviation **r-r**] Tap the right *R hand,* palm facing down and the fingers pointing forward, downward first in front of the right side of body and then again slightly to the right.

rest room[2] *n.* See sign for TOILET.

result *n.*
[Initialized sign similar to sign for **end**[1]] Move the fingertips of the right *R hand,* palm facing down, along the length of the index finger of the left *B hand,* palm facing in, and then down off the fingertips.

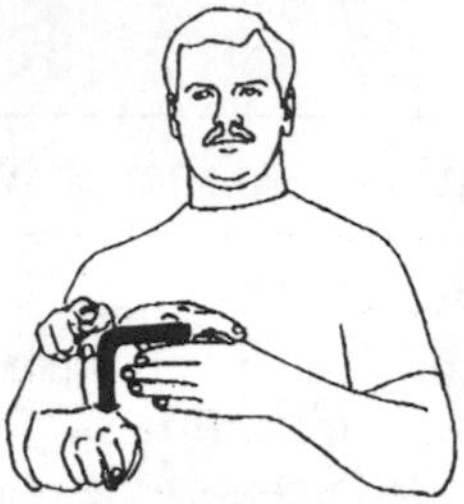

retail *v.* See sign for SELL.

retain *v.* See sign for SAVE[2].

retaliate *v.* See sign for REVENGE.

retire *v.*
[Initialized sign similar to sign for **holiday**] Touch the extended thumbs of both *R hands,* palms facing each other, against each side of the chest.

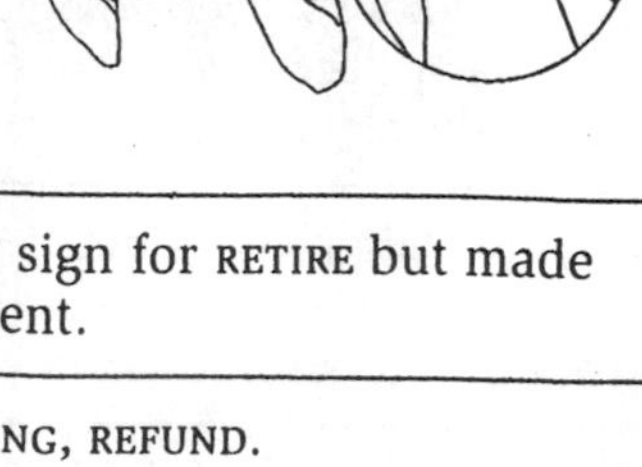

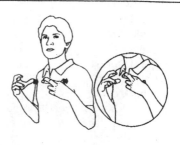

retirement *n.* Similar to sign for RETIRE but made with a double movement.

return *v.* See sign for BRING, REFUND.

reveal *v.* See signs for ANNOUNCE, TELL[1].

revenge *n.* Same sign used for: **avenge, get even, retaliate, vengeance.**

[Suggests two people striking each other] Beginning with both *modified X hands* in front of the chest, left hand above the right hand and palms facing each other, bring the right hand upward until the knuckles of both the hands touch.

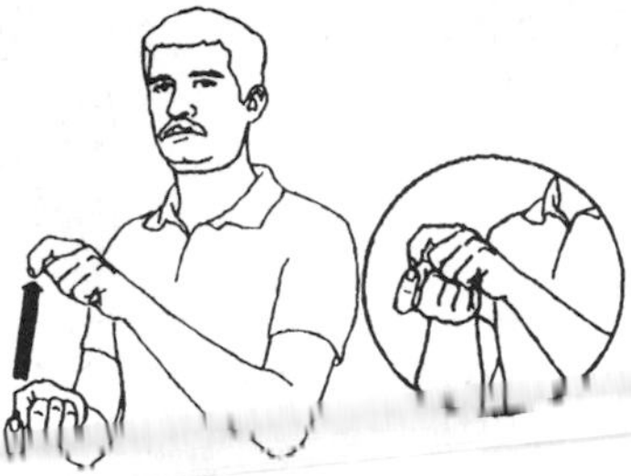

revenue *n.* See sign for INCOME[1].

reverberate *v.* See sign for BELL. Related form: **reverberation** *n.*

revoke *v.* See sign for TEAR.

reward *n.,v.* See sign for GIFT.

ribbon *n.* See sign for BOW[2].

rich *adj.* Same sign used for: **wealth.**

[Represents a pile of money in one's hand] Beginning with the little-finger side of the right *S hand,* palm facing left, in the open left palm held in front of the body, raise the right hand a short distance while opening into a *curved 5 hand,* palm facing down.

rid *v.* See sign for ELIMINATE[1].

ride in a car, truck, etc.

[Represents a person sitting in a vehicle] With the fingers of the right *bent U hand,* palm facing down, hooked over the thumb of the left *C hand,* palm facing right, move the hands forward from in front of the body.

ridiculous *adj.* See sign for SILLY.

right[1] *n., adj., adv.*

[Initialized sign showing a right direction] Move the right *R hand,* palm facing forward, from in front of the right side of the body to the right a short distance.

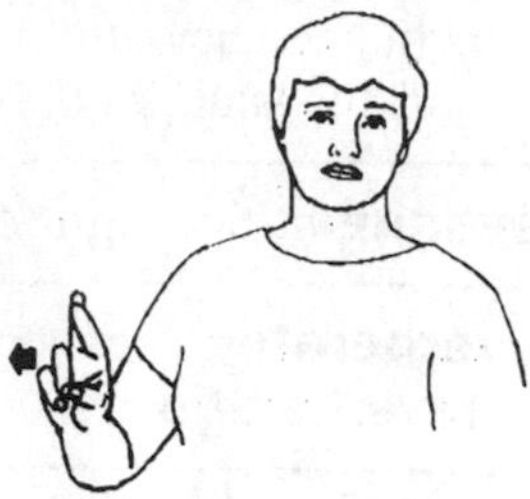

right[2] *n.* Same sign used for: **all right, privilege.**

[Shows the approved path] Slide the little-finger side of the right *open hand,* palm facing left, in an upward arc across the upturned left palm held in front of the body.

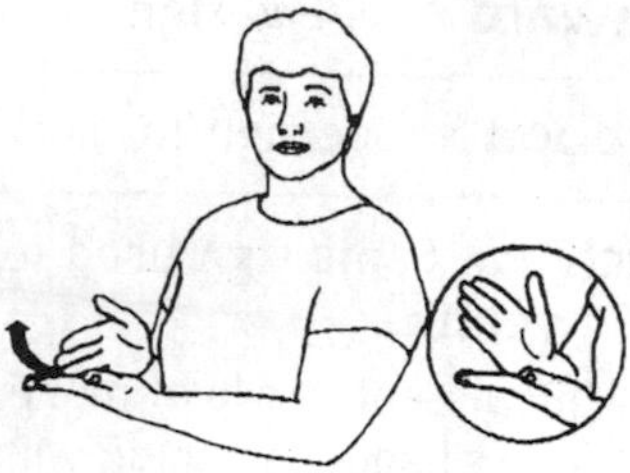

right[3] *adj.* Same sign used for: **accurate, correct.**

With the index fingers of both hands extended forward at right angles, palms angled in and right hand above left, bring the little-finger side of the right hand sharply down across the thumb side of the left hand.

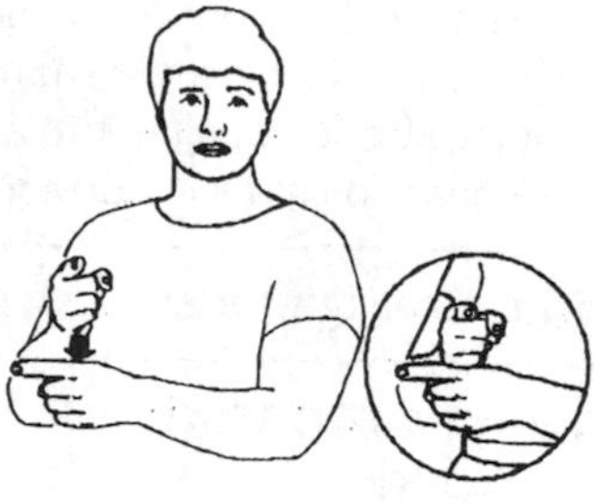

rigid *adj.* See sign for FREEZE.

ring *v., n.* See sign for BELL.

riot *v., n.* See signs for COMPLAIN, MESSY.

rip *v.* See sign for TEAR.

rise *v., n.* See sign for RAISE.

risk *n.* See sign for DANGER.

rival *n.* See sign for ENEMY.

river *n.*

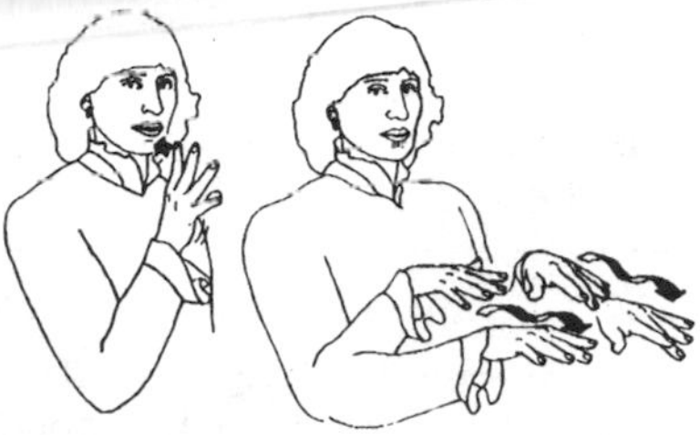

[**water** + a gesture showing the movement of waves] Tap the index-finger side of the right *W hand,* palm facing left, against the chin with a double movement. Then move both *5 hands,* palms facing down, forward from in front of the chest with an up-and-down wavy movement.

road *n.* Same sign used for: **path, route, street, way.**

[Indicates the shape of a road] Move both *open hands* from in front of each side of the body, palms facing each other, forward with a parallel movement.

roam *v.* Same sign used for: **adrift, wander.**

[Represents the aimless movement of a roaming person] Beginning with the extended right index finger pointing up in front of the right shoulder, palm facing forward, move the hand to in front of the chest and then outward again in a large arc.

roar *v., n.* See sign for SCREAM.

rob *v.* Related form: **robbery.** Same sign used for: **burglary, hold up, raid.**

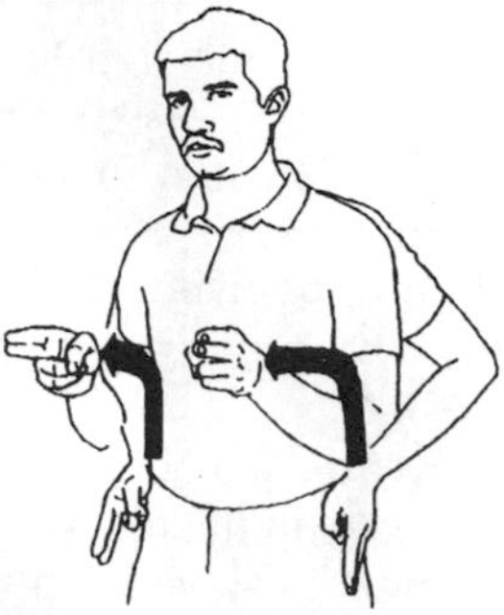

[Represents pulling out one's guns for a robbery] Beginning with both *H hands* in front of each side of the waist, palms facing each other and fingers pointing down, twist the wrists upward, bringing the hands up in front of each side of the body, palms facing each other and fingers pointing forward.

rock[1] *n.* Same sign used for: **stone.**

[Indicates the hardness of a rock] Tap the back of the right *S hand,* palm facing up, on the back of the left *S hand* held in front of the chest, palm facing down, with a repeated movement.

rock[2] *n.* See sign for METAL.

rod *n.* See signs for PIPE[1], STICK[2].

romp *v., n.* See sign for PLAY[1].

room *n.* See sign for BOX. Same sign used for: **package, present.**

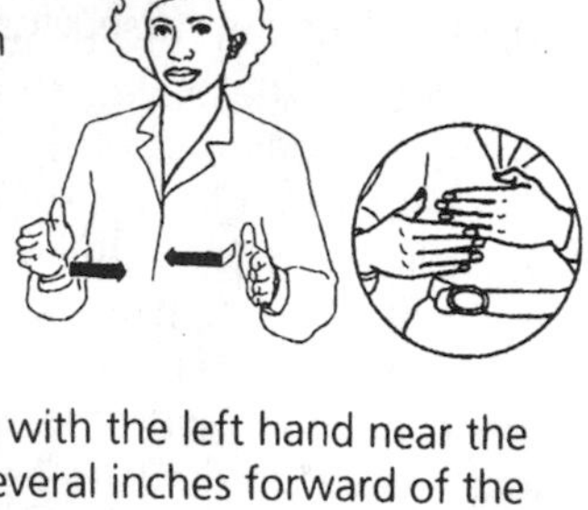

[Shows the four walls of a room] Beginning with both *open hands* in front of each side of the chest, palms facing each other and fingers pointing forward, move the hands in opposite directions by bending the wrists, ending with the left hand near the chest and the right hand several inches forward of the left hand, both palms facing in.

rot *v., n.* See sign for WEAR OUT. Related form: **rotten** *adj.*

rough *adj.* Same sign used for: **approximate, coarse, draft, estimate.**

[Indicates a rough, scratchy surface] Move the fingertips of the right *curved 5 hand,* palm facing down, from the heel to the fingertips of the upturned left *open hand* held in front of the body.

round[1] *n.*

[Initialized sign similar to sign for **circle**[1]] Move the extended fingers of the right *R hand* from pointing down in front of the body in a large flat circle in front of the body.

round[2] *adj.* See sign for CIRCLE[1].

route *n.* See sign for ROAD.

routine *n.* See sign for DAILY.

row[1] *n.*

[Represents legs sitting in a row] Beginning with the index–finger sides of both *bent V hands* touching in front of the body, palms facing down, move the hands apart to in front of each side of the body.

row[2] *n.* See sign for LINE UP.

royalty *n.* See sign for PENSION.

rub *v.* See signs for WASH, WIPE.

rude *adj.* See sign for MEAN[1].

ruin[1] *v.* Same sign used for: **spoil.**

[A ripping movement] Slide the little-finger side of the right *X hand,* palm facing left, across the index–finger side of the left *X hand,* palm facing right.

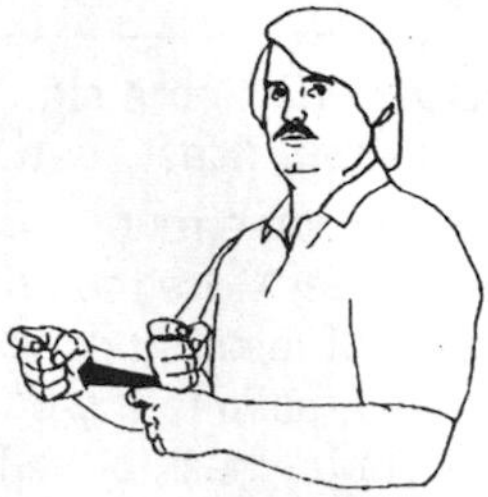

ruin[2] *v.* See sign for DAMAGE.

rule *v.* See sign for MANAGE.

rumor *n.* See sign for GOSSIP[1].

run[1] *v.*

[Represents one's legs moving when running] With the index finger of the right *L hand,* palm facing left and index finger pointing forward, hooked on the thumb of the left *L hand,* palm facing right and index finger pointing forward, move both hands forward.

run[2] *v.* See sign for LEAK[1].

run[3] *v.* Same sign used for: **operate.**

[Represents the smooth operation of an assembly line] Brush the palm of the right *open hand* upward with a double movement across the left *open hand,* palms facing each other and fingers pointing forward.

run[4] *v.* See sign for MACHINE.

run around *v. phrase.* Same sign used for: **fool around, tour, travel.**

[Shows movement in different directions] With the left extended index finger pointing up in front of the body and the right extended index finger pointing down above it, both palms facing in, move both hands in alternate circles in front of the body.

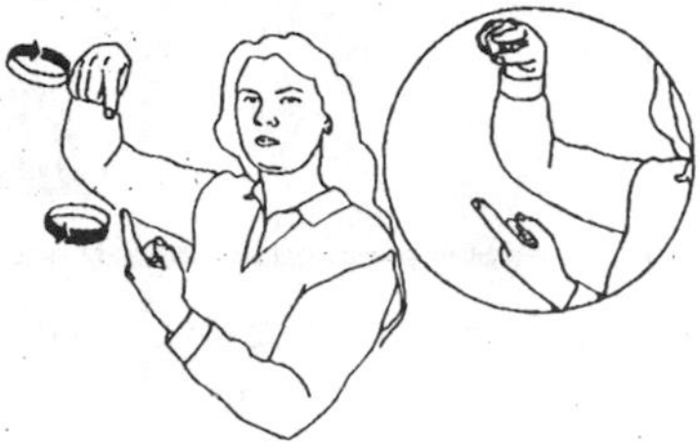

run away *v. phrase.* Same sign used for: **escape, get away, split** (*slang*).

[Represents one moving away quickly] Move the extended right index finger, palm facing left and finger pointing up, from between the index and middle fingers of the left *5 hand,* palm facing down in front of the chest, forward with a deliberate movement.

run out of *v. phrase.* Same sign used for: **all gone, deplete, use up.**

[Indicates grabbing everything so that nothing is left] Beginning with the little-finger side of the right *5 hand,* palm facing in, on the heel of the left *open hand,* palm facing up, bring the right hand forward to the left fingertips while changing into an *S hand.*

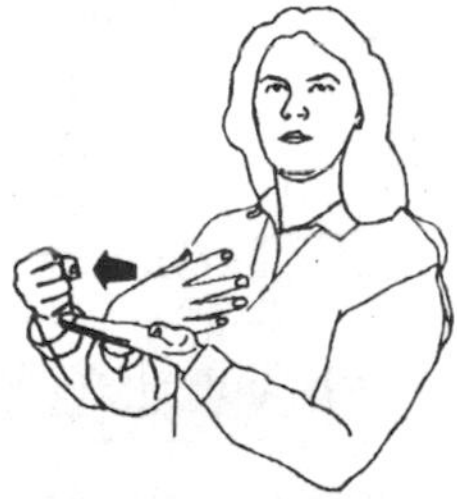

run over *v. phrase.* See sign for OVERFLOW.

rush *v., n.* See sign for HURRY.

sad *adj.* Same sign used for: **grave.**

[The hands seem to pull the face down to a sad expression] Move both *5 hands* from in front of each side of the face, palms facing in and fingers pointing up, downward a short distance.

safe *adj.* See sign for SAVE[1].

sail *n.* See sign for BOAT. Related form: **sailing** *n.*

salad *n.*

[Mime tossing a salad] Move both *curved hands,* palms facing up and fingers pointing toward each other, from in front of each side of the body toward each other with a double movement.

salary *n.* See signs for EARN, INCOME[1].

sale *n.* See sign for SELL.

salt *n.*

[Represents tapping out salt from a shaker on one's food] Alternately tap the fingers of the right *V hand* across the back of the fingers of the left *V hand,* both palms facing down.

salvation *n.* See sign for SAVE[1].

same *adj.* See sign for ALIKE, STANDARD.

sandwich *n.*

[Represents a sandwich being eaten] With the palms of both *open hands* together, right hand above left, bring the fingers back toward the mouth with a short double movement.

satisfy *v.* Related form: **satisfaction** *n.* Same sign used for: **appease, content, contentment.**

[A settling down of feelings] Beginning with both *B hands* in front of the chest, right hand above the left hand and both palms facing down, bring the index-finger sides of both hands against the chest.

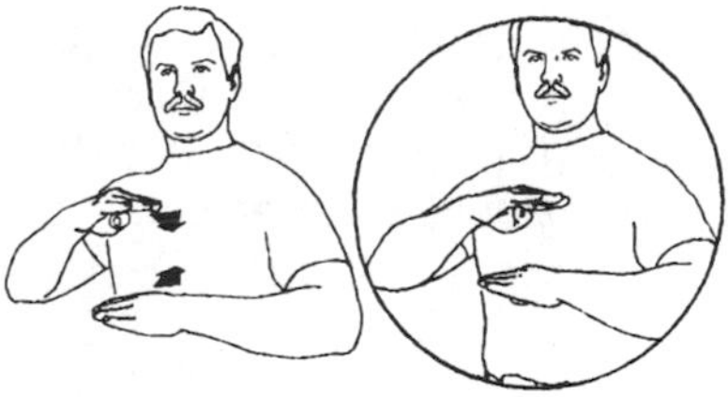

Saturday *n.*

[Initialized sign] Move the right *S hand,* palm facing back, in a small circle in front of the right shoulder.

save[1] *v.* Same sign used for: **free, freedom, liberate, liberty, safe, salvation, secure, security.**

[Initialized sign representing breaking the chains of captivity] Beginning with both *S hands* crossed at the wrists in front of the chest, palms facing in opposite directions, twist the wrists and move the hands apart, ending with the hands in front of each shoulder, palms facing forward.

save[2] *v.* Related form: **savings** *pl. n.* Same sign used for: **preservation, preserve, restore, retain, storage, store, stuff.**

[The *S hand* holds one's savings behind the bars of a bank cage] Tap the fingers of the right *V hand* with a double movement on the back of the fingers of the left *V hand,* both palms facing in.

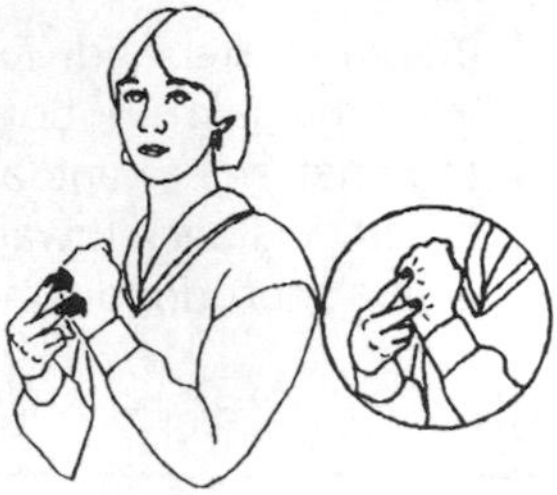

say *v.* Same sign used for: **comment, remark, remarks, state.**

[Points to where words are said] Tap the extended right index finger, palm facing in, on the chin with a double movement.

scalp *n.* See sign for BALD.

scant *adj.* See sign for TINY.

scared *adj.* See signs for AFRAID, FEAR.

scent *n., v.* See sign for SMELL.

schedule[1] *n.* Same sign used for: **chart, graph.**

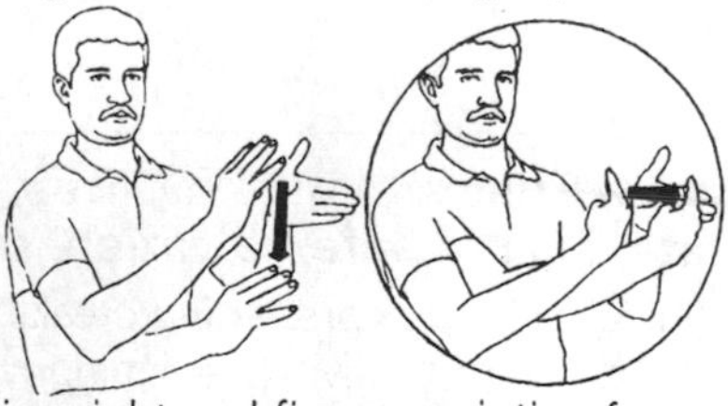

[Shows the rows and columns on a schedule] Beginning with the left *open hand* held in front of the left shoulder, palm facing right and fingers pointing forward, bring the fingers of the right *4 hand,* palm facing left, down the heel of the left hand, and then drag the back of the right fingers across the length of the left palm from the heel to the fingertips.

schedule[2] *n.* See signs for PLAN.

school *n.*
[A teacher claps for attention] Tap the fingers of right *open hand,* palm facing down, with a double movement on the upturned palm of left *open hand.*

scissors *n.*
[Mime cutting with scissors] Open and close the index and middle fingers of the right *V hand,* palm facing in and fingers pointing left, with a repeated movement.

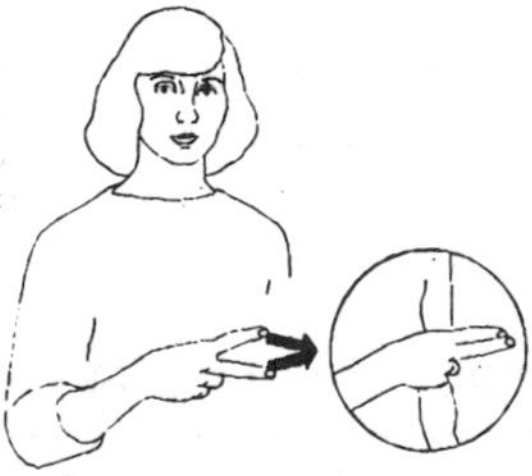

scold *v.* Same sign used for: **admonish.**
[Natural gesture for scolding someone] Move the extended right index finger from in front of the right shoulder, palm facing left and finger pointing up, forward with a double movement.

score *n., v.* See sign for LIST.

scramble *v.* See sign for MIX[1].

scream *v., n.* Same sign used for: **cry, roar, shout, yell.**
[The hand seems to take a loud sound from the mouth and direct it outward] Beginning with the fingers of the right *C hand* close to the mouth, palm facing in, bring the hand forward and upward in an arc.

scribble *v.* See sign for WRITE.

seal *n., v.* See sign for STAMP[2].

seal one's lips See sign for SHUT UP.

search for *v. phrase.* See sign for LOOK FOR.

seasoning *n.*

[Mime shaking seasoning on food] Shake the right *curved hand,* palm facing forward and fingers pointing left, downward in front of the chest with a double movement.

seat *n.* See sign for CHAIR.

second-hand *adj.* Same sign used for: **used.**

[Two fingers turned over, indicating a second use] Beginning with the right *L hand* in front of the right side of the chest, palm facing down and index finger pointing forward, twist the wrist up and down with a double movement.

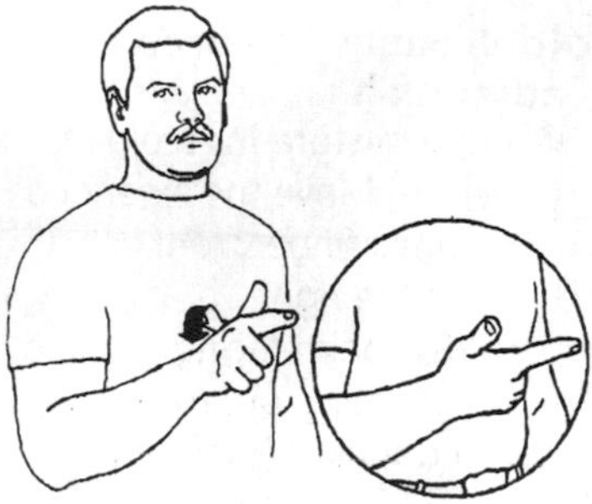

second the motion

[Two fingers waving for attention during a parliamentary procedure] Beginning with the right *L hand* in front of the right side of the head, palm facing left and index finger pointing up, move the hand deliberately forward while tipping the hand downward, ending with the index finger pointing forward.

secret *adj., n.* Same sign used for: **classified, confidential, privacy, private.**

[The movement seems to silence the lips to keep a secret] Tap the thumb side of the right *A hand,* palm facing left, against the mouth with a repeated movement.

secretary *n.*

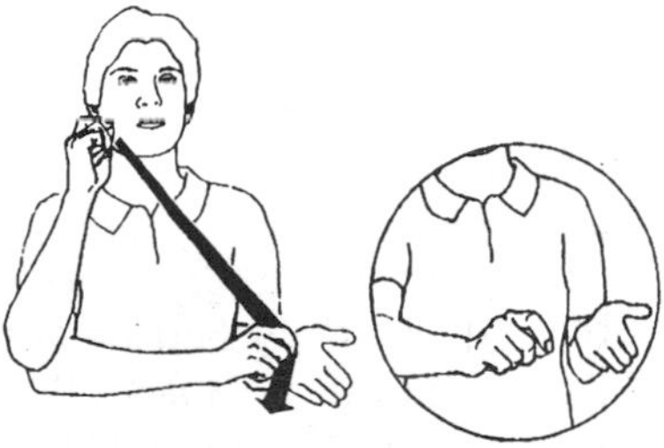

[The hand seems to take words from the mouth and write them on paper] Bring the right *modified X hand* from near the right side of the chin downward across the palm of the left *open hand* from the heel to off the fingertips.

section *n.* See signs for CLASS, PART[1].

secure *v.* See sign for SAVE[1]. Related form: **security** *n.*

security *n.* See signs for DEFEND, POLICE, SAVE[1].

see *v.* Same sign used for: **sight, visualize.**

[The fingers follow the direction of vision from the eyes] Bring the fingers of the right *V hand* from pointing at the eyes, palm facing in, forward a short distance.

seem *v.* Same sign used for: **apparently, appear, look like.**

[Looking in a mirror] Beginning with the right *open hand* near the right shoulder, palm facing forward and fingers pointing up, turn the hand so the palm faces back.

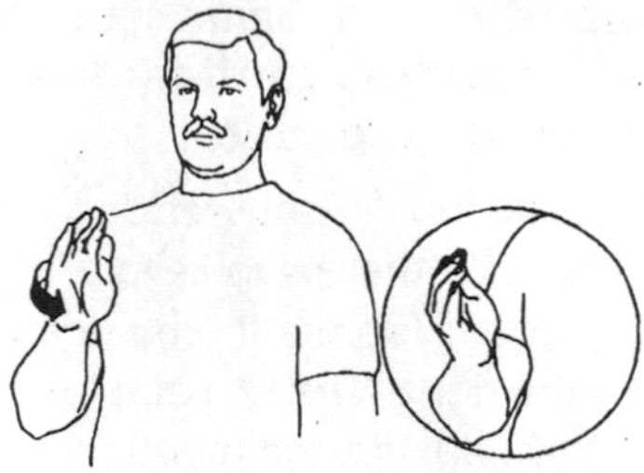

segment *n.* See sign for PART[1].

seize *v.* See sign for CAPTURE.

seldom *adv.*
[**once** formed with a rhythmic repeated movement] Bring the extended right index finger, palm facing in, downward against the upturned palm of the left *open hand* and then swing it upward in a slow upward arc with a double movement.

select *v.* See signs for APPOINT, CHOOSE.

self *n.* See sign for OWN.

selfish *n.* See sign for GREEDY.

sell *v.* Same sign used for: **distribute, merchandise, peddle, retail, sale.**
[The hands seem to hold something out for inspection in order to sell it] Beginning with both *flattened O hands* held in front of each side of the chest, palms facing down and fingers pointing down, swing the fingertips forward and back by twisting the wrists upward with a double movement.

send *v.* See sign for MAIL[1].

send out *v. phrase.* See sign for MAIL[1].

sensation *n.* See sign for FEEL.

sense *v., n.* See signs for FEEL, MIND.

sentence *n.* Same sign used for: **statement.**

[Represents stretching out words into a sentence] Beginning with the thumbs and index fingers of both *F hands* touching in front of the chest, palms facing each other, pull the hands apart with a wiggly movement, ending in front of each side of the chest.

separate *v., adj.* Related form: **separation** *n.*

[Things pulled apart] Beginning with the knuckles of both *A hands* touching in front of the chest, palms facing in, bring the hands apart.

series *n.* See sign for CLASS.

serious *adj.* Same sign used for: **severe.**

[Drilling a serious point in] With the extended right index finger touching the chin, palm facing left, twist the right hand, ending with the palm facing back.

serve *v.* Related form: **service** *n.* Same sign used for: **host.**

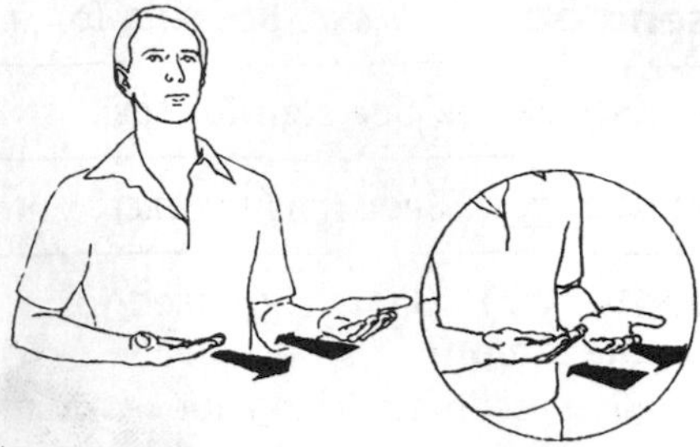

[The hands seem to carry something to serve it] Beginning with both *open hands* in front of each side of the body, palms facing up and right hand closer to the body than the left, move the hands forward and back with an alternating movement.

set *v.* See sign for PUT.

set off *v. phrase.* See sign for ZOOM.

settle or **settle down** *v.* Same sign used for: **calm, calm down, quiet down, relax.**

[Natural gesture for calming someone down] Beginning with both *5 hands* in front of each side of the chest, palms facing down, move the hands slowly down to in front of each side of the waist.

several *adj.* See sign for FEW.

severe *adj.* See sign for SERIOUS.

sex *n.* Related form: **sexual** *adj.*

[Denotes the male and female areas of the head] Touch the index-finger side of the right *X hand,* first to near the right eye and then to the lower chin, palm facing forward.

sham *n.* See sign for FAKE.

shame *n.* See sign for ASHAMED. Related form: **shameful** *adj.*

shape *n.* Same sign used for: **form, image.**

[The hands outline the image of a shape] Beginning with both *10 hands* in front of each side of the chest, palms facing forward, bring the hands downward with a wavy movement, ending in front of each side of the waist.

share *v.* Same sign used for: **change.**

[The hand moves back and forth as if to share a portion of something] Move the little-finger side of the right *open hand,* palm facing in, back and forth with a double movement at the base of the index finger of the left *open hand,* palm facing in.

sharp *adj.* Same sign used for: **keen.**

[Feeling something sharp] Flick the bent middle finger of the right *5 hand,* palm facing down, forward off the back of the left *open hand* held in front of the body.

shave *v.* Same sign used for: **razor.**

[Represents holding a hand razor to shave] Move the knuckles of the right *Y hand,* palm facing left, downward on the right cheek with a repeated movement.

she *pron.* See sign for HE.

shed *v.* See sign for BLOOD.

sheriff *n.* See sign for POLICE.

shield *v.* See sign for DEFEND.

shift *v.* See sign for CHANGE[1].

shiny *adj.* Related form: **shine** *n., v.* Same sign used for: **glitter, glossy, glow, sparkle.**

[Indicates the glare reflecting off something shiny] Beginning with the bent middle finger of the right *5 hand,* palm facing down, touching the back of the left *open hand,* palm facing down, bring the right hand upward in front of the chest with a wiggly movement.

ship *n.* See sign for BOAT.

shirk *v.* See sign for AVOID.

shirt *n.*

[Indicates the location of a shirt] Pull a small portion of clothing from the upper right chest forward with the fingers of the right *F hand,* palm facing in, with a double movement.

shiver *v., n.* See sign for COLD[2].

shoe *n.*

[Represents clicking the heels of shoes together] Tap the index-finger sides of both *S hands* together in front of the chest with a double movement, palms facing down.

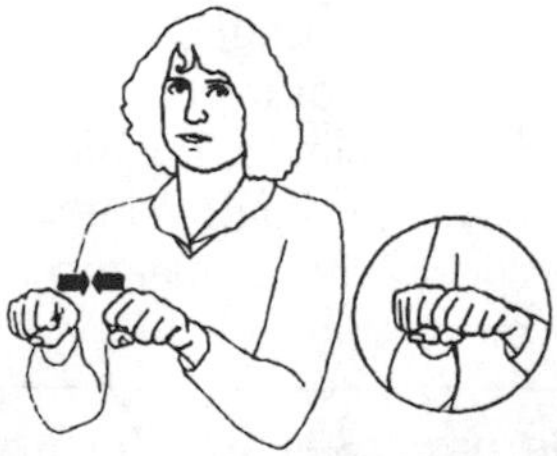

shoot *v.* See sign for TAKE PICTURES.

shop[1] *v.* Related form: **shopping** *n.*

[The hand takes money and gives it in payment] Beginning with the back of the right *flattened O hand,* palm facing up, across the palm of the left *open hand,* palm facing up, move the right hand forward and slightly upward with a double movement.

shop[2] *n.* See sign for STORE.

shoplift *v.* See sign for STEAL.

short[1] *adj.* Related form: **shortage** *n.* See also sign for BRIEF[1]. Same sign used for: **soon, temporary.**

[The fingers measure off a short distance] Rub the middle-finger side of the right *H hand,* palm angled left, back and forth with a repeated movement on the index-finger side of the left *H hand,* palm angled right.

short[2] *adj.* See signs for LITTLE[1], THIN[1].

shortly *adv.* See sign for SOON[1].

should *auxiliary v.* See sign for NEED.

shout *v.* See sign for SCREAM.

show[1] *v.* Same sign used for: **demonstrate, example, expose, indicate, indication, portray.**

[The finger points to something in the hand and moves it to show it to someone else] With the extended right index finger, palm facing in, touching the open left palm, move both hands forward a short distance.

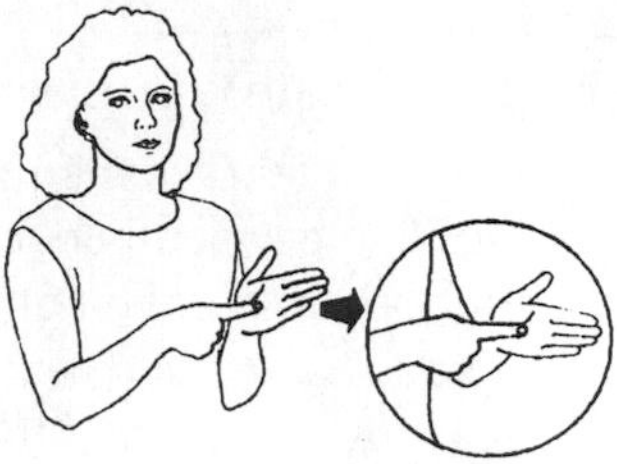

show[2] *v.* (*alternate sign, used when something is shown to many people*) Same sign used for: **exhibit.**

[Represents showing something around to many people] With the extended right index finger, palm facing in, touching the open left palm, move both hands in a flat circle in front of the body.

show[3] *n.* See sign for ACT[2], FILM.

shower *n., v.*

[Represents water coming down from a shower head] Beginning with the right *O hand* above the right side of the head, palm facing down, open the fingers into a *5 hand* with a double movement.

show off *v. phrase.* See sign for BRAG.

show up *v. phrase.* Same sign used for: **appear, come up, incident, materialize, occur, pop up, surface, turn up.**

[Represents something popping up into sight] Push the extended right index finger, palm angled left, upward between the index finger and middle finger of the left *open hand,* palm facing down.

shrink *v.* See sign for [illegible]

shut up *v. phrase.* Same sign used for: **keep quiet, seal one's lips.**

[Represents closing one's mouth to shut it up] Beginning with the thumb of the *flattened C hand* touching the chin, palm facing in, close the fingers to the thumb, forming a *flattened O hand.*

shy *adj.* See sign for ASHAMED.

sick *adj.* Related form: **sickness** *n.* Same sign used for: **ill, illness, malady.**

[The finger used to indicate feeling touches the forehead to show that a person doesn't feel well] Touch the bent middle finger of the right *5 hand,* palm facing in, to the forehead.

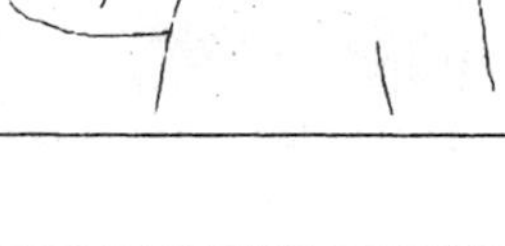

sight *n.* See sign for SEE.

sign[1] *v., n.*

[Represents one's hands moving when using sign language] Beginning with both extended index fingers pointing up in front of each side of the chest, palms facing forward and the left hand higher than the right hand, move the hands in large alternating circles toward the chest.

sign[2] *v.* Same sign used for: **register.**

[Represents placing one's name on a piece of paper] Place the extended fingers of the right *H hand*, palm facing down, firmly down on the upturned palm of the left *open hand* held in front of the chest.

---

sign[3] *n.* See sign for SQUARE.

---

signature *n.* Same sign as for SIGN[2] but made with a double movement.

---

significant *adj., n.* See sign for IMPORTANT. Related form: **significance** *n.*

---

silence *n.* See sign for QUIET.

---

silent *adj.* Same sign used for: **calm, calm down, mute, quiet, still.**

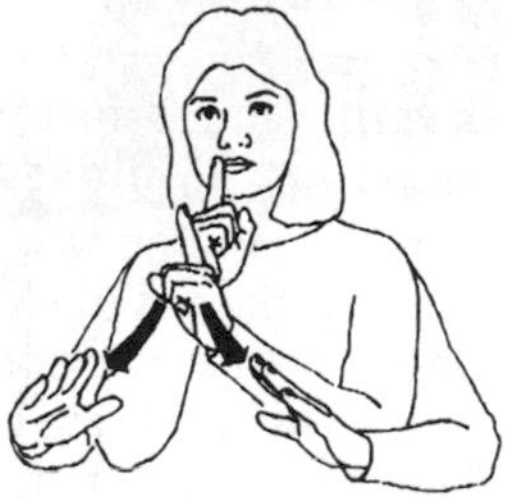

[The fingers seem to silence the mouth, and the hands move down as if to show quiet] Beginning with both extended index fingers pointing up in front of the mouth, right hand closer to the face than the left hand and palms facing in opposite directions, bring the hands downward and outward, ending with both *open hands* in front of each side of the chest, palms angled down.

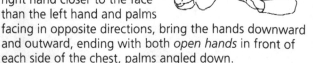

silly *adj.* Same sign used for: **ridiculous.**

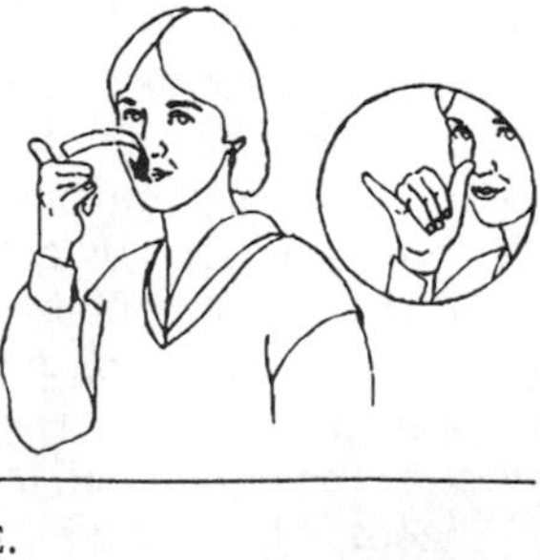

[Looking past something worthless] Beginning with the right *Y hand* in front of the face, palm facing in, twist the wrist outward with a double movement, brushing the right thumb across the nose with each movement.

---

similar *adj.* See signs for ALIKE.

simple[1] *adj.*

[A simple movement] Beginning with both *F hands* in front of the body, right hand higher than the left hand and palms facing in opposite directions, bring the right hand down, striking the fingertips of the left hand as it passes.

simple[2] *adj.* See sign for EASY.

sin *n., v.* Same sign used for: **trespass.**

[The fingers move in opposition to each other as do good and evil] Beginning with both extended index fingers angled upward in front of each side of the chest, palms facing in, move the hands toward each other in double circular movement.

since[1] *prep.* Same sign used for: **been, ever since, lately.**

[Shows passage of time from the past to the present] Move the extended index fingers of both hands from touching the upper right chest, palms facing in, forward in an arc, ending with the index fingers angled forward and the palms angled up.

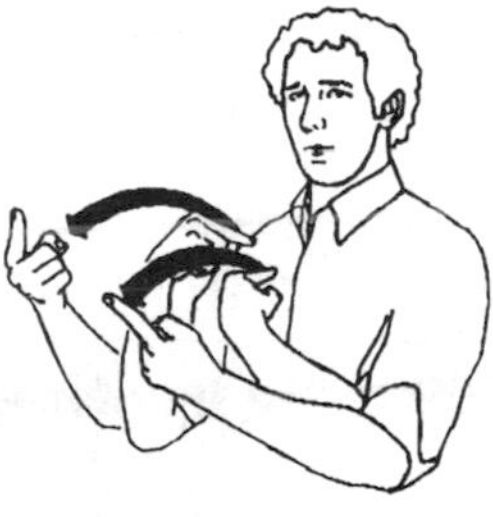

since[2] *conj.* See sign for BECAUSE.

sing *v.* See sign for MUSIC.

sister *n.*

[The female area of the head plus a sign similar to **same** indicating a girl in the same family] Beginning with the thumb of the right *L hand* touching the right side of the chin, palm facing left, move the right hand downward, ending with the little-finger side of the right *L hand* across the thumb side of the left *L hand* held in front of the chest, palms facing right.

sit *v.*
[The bent fingers represent one's legs dangling from the edge of a seat] Hook the fingers of the right *curved U hand,* palm facing down, perpendicular to the fingers of the left *U hand* held in front of the chest, palm facing down and fingers pointing right.

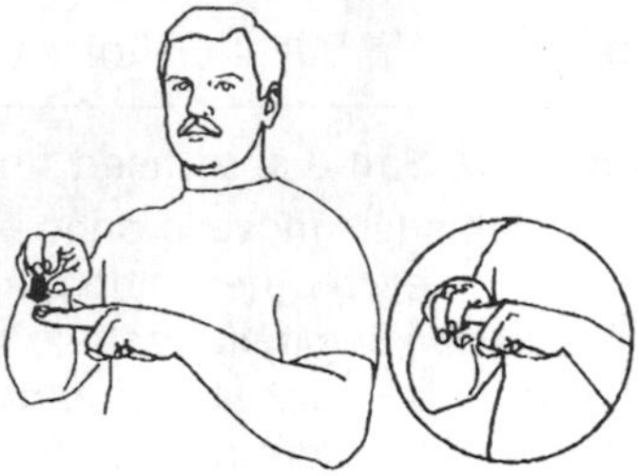

size[1] *n.*
[The hands seem to measure out a size] Beginning with the thumbs of both *Y hands* touching in front of the chest, palms facing down, bring the hands apart to in front of each side of the chest.

size[2] *n.* See sign for MEASURE.

sketch *n.* See sign for ART.

skill *n.* Related form: **skilled** *adj.* Same sign used for:
ability, able, agile, capable, efficient, enable, expert, handy, proficient, talent.
[The edge of the hand is honed as are skills] Grasp the little-finger side of the left *open hand* with the curved right fingers. Then pull the right hand forward while closing the fingers into the palm.

skip *v.* See also sign for ABSENT. Same sign used for: **lack, miss.**

[Points out the hiding finger] Beginning with the left *5 hand* held across the chest, middle finger bent downward, move the extended right index finger, palm facing left and finger pointing forward, from right to left in front of the chest, hitting the bent left middle finger as it passes.

skirt *n.*

[The location of a skirt] Brush the thumbs of both *5 hands,* palms facing in and fingers pointing down, from the waist downward and outward with a repeated movement.

slacks *pl. n.* See sign for PANTS.

slaughter *v.* See sign for KILL.

sleep *v., n.* Same sign used for: **doze, slumber.**

[The hand brings the eyes and face down into a sleeping position] Bring the right *open hand,* palm facing left and fingers point up, in against the right cheek.

slim *adj.* See sign for DIET.

slothful *adj.* See sign for LAZY.

slow *adj.* Related form: **slowly** *adj.*

[Demonstrates a slow movement] Pull the fingertips of

the right *5 hand,* palm facing down, from the fingers toward the wrist of the back of the left *open hand,* palm facing down.

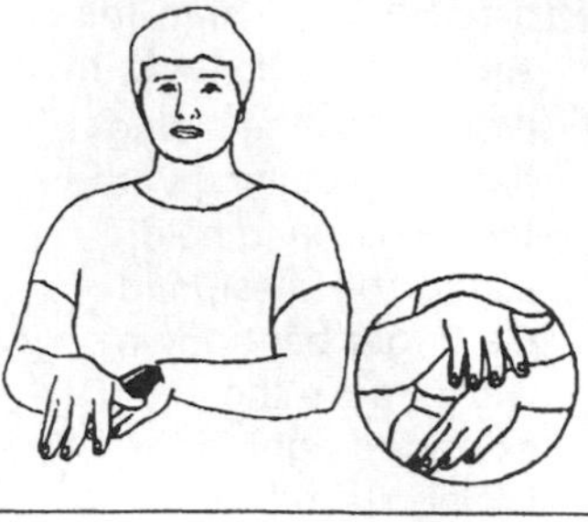

slumber *n.* See sign for SLEEP.

small *adj.* See also signs for LITTLE[1], TINY. Same sign used for: **meager, mini.**

[Shows a small size] Beginning with both *open hands* in front of each side of the chest, palms facing each other and fingers pointing forward, bring the palms close to each other in front of the chest.

smart *adj.* See also sign for SCHOLARLY. Same sign used for: **brilliant, clever, intelligence, intelligent, quick-witted.**

[Indicates brightness coming from the brain] Bring the bent middle finger of the right *5 hand* from touching the forehead, palm facing in, forward with a wavy movement.

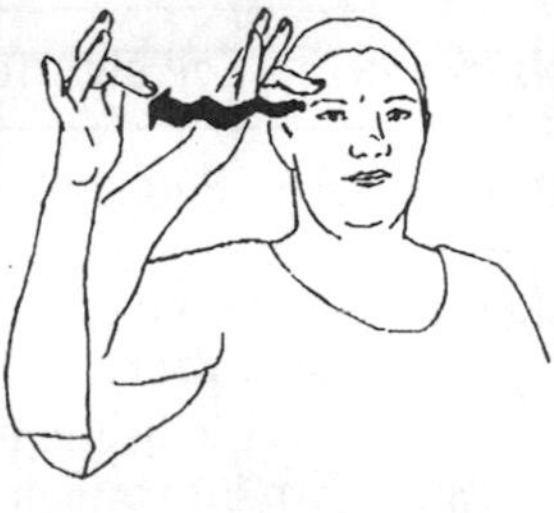

smell *v., n.* Same sign used for: **fragrance, fume, odor, scent.**

[Represents bringing something from in front of the nose to smell it] Brush the fingers of the right *open hand,* palm facing in, upward in front of the nose with a double movement.

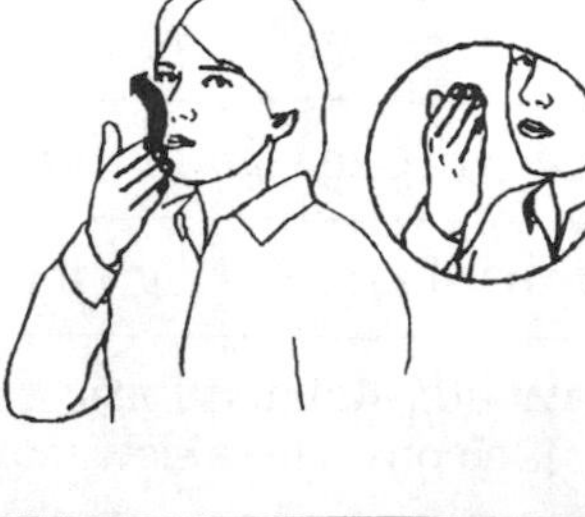

smile *v., n.* Same sign used for: **grin.**

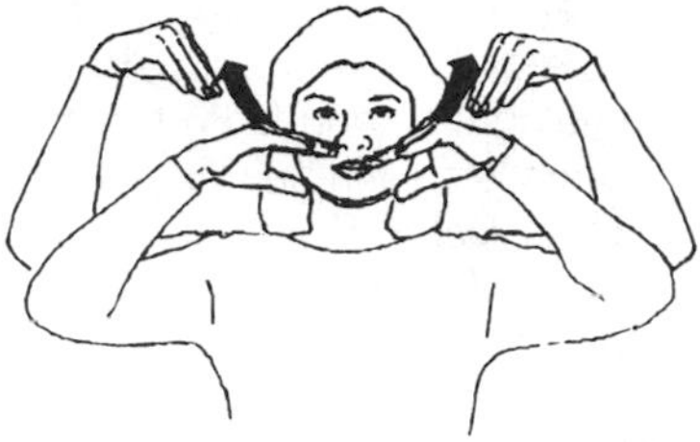

[The shape of the mouth when smiling] Beginning with both *flattened C hands* near each side of the mouth, palms facing each other, pull the fingers back and upward past each cheek in the shape of a smile while pinching the fingers together, forming *flattened O hands* near each side of the head, palms facing down.

---

smoke[1] *v.* Related form: **smoking** *n.*

[Mime smoking a cigarette] Beginning with the fingers of the right *V hand* touching the right side of the mouth, palm facing in, bring the hand forward with a double movement.

---

smoke[2] *n.*

[Shows the movement of smoke upward from a fire] Beginning with the right *curved 5 hand* above the left *curved 5 hand,* palms facing each other in front of the chest, move the hands in repeated flat circles in opposite directions.

---

smooth *adj.*

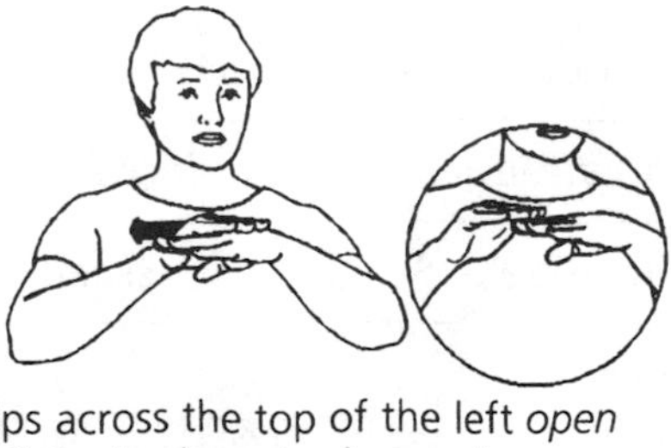

[Demonstrates a smooth flat surface] Move the fingers of the right *open hand,* palm facing down, from the wrist to the fingertips across the top of the left *open hand* held in front of the body, palm facing down.

snack *v., n.*

[Demonstrates picking up a snack to eat it] Move the fingertips of the right *F hand* from touching the open left palm held in front of the chest, palms facing each other, upward to the mouth with a double movement.

snoop *v.* See sign for NOSY.

snow *n.,v.*

[Represents snow on one's shoulder + the movement of snow falling] Beginning with the fingers of both *5 hands* touching each shoulder, palms facing down, turn the hands forward and bring the hands slowly down to in front of each side of the body while wiggling the fingers as the hands move.

soap *n.*

[Represents rubbing soap on one's hands] Wipe the fingers of the right *bent hand* on the palm of the left *open hand* from the fingers to the heel with a double movement, bending the right fingers back into the palm each time.

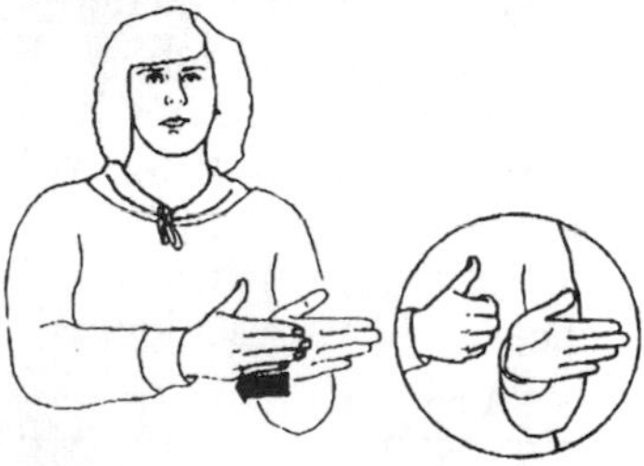

so-called *adj.* See sign for TITLE.

socialize *v.* See sign for ASSOCIATE.

sock *n.*

[Suggests needles used for knitting socks] Rub the sides of both extended index fingers back and forth with an alternating movement, palms facing down and fingers pointing forward in front of the body.

soda pop *n.* Alternate forms: **soda, pop.** Same sign used for: **soft drink.**

[Represents recapping a soda pop bottle] Insert the bent middle finger of the right *5 hand,* palm facing down, into the hole formed by the left *O hand,* palm facing right. Then slap the right *open hand,* palm facing down, sharply on the thumb side of the left *O hand.*

soft *adj.* Same sign used for: **gentle, mellow, tender.**

[The hands seem to feel something soft] Beginning with both *curved 5 hands* in front of each side of the chest, palms facing up, bring the hands down with a double movement while closing the fingers to the thumbs each time.

softball *n.* See sign for BASEBALL.

soft drink *n.* See sign for SODA POP.

soil *n.* See sign for DIRT.

soiled *adj.* See sign for DIRTY.

solely *adv.* See sign for ALONE.

solid *adj.* See signs for HARD[1], STRONG[1], STURDY[1].

solidify *v.* See sign for FREEZE.

some *adj.* Same sign used for: **part.**

[The hand seems to divide an object] Pull the little-finger side of the right *bent hand,* palm facing left, across the palm of the left *open hand,* palm facing up and fingers pointing forward.

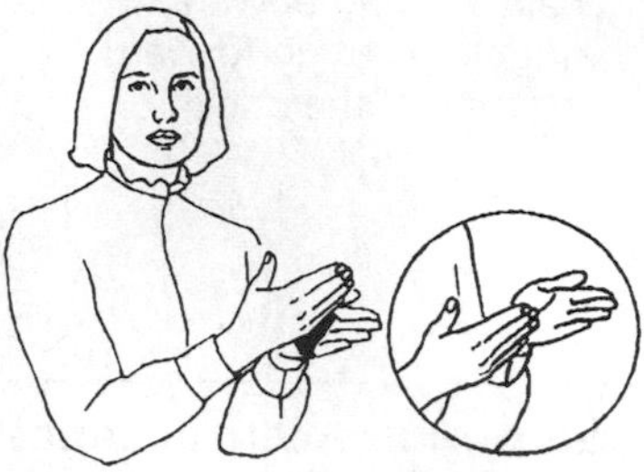

sometimes *adv.* Same sign used for: **occasional.**

[Similar to sign for **once** except repeated to indicate reoccurrence] Bring the extended right index finger, palm facing in, downward against the upturned palm of the left *open hand* and up again in a rhythmic repeated circular movement.

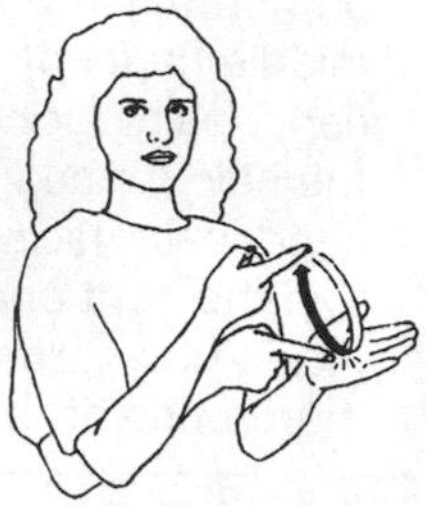

son *n.*

[A shortened form of the combination of the signs for **boy** and **baby**] Beginning with the fingertips of the right *B hand* against the forehead, palm facing left, bring the right hand downward, ending with the bent right arm cradled in the bent left arm held across the body, both palms facing up.

song *n.* See sign for MUSIC.

soon[1] *adv.* Same sign used for: **near future, in the; shortly.**

[The movement is close, indicating immediacy] Touch the fingertips of the right *F hand,* palm facing in, to the middle of the chin.

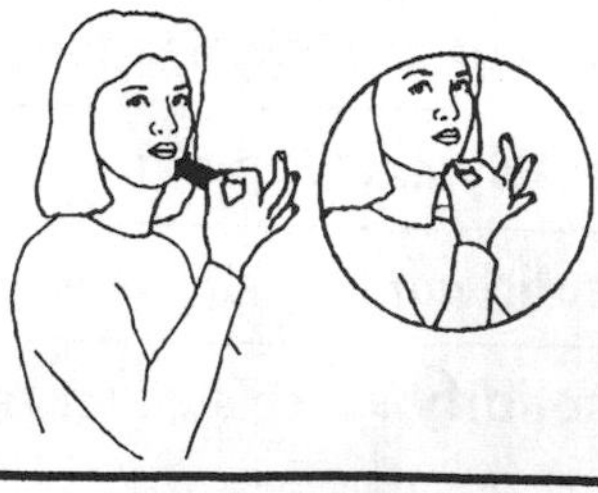

soon[2] *adv.* See sign for SHORT[1].

sordid *adj.* See sign for AWFUL.

sorry *adj.* Related form: **sorrow** *n.* Same sign used for: **apologize, apology, penitence, penitent, regret, repent.**

[Indicates rubbing the chest in sorrow] Rub the palm side of the right *A hand* in a large circle on the chest with a repeated movement.

sort[1] *n.* See sign for KIND[2].

sort[2] *v.* See sign for FILE[1].

sort of See sign for FAIR[1].

so-so *adj.* See sign for FAIR[1].

sound *n.* See signs for HEAR, NOISE.

soup *n.*

[Mime eating soup with a spoon] With the thumb extended, move the fingers of the right *U hand* from touching the palm of the left *open hand* upward to the mouth, both palms facing up.

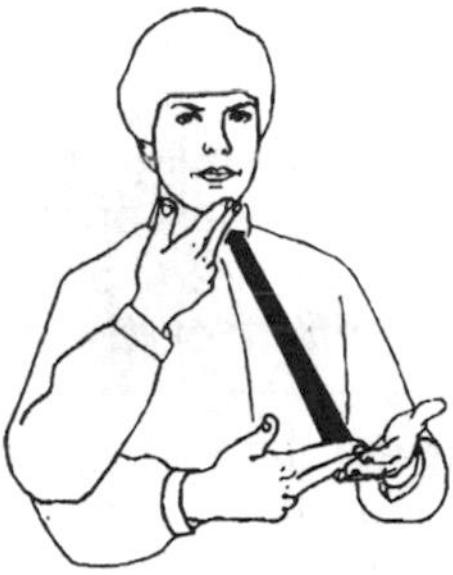

source *n.* See sign for START.

space *n.* See sign for AREA.

sparkle *v.* See sign for SHINY.

speak[1] *v.* Same sign used for: **talk.**

[Represents words coming from the mouth] Beginning

with the index-finger side of the right *4 hand* touching the chin, palm facing left, move the hand forward with a repeated movement.

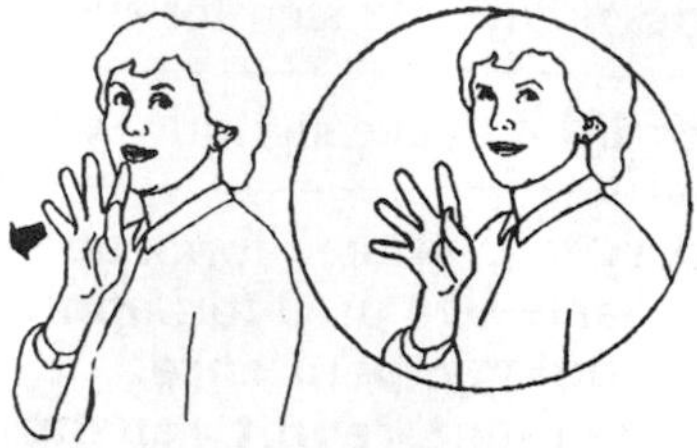

speak[2] *v.* Same sign used for: **address, lecture, presentation, speech.**

[Waving the hand when making a point] Beginning with the right *open hand* near the right side of the head, palm facing left and fingers pointing up, twist the wrist to move the fingers forward and back with a short repeated movement.

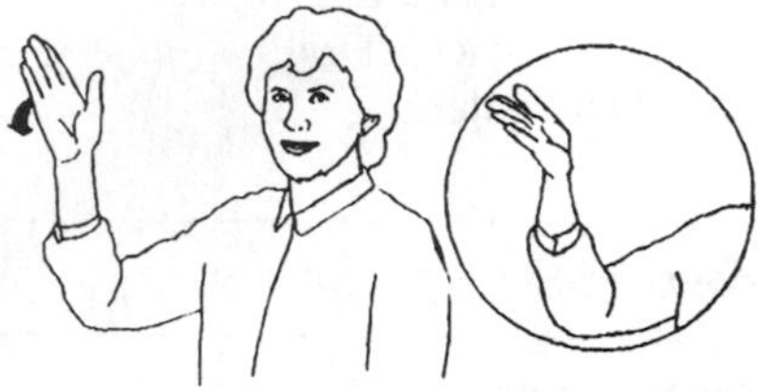

special *adj.* Same sign used for: **especially, unique.**

[Demonstrates pulling one thing out that is special] Grasp the left extended index finger, palm facing in and finger pointing up, with the fingers of the right *G hand* and pull upward in front of the chest.

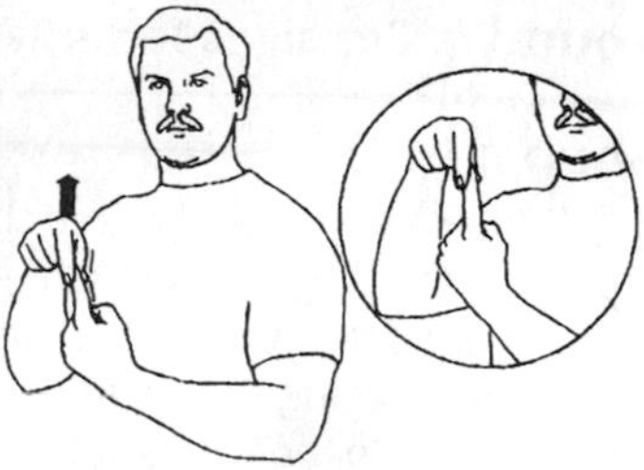

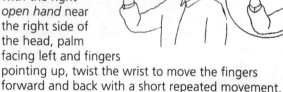

specialize *v.* Related form: **specialty** *n.* Same sign used for: **field, major, straight.**

[Suggests going in a specific direction] Slide the little-finger side of the right *B hand,* palm facing left and fingers pointing forward, along the index-finger side of the left *B hand* held in front of the chest, palm facing right and fingers pointing forward.

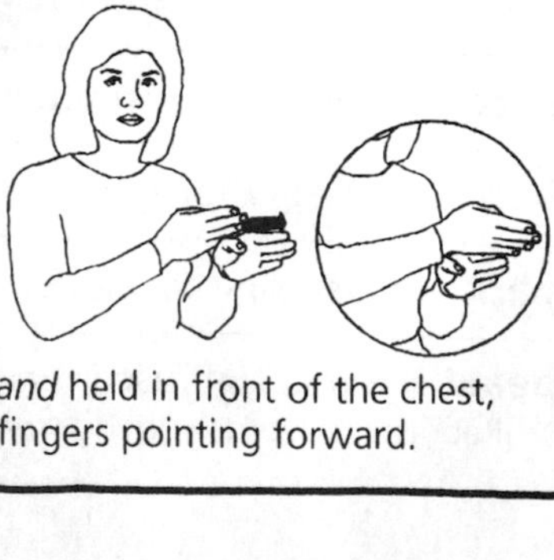

specific *adj.* See sign for POINT[1].

speech *n.* See sign for SPEAK[2].

spend *v.*

[Represents money slipping through one's hands] Beginning with both *curved hands* in front of each side of the chest, right hand nearer the chest than the left hand and both palms facing up, move the hands forward while moving the thumbs across the fingers, ending with *10 hands.*

split[1] *n., v.* See sign for DIVIDE.

split[2] *Slang.* See sign for RUN AWAY.

split up *v. phrase.* See sign for DIVIDE.

spoil *v.* See sign for RUIN[1].

sponsor *v.* See sign for SUPPORT.

spoon *n.*

[The fingers represent a spoon scooping up food] Wipe the backs of the fingers of the right *U hand,* palm facing up and thumb extended, across the upturned palm of the left *open hand* from the fingers to the heel with a double movement.

spot n. Same sign used for: **stain.**

[Shape and location of a spot] Touch the thumb side of the right *F hand* to the left side of the chest, palm facing left.

spread *v.* Same sign used for: **disseminate, distribute.**

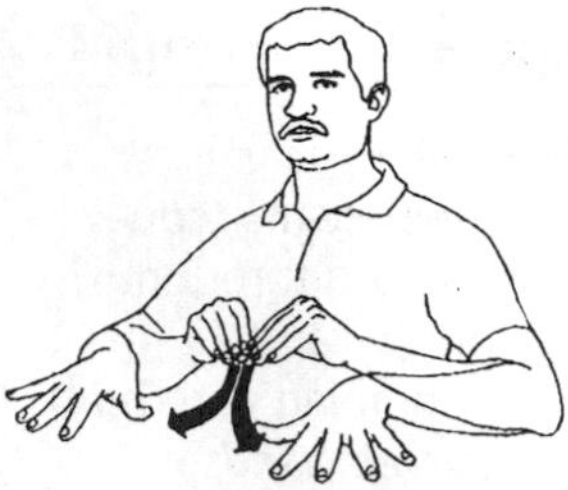

[Demonstrates something spreading outward] Beginning with the fingertips of both *flattened O hands* touching in front of the chest, palms facing down, move the hands forward and away from each other while opening into *5 hands* in front of each side of the body, palms facing down.

spring *n.*

[Similar to sign for **grow** except with a double movement] Beginning with the right *flattened O hand,* palm facing up, being held by the left *C hand,* palm facing in, move the right hand upward with a double movement, opening into a *5 hand* each time.

sprout *v.* See sign for GROW.

squabble *v.* See sign for ARGUE.

square *n., adj.* Same sign used for: **sign.**

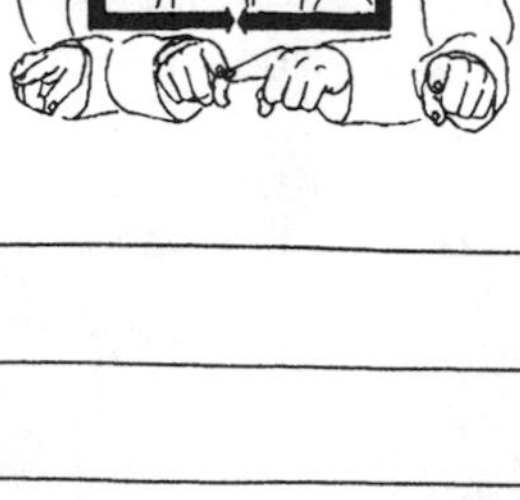

[Draw a square in the air] Beginning with both extended index fingers touching in front of the upper chest, palms angled forward and fingers pointing upward, bring the hands straight out to in front of each shoulder then straight down, and finally back together in front of the waist.

squeeze *n.* See sign for BRIEF.

stain *n.* See sign for SPOT.

staircase *n.* See sign for STAIRS.

stairs *n.* Same signs used for: **staircase, stairway.**

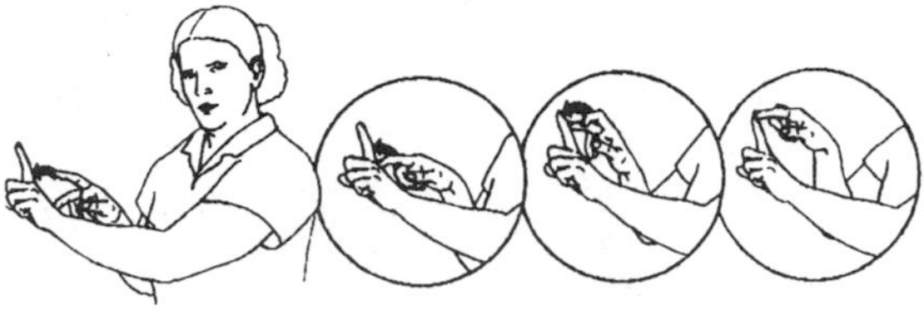

[Demonstrates the action of walking up stairs] Move the fingertips of the right *bent V hand,* palm facing forward, in an alternating crawling movement up the extended left index finger, palm facing forward.

---

stairway *n.* See sign for STAIRS.

---

stall *v.* See sign for HOLD².

---

stamp¹ *n., v.* Same sign used for: **postage, postage stamp.**

[The fingers seem to lick a stamp and place it on an envelope] Move the fingers of the right *H hand* from the mouth, palm facing in, down to land on the fingers of the left *open hand,* palm facing up, in front of the body.

---

stamp² *n., v.* Same sign used for: **brand, guarantee, seal.**

[Mime stamping something with a rubber stamp] Move the right *S hand,* palm facing left, from in front of the chest downward, ending with the little-finger side of the right *S hand* on the upturned palm of the left *open hand.*

---

stand *v.*

[The fingers represent erect legs] Place the fingertips of the right *V hand,* palm facing in and fingers pointing down, on the up-turned palm of the left *open hand* held in front of the body.

standard *n., adj.* Related form: **standardized** *adj.* Same sign used for: **common, same.**
[**same**[1] formed with a large circular movement to indicate everything is the same] Beginning with both *Y hands* in front of the body, palms facing down, move the hands in a large flat circle.

stand for *v. phrase.* See sign for MEAN[2].

staple *v.* Same sign as for STAPLER but formed with a single movement.

stapler *n.*
[Mime pushing down on a stapler] Press the heel of the right *curved 5 hand,* palm facing down, on the heel of the left *open hand,* palm facing up, with a double movement.

star *n.*
[Striking flints to create sparks that look like stars] Brush the sides of both extended index fingers against each other, palms facing forward, with an alternating movement as the hands move upward in front of the face.

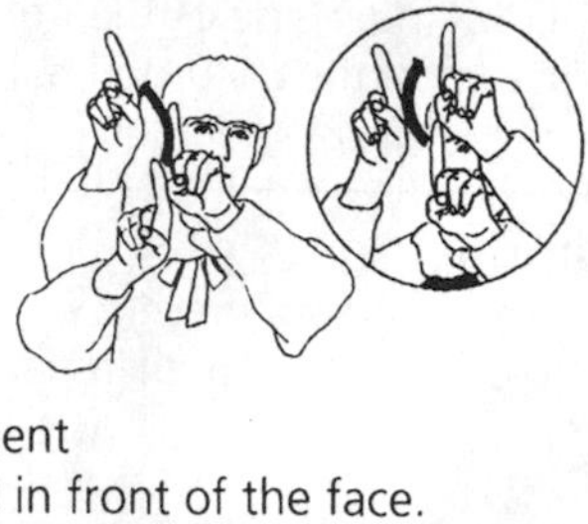

start *n.* Same sign used for: **beginning, origin, origination, source.**

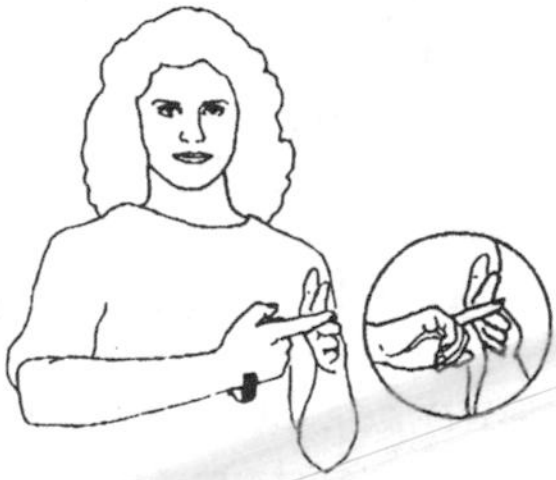

[Represents turning a key to start ignition] Beginning with the extended right index finger, palm facing in, inserted between the index and middle fingers of the left *open hand,* palm facing right and fingers pointing forward, twist the right hand back, ending with the palm angled forward.

startle *v.* See sign for SURPRISE.

starved *adj.* See sign for HUNGRY.

state *v.* See sign for SAY.

statement *n.* See sign for SENTENCE.

stay *v.* Same sign used for: **remain.**

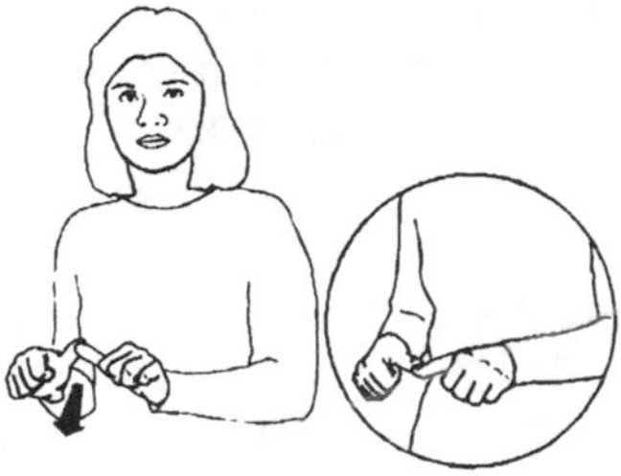

[Continuity of movement] With the thumb of the right *10 hand* on the thumb-nail of the left *10 hand,* both palms facing down in front of the chest, move the hands forward and down a short distance.

steadfast *adj.* See sign for CONSTANT.

steady *adj.* See sign for CONSTANT.

steal *v.* Same sign used for: **burglary, pillage, shoplift, theft.**

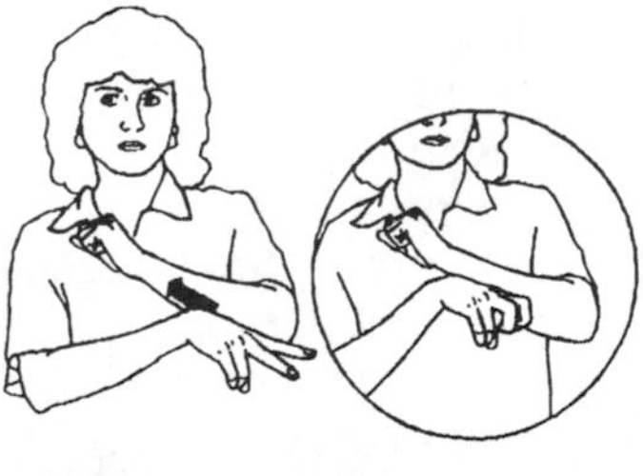

[The fingers seem to snatch something] Beginning with the index-finger side of the right *V hand,* palm facing down, on the elbow of the bent left arm, held at an upward angle across the chest, pull the right hand upward toward the left wrist while bending the fingers in tightly.

steel *n.* See sign for METAL.

steer *v.* See sign for LEAD.

stern *adj.* See sign for STRICT.

stick[1] *v.* Same sign used for: **adhere, adhesive, expose, fasten.**

[Demonstrates something sticky causing the finger and thumb to stick together] With the thumb of the right *5 hand,* palm facing down, touching the palm of the left *open hand,* palm facing up, close the right middle finger down to the thumb.

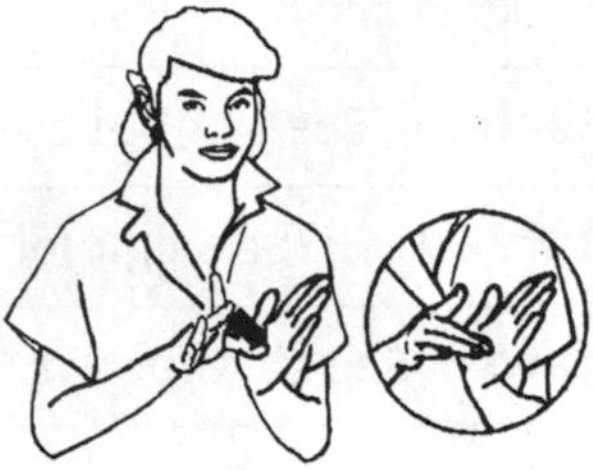

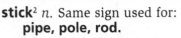

stick[2] *n.* Same sign used for: **pipe, pole, rod.**

[Shape of a stick] Beginning with the thumb sides of both *F hands* touching in front of the chest, palms facing forward, move the hands apart.

sticky *adj.* Same sign as for STICK[1] but formed with a double movement.

still[1] *adv.* See also sign for YET.

[Formed with a continuing movement to show passage of time] Move the right *Y hand,* palm facing down, from in front of the right side of the body forward and upward in an arc.

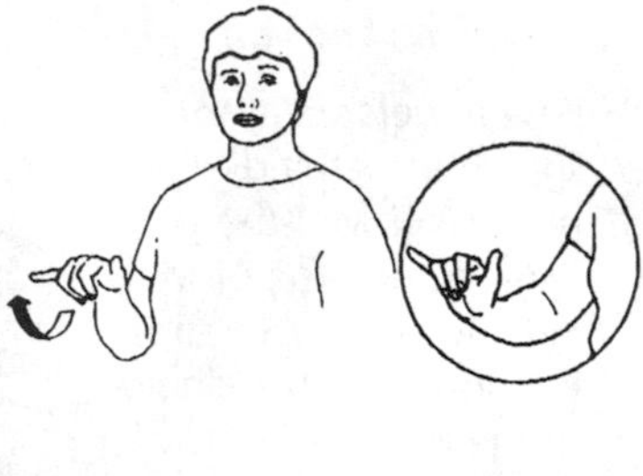

still[2] *adj.* See signs for QUIET, SILENT.

stingy *adj.* (alternate sign)
Same sign used for: **tightwad** (*informal*).

[Clutching a prized item] Beginning with the fingers of the right *curved 5 hand* in front of the chin, palm facing in, bring the hand downward while closing into an *S hand.*

stir *v.* See signs for BEAT[1], MESSY, MIX[1].

stocks *pl. n.* See sign for INVEST.

stone *n.* See sign for ROCK[1].

stop[1] *v.* Same sign used for: **cease, halt, quit.**

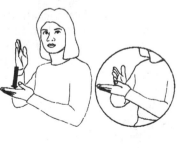

[Demonstrates an abrupt stopping movement] Bring the little-finger side of the right *open hand,* palm facing left and fingers pointing up, sharply down on the upturned palm of the left *open hand* held in front of the body.

stop[2] *v.* See sign for DESIST.

storage *n.* See sign for SAVE[2].

store[1] *n.* Same sign used for: **market, mart, shop.**
[The hands seem to hold merchandise out for inspection and sale] Beginning with both *flattened O hands* in front of each side of the body, palms facing down and fingers

pointing down, swing the fingers forward and back from the wrists with a repeated movement.

store[2] *v.* See sign for SAVE[2].

storm *n.* See signs for MESSY, WIND.

story *n.* Same sign used for: **parable, phrase, prose, remarks, tale.**

[The hands seem to pull out sentences to form a story] Beginning with both *flattened C hands* in front of the chest, palms facing each other and the right hand slightly over the left hand, close the fingertips to the thumbs of each hand and then pull the hands straight apart in front of each shoulder with a double movement.

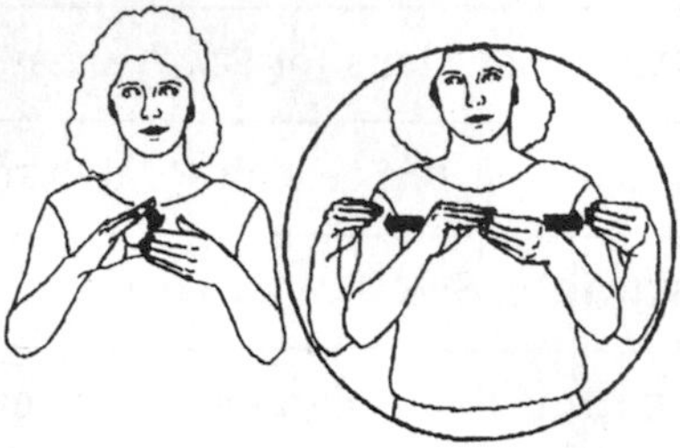

straight[1] *adj., adv.* Same sign used for: **direct.**

[Indicates a straight direction] Beginning with the index-finger side of the right *B hand* against the right shoulder, palm facing left and fingers pointing up, move the hand straight forward by bending the wrist down.

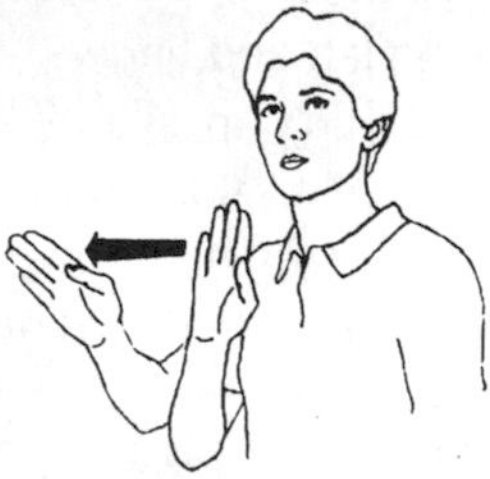

straight[2] *adj., adv.* See sign for SPECIALIZE.

stranded *adj.* See sign for STUCK.

strange *adj.* Same sign used for: **bizarre, freak, odd, peculiar, queer, unusual.**

[Something distorting one's vision] Move the right *C hand* from near the right side of the face, palm facing left, downward in an arc in front of the face, ending near the left side of the chin, palm facing down.

street *n.* See sign for ROAD.

strength *n.* See signs for POWER[1], STRONG[1], WELL[1].

stress *n.* See sign for IMPRESSION.

stretch[1] *v.* Same sign used for: **elastic.**

[Mime stretching out some elastic] Beginning with the knuckles of both *S hands* touching in front of the chest, palms facing in, bring the hands apart to in front of each side of the chest with a double movement.

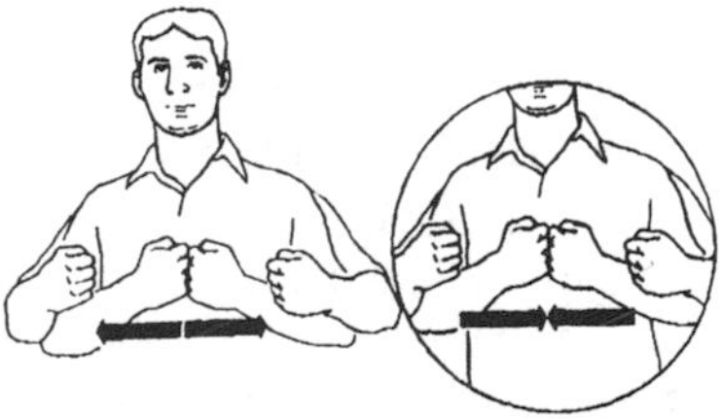

stretch[2] *v.* See sign for EXAGGERATE.

strict *adj.* Same sign used for: **bold, firm, stern.**

Strike the index-finger side of the right *bent V hand* against the nose with a deliberate movement, palm facing left.

strike *v.* See signs for COMPLAIN, HIT.

string *n.* See sign for LINE.

strip *v.* See sign for TEAR.

strive *v.* See sign for TRY.

oll *v.* See sign for WALK.

strong[1] *adj.* Same sign used for: **power, solid, strength.**

[Initialized sign formed similar to **power**[1]] Beginning with the index-finger side of the right *S hand* near the left shoulder, palm facing left, move the right hand down in an arc, ending with the little-finger side of the right *S hand* touching near the crook of the left arm, palm facing up.

strong[2] *adj.* See sign for POWERFUL, WELL[1].

struggle *v., n.* Same sign used for: **antagonism, at odds, banter, conflict, controversy, opposition.**

[Represents opposing forces struggling] Beginning with both extended index fingers pointing toward each other in front of the chest, palms facing in and right hand closer to the body than the left hand, move the hands back and forth simultaneously with a double movement.

stubborn *adj.* See sign for DONKEY.

stuck *adj.* Same sign used for: **confined, pregnant, rape, stranded, trapped.**

[Indicates where food gets stuck in the throat] Move the fingertips of the right *V hand,* palm facing down, against the throat with a deliberate movement.

student *n.* See sign for PUPIL[1].

study *v., n.*
[Eyes scanning information held in the hand in order to learn it] While wiggling the fingers, move the right *5 hand,* palm facing down, with a double movement toward the left *open hand* held in front of the chest, palm facing up.

stuff *n.* See sign for SAVE[2].

stuffed *adj.* See sign for FULL[1].

stupid *adj.* See sign for DUMB.

sturdy[1] *adj.* Same sign used for: **solid, tough.**
[Striking something that is sturdy] Move the right *S hand* from in front of the right side of the chest, palm facing in, in a downward arc across the back of the left *S hand* held in front of the chest, palm facing down, and back again.

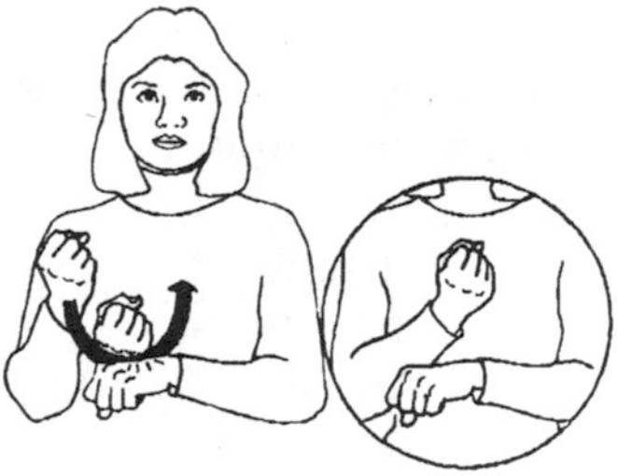

sturdy[2] *adj.* See sign for POWER[1].

subdue *v.* See sign for DEFEAT.

subject *n.* See sign for TITLE.

submit *v.* See signs for ADMIT, SUGGEST. Related form: **submission** *n.*

subscribe *v.* See sign for PENSION.

substitute *v.* See sign for TRADE. Related form: **substitution** *n.*

subtract *v.* Same sign used for: **deduct, discount, eliminate, exempt.**

[Demonstrates removing something] Beginning with the fingertips of the right *curved 5 hand* touching the palm of the left *open hand* held in front of the left side of the chest, palm facing right and fingers pointing up, bring the right hand down off the base of the left hand while changing into an *S hand.*

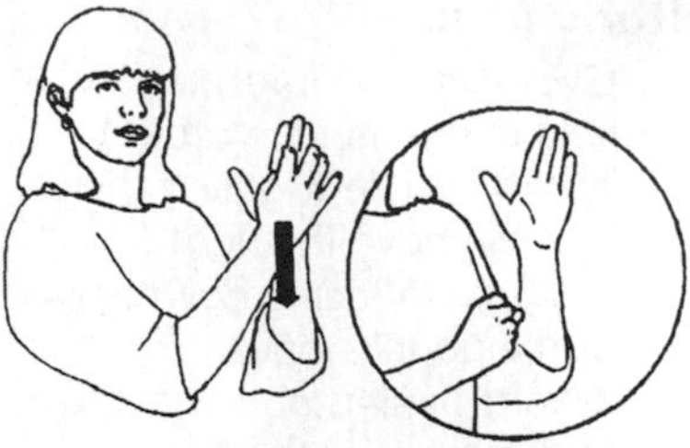

succeed *v.* See sign for FINALLY.

success *n.* See sign for ACHIEVE.

successful *adj.* Related forms: **succeed** *v.*, **success** *n.* See also sign for ACHIEVE. Same sign used for: **accomplish, accomplishment, achievement, prosper, triumph.**

[Moving to higher stages] Beginning with both extended index fingers pointing up in front of each shoulder, palms facing back, move the hands in double arcs upward and back, ending near each side of the head.

sudden *adj., adv.* See sign for FAST.

suffer *v.*

[Similar to **hurt**[2] except formed with a double movement] Beginning with the thumb of the right *A hand* touching the chin, palm facing left, twist the hand to the left with a double movement.

sufficient *adj.* See sign for ENOUGH.

sugar *n.* See sign for CANDY.

suggest *v.* Related form: **suggestion** *n.* Same sign used for: **appeal, bid, motion, offer, nominate, petition, proposal, propose, provide, submit, submission.**

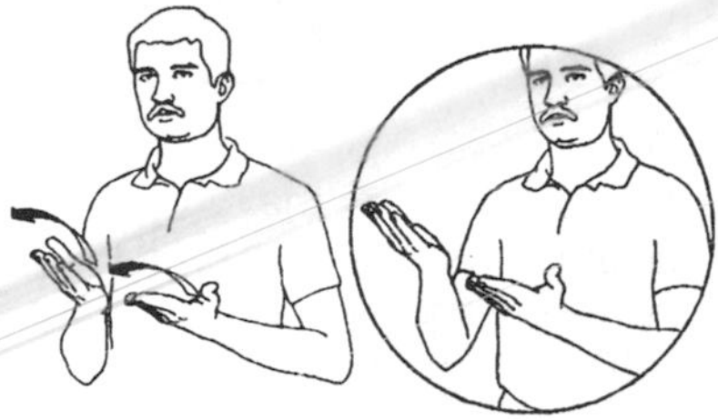

[The hands seem to put forward a suggestion] Beginning with both *open hands* in front of each side of the chest, palms facing up and fingers pointing forward, move the hands simultaneously upward in an arc.

suit[1] *n.* See signs for AGREE, FIT[1], MATCH.

suit[2] *n.* See sign for CLOTHES.

suitcase *n.* See sign for PURSE.

summarize *v.* See sign for BRIEF.

summer *n.*

[Represents wiping sweat from the brow] Bring the thumb side of the extended right index finger, palm facing down and finger pointing left, across the forehead while bending the index finger into an *X hand.*

summon *v.* See sign for CALL[1].

sun *n.*

[Represents shielding one's eyes from the sun] Tap the thumb and index finger of the right *C hand,* palm facing forward, against the right side of the head with a double movement.

Sunday *n.*

[The movement of the hands shows reverence and awe] Beginning with both *open hands* in front of each shoulder, palms facing forward and fingers pointing up, move the hands forward and back with a small double movement.

sundown *n.* See sign for SUNSET.

sunrise *n.* Same sign used for **dawn**.

[Represents the sun coming up over the horizon] Bring the index-finger side of the right *F hand,* palm facing left, upward past the little-finger side of the left *open hand,* palm facing down and fingers pointing right, held across the chest, ending with the right *F hand* in front of the face.

sunset *n.* Same sign used for: **sundown.**

[Represents the sun going down below the horizon] Move the thumb side of the right *F hand*, palm facing left, downward past the little-finger side of the left *open* hand held across the chest, palm facing down and fingers pointing right.

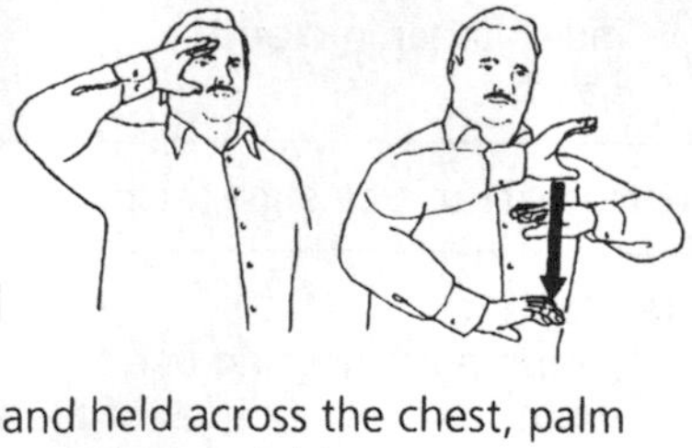

superb *adj.* Same sign used for: **excellent, fantastic, okay.**
[Natural gesture to indicate something is superb] Move the right *F hand,* palm facing left, forward with a short double movement in front of the right shoulder.

superintendent *n.* See sign for PRESIDENT.

superior *n.* See sign for CHIEF[1].

supervise *v.* See sign for CARE[1].

supplement *v.* See sign for ADD.

supply *v.* See sign for FEED.

support *v., n.* Same sign used for: **advocate, allegiance, backup, boost, fund, in behalf of, in favor of, sponsor.**
[Initialized sign similar to sign for **help**] Push the knuckles of the right *S hand,* palm facing left, upward under the little-finger side of the left *S hand,* palm facing in, pushing the left hand upward a short distance in front of the chest.

suppose *v.* Same sign used for: **if, in case of.**
[Indicates a thought coming from the mind] Move the extended little finger of the right *I hand,* palm facing in, forward from the right side of the forehead with a short double movement.

suppress *v.* See sign for CONTROL[1]. Related form: **suppression** *n.*

supreme *adj.* See sign for ADVANCED.

sure[1] *adj.* Same sign used for: **certain.**

[Indicates that facts are coming straight from the mouth] Move the extended right index finger from in front of the mouth, palm facing left and finger pointing up, forward with a deliberate movement.

sure[2] *adj.* See sign for HONEST.

surface *v.* See sign for SHOW UP.

surgery *n.* See sign for OPERATE[1].

surprise *n., v.* Same sign used for: **amaze, amazement, astound, bewilder, startle.**

[Represents the eyes widening in surprise] Beginning with the index fingers and thumbs of both hands pinched together near the outside of each eye, palms facing each other, flick the fingers apart, forming *L hands* near each side of the head.

survive *v.* See sign for LIVE. Related form: **survival** *n.*

suspend v. See sign for HOLD[2].

swap *v.* See sign for TRADE.

swear *v.* See sign for CURSE.

sweat *v., n.* Same sign used for: **perspire, perspiration, toil.**

[Represents sweat coming from one's brow] Beginning with both *S hands* in front of each side of the forehead, move the hands forward while opening into *curved hands,* palms facing down and fingers pointing toward each other.

sweep *v.* See sign for BROOM.

sweet *adj.* Same sign used for: **gentle.**

[Licking something sweet from the fingers] Wipe the fingertips of the right *open hand,* palm facing in and fingers pointing up, downward off the chin while bending the fingers.

sweetheart *n.* Same sign used for: **beau, lover.**

[Two people nodding toward each other] With the knuckles of both *10 hands* together in front of the chest, palms facing in and thumbs pointing up, bend the thumbs downward toward each other with a double movement.

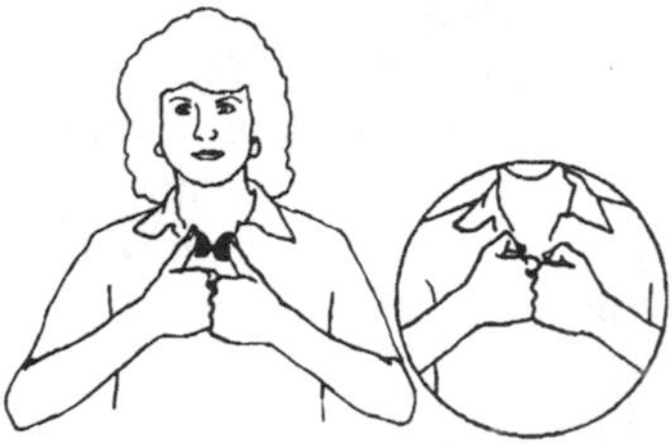

swim *v.* Related form: **swimming** *n.*

[Demonstrates the movement of the hands when swimming] Beginning with the fingers of both *open hands* crossed in front of the chest, palms facing down, move the hands apart to each side with a double movement.

switch *v.* See signs for CHANGE[1], TRADE.

syrup *n.* See sign for GRAVY.

table[1] *n.*

[Represents the flat surface of a table top] Beginning with the bent arms of both *open hands* across the chest, right arm above the left arm, move the right arm down with a short double movement.

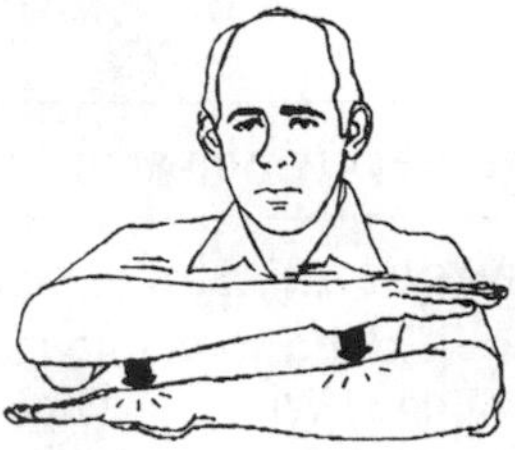

table[2] *n.* See sign for DESK.

tag *n.* See sign for LABEL.

take *v.* Same sign used for: **acquire, adopt, assume, assumption, takeover, take up.**

[The hands seem to take up something] Beginning with both *curved 5 hands* in front of each side of the body, palms facing down, move the hands upward toward the body while changing into *S hands.*

take advantage of See signs for ADVANTAGE[1].

take care of See sign for CARE[1].

take off *v. phrase.* Same sign for: **remove, undress.**

[Mime taking off one's clothes] Beginning with the fingers of both *curved hands* on each side of the chest, palms facing in, bring the hands outward to in front of each shoulder while closing into *S hands*, palms facing each other.

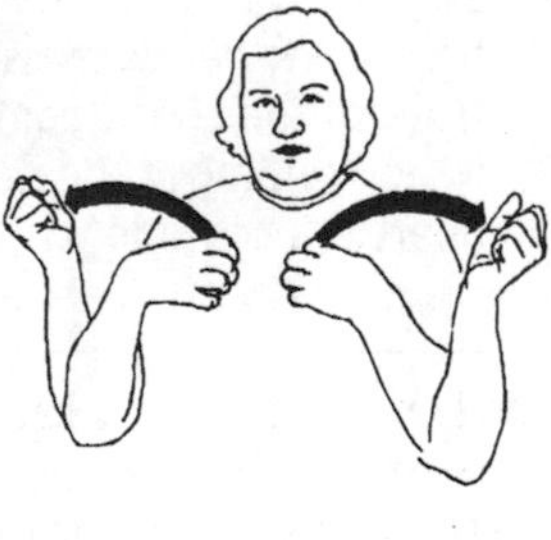

takeover *n.* See signs for CAPTURE, TAKE.

take pictures Same sign used for: **photograph, shoot.**

[Represents the shutter on a camera opening and closing] Beginning with both *modified C hands* near the outside of each eye, palms facing each other, bend the right index finger downward.

take up *v. phrase.* See sign for TAKE.

tale *n.* See sign for STORY.

talent *n.* See sign for SKILL.

talk[1] *v.*

[Shows words coming from the mouth] Beginning with the index-finger side of the right *4 hand* in front of the mouth, palm facing left and fingers pointing up, move the hand forward with a double movement.

talk[2] *v.* See signs for BLAB, CHAT[1], SPEAK[1]. Related form: **talkative** *adj.*

tardy *adj.* See sign for LATE.

target *n.* See signs for GOAL, POINT.

task *n.* See sign for WORK.

taste *n., v.*

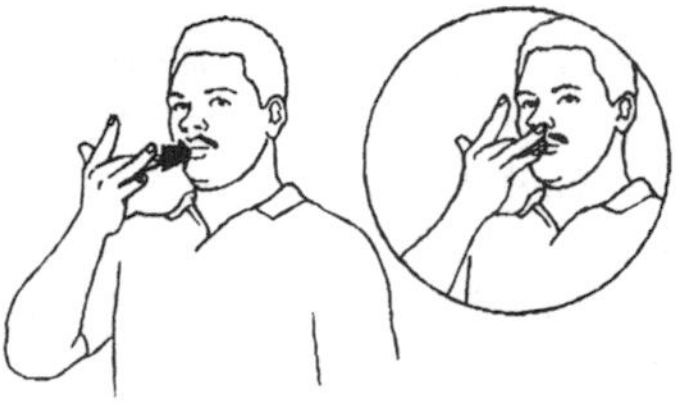

[The finger used for feeling points toward the sense of taste] Touch the bent middle finger of the right *5 hand,* palm facing in, to the lips.

[illegible]y *adj.* See sign for DELICIOUS.

[illegible]x *adj.* See sign for COST.

taxi *n.* See sign for CAB.

tea *n.*

[Mime dipping a tea bag in hot water] With the fingertips of the right *F hand,* palm facing down, inserted in the hole formed by the left *O hand* held in front of the chest, palm facing in, move the right hand in a small circle.

teach *v.* Same sign used for: **educate, education, indoctrinate, indoctrination, instruct, instruction.**

[The hands seem to take information from the head and direct it toward another person] Move both *flattened O hands,* palms facing each other, forward with a small double movement in front of each side of the head.

tear *v.* Same sign used for: **revoke, rip, strip, torn.**

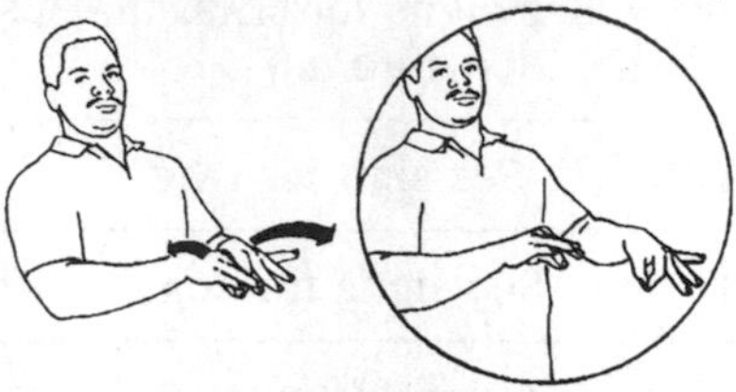

[Mime ripping a piece of paper] Beginning with the index-finger sides of both *F hands* touching in front of the chest, palms facing down, move the right hand back toward the body with a deliberate movement while moving the left hand forward.

tear apart *v. phrase.* See sign for BREAK.

tear down *v. phrase.* See sign for BREAK DOWN.

tease *v.* Related form: **teasing** *n.* Same sign used for: **jest, kid, kidding.**

[The hand seems to direct jabbing remarks at someone] Push the little-finger side of the right *X hand,* palm facing left, forward with a repeated movement across the index-finger side of the le

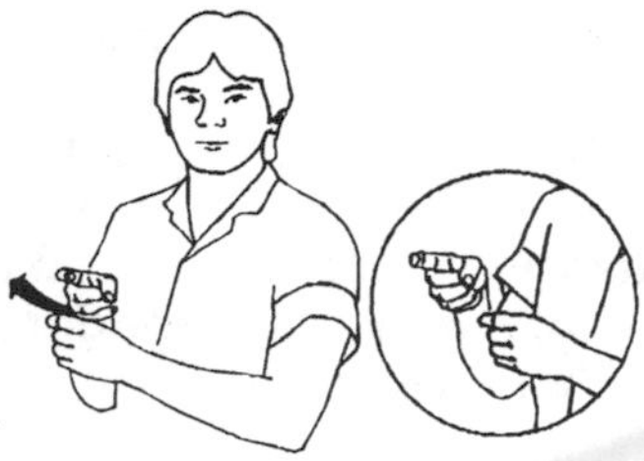

teeny *adj.* See sign for TINY.

telephone *n., v.* Same sign used for: **call, phone.**

[Represents holding a telephone receiver to the ear] Tap the knuckles of the right *Y hand,* palm facing in, with a double movement on the lower right cheek, holding the right thumb near the right ear and the little finger in front of the mouth. The same sign is used for the verb, as in *to telephone my sister*, but the sign is made with a single movement.

tell[1] *v.* Same sign used for: **reveal.**

[Represents words coming from the mouth toward another person] Beginning with the extended right index finger near the chin, palm facing in and finger pointing up, move the finger forward in an arc by bending the wrist, ending with the finger angled forward.

tell[2] *v.* See sign for ANNOUNCE.

temporary *adj.* See sign for SHORT[1].

ten cents *pl. n.* See sign for DIME.

tender *adj.* See sign for SOFT.

terminate *v.* See signs for ELIMINATE[1], FIRE[2].

terrible *adj.* See sign for AWFUL.

test *n., v.* Same sign used for:
examine, examination, inquire, quiz.

[Draw a question mark in the air + a gesture representing distributing the test to a group] Beginning with both extended index fingers pointing up in front of the head, palms facing forward, bring the hands in arcs to the side and then downward while bending the index fingers into *X hands* and continuing down while throwing the fingers open into *5 hands* in front of the body, palms facing down and fingers pointing forward.

text *n.* See sign for WORD.

thank *v.* Same sign used for:
thank you.

[The hand takes gratitude from the mouth and presents it to another] Move the fingertips of the right *open hand,* palm facing in and fingers pointing up, from the mouth forward and down, ending with the palm angled up in front of the chest.

thank you See sign for THANK.

Thanksgiving *n.*

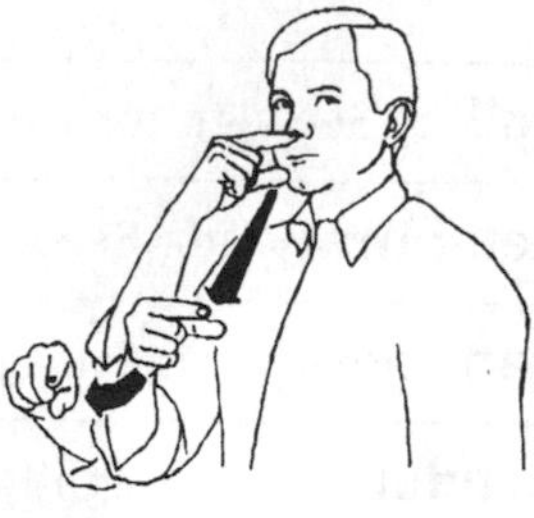

[Represents the shape of a turkey's wattle] Beginning with the right *G hand* in front of the nose, palm facing left, bring the hand downward in an arc with a double movement, bringing the hand forward in front of the chest each time.

that *pron., adj.*

[Points out something in the hand] Bring the palm side of the right *Y hand* with a deliberate movement down to land on the palm of the left *open hand* held in front of the chest, palm facing up.

theater *n.* See sign for ACT[2].

theft *n.* See sign for STEAL.

their *pron.* Related form: **theirs** *pron.*

[Points toward the referents being discussed] Move the right *open hand,* palm facing forward and fingers pointing up, from in front of the right side of the body outward to the right.

them *pron.* Same sign used for: **these, they.**

[Points toward the referents being discussed] Move the extended right index finger, palm facing down and finger pointing forward, from in front of the right side of the body outward to the right.

theme *n.* See signs for QUOTATION, TITLE.

themselves *pl. pron.*

[This hand shape is used for reflexive pronouns and is directed toward the referents being discussed] Move the right *10 hand* from in front of the right side of the body, palm facing left, outward to the right.

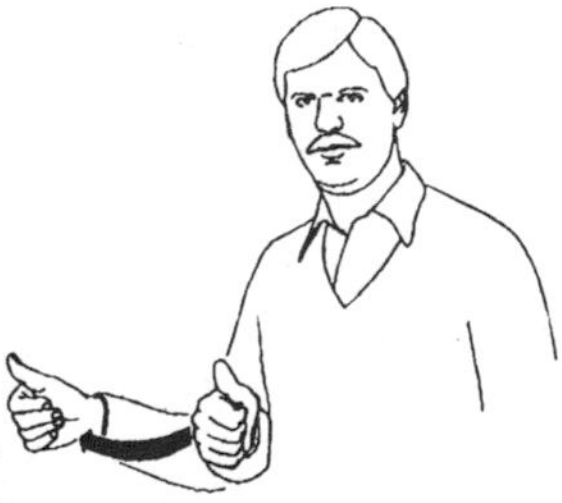

ı *adv.* See signs for FINISH[1], OR.

ere *adv.* Same sign used for: **point.**

[Points to a specific place away from the body] Push the extended right index finger from in front of the right shoulder forward a short distance, palm facing forward and finger pointing forward.

these *pron.* See sign for THEM.

they *pron.* See sign for THEM.

thick *adj.*

[Shows the thickness of a thick layer] Slide the thumb side of the right *modified C hand,* palm facing forward, from the wrist across the back of the left *open hand* held in front of the chest, palm facing down.

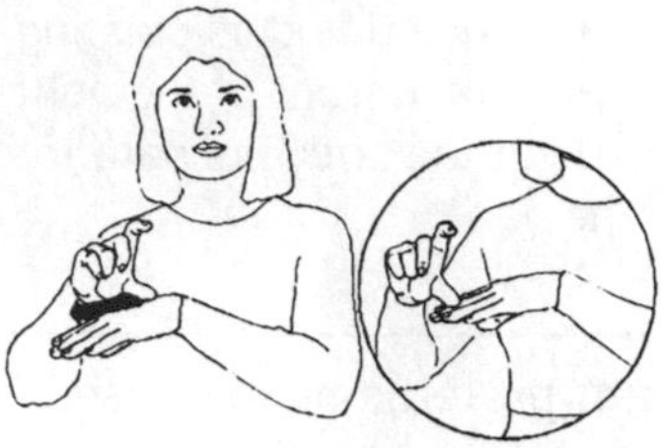

thin[1] *adj.* Same sign used for: **short.**

[Shows the thickness of a thin layer] Slide the thumb side of the right *G hand,* palm facing forward, from the wrist to the fingers of the left *open hand* held in front of the chest, palm facing down.

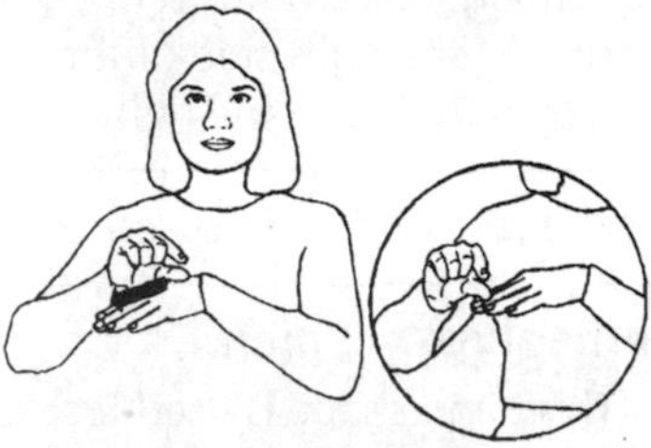

thin[2] *adj.* (alternate sign)

[Indicates something or someone that is very thin] Beginning with the extended little fingers of both *I hands* touching in front of the chest, right hand above the left hand and palms facing in, bring the right hand upward and the left hand downward.

thin[3] *adj.* See sign for DIET.

thing *n.*

[Something in the hand] Bring the right *open hand,* palm facing up and fingers pointing forward, from in front of the body in a large arc to the right.

think[1] *v.*

[Indicates the location of the mind] Tap the extended right index finger, palm facing in, to the right side of the forehead with a short double movement.

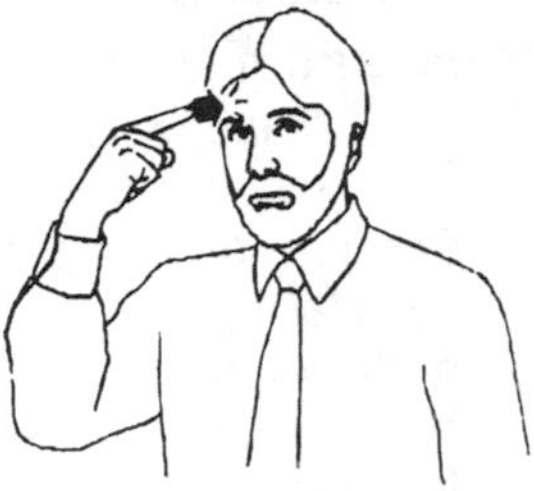

think[2] *v.* See signs for CONCERN[1], WONDER.

think about *v. phrase.* See sign for WONDER.

thinking *n.* See sign for WONDER.

third *adj.* See sign for ONE THIRD.

thirsty *adj.* Related form: **thirst** *n.* Same sign used for: **parched.**

[Indicates a dry throat] Move the extended right index finger, palm facing in and finger pointing up, downward on the length of the neck, bending the finger down as it moves.

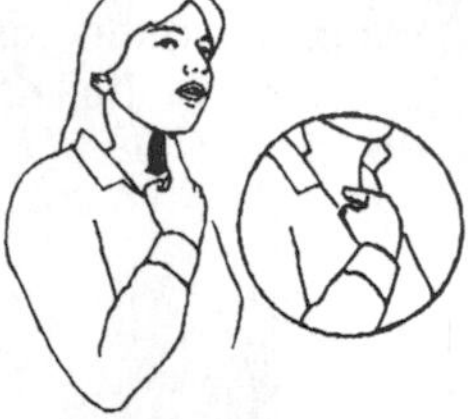

this *pron., adj.*

[Points to a specific thing held in the hand] Move the extended right index finger, palm facing down and finger pointing down, from in front of the chest in a circular movement and then down to touch the left *open hand* held in front of the body, palm facing up.

thousand *n., adj.*

[An *M hand* representing *mille*, the Latin word for thousand] Bring the fingertips of the right *bent hand,* palm facing left, against the palm of the left *open hand* held in front of the body, palm facing right and fingers pointing forward.

thread *n.* See signs for CORD, LINE.

threat *n.* See sign for DANGER.

thrifty *adj.* See sign for GREEDY.

through *prep.* Same sign used for: **via.**

[Demonstrates movement through something] Slide the little-finger side of the right *open hand,* palm facing in and fingers angled to the left, between the middle

finger and ring finger of the left *open hand* held in fr
of the chest, palm facing right and fingers pointing up

throw *v.* Same sign used for: **cast, dump, pitch, throw away, toss.**
[Mime throwing something] Beginning with the right *S hand* in front of the right shoulder, palm facing forward, move the hand forward and downward while opening into a *5 hand,* palm facing down.

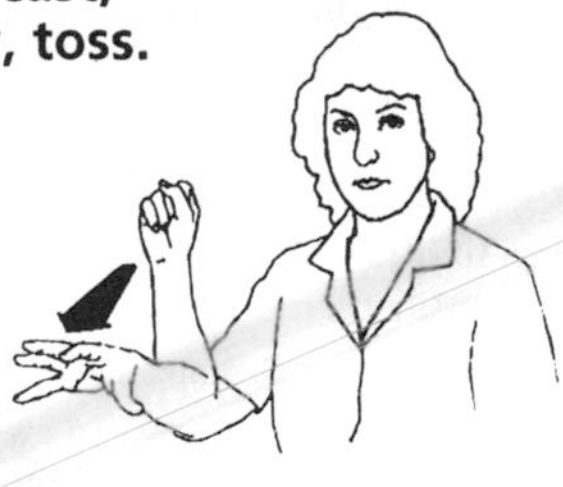

throw away *v. phrase.* See sign for THROW.

throw out *v. phrase.* See sign for ABANDON.

Thursday *n.*
[Abbreviation **t-h**] Beginning with the right *T hand* in front of the right shoulder, palm facing left, flick the index and middle fingers forward, forming an *H hand.*

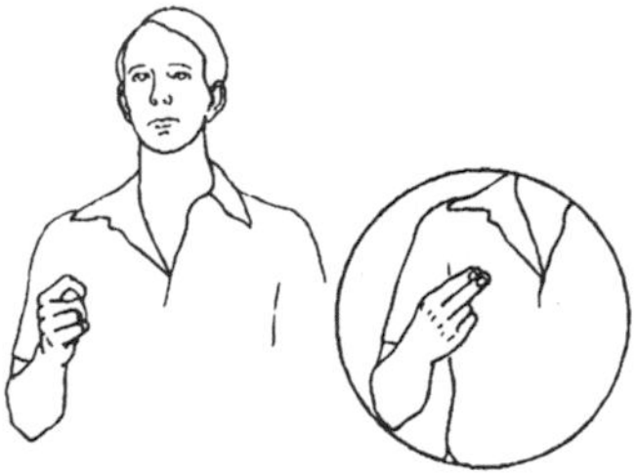

tie *v.* See sign for NECKTIE.

tight *adj.* See sign for GREEDY.

tightwad *n. Informal.* See sign for STINGY.

time *n.*
[Indicates the location of a person's watch] Tap the bent index finger of the right *X hand,* palm facing down, with a double movement on the wrist of the left wrist held in front of the chest, palm facing down.

timid *adj.* See sign for AFRAID.

y *adj.* See also sign for SMALL[1]. Same sign used for: **little bit, puny, scant, teeny.**

[Shows a tiny movement] Beginning with the right *6 hand* in front of the right side of the chest, palm facing up, flick the thumb off the little finger with a quick movement.

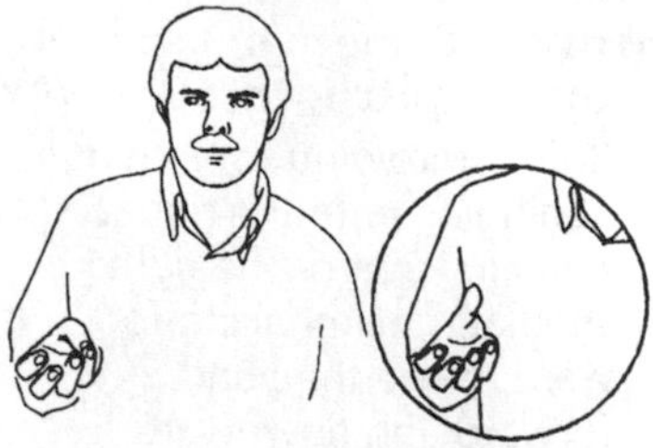

---

tired *adj.* Same sign used for: **exhausted, fatigue, weary.**

[The hands show that energy has dropped in the body] Beginning with the fingertips of both *bent hands* on each side of the chest, palms facing in, roll the hands downward on the fingertips, ending with the little-finger sides of both hands touching the chest, palms facing outward.

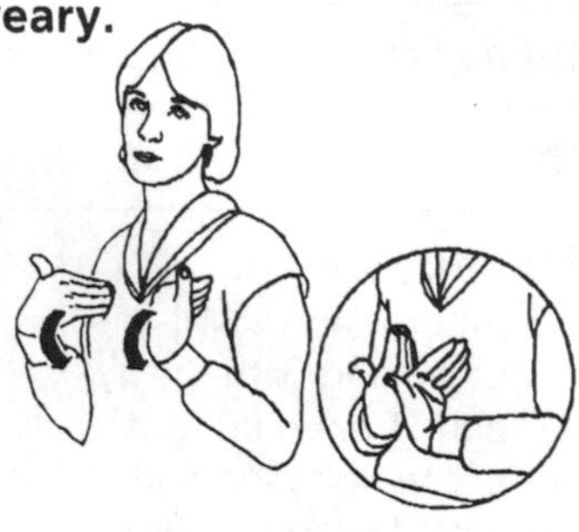

---

tissue *n.* Same sign used for: **Kleenex** (*trademark*).

[**cold**[1] + **paper**] Bring the index finger and thumb of the right *G hand,* palm facing in, downward on each side of the nose with a double movement, pinching the fingers together each time. Then brush the heel of the right *open hand,* palm facing down and fingers pointing left, with a double movement on the heel of the left *open hand* held in front of the body, palm facing up and fingers pointing right.

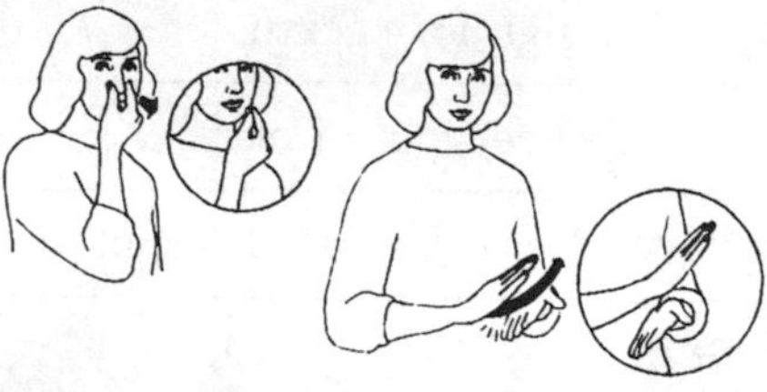

---

title *n.* Same sign used for: **entitle, quotes, so-called, subject, theme, topic.**

[Represents quotation marks around a title] Beginning

with both *bent V hands* near each side of the head, palms facing forward, twist the hands while bending the fingers down, ending with the palms facing back.

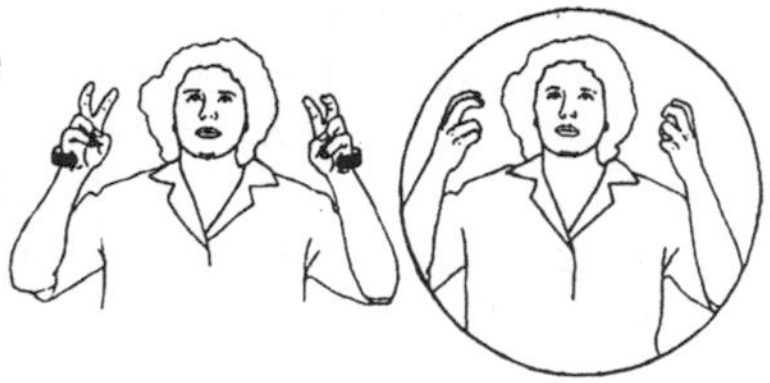

today *n., adv.*
[Sign similar to **now** except with a double movement] Bring both *Y hands,* palms facing up, with a short double movement downward in front of each side of the body.

together *adv.*
[Sign similar to **with**[1] except with a circular movement indicating duration] With the palm sides of both *A hands* together in front of the body, move the hands in a flat circle.

toil *n.* See sign for SWEAT.

toilet *n.* Same sign used for: **bathroom, lavatory, rest room, washroom.**
[Initialized sign] Move the right *T hand,* palm facing forward, from side to side in front of the right shoulder with a repeated shaking movement.

tolerant *adj.* See sign for PATIENT[1].

tolerate *v.* See sign for CONTROL[1]. Related form: **tolerant** *adj.*

tomorrow *n., adv.*
[The sign moves forward into the future] Move the palm side of the right *10 hand,* palm facing left, from the right side of the chin forward while twisting the wrist.

tonight *n.* See sign for NIGHT.

too much See signs for EXCESS, OVER[1].

top *n., adj.*
[The location on the top of something] Bring the palm of the right *open hand,* palm facing down and fingers pointing left, downward on the fingertips of the left *open hand* held in front of the chest, palm facing right and fingers pointing up.

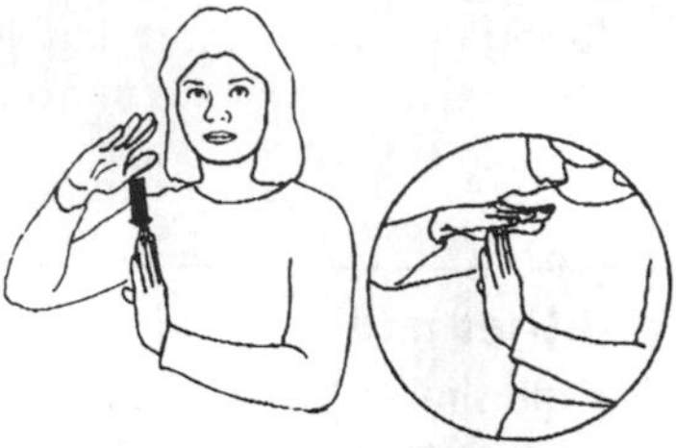

topic *n.* See sign for TITLE.

torn *adj.* See sign for TEAR.

toss *v.* See sign for THROW.

touch *v., n.*
[Demonstrates touching something, with the middle finger used frequently to indicate feelings] Bring the bent middle finger of the right hand, palm facing down, downward to touch the back of the left *open hand* held in front of the body, palm facing down.

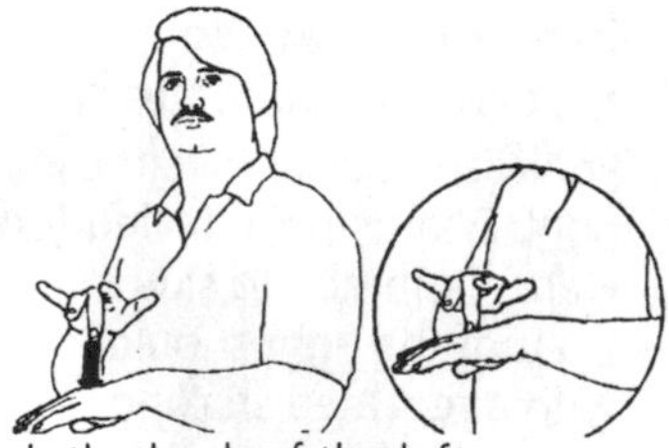

tough *adj.* See sign for STURDY[1].

tour *n.* See sign for RUN AROUND.

tow *v.* See sign for DRAG.

toward *prep.*

[Demonstrates a movement toward something] Beginning with the extended right index finger in front of the right shoulder, palm facing left, move the hand in an arc to the left, ending with the right extended index finger touching the left extended index finger pointing up in front of the left side of the body, palm facing right.

towel *n.*

[Mime drying one's back with a towel] Beginning with the right *S hand* above the right shoulder, palm facing forward, and the left *S hand* near the left hip, palm facing back, move the hands simultaneously upward and downward at an angle with a repeated movement.

town *n.* Same sign used for: **community, village.**

[Represents the rooftops in a town] Tap the fingertips of both *open hands* together in front of the chest with a double movement, palms facing each other at an angle.

trade *v.* Same sign used for: **budget, exchange, replace, substitute, substitution, swap, switch.**

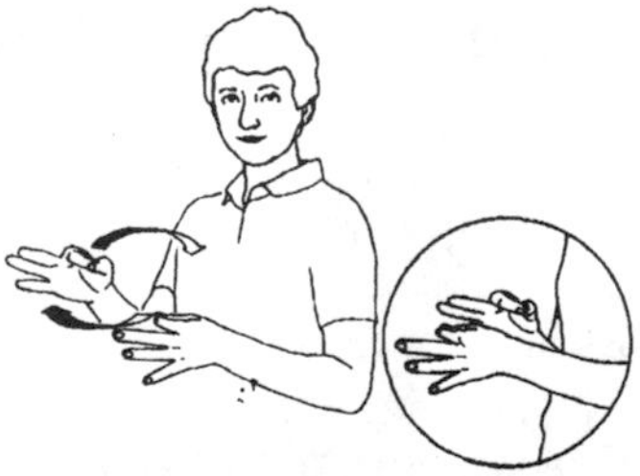

[Demonstrates moving something into another thing's place] Beginning with both *F hands* in front of the body, palms facing each other and right hand somewhat forward of the left hand, move the right hand back toward the body in an upward arc while moving the left hand forward in a downward arc.

traffic *n.*

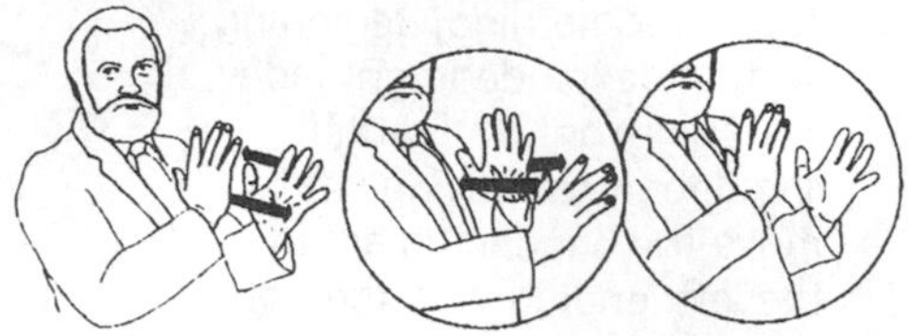

[Represents many vehicles moving quickly past each other in both directions] With both *5 hands* in front of the chest, palms facing each other and fingers pointing up, move the right hand forward and the left hand back with a repeated alternating movement, brushing palms as they pass each time.

trail *v.* See sign for FOLLOW.

trailer *n.* See sign for TRUCK.

train *n.* Same sign used for: **go by train, railroad, travel by train.**

[Represents the crossties on a railroad track] Rub the fingers of the right *H hand* back and forth with a repeated movement on the fingers of the left *H hand* held in front of the body, both palms facing down.

training *n.* See sign for PRACTICE.

tranquil *adj.* See sign for QUIET.

transport *v.* See sign for BRING.

trapped *adj.* See sign for STUCK.

travel *v.* See sign for RUN AROUND.

travel by train See sign for TRAIN.

tree *n.*

[Represents a tree trunk and branches at the top] Beginning with the elbow of the bent right arm resting on the back of the left *open hand* held across the body, twist the right *5 hand* forward and back with a small repeated

trespass *n.* See sign for SIN.

trial *n.* See sign for JUDGE.

tribute *n.* See sign for GIFT.

triumph *n.* See sign for SUCCESSFUL.

trouble[1] *n.* Same sign used for: **anxious, care, concern, worry.**

[Represents problems coming from all directions] Beginning with both *B hands* near each side of the head, palms facing each other, bring the hands toward each other with a repeated alternating movement, crossing the hands in front of the face each time.

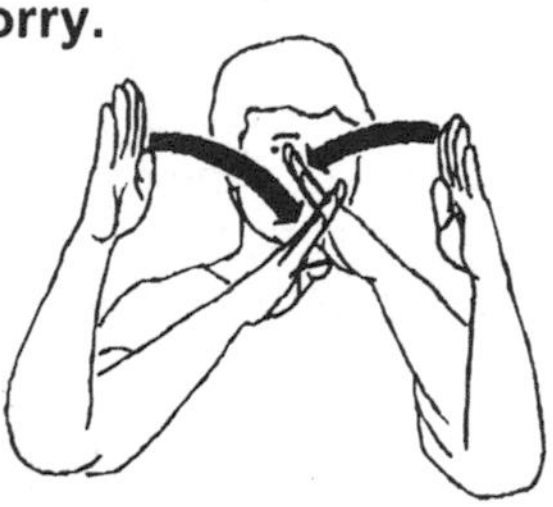

trouble[2] *n.* See sign for DIFFICULT.

trousers *n.* See sign for PANTS.

truck *n.* Same sign used for: **trailer.**

[Initialized sign similar to sign for **bus**] Beginning with the little-finger side of the right *T hand,* palm facing left, touching the index-finger side of the left *T hand,* palm facing right, move the right hand back toward the chest while the left hand moves forward.

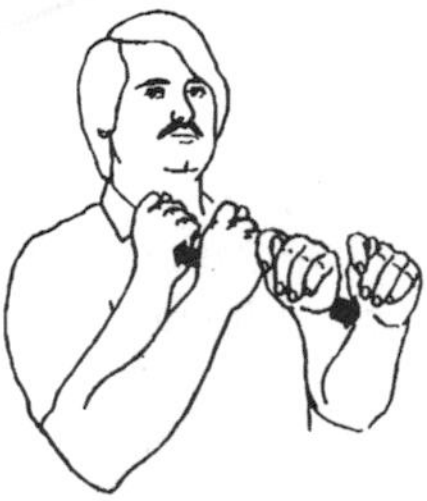

true *adj.* Same sign used for: **actual, actually,**

certain, certainly, truly.
[Represents words coming from the mouth] Move the side of the extended right index finger from in front of the mouth, palm facing left and finger pointing up, forward in an arc.

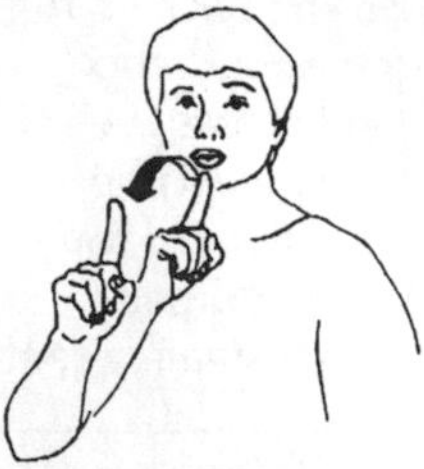

truly *v.* See sign for TRUE.

trust *n.* See sign for CONFIDENT.

truth *n.* Same sign used for: **fact, really.**
[Represents the truth coming straight from the mouth] Move the extended right index finger from pointing up in front of the mouth, palm facing left, forward with a deliberate movement.

try *v.* Same sign used for: **attempt, strive.**
[The hands push forward indicating effort] Move both *S hands* from in front of each side of the body, palms facing each other, downward and forward in simultaneous arcs.

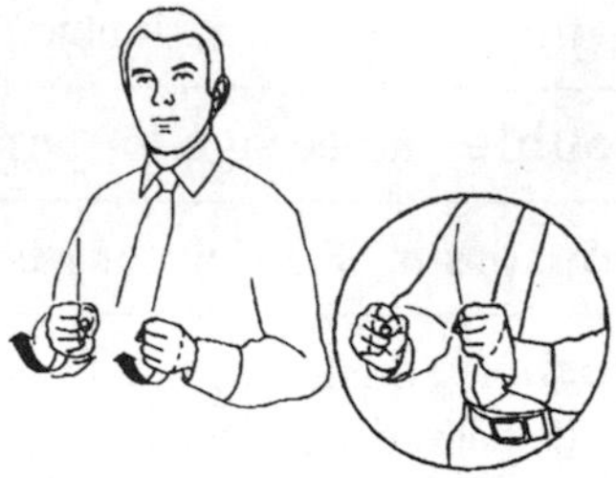

Tuesday *n.*
[Initialized sign] Move the right *T hand,* palm facing in, in a circle in front of the right shoulder.

turn *n.* See also sign for CHANGE[1]. Same sign used for: **alternate, next.**

[Indicates alternating positions in order to take turns] Move the right *L hand* from in front of the body, palm angled left, to the right by flipping the hand over, ending with the palm facing up.

turn down *v. phrase.* See sign for REJECT.

turn into *v. phrase.* See sign for BECOME.

turn over *v. phrase.* See sign for COOK.

turn up *v. phrase.* See sign for SHOW UP.

twenty-five cents *pl. n.* See sign for QUARTER[1].

type[1] *v.* Related form: **typing** *v.*

[Mime typing] Beginning with both *curved 5 hands* in front of the body, palms facing down, wiggle the fingers with a repeated movement.

type[2] *n.* See sign for FAVORITE[1]. Related form: **typical** *adj.*

type[3] *n.* See sign for KIND[2].

ugly *adj.*

Beginning with the extended right index finger in front of the left side of the face, palm facing left and finger pointing left, move the hand to the right side of the face while bending the index finger to form an *X hand.*

unaware *adj.* See sign for DON'T KNOW.

uncertain *adj.* See sign for RESIST.

uncle *n.*

[Initialized sign formed near the male area of the head] Shake the right *U hand,* palm facing forward and fingers pointing up, near the right side of the forehead.

unconscious *adj.* See sign for DON'T KNOW.

under *prep.*

[Shows a location under something else] Move the right *10 hand,* palm facing left, from in front of the chest downward and forward under the left *open hand* held in front of the chest, palm facing down and fingers pointing right.

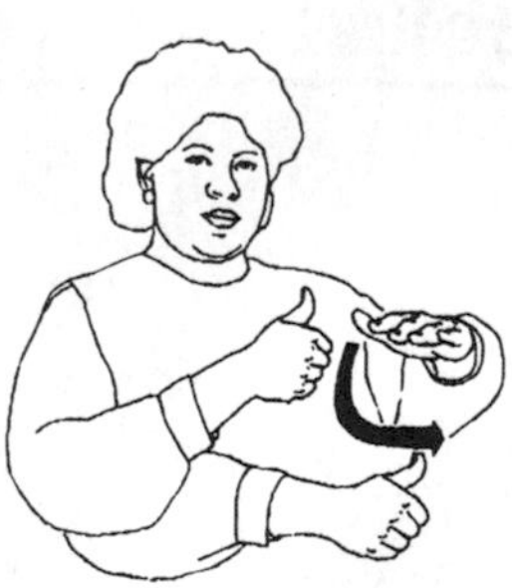

understand *v.* Same sign used for: **apprehend, comprehend, perceive.**

[Comprehension seems to pop into one's head] Beginning with the right *S hand* near the right side of the forehead, palm facing left, flick the right index finger upward with a sudden movement.

undress *v.* See sign for TAKE OFF.

union *n.* See sign for COOPERATION.

unique *adj.* See sign for SPECIAL.

unite *v.* See sign for BELONG.

unity *n.* See sign for COOPERATION.

universal *adj.* See sign for COOPERATION.

unknown *adj.* See sign DON'T KNOW.

unusual *adj.* See sign for STRANGE.

up *adv., prep.*

[Points up] With the right extended index finger pointing up in front of the right shoulder, palm facing forward, move the right hand upward a short distance.

upstairs *adv.* Same sign as for UP but made with a double movement. Same sign used for: **upward.**

up to See sign for MAXIMUM.

urgent *adj.* See signs for HURRY, NOW.

pron.

[Initialized sign similar to sign for **we**] Touch the index-finger side of the right *U hand,* palm facing left and fingers pointing up, to the right side of the chest. Then twist the wrist and move the hand around to touch the little-finger side of the right *U hand* to the left side of the chest, palm facing right.

use *v.*

[Initialized sign] Move the right *U hand,* palm facing forward and fingers pointing up, in a repeated circle over the back of the left *S hand* held in front of the chest, palm facing down, hitting the heel of the right hand on the left hand each time as it passes.

used *adj.* See sign for SECOND-HAND.

used to *adj. phrase.* Same sign used for: **usual, usually.**

[Initialized sign similar to sign for **habit**] With the heel of the right *U hand,* palm facing forward and fingers pointing up, on the back of the left *S hand* held in front of the chest, palm facing down, move both hands downward.

use up *v. phrase.* See sign for RUN OUT OF.

usual *adv.* See signs for DAILY, USED TO. Related form: **usually** *adv.*

vacant *adj.* See sign for EMPTY. Related form: **vacancy** *n.*

vacation *n.*

[Thumbs in the straps of one's overalls as a symbol of leisure] With the thumbs of both *5 hands* near each armpit, palms facing in and fingers pointing toward each other, wiggle the fingers with a repeated movement.

vacuum *v.*

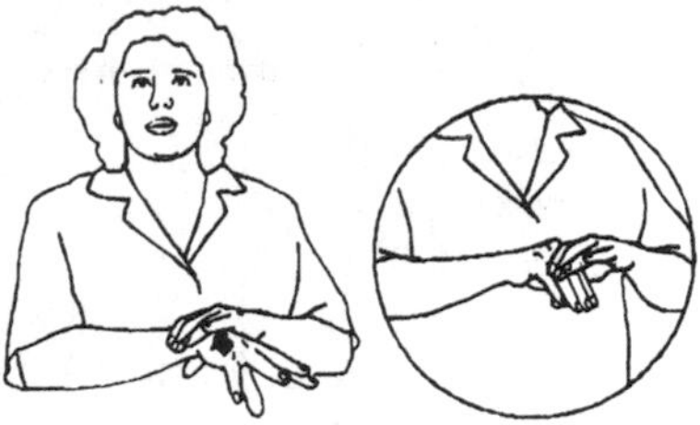

[Demonstrates the action of a vacuum drawing in dirt] With the fingertips of the right *flattened C hand* on the fingers of the left *open hand* held in front of the chest, palm facing up and fingers pointing forward, close the right fingers with a double movement while sliding across the left palm, forming a *flattened O hand* each time.

vague *adj.* Same sign used for: **ambiguous, blurry, fade, hazy, illegible.**

[Represents a blurring of the facts] With the palms of both *5 hands* together at angles in front of the chest, move both hands in circular movements going in opposite directions rubbing the palms against each other.

value *adj.* See sign for IMPORTANT.

vanilla *n., adj.*
[Initialized sign] Shake the right *V hand,* palm facing forward and fingers pointing up, from side to side with a small double movement in front of the right shoulder.

vanish *v.* See sign for DISAPPEAR[1].

vanquish *v.* See sign for DEFEAT.

variety *n.* Same sign used for: **and so-forth, random, range.**
[Pointing out many things] Beginning with the extended index fingers of both hands touching in front of the chest, palms facing down, move the hands apart while bending the index fingers downward, forming *X hands* with a repeated movement, ending with the hands in front of each side of the chest.

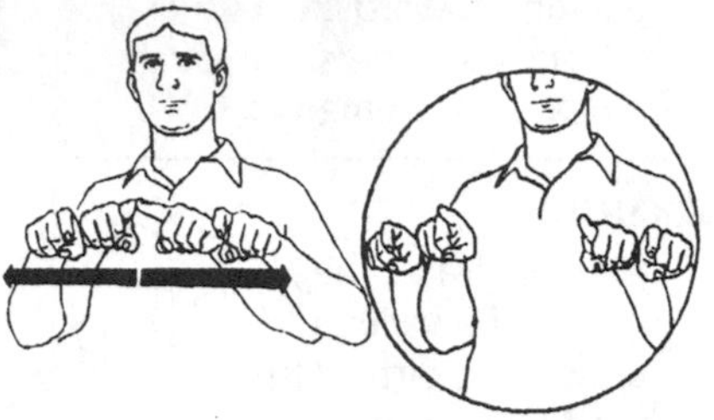

vegetable *n.*
[Initialized sign] Beginning with the index finger of the right *V hand,* palm facing forward, touching the right side of the chin, twist the wrist to turn the palm back and touch the middle finger to the right side of the chin, ending with the palm facing back.

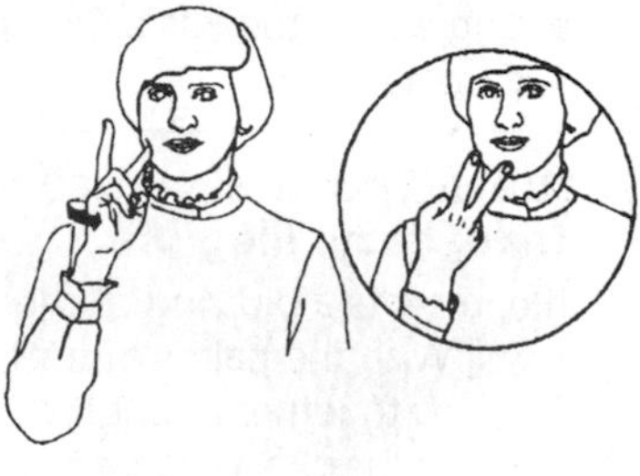

vengeance *n.* See sign for REVENGE.

versus *prep.* See sign for CHALLENGE.

very *adv.*

[Initialized sign similar to sign for **much**] Beginning with the fingertips of both *V hands* touching in front of the chest, palms facing each other, bring the hands apart to in front of each shoulder.

veto *v.* See sign for REJECT.

via *prep.* See sign for THROUGH.

view *v.* See sign for LOOK OVER.

village *n.* See sign for TOWN.

visit *v., n.*

[Initialized sign] Beginning with both *V hands* in front of each side of the chest, palms facing in and fingers pointing up, move the hands in alternating repeated movements.

visualize *adj.* See sign for SEE.

voice *n.* Related forms: **vocal, vocalize.**

[Initialized sign showing the location of one's voice] Move the fingertips of the right *V hand,* palm facing down, upward on the throat with a double movement.

void *adj.* See sign for EMPTY.

volunteer *v.* See sign for APPLY[2].

wacky *Slang. adj.* See sign for CRAZY.

wager *n.* See sign for BET.

wages *pl. n.* See signs for EARN, INCOME[1].

wait *v., n.*

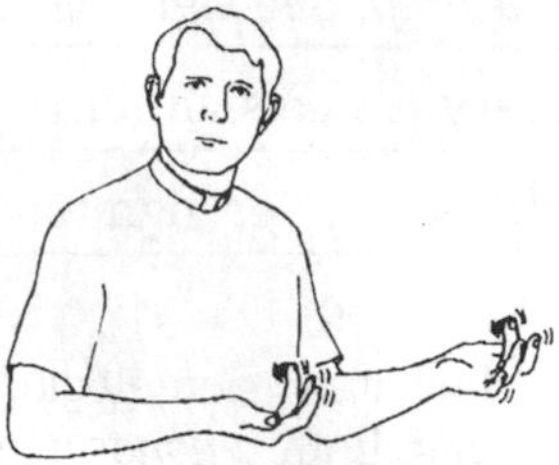

[Seems to be twiddling the finger while waiting impatiently] Beginning with both *curved 5 hands* in front of the body, palms facing up, wiggle the middle fingers with a repeated motion.

waive *v.* See sign for DISMISS.

wake up *v. phrase.* See sign for AWAKE.

walk *v.* Same sign used for: **stroll, wander.**

[Represents a person's legs moving when walking] Beginning with both *open hands* in front of each side of the body, left palm facing in and fingers pointing down and right palm facing down and fingers pointing forward, move the fingers of both hands up and down with an alternating movement by bending the wrists.

wander *v.* See signs for ROAM, WALK.

want *v.* Same sign used for: **desire, passion.**

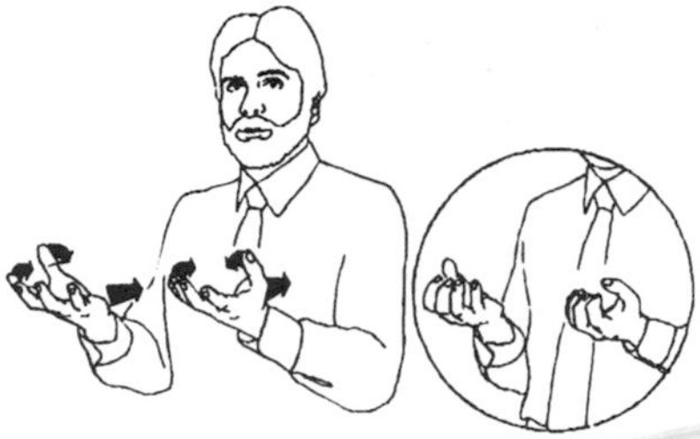

[Represents bringing a wanted thing toward oneself] Beginning with both *5 hands* in front of the body, palms facing up and fingers pointing forward, bring the hands back toward the chest while constricting the fingers toward the palms.

war *n.* See sign for BATTLE.

warm *adj.* Related form: **warmth** *n.*

[Using one's breath to warm the hand] Beginning with the fingers of the right *E hand* near the mouth, palm facing in, move the hand forward in a small arc while opening the fingers into a *C hand.*

warn *v.* Related form: **warning** *n.* Same sign used for: **caution, rebuke.**

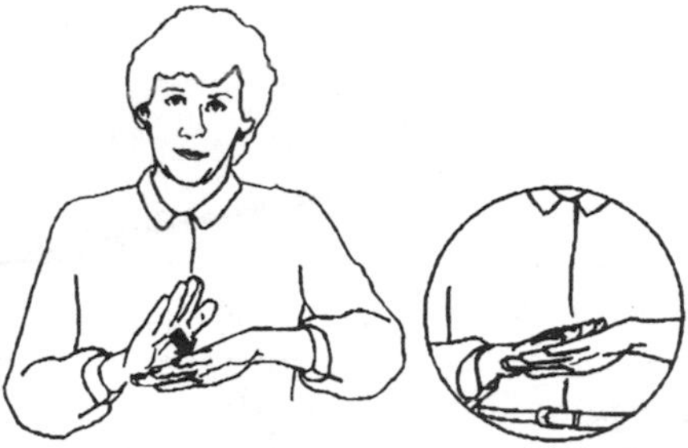

[Indicates tapping someone on the hand as a warning] Tap the palm of the right *open hand* with a double movement on the back of the left *open hand* held in front of the chest, both palms facing down.

was *v.* See sign for AGO.

wash *v.* Same sign used for: **rub.**

[Demonstrates the action of rubbing something to wash it] Rub the palm side of the right *A hand* with a repeated movement across the palm side of the left *A hand,* palms facing each other.

washroom *n.* See sign for TOILET.

watch[1] *v.*

[Represents the eyes looking at something] Beginning with the right *V hand* in front of the right side of the face, palm facing down and fingers pointing forward, move the hand forward.

watch[2] *v.* See sign for ATTENTION.

water *n.*

[Initialized sign] Tap the index-finger side of the right *W hand,* palm facing left, against the chin with a double movement.

way *n.* See sign for ROAD.

we *pron.*

[Points to self and encompasses others in near area] Touch the extended right index finger, palm facing down, first to the right side of the chest and then to the left side of the chest.

weak *adj.* Related form: **weakness** *n.* Same sign used for: **fatigue, feeble.**

[The fingers collapse as if weak] Beginning with the fingertips of the right *5 hand,* palm facing in, touching the palm of the left *open hand* held in front of the chest, move the right hand downward with a double movement, bending the fingers each time.

wealth *n.* See sign for RICH.

wear out *v. phrase.* Same sign used for: **decay, rot, rotten.**

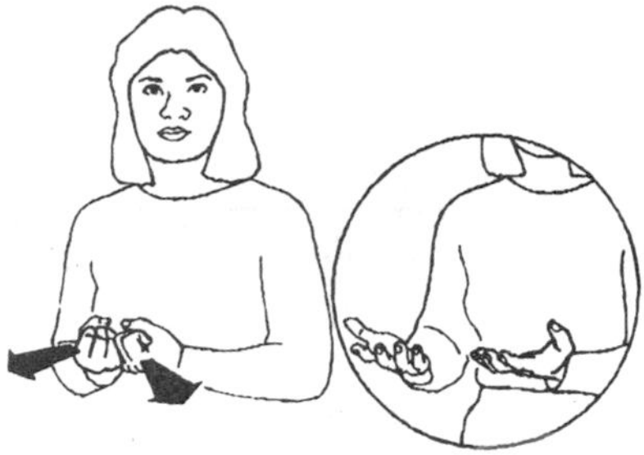

[Shows something coming apart] Beginning with both *S hands* together in front of the chest, palms facing up, move the hands forward with a sudden movement while opening into *5 hands,* palms facing up.

weary *adj.* See sign for TIRED.

weather *n.*

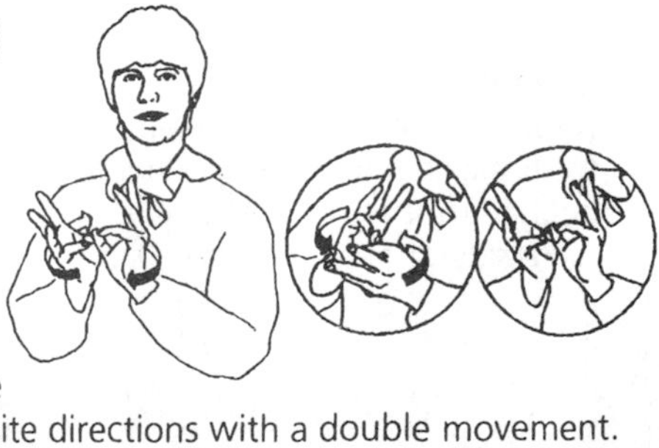

[Initialized sign] With the fingertips of both *6 hands* together in front of the chest, palms facing each other, twist the hands in opposite directions with a double movement.

wedding *n.* Related form: **wed** *v.*

[Represents bringing the bride's and groom's hands together during a wedding] Beginning with both *open hands* hanging down in front of each side of the chest, palms facing in and fingers pointing down, bring the fingers upward toward each other, meeting in front of the chest.

Wednesday *n.*

[Initialized sign] Move the right *W hand,* palm facing in and fingers pointing up, in a circle in front of the right shoulder.

week *n.* Same sign used for: **one week.**

[The finger moves along the days of one week on an imaginary calendar] Slide the palm side of the right *1 hand* from the heel to the fingers of the left *open hand* held in front of the chest, palm facing in.

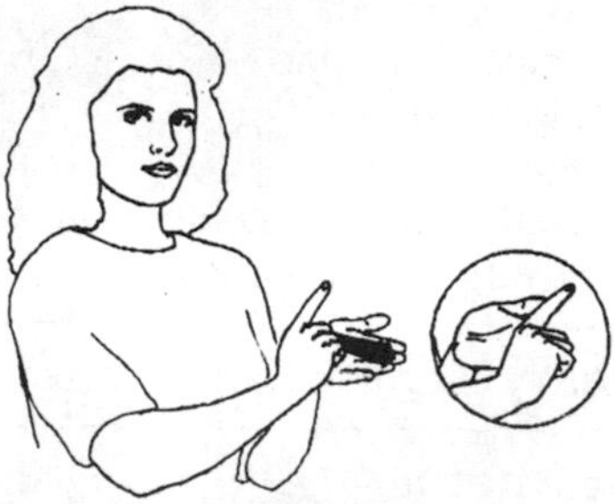

weekend *n.*

[**week** + **end**[1]] Slide the palm side of the right *1 hand* from the heel to the fingertips of the left *open hand* held in front of the chest, palm facing in. Then move the palm side of the right *open hand* downward along the fingertips of the left *open hand* held in front of the chest, palm facing right.

weep *v.* See sign for CRY[1].

weigh *v.* Related form: **weight** *n.* Same sign used for: **pound.**

[The fingers seem to balance something as if on a scale] With the middle-finger side of the right *H hand* across the index-finger side of the left *H hand,* palms angled toward each other, tip the right hand up and down with a repeated movement.

welcome *v., n., adj., interj.* See sign for INVITE.

welfare *n.* See sign for PENSION.

well[1] *adj., adv.* Same sign used for: **bold, cure, heal, healthy, strength, strong.**

[The hands seem to pull health from the body] Beginning with the fingertips of both *5 hands* on each side of the chest, palms facing in and fingers pointing up, bring the hands forward with a deliberate movement while closing into *S hands.*

well[2] *adj.* See sign for GOOD.

were *v.* See sign for AGO.

wet *adj.* Same sign used for:
damp, dew, humid, misty, moist, moisten, moisture.

[The hands seem to feel something wet] Beginning with the right *5 hand* near the right side of the chin, palm facing left, and the left *5 hand* in front of the left side of the chest, palm facing up, bring the hands downward while closing the fingers to the thumbs.

what *pron.*

[The fingers on the left hand are choices pointed out by the right hand] Bring the extended right index finger, palm facing left, downward across the left *open hand* held in front of the chest, palm facing up.

whatever *pron.* See sign for ANYWAY.

when *adv.*

[A continuous movement showing duration of time] Beginning with the extended right index finger in front of the chest, palm facing down and finger pointing forward, and the left extended index finger in front of the lower chest, palm facing in and finger pointing right, move the right index finger in a circular movement down to land on the left index finger.

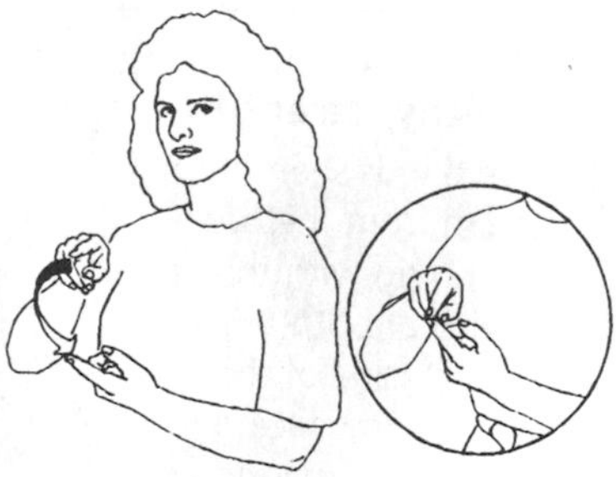

where *adv.*

[Indicates one direction and then another] Move the extended right index finger, palm facing forward and finger pointing up, with a short double movement from side to side in front of the right shoulder.

whether *pron.* See sign for WHICH.

which *pron., adj.* Same sign used for: **either, whether.**

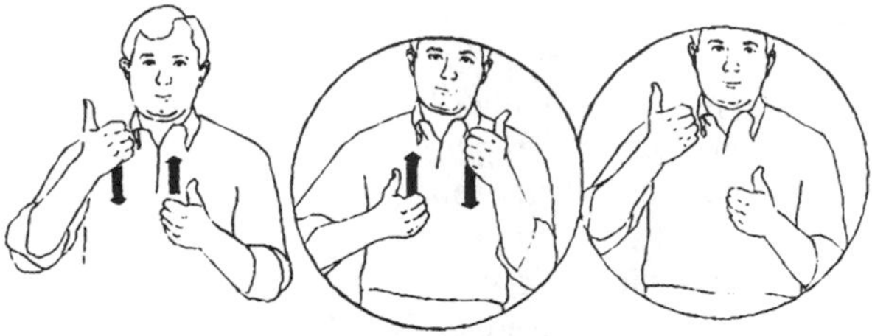

[The movement indicates indecision] Beginning with both *10 hands* in front of each side of the chest, palms facing each other and right hand higher than the left hand, move the hands up and down in front of the chest with an alternating movement.

while *conj.* See sign for DURING.

while ago, a See sign for JUST.

white *adj.*

[The downy breast of a swan] Beginning with the fingertips of the right *5 hand* on the chest, palm facing in, pull the hand forward while closing the fingers into a *flattened O hand.*

who *pron.* Same sign used for: **whom.**
[Outlines the verbal formation of the word **who**] With the thumb of the *modified C hand* touching the chin, palm facing left, bend the index finger up and down with a double movement.

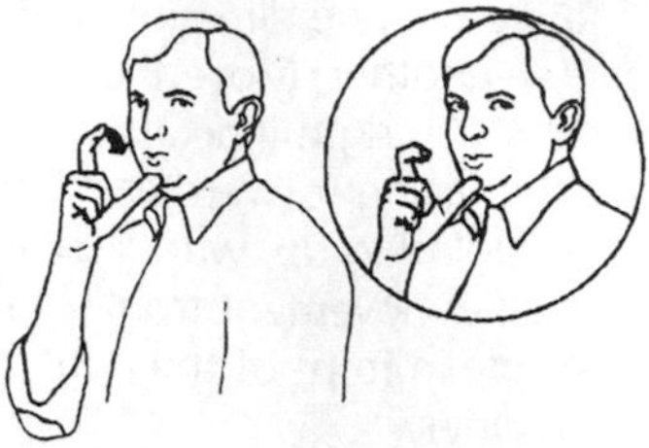

whole *adj., n.* See sign for ALL.

whom *pron.* See sign for WHO.

why *adv.*
[Taking information and presenting it for examination] Beginning with the fingertips of the right *bent hand* touching the right side of the forehead, palm facing down, move the hand forward with a deliberate movement while changing into a *Y hand.*

wicked *adj.* See sign for BAD.

wide *adj.* Same sign used for: **broad, general.**
[Indicates a wide space] Beginning with both *open hands* in front of each side of the body, palms facing each other and fingers pointing forward, move the hands away from each other outward to the sides of the body.

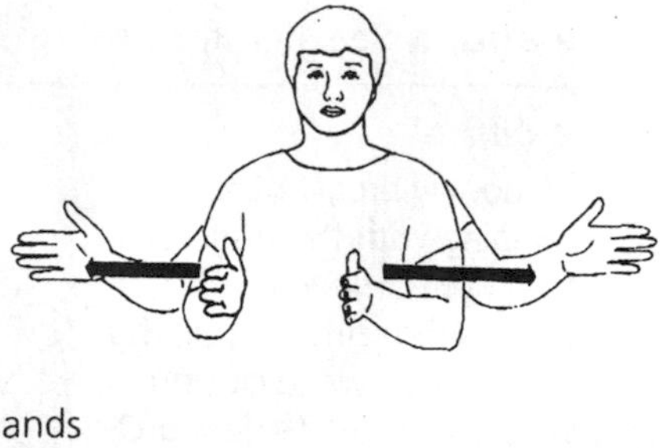

wife *n.*

[The hand moves from near the female area of the head + **marry**] Move the right *curved hand* from near the right side of the chin, palm facing forward, downward to clasp the left *curved hand* held in front of the body.

will *v.*

[The hand moves into the future] Move the right *open hand,* palm facing left and fingers pointing up, from the right side of the chin forward while turning the fingers forward.

willing *adj.* See sign for ADMIT.

will not See sign for WON'T.

win *v., n.*

[Grabbing the golden ring on a carousel] Beginning with the right *5 hand* in front of the right shoulder, palm facing forward and fingers pointing up, and the left *5 hand* in front of the body, palm facing right and fingers pointing forward, sweep the right hand downward in an arc across the index-finger side of the left hand while changing both hands into *S hands* and bringing the right hand upward in front of the chest.

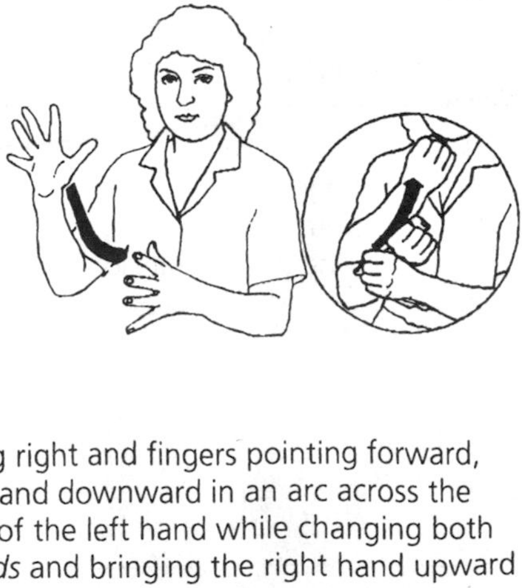

wind *n.* Same sign used for: **storm.**

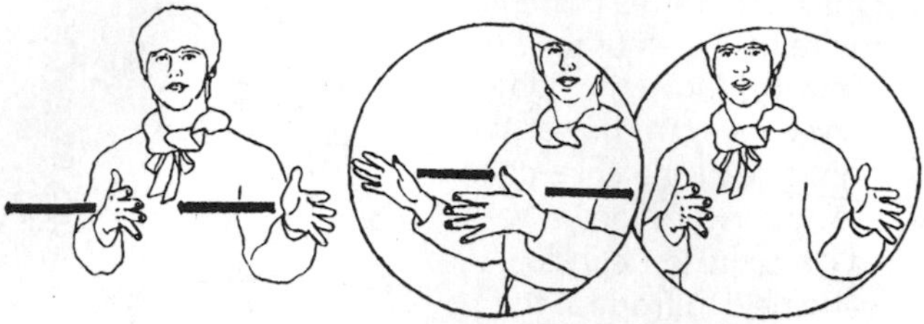

[Represents the action of wind blowing] Beginning with both *5 hands* in front of the left side of the body, palms facing each other and fingers pointing forward, move the hands back and forth in front of the chest with a repeated movement.

wind up *v. phrase.* See sign for END[1].

window *n.*

[Represents closing a window] Bring the little-finger side of the right *open hand* down sharply with a double movement on the index-finger side of the left *open hand,* both palms facing in and fingers pointing in opposite directions.

wine *n.*

[Initialized sign] Move the right *W hand,* palm facing left, in a small circle near the right side of the chin.

wings *pl. n.,* See sign for FLY.

winter[1] *n.*

[Initialized sign similar to sign for **cold**[2]] Beginning with both *W hands* in front of the body, palms facing each other, move the hands toward each other with a shaking repeated movement.

winter[2] *n.* See sign for COLD[2].

wipe *v.* Same sign used for: **rub**.

[Demonstrates the action of wiping something] Wipe the palm side of the right *A hand* with a repeated movement back and forth on the left *open hand* held in front of the body, palm facing up.

wire *n.* See sign for CORD.

wise *adj.* Related form: **wisdom** *n.*

[Shows the depth of wisdom in the brain] Move the right *X hand,* palm facing left, up and down with a double movement in front of the right side of the forehead.

wish *v., n.* Same sign used for: **desire.**

[The fingers outline the path of craving for something] Move the fingers of the right *C hand,* palm facing in, downward on the chest a short distance.

with *prep.*

[Indicates two things coming together so they are with one another] Beginning with both *A hands* in front of the chest, palms facing each other, bring the hands together.

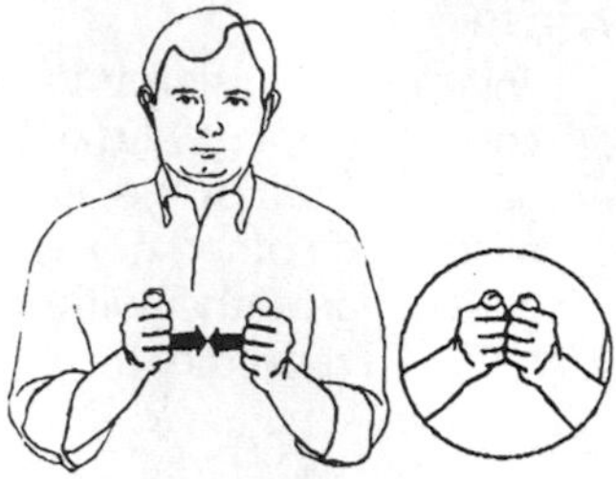

withdraw *v.* See signs for DISCONNECT, LEAVE[1].

within *prep.* See sign for INCLUDE.

woman *n.*

[A gesture beginning near the female area of the head + **polite**] Beginning with the extended thumb of the right *open hand* touching the right side of the chin, palm facing left, bring the hand downward to touch the thumb again in the center of the chest.

wonder *v.* Same sign used for: **consider, contemplate, meditate, ponder, reflect, think, think about, thinking.**

[Represents thoughts going around in one's head] Move the extended right index finger, palm facing in, in a small circle near the right side of the forehead with a repeated movement.

wonderful *adj.* Same sign used for: **amaze, excellent, fantastic, great, incredible, marvel, marvelous, remarkable.**

[A gesture of awe and wonder] Move both *5 hands,* palms facing forward and fingers pointing up, from in front of each side of the head forward with a short double movement.

won't *contraction.* Same sign used for: **refuse, will not.**

[Natural gesture for refusing to do something] Beginning with the right *10 hand* in front of the right shoulder, palm facing left, move the hand deliberately back toward the shoulder while twisting the wrist up.

word *n.* Same sign used for: **text.**

[Measures the size of a word] Tap the extended fingers of the right *G hand,* palm facing left, with a double movement against the extended left index finger pointing up in front of the left side of the chest, palm facing right.

work *n., v.* Same sign used for: **active, employment, job, labor, occupation, task.**

[Demonstrates repetitive action] Tap the heel of the right *S hand,* palm facing forward, with a double movement on the back of the left *S hand* held in front of the body, palm facing down.

work out See sign for EXERCISE[1].

world *n.*
[Initialized sign indicating the movement of the earth around the sun] Beginning with both *W hands* in front of the body, palms facing each other, move the right hand upward and forward in an arc as the left hand moves back and upward around the right hand, exchanging positions.

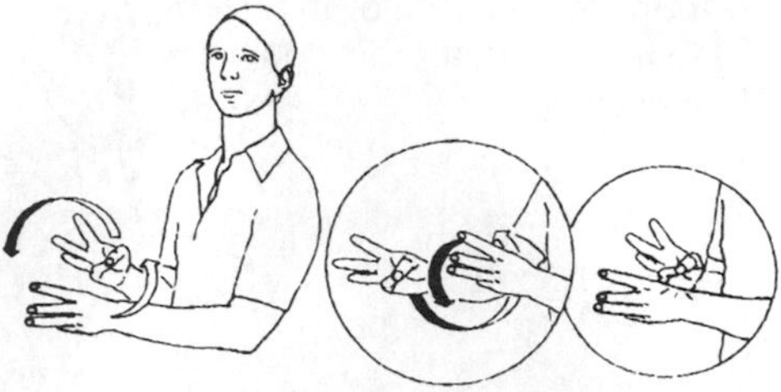

worry *v.* See sign for TROUBLE[1].

worth *n., prep.* See sign for IMPORTANT.

wound *v., n.* See sign for HURT.

write *v.* Related form: **written** *adj.* Same sign used for: **edit, scribble.**
[Mime writing on paper] Bring the fingers of the right *modified X hand*, palm facing left, with a wiggly movement from the heel to the fingers of the left *open hand* held in front of the body, palm facing up.

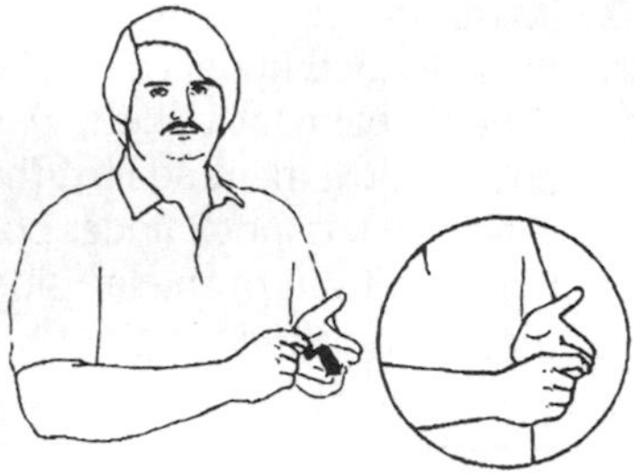

wrong *adj.* Same sign used for: **incorrect.**
[Similar to sign for **mistake** but with a single movement] Place the middle fingers of the right *Y hand,* palm facing in, against the chin with a deliberate movement.

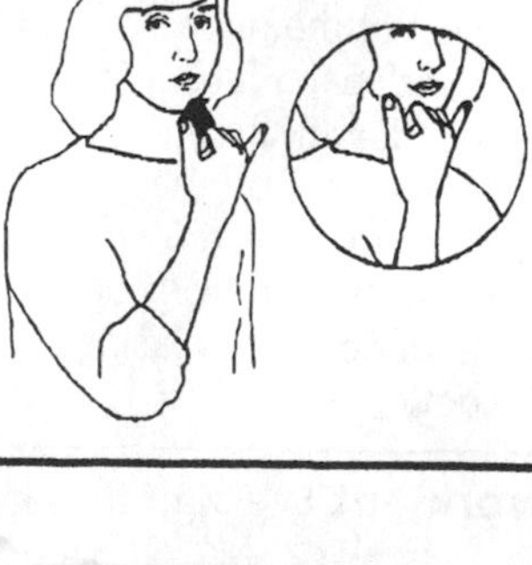

xylophone *n.*

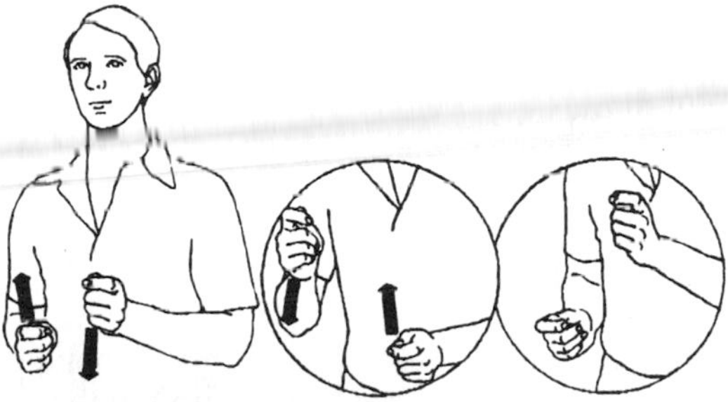

[Mime playing a xylophone] Beginning with the palms of both *modified X hands* facing each other in front of each side of the body, move the hands up and down with an alternating movement.

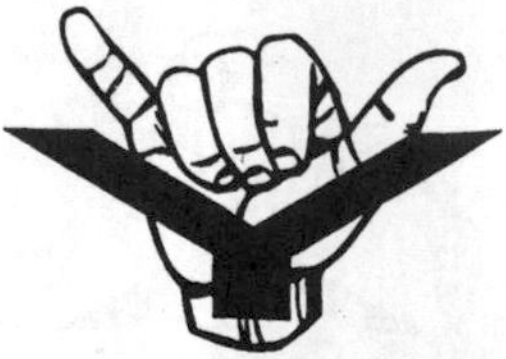

yeah *adv. Informal.* See sign for YES.

year *n.*

[Represents the movement of the earth around the sun] Beginning with the right *S hand,* palm facing left, over the left *S hand,* palm facing right, move the right hand forward in a complete circle around the left hand while the left hand moves in a smaller circle around the right hand, ending with the little-finger side of the right hand on the thumb side of the left hand.

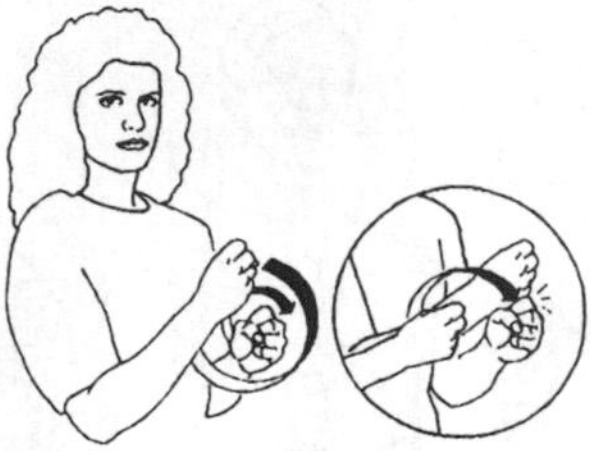

yearn *v.* See sign for HUNGRY.

yell *v.* See sign for SCREAM.

yellow *adj.*

[Initialized sign] Move the right *Y hand,* palm facing left, with a twisting double movement.

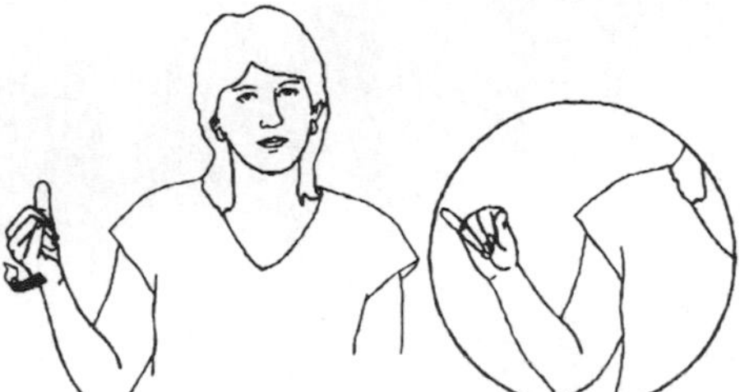

yes *adv.* Same sign used for: **yeah** (*informal*).

[Represents a person's head nodding in approval] Move the right *S hand,* palm facing forward, up and down in front of the right shoulder by bending the wrist with a repeated movement.

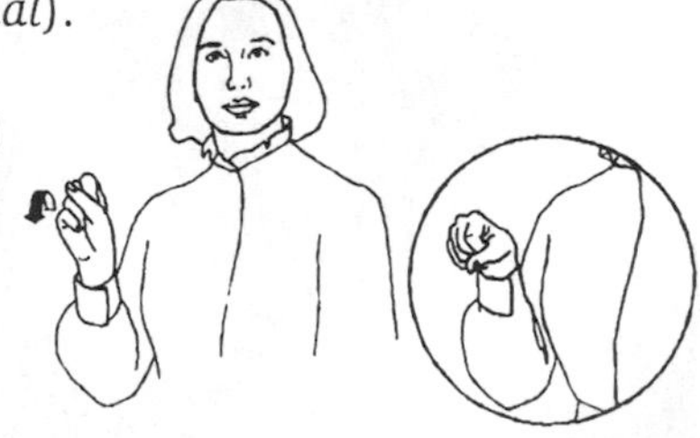

yesterday *n., adv.*

[Initialized sign moving back into the past] Move the thumb of the right *Y hand,* palm facing forward, from the right side of the chin up to the right cheek.

yet *adv.* See also sign for STILL[1].

[The hand gestures back into the past] Bend the wrist of the right *open hand,* palm facing back and fingers pointing down, back with a double movement near the right side of the waist.

you *pron.*

[Point toward the referent] Point the extended right index finger, palm facing down, toward the person being talked to.

young *adj.* Same sign used for: **youth.**

[Represents bringing up youthful feelings in the body] Beginning with the fingers of both *bent hands* on each side of the chest, palms facing in, brush the fingers upward with a double movement.

your *pron.* Related form:
yours *pron.*
[The hand moves toward the referent] Push the palm of the right *open hand,* palm facing forward and fingers pointing up, toward the person being talked to.

you're too late. See sign for MISS².

yourself *pron.*
[This hand shape is used for reflexive pronouns and moves toward the referent] Push the extended thumb of the right *10 hand,* palm facing left, forward with a double movement toward the person being talked to.

youth *n.* See sign for YOUNG.

zeal *n.* Same sign used for: **aspiration, aspire, eager, enthusiastic, motivation, motive.**

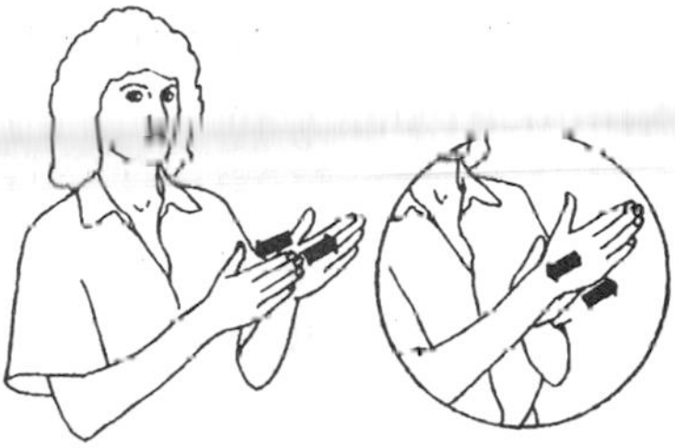

[Rubbing the hands together in eagerness] Rub the palms of both *open hands,* palms facing each other, back and forth against each other with a double alternating movement.

---

zip *v.* Same sign as for **zipper** but formed with a single movement.

---

zipper *n.*

[Mime pulling a zipper up and down] With the right *modified X hand,* palm facing down, move the right hand up and down with a double movement in front of the chest.

---

zoom *v.* Same sign used for: **set off.**

[Represents something getting smaller as it goes off into the distance] Beginning with the thumb of the right *G hand,* palm facing forward, at the base of the extended left index finger held in front of the chest, palm facing down and finger pointing right, move the right thumb across the length of the left index finger, closing the right index finger and thumb together as the hand moves to the right.

Manual Alphabet

The American Manual Alphabet is a series of handshapes used to represent each letter of the English alphabet. Many countries have their own manual alphabets, just as they have their own sign languages. It is important to note that although English is spoken in the United States and in England, the English Manual Alphabet, which is formed by using two hands, is very different from the American Manual Alphabet.

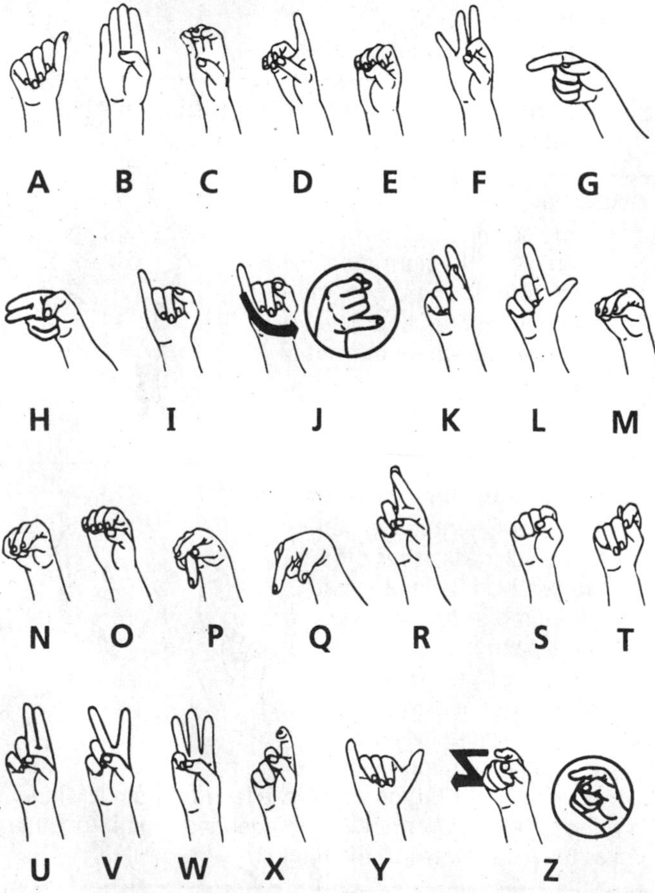